P9-DGQ-549

VOICES of FREEDOM

Sources in American History

PRENTICE HALL, Englewood Cliffs, New Jersey

E&H

Emory & Henry
College

WITHDRAWN

Frederick T. Kelly
Library

Emory, Virginia 24327-0947

© 1987 GAYLORD

VOICES OF FREEDOM
SOURCES IN AMERICAN HISTORY

Designed and produced by Cover to Cover, Inc.

© 1987 by Prentice Hall, Inc., Englewood Cliffs,
New Jersey 07632. All rights reserved. No part of this book
may be reproduced in any form or by any means without
permission in writing from the publisher. Printed in the
United States of America.

ISBN 0-13-943655-3

10   9   8   7   6   5   4

Illustration credits appear on page 351.

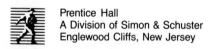
Prentice Hall
A Division of Simon & Schuster
Englewood Cliffs, New Jersey

CONTENTS Part One

E 175.3
1. V65

THEME 1

The World of the Americas 13

THEME 2

Settling the New World 30

EMORY AND HENRY LIBRARY

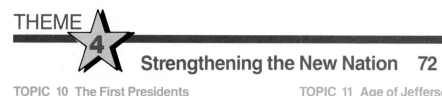

THEME 5

A Growing Nation   89

THEME 6

The Nation Divided   112

CONTENTS Part Two

THEME 2 Entering a Modern Age 176

THEME 3 The Roaring Twenties 207

THEME 4

A Time of Trial 227

THEME 5

The United States in a Changing World 270

Skill Lessons   329

TO THE STUDENT

Voices of Freedom: Sources in American History is a vivid collection of the raw materials of American history—the expressions of Americans about their land and its history. It contains a rich variety of letters and diaries, cartoons and drawings, poetry and documents. Many are accompanied by colorful photographs.

Voices of Freedom uses both primary and secondary sources. Primary sources are original materials, such as a letter, a diary entry, or a cowboy song, taken directly from the real-life experiences of people. Paintings, photographs, and drawings are also primary sources if they were produced during the period being studied. Secondary sources represent the views of people living at another time or of someone who did not actually witness the events. Both primary and secondary sources help you understand and appreciate history.

The book has two parts. Part One covers the period from the first Americans through Reconstruction. Part Two begins in 1861 and continues to the present. Each part is divided into themes that cover major periods of American history. The themes in turn contain topics that describe shorter time periods.

An *Introduction* to each source gives background information about the historical period, the artist or writer, and the situation that inspired the work. The *Vocabulary* section, which follows, highlights words you may want to look up before you read the source. Following each source, a *Reading Review* helps you interpret and analyze what you have read. It includes important skills such as finding the main idea, recognizing a point of view, making inferences, comparing, summarizing, relating cause and effect, and drawing conclusions. Other valuable skills are included in the section of Skill Lessons beginning on page 329. This section provides review and reinforcement of skills needed to master critical thinking. By thinking critically about the sources of American history, you will develop a deeper appreciation of the traditions and values of our nation.

Part One

The World of the Americas

Topic

1 The American Land (Prehistory–Present)

★ 1-1 America the Beautiful ★

Introduction The beauty and majesty of the American land has captured the imagination of people from the first Americans to Americans of the 1980s. In 1911, Katharine Lee Bates, a poet and professor of English at Wellesley College, wrote the words to this song, "America the Beautiful." In them she celebrated her country's beauty and its noble history.

Vocabulary Before you read the selection, find the meaning of these words in a dictionary: spacious, alabaster.

O beautiful for spacious skies,
For amber waves of grain,
For purple mountain majesties
Above the fruited plain!
America! America!
God shed His grace on thee,
And crown thy good with
    brotherhood,
From sea to shining sea!

O beautiful for pilgrim feet,
Whose stern, impassion'd stress
A thoroughfare for freedom beat
Across the wilderness!
America! America!
God mend thine ev'ry flaw,
Confirm thy soul in self-control,
Thy liberty in law!

O beautiful for heroes proved,
In liberating strife,
Who more than self their country
    loved,
And mercy more than life!
America! America!
May God thy gold refine,
Till all success be nobleness,
And ev'ry gain divine!

O beautiful for patriot dream
That sees beyond the years
Thine alabaster cities gleam
Undimm'd by human tears!
America! America!
God shed His grace on thee,
And crown thy good with
    brotherhood,
From sea to shining sea!

READING REVIEW ★ ★ ★ ★ ★ ★ ★

1. What virtue does the songwriter feel "crowns" all of America's other good points?

2. Some people have proposed that "America the Beautiful" be made the national anthem. (a) Do you agree? (b) What is the national anthem?

3. **Understanding geography.** List the physical regions of North America that are described in the song.

★ ★ ★ ★ ★ ★ ★ ★ ★ ★ ★ ★ ★ ★ ★ ★ ★ ★ ★

★   1-2   A European View of North America   ★

Introduction Fur traders were the first Europeans to explore the heartland of North America and the Rocky Mountains to the west. In 1793, Alexander Mackenzie, a Scotsman, blazed a trading trail to the Rockies and across them to the Pacific. This selection from the journal Mackenzie kept on his trip describes the land as he approached the Rockies.

Vocabulary Before you read the selection, find the meaning of these words in a dictionary: strata, saline, ascending, precipice, verdure.

May 9, 1793 The canoe was put into the water: her dimensions were 25 feet long within, exclusive of the curves of stem and stern, 26 inches hold, and 4 feet 9 inches beam. At the same time she was so light that two men could carry her on a good road three or four miles without resting.

In this slender vessel, we shipped provisions, goods for presents, arms, ammunition, and baggage, to the weight of 3,000 pounds, and an equipage of ten people, with two Indians as hunters and interpreters.

May 10 Where the earth has given way, the face of the cliffs shows numerous strata, consisting of reddish earth and small stones, bitumen, and a grayish earth below which, near the water edge, is a red stone.

At half-past six in the afternoon the young men landed, when they killed an elk and wounded a buffalo. In this spot we formed our encampment for the night.

From the place which we quitted this morning, the west side of the river displayed a succession of the most beautiful scenery I had ever beheld.

The ground rises at intervals to a considerable height, and at every interval or pause in the rise, there is a very gently ascending space or lawn, which is alternated with abrupt precipices to the summit. This magnificant theater of nature has all the decorations which the trees and animals of the country can afford it. Groves of poplars in every shape vary the scene, and their intervals are enlivened with vast herds of elks and buffaloes—the former choosing the steeps and uplands and the latter preferring the plains. At this time the buffaloes were attended with their young ones, who were frisking about them.

The whole country displayed an exuberant verdure. The trees that bear a blossom were advancing fast to that delightful appearance, and the velvet rind of their branches, reflecting the oblique rays of a rising or setting sun, added a splendid gaiety to the scene, which no expressions of mine are qualified to describe. The east side of the river consists of a range of high land covered with the white spruce and the soft birch, while the banks abound with the alder and the willow. The water continued to rise and, the current being strong, we made a greater use of setting poles than paddles.

May 12 The land on both sides of the river, during the two last days, is very much elevated, but particularly in the latter part of it. On the western side it presents in different places white, steep, and lofty cliffs. Our view being confined by these circumstances, we did not see so many animals as on the tenth. Between these lofty boundaries, the river becomes narrow, and in a great measure free from islands, for we had passed only four. The stream, indeed, was not more than from 200 to 300 yards broad, whereas before these cliffs pressed upon it, its breadth was twice that extent and sprinkled with islands.

May 16 The land above the spot where we camped spreads into an extensive plain and stretches on to a very high ridge, which in some parts presents a face of rock but is principally covered with verdure and varied with the poplar and white birch tree.

The country is so crowded with animals as to have the appearance in some places of a stall yard, from the state of the ground and the quantity of dung which is scattered over it. The soil is black and light. We this day saw two grizzly and hideous bears.

May 17 It froze during the night, and the air was sharp in the morning, when we continued our course, making good 11 miles during the forenoon. At two in the afternoon the Rocky Mountains appeared in light, with their summits covered with snow, bearing southwest by south. They formed a very agreeable object to every person in the canoe, as we attained the view of them much sooner than we expected.

Adapted from Alexander Mackenzie, *Voyage from Montreal on the River St. Laurence Through the Continent of North America to the Frozen and Pacific Oceans,* 1801.

READING REVIEW ★ ★ ★ ★ ★ ★ ★

1. What animals did Mackenzie's party see on the journey toward the Rockies?
2. What means of transportation did Mackenzie use to make his trip west?
3. **Applying information.** How did the American land itself help Mackenzie's party on their journey?

★ ★ ★ ★ ★ ★ ★ ★ ★ ★ ★ ★ ★ ★ ★ ★ ★

As explorers pushed westward across North America, they were struck by the variety and numbers of animals. This antelope is grazing on the northern plains.

Introduction Much of the United States has a climate with mild temperatures and enough rainfall to grow crops. The first Americans, like Americans for centuries since, used the warm sunshine and rain to grow food. The prayer to the sun printed below is from the Native American nation of the Havasupai.

Vocabulary Before you read the selection, find the meaning of this word in a dictionary: irrigate.

Sun, my relative
Be good coming out
Do something good for us.

Make me work,
So I can do anything in the garden
I hoe, I plant corn, I irrigate.

You, sun, be good going down at
    sunset

We lie down to sleep
I want to feel good.

While I sleep you come up.
Go on your course many times.
Make good things for us men.

Make me always the same as I am
    now.

From Leslie Spier, *Havasupai Ethnography* (New York: American Museum of Natural History, 1977).

READING REVIEW★ ★ ★ ★ ★ ★ ★

1. What is the sun supposed to do in daytime?
2. What seems to have been a chief crop of the Havasupai?
3. **Relating past to present.** Do you think the sun is as important to Americans today as it was to the first Americans? Explain.

★ ★ ★ ★ ★ ★ ★ ★ ★ ★ ★ ★ ★ ★ ★ ★

Topic 2 The First Americans (Prehistory–1600)

Introduction Legends passed down from generation to generation are an important source of knowledge about early peoples in North America. By studying oral legends, you can learn about a group's culture. The legend printed here is from the Arapahos, who lived on the western plains. Today their descendants live mostly in Wyoming and Oklahoma.

Vocabulary Before you read the selection, find the meaning of these words in a dictionary: enclosure, windward, flint, tinder.

A man tried to think how the Arapahos might kill buffalo. He was a hard thinker who would go off for several days to fast and think. At last he dreamed that a voice spoke to him and told him what to do.

Going back to his people, he made an enclosure of trees set in the ground with willows wound between them. Then four runners who never tired were sent out to the windward of the herd of buffalo, two of them on each side of the herd. They drove the animals toward the enclosure and into it. Then the people drove the buffalo around inside until a heavy cloud of dust rose. Unable to see in the dust, the animals ran over the cliff and were killed.

At that time the people had nothing to cut their meat with. Another man took a buffalo shoulder blade and cut out a narrow piece of it with flint. This he sharpened until it was a good knife. He also made a knife from flint by flaking it into shape. All the people learned how to make knives.

This man made the first bow and arrows also. He made the first arrow point from the short rib of a buffalo. With his bow and four arrows, he went off alone and waited in the woods at a buffalo path. When a buffalo came along the path, he shot; the arrow disappeared in the body and the animal fell dead. Then he killed three others. He went back to camp and told his people: "Harness the dogs; there are four dead buffalo in the woods." Thereafter the Arapahos were able to get meat without driving the buffalo into an enclosure.

In the early days, people used the fire drill. A man, another hard thinker, went off alone to think. He learned that certain stones, when struck, would give a spark, and that this spark would light tinder. He gathered stones and filled a small horn with dry, soft wood. Then he went home.

His wife said to him, "Please make a fire." So he took out his horn and his flint stones, struck a spark, blew it, put grass on it, and soon, to the surprise of all who saw it, he had a fire.

The buffalo had a central place in the lives of Plains Indians. This Blackfoot shield is made of buffalo hide and shows a buffalo in the center.

Making a fire in this way was so much easier than using a fire drill that soon all the people did it.

These three men—the one who made the first enclosure for buffalo, the one who made the first knife and the first bow and arrows, and the one who showed people how to make fire easily—they were the men who brought our people to the condition in which they live now.

Adapted from *Indian Legends from the Northern Rockies,* by Ella E. Clark. Copyright © 1966 by the University of Oklahoma Press.

READING REVIEW ★ ★ ★ ★ ★ ★ ★

1. (a) How did the Arapahos first kill buffalo? (b) What was the second method?
2. Why were the three men described in the legend important to the Arapahos?
3. **Using oral history.** What does the legend tell you about Arapaho life?

★ ★ ★ ★ ★ ★ ★ ★ ★ ★ ★ ★ ★ ★ ★ ★ ★ ★ ★ ★

★   2-2   **Prayer to the Young Cedar**   ★

Introduction The peoples of the Northwest Coast, like all the early peoples of North America, had a close relationship with nature. Women used cedar bark to make baskets, clothes, and blankets. Before peeling the bark from a tree, a woman would say a prayer such as the one that follows.

Vocabulary Before you read the selection, find the meaning of this word in the dictionary: pity.

Among the things Northwest Coast Indians made from the cedar tree were canoes like the elaborately carved and painted one shown here. The Indians in the foreground are fishing for salmon.

Look at me, friend!
I come to ask for your dress,
For you have come to take pity on us;
For there is nothing for which you
    cannot be used, . . .
For you are really willing to give us
    your dress,
I come to beg you for this,
Long Life Maker,
For I am going to make a basket for
    lily roots out of you.
I pray you, friend, not to feel angry
On account of what I am going to do to
    you;
And I beg you, friend, to tell our
    friends about what I ask of you.
Take care, friend!

Keep sickness away from me,
So that I may not be killed by sickness
    or in war, O friend!

From *American Indian Prose and Poetry,* ed. Margot Astrov (New York: Capricorn Books, 1962). Copyright 1946 by Margot Astrov.

READING REVIEW ★ ★ ★ ★ ★ ★ ★

1. What does the woman mean when she talks about the cedar's "dress"?
2. What is she going to do with the cedar's "dress"?
3. **Understanding other cultures.** Why do you think the woman prays to the tree before peeling its bark?

★ ★

★   2-3   Keeping a Heritage Alive   ★

Introduction Much of what is known about the first Americans is based on the legends and stories kept alive by later generations. In this selection, Ohiyesa, a Sioux, tells how young boys learned the history of their people to keep it alive for future generations.

Vocabulary Before you read the selection, find the meaning of these words in a dictionary: systematic, instituted, confer, sustenance.

It is commonly supposed that there is no systematic education of their children among the people of this country. Nothing could be farther from the truth. All the customs of this people were held to be divinely instituted. Those in connection with the training of children were carefully followed and passed from one generation to the next.

The expectant parents jointly bent all their efforts to the task of giving the newcomer the best they could gather from a long line of ancestors. An expectant mother would often choose one of the greatest characters of her family and tribe as a model for her child. This hero was daily called to mind. She would gather from tradition all of his noted deeds and daring exploits, rehearsing them to herself when alone.

The Indians believed, also, that certain kinds of animals would confer peculiar gifts upon the unborn, while others would leave so strong an adverse impression that the child might become a monstrosity. A case of harelip was commonly blamed on the rabbit. It was said that a rabbit had charmed the mother and given to the baby its own features.

Scarcely was the young warrior ushered into the world when he was met by lullabies that speak of wonderful exploits in hunting and war. Those ideas which so fully occupied his mother's mind before his birth are now put into words by all about the child, who is as yet quite unresponsive to their appeals to his honor and ambition. He is called the future defender of his people, whose lives may depend upon his courage and skill. If the child is a girl, she is at once addressed as the future mother of a noble race.

In hunting songs, the leading animals are introduced. They come to the boy to offer their bodies for the sustenance of his tribe. The animals are re-garded as his friends and spoken of almost as tribes of people.

Very early, the Indian boy assumed the task of preserving and transmitting the legends of his ancestors and his race. Almost every evening a myth or a true story of some deed done in the past was narrated by one of the parents or grandparents, while the boy listened with parted lips and glistening eyes. On the following evening, he was usually required to repeat it. If he was not an apt scolar, he struggled long with his task. But, as a rule, the Indian boy is a good listener and has a good memory, so that the stories are tolerably well mastered.

This sort of teaching at once enlightens the boy's mind and stimulates his ambition. His idea of his own future career becomes a vivid and irresistible force.

Adapted from *Cry of the Thunderbird: The American Indian's Own Story*, Edited and with an Introduction and Commentary by Charles Hamilton. New Edition Copyright © 1972 by the University of Oklahoma Press.

READING REVIEW ★ ★ ★ ★ ★ ★ ★

1. How did a mother call on the heritage of the people even before the baby was born?

2. How did a young boy learn about the history of his people?

3. **Relating past to present.** Compare the way young people today learn about their heritage with the way the young Sioux learned about theirs.

★ ★ ★ ★ ★ ★ ★ ★ ★ ★ ★ ★ ★ ★ ★ ★ ★ ★

★ 2-4 **Founding the League of the Iroquois** ★

Introduction About 1570, five Iroquois nations—the Mohawk, the Seneca, the Cayuga, the Oneida, and the Onondaga—formed the League of the Iroquois. They wanted to stop the fighting among the nations. According to legend, a Mohawk leader named Hiawatha helped found the league. Chief Elias Johnson relates the legend in this selection.

Vocabulary Before you read the selection, find the meaning of these words in a dictionary: tremble, habitation, annihilated.

The council met. Hiawatha entered the assembly with even more than ordinary attention. Every eye was fixed upon him when he began to address the council in the following words.

"Friends and Brothers: You being members of many tribes, you have come from a great distance. The voice of war has aroused you up. You are afraid for your homes, your wives, and your children. You tremble for your safety. Believe me, I am with you. My heart beats with your hearts. We are one. We have one common object. We come to promote our common interest and to determine how this can be best done.

"To oppose those hordes of northern tribes, singly and alone, would prove certain destruction. We can make no progress in that way. We must unite ourselves into one common band of brothers. We must have but one voice. Many voices make confusion. We must have one fire, one pipe, and one war club. This will give us strength. If our warriors are united, they can defeat the enemy and drive them from our land; if we do this, we are safe.

"Onondaga, you are the people sitting under the shadow of the Great Tree, whose branches spread far and wide, and whose roots sink deep into the earth. You shall be the first nation, because you are warlike and mighty.

"Oneida, you, the people who recline your bodies against the Everlasting Stone that cannot be moved, shall be the second nation, because you always give good counsel.

"Seneca, you, the people who have your habitation at the foot of the Great Mountain and are overshadowed by its crags, shall be the third nation, because you are all greatly gifted in speech.

"Cayuga, you, whose dwelling is in the Dark Forest, and whose home is everywhere, shall be the fourth nation, becauses of your superior cunning in hunting.

"Mohawk, you, the people who live in the open country and possess much wisdom, shall be the fifth nation, because you understand better the art of raising corn and beans and making cabins.

"You five great and powerful nations, with your tribes, must unite and have one common interest, and no foe shall disturb or subdue you.

"And you of the different nations of the south, and you of the west, may place yourselves under our protection, and we will protect you. We earnestly desire the alliance and friendship of you all.

"If we unite in one band the Great Spirit will smile upon us, and we shall be free, prosperous, and happy; but if we shall remain as we are we shall earn his displeasure. We shall be enslaved, and perhaps annihilated forever.

"Brothers, these are the words of Hiawatha. Let them sink deep into your hearts. I have done."

A deep and impressive silence followed the delivery of this speech. On the following day the council again assembled to act on it. The union of the tribes into one confederacy was discussed and unanimously adopted.

Adapted from *Cry of the Thunderbird: The American Indian's Own Story,* Edited and with an Introduction and Commentary by Charles Hamilton. New Edition Copyright © 1972 by the University of Oklahoma Press.

READING REVIEW ★ ★ ★ ★ ★ ★ ★

1. What five nations did Hiawatha speak to?
2. Why did he urge them to unite?
3. **Making a review chart.** Make a chart with two columns. In the first column, list the five nations. In the second, describe the contribution Hiawatha thought each would make to the league.

★ ★ ★ ★ ★ ★ ★ ★ ★ ★ ★ ★ ★ ★ ★ ★ ★ ★

Introduction The Incas developed farming methods that allowed them to grow ample food for all the people. The Sapa Incas, called the Inca in this selection, strictly controlled how the land was used and how food and clothing was distributed. In the early 1600s, Garcilaso de la Vega described how this was done. De la Vega was the son of an Inca princess and a Spanish army officer.

Vocabulary Before you read the selection, find the meaning of these words in a dictionary: torrid, arduous, arable, vassals, uncultivated.

The Incas had a sophisticated culture, as their farming methods show. Inca artists were also highly skilled. This silver alpaca was made by an Inca silversmith.

When the Inca had conquered a new province, he immediately sent engineers there, who were specialized in building canals for irrigation, in order to increase the corn acreage, which otherwise could not flourish in these torrid lands. In the same way, he irrigated the prairie lands, as may be seen today from the evidence of canals that still exist all over Peru. On the mountainsides, on the peaks, and on all rocky surfaces, they built terraces, sustained by stone walls, which they filled with light soil brought from elsewhere. These terraces grew wider from the top to the bottom of the slope, where some were as much as 240 acres in size.

These were arduous undertakings, but they made it possible to give the maximum development to the tiniest plots of barren land. Indeed, it often happened that they would build canals 15 to 20 leagues long to irrigate only a few acres of land.

Community records of landholdings were carefully kept up to date in all the provinces and villages, and arable land was divided into three parts: that belonging to the Sun, that of the Inca, and that of his vassals. This latter part was calculated to permit each village to provide for its own needs. In case there was an increase in population, the Inca reduced the surface of his own holdings. Thus it may be said that he kept for himself only that part that, without him, would have remained uncultivated. The major part of the terrace crops belonged to the king and to the Sun, which was only normal, inasmuch as it was the Inca who had had the terraces built.

Adapted from *The Royal Commentaries of the Inca Garcilaso de la Vega, 1539–1616*, ed. Alain Gheerbrant (New York: The Orion Press, 1961).

READING REVIEW ★ ★ ★ ★ ★ ★

1. How did the Incas build terraces?
2. How did the Incas make sure that each village would have enough food?
3. **Understanding geography.** What geographical features of the Inca empire made it necessary for the Incas to build terraces and irrigate the land?

★ ★ ★ ★ ★ ★ ★ ★ ★ ★ ★ ★ ★ ★ ★ ★ ★

Topic

3 Europeans Explore America (1000–1650)

★ 3-1 Leif Ericson Explores Vinland ★

Introduction The story of Leif Ericson's trip to North America was passed on from generation to generation in Viking sagas such as this one. Sagas were the stories the Vikings told of their early leaders. They presented the facts of a story in a way that emphasized the romantic or noble aspects of a hero and his adventures.

Vocabulary Before you read the selection, find the meaning of these words in a dictionary: counsel, foster.

There was now much talk about voyages of discovery. Leif, the son of Eric the Red, of Brattahild, went to Biarni Heriulfson and bought the ship from him. He hired men for it, so that there were 35 men in all.

Now they sailed into the open sea with a northeast wind. They were days at sea before they saw land. They came to an island which lay to the east of the land. They went up and looked round them in good weather, and saw that there was dew upon the grass. And so it happened that they touched the dew with their hands and raised the fingers to the mouth. They thought that they had never before tasted anything so sweet.

After this they took counsel, and decided to remain there for the winter, and built large houses. There were many salmon in the river and in the lake, and larger salmon than they had seen before. The nature of the country was, as they thought, so good that cattle would not require house feeding in winter, for no frost came in the winter, and little did the grass wither there. Day and night were more equal than in Greenland, for on the shortest day the sun was above the horizon from half past seven in the forenoon till half past four in the afternoon.

It happened one evening that a man of the party was missing. He was Tyrker the German. Leif took this much to heart, for Tyrker had been long with his father and him, and had loved Leif much in his childhood. Leif now took his people severely to task. He prepared to seek for Tyrker, and took 12 men with him. But when they had got a short way from the house, Tyrker came towards them and was joyfully received.

Then Leif said to him: "Why were thou so late, my foster father, and separated from the party?"

"I have not been much farther off, but still I have something new to tell of. I found vines and grapes."

"But is that true, my foster father?" said Leif.

"Surely it is true," Tyrker replied, "for I was raised in a land where there are many vines and grapes."

Now a cargo was cut down for the ship, and when the spring came they got ready and sailed away; and Leif gave the land a name after its qualities, and called it Vinland.

Adapted from *The Voyages of the Northmen to America*, 1877.

READING REVIEW ★ ★ ★ ★ ★ ★ ★

1. What made Vinland an inviting place?
2. Leif Ericson named Vinland after what grew there. What else could a place be named for? Give an example.
3. **Analyzing a primary source.** How does this saga present Leif Ericson in a romantic or noble light?

★ ★ ★ ★ ★ ★ ★ ★ ★ ★ ★ ★ ★ ★ ★ ★ ★ ★

Introduction The stories Marco Polo told about his travels in Asia played a key role in inspiring Europeans to explore new and distant lands. Early explorers and geographers also turned to Marco Polo's accounts to help them in their ventures into these new lands. This selection is from accounts of his journeys in *The Book of Marco Polo.*

Vocabulary Before you read the selection, find the meaning of these words in a dictionary: sufficient, flax, gratification.

You must know that the city of Cambaluc has so many houses, and such a vast population inside the walls and outside, that it seems quite past all possibility. There is a suburb outside each of the 12 gates. These suburbs are so great that they contain more people than the city itself. In those suburbs live the foreign merchants and travelers who have come to bring presents to the emperor, or to sell articles at court, or because the city affords so good a mart to attract traders.

To this city also are brought articles of greater cost and rarity, and in greater abundance, than to any other city in the world. For people of every description, and from every region, bring things (including all the costly wares of India, as well as the fine and precious goods of Cathay [China] itself with its provinces).

As sample, I tell you, no day in the year passes that there do not enter the city 1,000 cartloads of silk alone, from which are made quantities of cloth of silk and gold, and of other goods. And this is not to be wondered at; for in all the countries around about there is no flax, so that everything has to be made of silk. It is true, indeed, that in some parts of the country there is cotton and hemp, but not sufficient for their wants. This, however, is not of much consequence, because silk is so abundant and cheap, and is a more valuable substance than either flax or cotton.

Round about this great city of Cambaluc there are some 200 other cities at various distances, from which traders come to sell their goods and buy others for their lords. And all find means to make their sales and purchases, so that the traffic of the city is passing great.

First and foremost, then, the document stated the city of Kinsay to be so great that it was 100 miles around. And there are in it 12,000 bridges of stone. For the most part they are so lofty that a great fleet could pass beneath them. And let no man marvel that there are so many bridges, for you see the whole city stands as it were in the water and surrounded by water, so that a great many bridges are required to give free passage about it.

Marco Polo's stories of wealth and luxury in Asia sparked interest among Europeans. This illustration of the wedding of Kublai Khan's son gives a sense of the splendor Polo described.

Topic 3

Inside the city there is a lake which has a compass of some 30 miles. All round it are built beautiful palaces and mansions, of the richest and most exquisite structure that you can imagine, belonging to the nobles of the city. In the middle of the lake are two islands, on each of which stands a rich, beautiful, and spacious building, furnished in such style as to seem fit for the palace of an emperor. And when any one of the citizens wanted to hold a marriage feast or to give any other entertainment, it used to be done at one of these palaces. And everything would be found there ready to order, such as silver plate, trenchers, and dishes, and whatever else was needful. The king made this provision for the gratification of his people and the place was open to everyone who desired to give an entertainment.

Adapted from *The Book of Ser Marco Polo*, introduction and notes by G. B. Parks (New York: Macmillan Publishing Co., Inc., 1929).

READING REVIEW ★ ★ ★ ★ ★ ★ ★

1. What attracted so many people to the city of Cambaluc?
2. Why were so many garments made of silk in Asia?
3. **Understanding geography.** The names of the cities Marco Polo describes are now Khanbalik (Cambaluc) and Hangchow (Kinsay). Locate Hangchow on a world map. Use the scale to find how far Hangchow is from Venice, where Marco Polo began his journey.

★ ★ ★ ★ ★ ★ ★ ★ ★ ★ ★ ★ ★ ★ ★ ★ ★ ★

★ 3-3 Columbus Lands in America ★

Introduction Today, October 12 is a national holiday. Each year on that day we celebrate Christopher Columbus's arrival in America. What was the first Columbus Day like? This selection, from Columbus's journal of his trip, gives a firsthand account of that day. The journal entry for the day records the first European impressions of Native Americans.

Vocabulary Before you read the selection, find the meaning of these words in a dictionary: hove to, standard, diverse, testimony, adjacent.

Friday, October 12 The vessels were hove to, waiting for daylight; and on Friday they arrived at a small island called, in the language of the Indians, Guanahani.* The admiral went on shore in the armed boat, and Martin Alonso Pinzon and Vincente Yanez, his brother, who was captain of the

*Now Watling Island, it was named San Salvador by Columbus.

Nina. The admiral took the royal standard, and the captains went with two banners of the green cross.

Having landed, they saw trees very green, and much water, and fruits of diverse kinds. The admiral called to the two captains. They said that they should bear faithful testimony that he, in presence of all, had taken possession of the said island for the king and for the queen.

Presently many people of the island assembled. What follows are the actual words of the admiral in his book of the first navigation and discovery of the Indies.

"I," he says, "wanted us to form a great friendship, for I knew that they were a people who could be more easily freed and converted to our holy faith by love than by force. So I gave to some of them red caps, and glass beads to put round their necks, and many other things of little value, which gave them great pleasure, and made them so much our friends that it was a marvel to see.

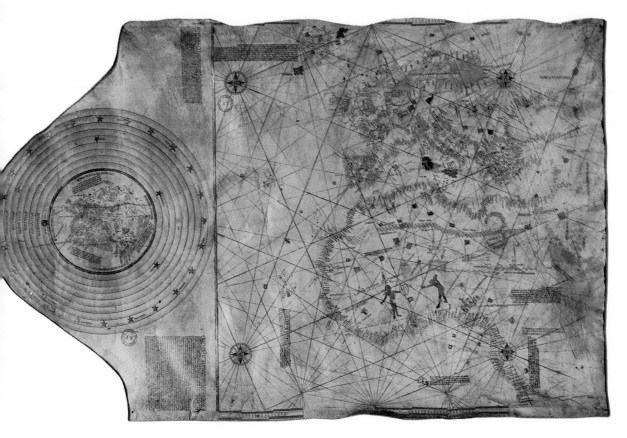

Historians think that this map, drawn on calfskin, may have been made by Christopher Columbus and taken along on the *Santa Maria* in 1492. The coastlines of Europe and Africa appear at right.

"They afterwards came to the ship's boats where we were, swimming and bringing us parrots, cotton threads in skeins, darts, and many other things. And we exchanged them for other things that we gave them, such as glass beads and small bells. In fine, they took all, and gave what they had with good will. It appeared to me to be a race of people very poor in everything.

"All I saw were youths, none more than 30 years of age. They are very handsome. Their hair is short and coarse, almost like the hairs of a horse's tail. They wear the hairs brought down to the eyebrows, except a few locks behind, which they wear long and never cut. They paint themselves black, and they are the color of the Canarians, neither black nor white. Some paint themselves white, others red, and others of what color they find. Some paint their faces, others the whole body, some only round the eyes, others only on the nose.

"They neither carry nor know of anything of arms, for I showed them swords, and they took them by the blade and cut themselves through ignorance. They have no iron, their darts being wands without iron, some of them having a fish's tooth at the end, and others being pointed in various ways.

"They are all of fair stature and size, with good faces, and well made. I saw some with marks of wounds on their bodies, and I made signs to ask what it was. And they gave me to understand that people from other adjacent islands came with the intention of seizing them, and that they defended themselves.

"They should be good servants and intelligent, for I saw that they quickly took in what was said to them. I believe that they would easily be made Christians, as it appeared to me that they had no religion. I will take, at the time of my departure, six of them for your Highnesses, that they may learn to speak. I saw no beast of any kind, except parrots, on this island."

The above is in the words of the admiral.

Adapted from *The Journal of Christopher Columbus*, 1893.

READING REVIEW ★ ★ ★ ★ ★ ★ ★

1. What was the first thing Columbus did when he landed?

2. Why did Columbus give the Indians beads and other trinkets?

3. **Drawing conclusions.** Columbus was trying to find the riches of Asia. How do you think this goal affected his attitude toward the Indians he found on Guanahani?

★ ★ ★ ★ ★ ★ ★ ★ ★ ★ ★ ★ ★ ★ ★ ★ ★ ★ ★

★ 3-4 Rescued by Indians ★

Introduction On November 6, 1528, Cabeza de Vaca and a party of about 80 men were shipwrecked on an island off the coast of Texas. The area was wild and unfamiliar. The men feared that the Indians who lived on the island might capture and kill them all. In this selection from his journal, de Vaca describes what happened.

Vocabulary Before you read the selection, find the meaning of these words in a dictionary: lament, sacrifice, victim.

I made the Indians understand by signs that our boat had sunk and three of our number had been drowned. The Indians, seeing what had befallen us and our state of suffering, sat down among us. From the sorrow and pity they felt, they all began to lament so earnestly that they might have been heard at a distance. They continued doing so for more than half an hour. It was strange to see these men, wild and untaught, howling like brutes over our misfortunes.

The cries having ceased, I talked with the Christians. I said that if it appeared well to them, I would beg these Indians to take us to their houses. Some, who had been in New Spain, replied that we ought not to think of it; for if they should do so, they would sacrifice us to their idols. But seeing no better course, and that any other led to a nearer and more certain death, I disregarded what was said and asked the Indians to take us to their dwellings. They indicated that it would give them delight.

Presently 30 men loaded themselves with wood and started for their houses, which were far off. We remained with the others until near night. Then, holding us up, they carried us with all haste. Because of the extreme coldness of the weather, they built four or five very large fires at intervals, and at each they warmed us. When they saw that we had regained some heat and strength, they took us to the next so swiftly that they hardly let us touch our feet to the ground.

In this manner we went as far as their village, where we found that they had made a house for us with many fires in it. An hour after our arrival, they began to dance and hold great rejoicing, which lasted all night, although for us there was no joy, festivity, nor sleep. We awaited the hour they should make us victims. In the morning they again gave us fish and roots, showing us such hospitality that we were reassured and lost somewhat the fear of sacrifice.

Adapted from "The Narrative of Alvar Nuñez Cabeca de Vaca," in *Spanish Explorers in the Southern United States,* ed. Frederick W. Hodge (New York: Barnes & Noble, 1959).

READING REVIEW ★ ★ ★ ★ ★ ★ ★

1. How did the Indians react to the sight of the shipwrecked Spaniards?
2. Who was reluctant to go to the Indians' houses? Why?
3. **Supporting generalizations.** List at least three things the Indians did that show they felt friendly towards the Spaniards.

★ ★ ★ ★ ★ ★ ★ ★ ★ ★ ★ ★ ★ ★ ★ ★ ★ ★ ★

★ 3-5 Cartier and the Indians of Canada ★

Introduction Explorer Jacques Cartier played a key role in the development of the two largest French Canadian cities—Québec and Montreal. During his time in North America, he also learned much about the culture of northern Indians. It was Cartier who first brought corn, one of the Indians' chief foods, to Europe. This selection, from a firsthand account of Cartier's second voyage to the New World, describes the visit to the site of Montreal.

Vocabulary Before you read the selection, find the meaning of these words in a dictionary: cunningly, chamber.

Cartier and other French explorers often traveled by canoe. When rapids appeared, the lightweight canoes could be portaged, or carried, to the next calm spot.

The next day very early in the morning, our captain very gorgeously attired himself. He caused all his company to be set in order to go to see the town of those people and a certain mountain that is somewhat near the city. We took with us three men of Hochelaga to bring us to the place. All along as we went we found the fairest and best country that possibly can be seen, full of great oaks under which the ground was all covered over with acorns.

We began to find large fields full of such corn as the country can yield. In the midst of those fields is the city of Hochelaga, placed near a great mountain. The mountain is tilled round about, very fertile. And on the top of it you may see very far. We named it Mount Royal. The city of Hochelaga is round, surrounded by timber.

There are in the town about 50 houses about 50 paces long and 12 or 15 broad. They are built all of wood, covered over with the bark of the wood as broad as any board, very finely and cunningly joined together. Within the houses, there are many rooms, lodgings, and chambers. In the middle of every one there is a great court, where they make their fire.

They have also on the top of their houses certain garrets, where they keep their corn to make their bread. They call it Carraconny. They have certain pieces of wood, made hollow, and on them, with mallets of wood, they beat their corn to powder. Then they make paste of it, and of the paste, cakes or wreaths. Then they lay them on a broad and hot stone, and cover it with hot stones. And so they bake their bread instead of in ovens.

Adapted from Richard Hakluyt, *The Third and Last Volume of the Voyages, Navigations, Traffiques, and Discoveries of the English Nation*, 1600.

READING REVIEW ★ ★ ★ ★ ★ ★ ★

1. Describe the houses in Hochelaga.
2. How did the Indians of Hochelaga bake their corn bread?
3. **Understanding geography.** What kind of landform do you think the city of Montreal was named for? Explain.

★ ★ ★ ★ ★ ★ ★ ★ ★ ★ ★ ★ ★ ★ ★ ★ ★ ★

★   **3-6   Skills Needed in the New World**   ★

Introduction Sailors skilled in the art of navigation were needed to guide explorers on their voyages to the New World. Once there, however, people with many other talents were needed if the explorers hoped to make a go of life in America. This selection contains a list compiled by the Englishman Richard Hakluyt of the various kinds of skilled workers he planned to include in an expedition to America.

Vocabulary Before you read the selection, find the meaning of these words in a dictionary: husbandmen, fortification, bulwarks, pike.

Sorts of men which are to go on this voyage

1. Men skillful in all mineral causes.
2. Fishermen, for sea fishings on the coasts, others for freshwater fishings.
3. Salt makers, to view the coast and see how rich the sea water there is.
4. Husbandmen, to view the soil and to decide what to till.
5. Vineyard men, to see how the soil may serve for the planting of vines.

Artists often accompanied early explorers and settlers to the New World. They drew pictures of Native Americans as well as sketches of plants and animals such as this crab.

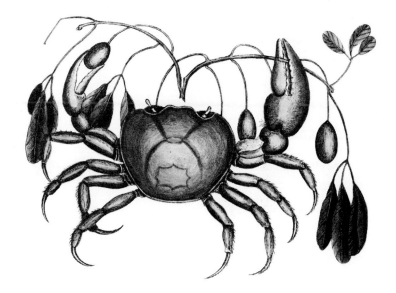

6. Men bred in the Shroff in South Spain, for discerning how olive trees may be planted there.

7. Others, for planting orange trees, fig trees, lemon trees, and almond trees.

8. Lime makers, to make lime for buildings.

9. Masons, carpenters, etc., for buildings there.

10. Brick makers and tile makers.

11. Men cunning in the art of fortification, that may choose places strong by nature to be fortified and that can plot out and direct workmen.

12. Choice spade men, to dig trenches cunningly and to raise bulwarks of earth for defense and offense.

13. Smiths, to forge the irons of the shovels and spades, and to make black bills and other weapons, and to mend many things.

14. Coopers, to make casks of all sorts.

15. Forgers of pikes' heads and of arrow heads, with Spanish iron and with all manner of tools to be carried with them.

16. Fletchers, to renew arrows, since archery prevaileth much against unarmed people and gunpowder may soon perish by setting on fire.

17. Bowyers also, to make bows there for need.

18. Makers of oars for boats and barges.

19. Shipwrights, to make barges and boats, and bigger vessels, if need be, to run along the coast and to pierce the great bays and inlets.

20. Turners, to turn targets [shields] of elm and tough wood for use against darts and arrows.

21. Tanners, to tan hides of buffs, oxen, etc.

22. Men skillful in burning of soap ashes and in making of pitch and tar and rosin to be fetched out of Prussia and Poland.

23. A skillful painter, to bring the descriptions of all beasts, birds, fishes, trees, towns, etc.

Adapted from John Brereton, *Discovery of the North Part of Virginia*, 1602.

READING REVIEW ★ ★ ★ ★ ★ ★

1. Name five types of equipment Hakluyt thought colonists would have to make.

2. (a) How does the last type of worker named differ from the rest? (b) Why did Hakluyt probably think this occupation was important?

3. **Building vocabulary.** Many common last names come from occupations. Use Hakluyt's list and a dictionary to find what these last names originally meant: Mason, Smith, Cooper, Fletcher, Turner.

★ ★ ★ ★ ★ ★ ★ ★ ★ ★ ★ ★ ★ ★ ★ ★ ★

Theme 2

Settling the New World

Topic 4 Planting Colonies (1530–1690)

★ 4-1 Hardships of the Atlantic Crossing ★

Introduction The men and women who made the first voyages across the Atlantic had to be hardy as well as brave. Conditions on board the early ships were grueling. This description of the crossing was written by Father Tomas de la Torre, a Spanish priest. De la Torre came to America in 1544 with Bartolomé de las Casas, the priest who tried to improve conditions among the Indians.

Vocabulary Before you read the selection, find the meaning of these words in a dictionary: habitat, entails, hardtack.

By the Grace of our Lord, on the morning of Wednesday, July 9, 1544, we hastily scrambled aboard the small boats that carried us out to the ships on which the remaining members of our order were booked for passage. Chief among us was the Bishop of Chiapas, the Very Reverend Bartolomé de las Casas. Having triumphed over the Council of the Indies, he came armed with royal authority to remedy the ills of the Indians and to free the slaves.

We soon realized that the sea was not man's natural habitat. Everyone became so seasick that nothing in the world could induce us to move from the spot where we lay.

A more befouled hospital and one so filled with the moans of the sick can hardly be imagined. Some sufferers were cooked alive in the heat below deck. The sun roasted others lying about the deck, where they were trod upon and trampled, and where they were so filthy that words cannot describe the scene. Bishop Las Casas gave the chickens he was bringing to the sufferers since the rest of us had not brought any.

To help those who are unfamiliar with life at sea understand something of the hardship and suffering that it entails, I shall set forth a few circumstances. First of all, a ship is a very narrow and stout prison from which no one can escape even if he wears no shackles or chains. Closely crowded in cramped quarters, heat and suffocation

Part One 30

are unbearable. The deck floor is usually one's bed. And though some passengers brought soft mats, ours were small, hard, and thinly stuffed with dog hair.

The thirst that one endures is unbelievable, and it is increased by our fare of hardtack and salt beef. Water is measured out a half azumbre [about a liter] a day. An infinite number of lice eat one alive, and clothing cannot be washed because salt water shrinks it. Everywhere bad odors pervade the ship, especially below deck. These annoyances and many other hardships are very common in shipboard life.

Adapted from Fray Francisco Ximénez, *Historia de la Provincia de San Vicente de Chiapas y Guatemala de la Orden de Predicadores,* Prólogo del Lic. Antonio Villacorta, C., 3 vols., 1929.

READING REVIEW ★ ★ ★ ★ ★ ★ ★

1. What did the diet of passengers on de la Torre's ship consist of?
2. (a) Why, according to de la Torre, was de las Casas making this trip to America? (b) What does de la Torre seem to think of de las Casas? (c) How can you tell?
3. **Summarizing.** Briefly, what were the things that made the Atlantic crossing unpleasant?

★ ★ ★ ★ ★ ★ ★ ★ ★ ★ ★ ★ ★ ★ ★ ★ ★ ★

★ 4-2 A Description of Mexico City ★

Introduction The Spanish colonies in the New World were the first European settlements to flourish here. By the mid-1500s, New Spain boasted cities, universities, and printing presses. The new colonial cities were especially impressive. In part, this was because they were often built on the sites of the great cities of the Aztecs and Incas. This description is of Mexico City, which was built on the foundations of the ancient Aztec capital, Tenochtitlan. It comes from a description by an English trader, Henry Hawks, who visited New Spain in 1567.

Vocabulary Before you read the selection, find the meaning of these words in a dictionary: victuals, divers.

Mexico is a great city. It has more than 50,000 households. There are not over 5,000 or 6,000 houses of Spaniards. All the others are the people of the country, which live under the Spaniards' laws. There are in this city stately buildings and many monasteries of friars and nuns which the Spaniards have made. The building of the Indians is somewhat beautiful outwardly, and within full of small rooms, with very small windows. This city stands in the middle of a great lake. And the water goes through all or most of the streets. There come small boats, which they call canoes. In them they bring all things necessary, such as wood and coals, and grass for their horses, stones and lime to build, and corn.

This city is subject to many earthquakes, which often cast down houses and kill people. This city is very well provided with water to drink and with all manner of victuals, such as fruits, fish, bread, hens and capons, guinea cocks and hens, and all other fowl. There are in this city every week three fairs or markets, which are attended by many people, Spaniards as well as the people of the country. There are in these fairs or markets all manner of things that may be invented to sell, and in especial things of the country.

Toward the north from Mexico, there are many silver mines. There is more silver found in these mines toward the north than there is in any other parts. These mines are commonly upon great hills and stony ground, very hard to work.

Out of some of the mines the Indians find a certain kind of earth of divers colours, wherewith they paint themselves in times of their dances and other pastimes which they use.

In this country of Nova Hispania, there are also mines of gold, although the gold be commonly found in rivers or very near rivers. And now in these days there is not so much gold found as there has been before.

There are many great rivers and great store of fish in them, not unlike our kinds of fish. And there are great woods and as fair trees as may be seen of divers sorts, especially fir trees, that may mast any ship that goes upon the sea, oaks and pineapples, and another tree which they call mesquite. It bears a fruit like a peapod, very sweet, which the wild people gather and keep all the year and eat instead of bread.

There is a great number of beasts or cattle in the country of Cibola, which were never brought there by the Spaniards but breed naturally in the country. They are like our oxen, saving that they have long hair like a lion and short horns, and they have upon their shoulders a bunch like a camel, which is higher than the rest of their body. They are very wild and swift in running. They call them the beasts or cattle of Cibola.

Adapted from Richard Hakluyt, *Principal Navigations,* 1589.

READING REVIEW ★ ★ ★ ★ ★ ★ ★

1. What animal is Hawks describing at the end of this passage?
2. What evidence is there in Hawks's description that Indian and Spanish influences mixed in the culture of New Spain?
3. **Comparing.** Compare Mexico City, as described here, with the ancient Aztec capital of Tenochtitlan, described in Chapter 2.

★ ★ ★ ★ ★ ★ ★ ★ ★ ★ ★ ★ ★ ★ ★ ★ ★ ★

★ 4-3 Marquette and Joliet ★

Introduction French traders in Canada heard stories of a great river to the south and west from the Indians with whom they traded. In 1673, the French colonial government asked Father Jacques Marquette and Louis Joliet to try to find this "Mississippi," the Indian word meaning "great river." Marquette knew several Indian languages, and Joliet was a skilled mapmaker. This selection is from the report Father Marquette wrote of their trip.

Vocabulary Before you read the selection, find the meaning of these words in a dictionary: league, reconnoiter, token.

The first nation that we came to was that of the Folle Avoine [Menominee]. I told these people of my design to go and discover remote nations, in order to teach them the mysteries of our holy religion. They were greatly surprised to hear it and did their best to prevent me from going. They told me that I would meet nations who would never show mercy to strangers, but break their heads without any cause; and that war was kindled between various peoples who lived along our route. This exposed us to the further danger of being killed by the bands of warriors who are ever in the field.

They also said that the great river was very dangerous; that it was full of horrible monsters, which ate men and canoes together; that there was even a demon who barred the way and swallowed up all who ventured to approach him; finally, that the heat was so bad in these countries that it would inevitably cause our death.

I thanked them for the good advice that they gave me, but told them that I could not follow it because the salvation of souls was at stake. For that I would be delighted to give my life.

Thus we left the waters flowing to Quebec, 400 or 500 leagues from here, to float on those that would take us through strange lands.

Finally on June 25 we saw on the water's edge some tracks of men, and a narrow and somewhat beaten path leading to a fine prairie. We stopped to examine it; and, thinking that it was a road which led to some village, we resolved to go and reconnoiter it.

Monsieur Joliet and I undertook this investigation—a rather hazardous one for two men who exposed themselves alone to the mercy of an unknown people. We silently followed the narrow path. After walking about two leagues, we discovered a village on the bank of a river. Then we heartily commended ourselves to God, and, after asking His aid, we went farther without being seen. We approached so near that we could even hear the savages talking. We therefore decided that it was time to reveal ourselves. This we did by shouting with all our energy, and stopped without going any farther. On hearing the shout, the savages quickly came out of their cabins. Having recognized us as Frenchmen, especially when they saw a black gown—or, at least, having no cause to distrust us since we were only two men and had given them notice of our arrival—they named four old men to come and speak to us.

Two of these old men bore tobacco pipes, finely decorated and adorned with various feathers. They walked

French settlers followed in the path blazed by explorers such as Marquette and Joliet. As this picture shows, it took brave, hardy men and women to adapt to the rugged life on the cold Canadian frontier.

slowly and raised their pipes toward the sun without saying a word. Finally, when they had drawn near, they stopped to look at us attentively. I spoke to them first and asked who they were. They replied that they were Illinois; and as a token of peace, they offered us their pipes to smoke. They afterward invited us to enter their village, where all the people impatiently awaited us.

Adapted from *The Jesuit Relations and Allied Documents,* ed. Reuben Gold Thwaites, 1900.

READING REVIEW ★ ★ ★ ★ ★ ★ ★

1. What dangers did the Menominee Indians warn the two Frenchmen about?
2. How did the Indians whom Marquette and Joliet met show that they meant the Frenchmen no harm?
3. **Making inferences.** Why did Father Marquette make this dangerous trip and take such risks as going alone into the Indian village?

★ ★ ★ ★ ★ ★ ★ ★ ★ ★ ★ ★ ★ ★ ★ ★ ★

Introduction After the rough first years of the Jamestown colony, when all but 60 of 900 settlers died, conditions gradually began to improve. Yet life in Virginia was still far from easy. Those who lived outside Jamestown faced great difficulties—shortages, illness, loneliness. Richard Frethorne describes this life in a letter he wrote to his parents in England in 1623. His life was especially difficult because he came to America as an indentured servant. (See page 117.)

Vocabulary Before you read this selection, find the meaning of these words in a dictionary: rogue, victuals, redeem, entreat.

Loving and kind father and mother:

My most humble duty remembered to you, hoping in God of your good health. This is to let you understand that I, your child, am in a most heavy case because of the nature of the country, which causes much sickness. When we are sick there is nothing to comfort us. Since I came out of the ship, I never ate anything but peas and loblollie (that is, water gruel). As for deer or venison, I never saw any since I came into this land. There is indeed some fowl. But we are not allowed to go and get it. We must work hard both early and late for a mess of water gruel and a mouthful of bread and beef.

We live in fear of the enemy every hour; we are but 32 to fight against 3,000 if they should come. And the nearest help that we have is 10 miles from us. When the rogues overcame this place the last time they slew 80 persons.

I have nothing to comfort me. I have nothing at all—no, not a shirt to my back but two rags, nor no clothes but one poor suit, nor but one pair of shoes, one pair of stockings, and one cap. My cloak was stolen by one of my own fellows. And to his dying hour, he would not tell me what he did with it. Some of my fellows saw him take butter and beef out of a ship, which my cloak, I doubt not, paid for.

I am not a quarter as strong as I was in England, and all is for want of victuals. I tell you that I have eaten more in one day in your home than I have here in a week. You have given more than my day's allowance to a beggar at the door.

If you love me you will redeem me suddenly, for which I do entreat and beg. And if you cannot get the merchants to redeem me for some little money, then for God's sake get a gathering or ask some good folks to lay out some little sum of money in meal and cheese and butter and beef. The answer of this letter will be life or death to me.

Your loving son,

Richard Frethorne

Virginia

3rd April, 1623

Adapted from Richard Frethorne, letter to his father and mother, 1623, in *The Records of the Virginia Company of London,* ed. Susan M. Kingsbury (New York: AMS Press, 1935).

READING REVIEW ★ ★ ★ ★ ★ ★ ★

1. What does Richard Frethorne ask his father to do for him?

2. What does Frethorne dislike most about his life in America?

3. **Comparing points of view.** (a) How did Richard Frethorne's experience with native Americans and his attitude toward them differ from that of Marquette? (b) How would you explain the difference?

★ ★ ★ ★ ★ ★ ★ ★ ★ ★ ★ ★ ★ ★ ★ ★ ★

Introduction Indians helped the Pilgrims survive in Plymouth. This friendly relationship between Indians and English was largely due to the good will of people on both sides. These passages are from a journal written by William Bradford, first governor of Plymouth Colony, and Edward Winslow, one of the colony's founders. Their journal is the only firsthand account of the Pilgrims' first weeks in America.

Vocabulary Before you read the selection, find the meaning of these words in a dictionary: rendezvous, carriage.

Friday, March 16

There presented himself a savage, which caused an alarm. He very boldly came all alone and along the houses straight to the rendezvous where we met him.

He greeted us in English and bade us welcome, for he had learned some broken English amongst the Englishmen that came to fish along the coast.

Samoset [the Indian] was a man free in speech, so far as he could express his mind, and of a seemly carriage. We questioned him of many things. He was the first savage we could meet withal.

These people are ill affected towards the English because of Hunt, a master of a ship, who deceived the people, and carried 20 away and sold them for slaves.

Thursday, March 22

About noon we met again about our public business, but we had scarce been an hour together but Samoset came again with Squanto, who was one of the 20 captives carried away by Hunt. He had been in England and could speak a little English. They brought with them some few skins of trade, and some red herrings newly taken and dried. After an hour their King came. Then we made a treaty of peace, which was:

1. That neither he nor any of his should do hurt to any of our people.

2. And if any of his did hurt to any of ours, he should send the offender that we might punish him.

3. If any did unjustly war against him, we would aid him; if any did war against us, he should aid us.

4. He should go to his neighbors to tell them of this, that they might not wrong us, but might be likewise included in the conditions of peace.

Many different Native American nations lived in North America when the Pilgrims and other Europeans arrived. This painting shows several Indians who have just sighted a European ship on the Hudson River. Such sights must have seemed alien and frightening at first.

5. That when their men came to us, they should leave their bows and arrows behind them, as we should do our muskets when we came to them.

So after all was done, the Governor conducted him to the brook, and there they embraced each other and he departed.

Adapted from William Bradford and Edward Winslow, *A Relation or Journal of the beginnings and proceedings of the English Plantation at Plimoth in New England by certaine English Adventurers,* 1622.

READING REVIEW ★ ★ ★ ★ ★ ★ ★

1. How did Samoset learn English?
2. What had happened to Squanto in the past that made his friendliness toward the Pilgrims surprising?
3. **Analyzing a primary source.** (a) In the peace treaty, what did the Indians agree to do that would benefit the English? (b) What did the English agree to do that would benefit the Indians? (c) Which side gained the most from the treaty?

★ ★ ★ ★ ★ ★ ★ ★ ★ ★ ★ ★ ★ ★ ★ ★ ★ ★

★ 4-6 What to Take to the New World ★

Introduction Many colonists had a hard time in America because they were not well prepared for their new life. They were used to a wide variety of available goods and services. Yet early colonists had to take with them or make themselves everything they would need in their new life.

The Reverend Francis Higginson decided to do what he could to help future colonists. In 1630, he published a book that contained this checklist of things to take to the New World.

Vocabulary Before you read the selection, find the meaning of these words in a dictionary: firkin, ell, frowers, trencher, kine.

Victuals for a whole year for a man, and so after the rate for more
8 bushels of meal
2 bushels of peas
2 bushels of oatmeal
1 gallon of aqua-vita
1 gallon of oil
2 gallons of vinegar
1 firkin of butter
   Apparel
1 Monmouth cap
3 falling bands
3 shirts
1 waistcoat
1 suit of canvas

1 suit of frieze
1 suit of cloth
3 pair of stockings
4 pair of shoes
2 pair of sheets
7 ells of canvas, to make a bed and bolster
1 pair of blankets
1 coarse rug
   Arms
1 armor, complete
1 long piece
1 sword
1 belt
1 bandoleer
20 pound of powder
60 pound of lead
1 pistol and goose shot
   Tools
1 broad hoe
1 narrow hoe
1 broad axe
1 felling axe
1 steel handsaw
1 whipsaw
1 hammer
1 spade
2 augers
4 chisels
2 piercers, stocked
1 gimlet
1 hatchet
2 frowers
1 handbill

1 grindstone
1 pickaxe
nails, of all sorts
  Household Implements
1 iron pot
1 kettle
1 frying pan
1 gridiron
2 skillets
1 spit
wooden platters
dishes
spoons
trenchers
  Spices
sugar
pepper
cloves
mace
cinnamon
nutmegs, fruit

Also, there are diverse other things necessary to be taken over to this plantation, [such] as books, nets, hooks and lines, cheese, bacon, kine, goats, etc.

Adapted from *Chronicles of the First Planters of the Colony of Massachusetts Bay,* ed. Alexander Young, 1846.

READING REVIEW ★ ★ ★ ★ ★ ★ ★

1. A bushel equals 32 quarts. How much oatmeal did Reverend Higginson assume a man would eat in a week?
2. What other important items do you think should have been included in the list?
3. **Classifying information.** Under which heading would Higginson have listed the following items: flour, salt, rope, towels, bucket?

★ ★ ★ ★ ★ ★ ★ ★ ★ ★ ★ ★ ★ ★ ★ ★ ★

Topic

5 English Colonies Take Root (1630–1750)

★ 5-1 A Slave's Ballad on an Indian Attack ★

Introduction In 1621, Pilgrims and Indians sat down together for the first Thanksgiving. Yet not long afterwards, this friendly beginning had given way to open hostility. New Englanders started to claim Indian land, and the Indians struck back in revenge. These attacks could be unexpected and frightening. The 1746 attack on the village of Deerfield, Massachusetts, was typical. One of the best descriptions of the event is the account given by Lucy Terry, a black slave. Terry wrote this account in the form of a ballad.

Vocabulary Before you read the selection, find the meaning of these words in a dictionary: ambush, valiant.

A 1704 Indian attack on Deerfield, Massachusetts, is shown in this painting. The town was destroyed and at least 50 colonists were killed.

August 'twas the twenty-fifth
Seventeen hundred forty-six
The Indians did in ambush lay
Some very valiant men to slay.
Twas nigh unto Sam Dickinson's mill
The Indians there five men did kill
The names of whom I'll not leave out.
Samuel Allen like a hero fought
And though he was so brave and bold
His face no more shall we behold.
Eleazer Hawks was killed outright
Before he had time to fight
Before he did the Indians see
Was shot and killed immediately.
Oliver Amsden he was slain
Which caused his friends much grief
    and pain.
Simeon Amsden they found dead
Not many rods off from his head.
Adonijah Gillet we do hear
Did lose his life which was so dear.
John Saddler fled across the water
And so escaped the dreadful slaughter.
Eunice Allen see the Indians coming

And hoped to save herself by running
And had not her petticoats stopt her
The awful creatures had not cotched her
And tommyhawked her on the head
And left her on the ground for dead.
Young Samuel Allen, Oh! lack-a-day
Was taken and carried to Canada.

Adapted from Lucy Terry, "A Slave Report in Rhyme on the Indian Attack on Old Deerfield, August 25, 1746."

READING REVIEW ★ ★ ★ ★ ★ ★ ★

1. What kind of weapons did the Indians use?
2. It seems that entire families were involved in the attack. Describe the fate of the Allens in your own words.
3. **Using a poem as a primary source.** What sort of relationship do you think Lucy had with her owners and with the other white families in Deerfield? Base your answers on evidence in the ballad.

★ ★ ★ ★ ★ ★ ★ ★ ★ ★ ★ ★ ★ ★ ★ ★ ★ ★

★ 5-2 Witchcraft in Massachusetts? ★

Introduction Not only uneducated people took part in the Salem witch hunt. Even the best-educated of Puritans believed in the devil and the possibility that he used ordinary men and women to do his work. Increase Mather was one of the intellectual leaders of the Massachusetts Bay Colony. Yet in 1684, Mather wrote a pamphlet warning his fellow citizens that the devil was at work in their midst. This selection is taken from that pamphlet.

Vocabulary Before you read the selection, find the meaning of these words in a dictionary: disquieted, bodkin, vanity, conjurer.

In the year 1679, the house of William Morse, in Newberry in New England, was strangely disquieted by a demon. After those troubles began, he did, by

the advice of friends, write down the particulars of those unusual accidents. And the account which he gives thereof follows:—

On December 8, in the morning, there were five great stones and bricks by an invisible hand thrown in at the west end of the house while the man's wife was making the bed. The bedstead was lifted up from the floor, and the bedstaff flung out of the window, and a cat was hurled at her. A long staff danced up and down in the chimney; a burnt brick and a piece of weatherboard were thrown in at the window.

In another evening, they went to bed undressed because of their late disturbances, and the man, wife, and boy presently felt themselves pricked. Upon searching, they found in the bed a bodkin, a knitting needle, and two sticks pointed at both ends. The man received also a great blow on his thigh and on his face, which fetched blood. And while he was writing, a candlestick was twice thrown at him; and a great piece of bark fiercely smote him; and a pail of water turned up without hands.

On December 26, the boy barked like a dog, and clucked like an hen; and after long being kept from speaking, said: "There's Powel, I am pinched." His tongue likewise hung out of his mouth so as that it could by no means be forced in till his fit was over, and then he said 'twas forced out by Powel.

Neither were there many words spoken by Satan all this time. Only once, having put out their light, they heard a scraping on the boards and then a piping and drumming on them, which was followed with a voice singing, "Revenge! Revenge! Sweet is revenge!" And they, being terrified by it, called upon God. Suddenly, with a mournful note, there were six times uttered such expressions as, "Alas! me knock no more! Me knock no more!" And now all ceased.

Thus far is the story concerning the demon of William Morse's house in Newberry. The true reason for these strange disturbances is as yet not certainly known. Some did suspect Morse's wife to be guilty of witchcraft.

One of the neighbors took apples which were brought out of that house, and put them into the fire—upon which, they say, their houses were much disturbed. I shall not here enlarge upon the vanity and superstition of such experiments, reserving that for another place.

Others were apt to think that a seaman, by some suspected to be a conjurer, set the devil to work thus to disquiet Morse's family. Or it may be some other thing, as yet kept hid in the secrets of Providence.

Adapted from Increase Mather, "An Essay for the Recording of Illustrious Providences," 1684.

READING REVIEW ★ ★ ★ ★ ★ ★ ★

1. Describe three of the events reported to be the work of a demon for which there could be a logical or scientific explanation.

2. (a) Does Mather think he is superstitious? (b) Do you think he is? Support your answers with evidence from the selection.

3. **Drawing conclusions.** What do you think might have happened to a woman named Powel at the time of the Salem witchcraft trials? Why?

★ ★ ★ ★ ★ ★ ★ ★ ★ ★ ★ ★ ★ ★ ★ ★ ★ ★ ★

Two New England colonies, Connecticut and Rhode Island, were set up by people who were discontent with life in Massachusetts Bay. Thomas Hooker, shown here moving to the Connecticut River Valley, thought that there should be limits on the power of the government.

Introduction The Dutch were eager for settlers to come to the colony of New Netherland and transform its vast expanses into productive farmland. Some wealthy people were lured by the promise of a large tract of land in return for starting a small private colony. Others, awed by the scope of such an undertaking, needed more encouragement. So in 1650, the Secretary of New Netherland, Cornelius Van Tienhoven, wrote a report that gave detailed advice on how to go about founding a colony in New Netherland. This selection is from that report.

Vocabulary Before you read the selection, find the meaning of these words in a dictionary: felled, palisades, hamlet, wainscot, spars.

Those who are obliged to work in the colonies ought to sail from this country in March or at the latest in April, so as to be able to plant garden vegetables, maize, and beans, and also to use the whole summer in clearing land and building cottages as I shall hereafter describe.

All, then, who arrive in New Netherland must immediately set about preparing the soil, so as to be able, if possible, to plant some winter grain. The trees are usually felled from the stump, cut up and burnt in the field, except such as are suitable for building—for palisades, posts, and rails. The farmer, having thus begun, must try every year to clear as much new land as he possibly can and sow it with such seed as he considers suitable.

It is not necessary that the farmer should take up much livestock in the beginning, since clearing land and other work do not permit him to save much hay or to build barns for stabling. One pair of draft horses or a yoke of oxen is necessary to take the planks for buildings or rails from the land to the place where they are to be set. The farmer can get all sorts of cattle in the course of the second summer, when he will have more leisure to cut and bring home hay and also to build barns and houses for men and cattle.

Before beginning to build it will above all things be necessary to select a well-located spot, either on some river or bay, suitable for the settlement of a village or hamlet. This is to be properly surveyed and divided into lots, with good streets according to the situation of the place. This hamlet can be fenced all around with high palisades or long boards and closed with gates, which is advantageous in case of attack by the natives.

Those in New Netherland and especially in New England, who have no means to build farmhouses at first, should dig a square pit in the ground, cellar fashion, six or seven feet deep and as long and as broad as they think

Much work was required before settlers could even begin to build or plant crops. One way of clearing land is shown here. First, strips of bark were cut around the trees to kill them. When dead, they were cut down. Finally, the stumps were burned.

proper. They should case the earth inside with wood all around the wall, and line the wood with the bark of trees or something else, to prevent the caving in of the earth. They should floor this cellar with plank and wainscot it overhead for a ceiling, raise a roof of spars, and clear up and cover the spars with bark or green sods—so that they can live dry and warm in these houses with their entire families for two, three, and four years.

The wealthy and principal men in New England, in the beginning of the colonies, began their first dwelling houses in this fashion for two reasons: firstly, in order not to waste time building, and secondly, in order not to discourage poorer laboring people whom they brought over in numbers from the fatherland. In the course of three or four years, when the country became adapted to agriculture, they built themselves handsome houses, spending on them several thousands.

Adapted from Cornelius Van Tienhoven, "Information Relative to Taking Up Land in New Netherland," in *The Documentary History of the State of New York*, ed. E. B. O'Callaghan, Vol. IV, 1851.

READING REVIEW ★ ★ ★ ★ ★ ★ ★

1. What sort of houses did Van Tienhoven encourage colonists to build at first?
2. Why does he recommend this type of housing?
3. **Understanding chronology.** In what order did Van Tienhoven suggest colonists undertake the following tasks: planting a garden, clearing land, building a house, buying cattle, preparing palisades and fence rails?

★ ★ ★ ★ ★ ★ ★ ★ ★ ★ ★ ★ ★ ★ ★ ★ ★ ★ ★

★　　5-4　　Bacon Rebels　　

Introduction The first rebellion of colonists against a British governor was that led by a fiery young Virginian, Nathaniel Bacon, in 1676. Bacon complained that the government had not helped the colonists defend themselves against Indian attacks, despite repeated promises to do so. Their patience exhausted, Bacon and his followers decided to take matters into their own hands. The result was fierce and frightening violence. This selection was written by a member of the Virginia legislature who witnessed much of the rebellion firsthand.

Vocabulary Before you read the selection, find the meaning of these words in a dictionary: redoubt, proclamation, procrastination.

In these frightful times the most exposed small families withdrew into our houses, which we fortified with palisades and redoubts. Neighbors joined their labors, taking their arms into the fields and setting sentinels. No man stirred out of doors unarmed. Indians were sighted, three, four, five, or six in a party, lurking throughout the whole land. Yet (what was remarkable) I rarely heard of any houses burnt, nor ever of any corn or tobacco cut up, or other injury done, besides murders, except the killing of a very few cattle and swine.

Frequent complaints of bloodshed were sent to Sir William Berkeley, the governor, from the heads of the rivers, which were often answered with promises of assistance.

The people at the heads of James and York Rivers grew impatient at the many slaughters of their neighbors. They rose for their own defense, choosing Mr. Bacon for their leader.

During these delays, with people often slain, the officers and 300 men, led by Mr. Bacon, met. They discussed the danger of going without a commission* on the one part, and the continual murders of their neighbors on the other part, and came to this resolution: to prepare themselves with supplies for a march, but in the meantime, to send again for a commission. If one could not be obtained by a certain day, they would proceed, commission or no commission.

This day ended and no commission came. So they marched into the wilderness in quest of these Indians. After this the Governor sent his proclamation, denouncing all rebels who should not return within a limited time. Most obeyed. But Mr. Bacon with 57 men proceeded until their provisions were near spent, without finding enemies. Then coming near a fort of friendly Indians, on the other side of the James River, they offered payment for provisions which these Indians kindly promised to give them on the morrow. But the Indians put them off with promises until the third day when they had eaten their last morsels. And now 'twas suspected these Indians had received private messages from the Governor which were the causes of these procrastinations. That evening a shot from the place they left on the other side of the river killed one of Mr. Bacon's men. This made them believe that those in the fort had sent for other Indians to come behind them and cut them off.

Thereupon they set fire to the palisades, stormed and burnt the fort and cabins, and (with the loss of three English) slew 150 Indians.

Adapted from *Beginning, Progress and Conclusion of Bacon's Rebellion in Virginia,* reprinted 1897.

---

*A commission refers to the official right to undertake certain actions, in this case to fight the Indians.

Bacon and his followers came from the recently settled backcountry of Virginia. Conditions in the wild and rugged backcountry were very different from those in the older coastal settlements. The failure of the colonial government to understand the differences helped create the frustration that led to Bacon's rebellion.

READING REVIEW ★ ★ ★ ★ ★ ★ ★

1. What had Indians done to anger the colonists?

2. What led Bacon to attack the Indians he did?

3. **Expressing an opinion.** (a) Do you think Bacon's actions were justified? Explain. (b) Why do you think the Indians were attacking the settlers?

★ ★ ★ ★ ★ ★ ★ ★ ★ ★ ★ ★ ★ ★ ★ ★ ★

Introduction Many colonists sympathized with Nathaniel Bacon's hostility towards the Indians they met in the New World. Others, however, saw the Indians as a friendly, even a noble people. Robert Beverley lived in Virginia at the same time as Bacon. Yet he had a very different attitude towards the same Indian nations that Bacon attacked. This selection is from a book Beverley wrote about Virginia.

Vocabulary Before you read the selection, find the meaning of these words in a dictionary: retinue, diverted, boisterous, melancholy.

The Indians are of the middling and large stature of the English. They are straight and well-proportioned, having the cleanest and most exact limbs in the world. They are so perfect in their outward frame that I never heard of one single Indian that was either dwarfish, crooked, bandy-legged, or otherwise misshapen.

Their color, when they are grown up, is a chestnut brown and tawny, but much lighter in their infancy. Their skin comes afterward to harden and grow blacker, by greasing and sunning themselves. They have generally coal black hair, and very black eyes. Their women are generally beautiful, possessing shape and features agreeable enough, and wanting no charm but that of education.

The men wear their hair cut after several fanciful fashions, sometimes greased and sometimes painted. The great men, or better sort, preserve a long lock behind for distinction. They pull their beards out by the roots with mussel shells. The women wear the hair of the head very long, either hanging at their backs, or brought forward in a single lock, bound up with a band of wampum or beads. Sometimes also they wear it neatly tied up in a knot behind. It is commonly greased, and shining black, but never painted.

They have a remarkable way of entertaining all strangers, which is performed after the following manner. First, the king or queen, with a guard and a great retinue, march out of the town, a quarter or half a mile, carrying mats. When they meet the strangers, they invite them to sit down upon those mats. Then they pass the ceremony of the pipe. They fill that pipe with the best tobacco they have, and then present it to the strangers, and smoke out of the same after them. Afterward, having spent about half an hour in serious conversation, they get up all together and march into the town.

Here the first compliment is to wash the courteous traveler's feet. Then he is entertained by a great number of attendants. After this he is diverted with antique Indian dances, performed both by men and women, and accompanied with great variety of wild music.

Their sports and pastimes are singing, dancing, instrumental music, and some boisterous games which are performed by running, catching, and leaping upon one another.

Their singing is not the most charming that I have heard. It consists much in raising the voice and is full of slow melancholy accents. However, I must admit even this music contains some wild notes that are pleasant.

Their dancing is performed either by few or a great company, but without much regard either to time or to steps. The first of these is by one or two persons, or at most by three. In the meanwhile, the company sit about them in a ring upon the ground, singing outrageously and shaking their rattles.

The other is performed by a great number of people, the dancers themselves forming a ring. Each has his rattle in his hand, or what other thing he fancies most, as his bow and arrows or his tomahawk. They also dress themselves up with branches of trees or some other strange costume.

Adapted from Robert Beverley, *The History of Virginia in Four Parts,* 1705.

READING REVIEW ★ ★ ★ ★ ★ ★ ★

1. What does Beverley think of the Indians' appearance?

2. How do the Indians of Virginia welcome strangers?

3. **Making inferences.** Beverley is not hostile to the Indians. But does he respect them? Explain.

★ ★ ★ ★ ★ ★ ★ ★ ★ ★ ★ ★ ★ ★ ★ ★ ★

★ 5-6 Contract of an Indentured Apprentice ★

Introduction Indentured servants agreed to work for a certain period of time in return for payment of their passage to America. Such arrangements were also made by colonists who wished to learn a particular craft or trade. These young people, called apprentices, would agree to work for a master craftsworker for a number of years in exchange for being taught that person's trade. This contract between an apprentice cordwainer, or leatherworker, and his master is typical of such agreements of indenture. The obligations of both people involved are spelled out in detail.

Vocabulary Before you read the selection, find the meaning of these words in a dictionary: consent, matrimony.

This indenture witnesses that William Matthews, son of Marrat of the city of New York, does voluntarily and of his own free will and by the consent of his mother put himself as an apprentice cordwainer to Thomas Windover.

He will serve from August 15, 1718, until the full term of seven years be completed and ended. During all of this term, the said apprentice shall faithfully serve his said master, shall faithfully keep his secrets, and gladly obey his lawful commands everywhere.

He shall do no damage to his said master, nor see any done by others without giving notice to his said master. He shall not waste his said master's goods nor lend them unlawfully to any. He shall not contract matrimony within the said term.

At cards, dice, or any other unlawful game, he shall not play with his own goods or the goods of others. Without permission from his master, he shall neither buy nor sell during the said term. He shall not absent himself day or night from his master's service without his permission, nor visit alehouses, but in all things he shall behave himself as a faithful apprentice toward his master all during his said term.

The said master, during the said term, shall, by the best means or methods, teach or cause the said apprentice to be taught the art or mystery of a cordwainer. He shall find and provide unto the said apprentice meat, drink, clothing, lodging, and washing fit for an apprentice. During the said term, every night in winter he shall give the apprentice one quarter of schooling. At the end of the said tèrm, he shall provide him with a decent new suit of clothes, four shirts, and two neckties.

Adapted from *Collections of the New York Historical Society for the Year 1909,* 1910.

1. In what ways did William Mathews's contract limit his actions?

2. Young Mathews's master owed him food, clothing, and lodging. What else did he owe his apprentice?

3. **Analyzing a primary source.** An indentured worker had to serve his master and obey him. Yet such a worker could still be said to be free. What lines in the contract support this fact?

★ ★ ★ ★ ★ ★ ★ ★ ★ ★ ★ ★ ★ ★ ★ ★ ★ ★ ★

Topic

6 Life in the Colonies (1630–1775)

★ 6-1 A Young Girl of Colonial Boston ★

Introduction By the 1700s, life in Boston was livelier and more leisurely than it had been for the earlier Puritan settlers. Yet Puritan influence remained strong. Seeing to the proper development of their minds and souls was still a priority with Bostonians. This selection is from the diary kept by an 11-year-old Boston girl in the mid–1700s. In it, Anna Green Winslow gives a glimpse of what life was like for a young girl.

Vocabulary Before you read the selection, find the meaning of these words in a dictionary: disabled, flax, exert.

January 4, 1772 I was dressed in my yellow coat, my black bib & apron, my shoes, the cap my Aunt Storer presented me with (blue ribbons on it) & a very handsome locket in the shape of a heart she gave me. And I would tell you that for the first time they all liked my dress very much.

January 11 I have attended my school every day this week except Wednesday afternoon. I made a visit to Aunt Suky, & was dressed just as I was to go to the ball. I heard Mr. Thacher preach our lecture last eve-

ning. I remember a great deal of the sermon, but don't have time to put it down.

February 9 I am disabled by a sore on my fourth finger & something like one on my middle finger from using my own pens. But altho' my right hand is in bandages, my left is free. My aunt says it will be a nice opportunity when it improves to learn to spin flax. I am pleased with the proposal & aim at present to exert myself for this purpose. I hope, when two or at most three months are past, to give

Young girls in the colonies spent much time at handiwork such as sewing, spinning, and knitting. Many made elaborate embroidered samplers to demonstrate their skill with a needle. Samplers were typical of the practical forms of art that developed in the colonies. This sampler was made in Connecticut in the 1700s.

you a visible demonstration of my skill in this art, as well as several others.

I have read my Bible to my aunt this morning (as is the daily custom) & sometimes I read other books to her.

February 21 My Grandmamma sent Miss Deming, Miss Winslow, & I one eighth of a dollar apiece for a New Year's gift. I have made the purchase I told you of a few pages ago, that is, last Thursday I purchased with my aunt Deming's leave a very beautiful white feather hat. I have long been saving my money to buy this hat.

February 22 I have spun 30 knots of linen and mended a pair of stockings for Lucinda, read a part of the *Pilgrim's Progress*, copied part of my text journal.

Played some, laugh'd enough, & I tell aunt it is all human nature, if not human reason.

Adapted from *Diary of Anna Green Winslow.*

READING REVIEW ★ ★ ★ ★ ★ ★

1. What place do clothes have in Anna's life? How does her attitude toward clothes compare with that of an 11-year-old girl today?
2. What role does Anna think playing, talking, and laughing should have in people's lives?
3. **Analyzing a primary source.** What evidence is there in Anna's diary that her family still feels that the life of the mind and of the soul are important?

★ ★ ★ ★ ★ ★ ★ ★ ★ ★ ★ ★ ★ ★ ★ ★ ★

★ **6-2 A Critical View of Philadelphia** ★

Introduction For the most part, people who settled in the Middle Colonies enjoyed a comfortable life. Travelers remarked especially on the agreeableness of life in Philadelphia, the region's largest city. But at least one observer had a less than flattering response to Philadelphia. A Scottish doctor, Alexander Hamilton, traveled to several colonial cities in 1744. This selection is from his account of his travels.

Vocabulary Before you read the selection, find the meaning of these words in a dictionary: regularity, obstinate, perpetual, nonresistance, traffic.

At my entering the city, I observed the regularity of the streets. But at the same time the majority of the houses were mean and low and much decayed, the streets in general not paved, very dirty, and covered with rubbish.

Thursday, June 7 I noticed one example of industriousness as soon as I got up and looked out my window, and that was the shops open at 5 in the morning.

Friday, June 8 I dined at a tavern with a very mixed company of different nations and religions. There were Scots, English, Dutch, Germans, and Irish; there were Roman Catholics, Church men, Presbyterians, Quakers, Methodists, Seventh-Day men, Moravians, Anabaptists, and one Jew. The whole company consisted of 25 planted round an oblong table in a great hall well-stocked with flies.

Saturday, June 9 The market in this city is perhaps the largest in North America. The street where it stands, called Market Street, is large and spacious, composed of the best houses in the city.

They have but one public clock here which strikes the hour but has neither hands nor dial plate. It is strange that they should want such an ornament and convenience in so large a place, but the chief part of the community are Quakers, who seem to shun ornament in their public buildings as well as in their apparel or dress.

The Quakers are the richest and the people of greatest interest in the government. Their House of Assembly is chiefly composed of them. They have the character of an obstinate, stiff-necked generation and are a perpetual trouble to their governors.

Here is no public storehouse of arms nor any method of defense, either for city or province, in case of the invasion of an enemy. This is owing to the obstinacy of the Quakers in maintaining their principle of nonresistance.

I never was in a place so populous where public diversions were found so little. There is no such things as assemblies of the gentry among them, for either dancing or music. Their chief employ, indeed, is trade and mercantile business, which turns their thoughts from these innocent amusements, for the most part so agreeable and entertaining to the young, and indeed, in the opinion of moderate people, so helpful in the improvement of politeness, good manners, and humanity.

Adapted from Alexander Hamilton, *Itinerarium*, 1907.

The influence of cultures other than the English was strongest in the Middle Colonies. This was especially true in New York, which had been a Dutch colony for years.

READING REVIEW ★ ★ ★ ★ ★ ★ ★

1. Name three things about Philadelphia that Hamilton admires.
2. What does Hamilton dislike about the Quakers?
3. **Recognizing a point of view.** Hamilton is dismayed to find that Philadelphia has no "public amusements." What does he say in defense of such amusements?

★ ★ ★ ★ ★ ★ ★ ★ ★ ★ ★ ★ ★ ★ ★ ★ ★ ★

★ 6-3 A Slave Describes the Middle Passage ★

Introduction The horrors endured by slaves on the Middle Passage from Africa to the New World can be most keenly realized by hearing them described firsthand. One slave who eventually wrote an account of his experiences was Gustavus Vasa. Vasa was captured by white slave traders when he was only 11. Young Vasa was industrious, however. After several years he was able to buy his freedom and acquire an education. This selection is from his autobiography.

Vocabulary Before you read the selection, find the meaning of these words in a dictionary: indulge, flog, loathsome.

When I was carried on board I was immediately handled and tossed up, to see if I were sound, by some of the crew. I was now persuaded that I had got into a world of bad spirits, and that they were going to kill me.

I was not long allowed to indulge my grief. I was soon put down under the decks. There, with the stench and crying together, I became so sick and low that I was not able to eat, nor had I the least desire to taste anything. But soon, to my grief, two of the white men offered me something to eat. On my refusing to eat, one of them held me fast by the hands and tied my feet, while the other flogged me severely.

I feared I should be put to death because the white people looked and acted, as I thought, in so savage a manner. I had never seen among any people such instances of brutal cruelty. And this was not only shown towards

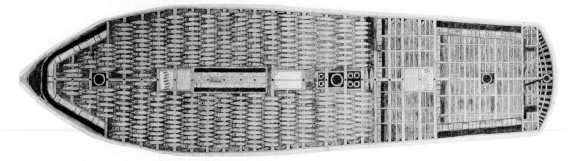

This diagram of the inside of a slave ship shows a loading plan for squeezing as many chained men and women as possible into the available space. Such severe overcrowding was but one part of the inhuman treatment slaves received on the Middle Passage.

us blacks, but also to some of the whites themselves. One white man in particular I saw flogged so unmercifully with a large rope that he died because of it; and they tossed him over the side as they would have done a brute. This made me fear these people the more.

The stench of the hold while we were on the coast was so intolerably loathsome that it was dangerous to remain there for any time. The closeness of the place and the heat of the climate, added to the number in the ship, which was so crowded that each had scarcely room to turn himself, almost suffocated us.

One day, when we had a smooth sea and moderate wind, two of my wearied countrymen, who were chained together, preferring death to such a life of misery, somehow made through the nettings and jumped into the sea. Immediately another quite dejected fellow, who on account of his illness was allowed to be out of irons,

also followed their example. And I believe many more would very soon have done the same if they had not been stopped by the ship's crew, who were instantly alarmed. There was such a noise and confusion among the people of the ship to stop and get the boat to go after the slaves. Two of the wretches were drowned, but they got the other, and afterwards flogged him unmercifully for preferring death to slavery.

Adapted from Gustavus Vasa, *The Interesting Narrative of the Life of Olandah Equiano or Gustavus Vasa, Written by Himself,* 1793.

READING REVIEW ★ ★ ★ ★ ★ ★ ★

1. What did the white traders do that especially aroused Vasa's fear?
2. Why did several of the slaves jump overboard?
3. **Drawing conclusions.** Why do you think the traders tried to keep the slaves alive, yet at the same time treated them so poorly?

★ ★ ★ ★ ★ ★ ★ ★ ★ ★ ★ ★ ★ ★ ★ ★ ★ ★ ★

★　　6-4　　Getting an Education in Virginia　　★

Introduction Except among the wealthy, schooling was often hard to come by in the middle and southern colonies. This selection, from the autobiography of Devereux Jarratt, tells of the problems faced by both those who wanted to learn and those who wanted to teach. Yet the selection also tells how the love of learning triumphs over great odds.

Vocabulary Before you read the selection, find the meaning of these words in a dictionary: scrawl, rhetoric, harrowed.

At 8 or 9 years old, I was sent to an English school in the neighborhood. And I continued to go to one teacher and another as opportunity arose, though not without great interruptions, till I was 12 or 13. In this time I learned to read the Bible and to write a sorry scrawl, and acquired some knowledge of arithmetic. With this small fund, I left school.

By the time I was 18 or 19, I wished for more knowledge, especially in figures. My friends, I dare say, thought me a scholar—but I knew better. I had not gone far in arithmetic, and was very superficial in the rules I had been hurried through. To understand figures well we reckoned the height of learning. Philosophy, rhetoric, logic, etc. we never heard of. There were no books on such subjects among us. Arithmetic was all and all. To acquire this, I borrowed a plain book. And while the horse, with which I harrowed or ploughed, was grazing an hour or two at noon, I frequently spent the time studying that book. And being now of an age for better discovering the nature of things, I made greater progress in the real knowledge and use of figures in one month than I had done in years while at school. But I had no thought, then, of becoming a teacher. Yet, while at the plough or ax, I seemed out of my element. Neither of these, as time showed, was the business for which I was designed.

I was so well skilled in the division of crops that, you may be sure, the fame of my learning sounded far. One Jacob Moon, living in Albemarle county, about 100 miles from New Kent, had also heard how learned I was. He sent me word that he should be glad to employ me as a schoolmaster, and supposed I might get as many pupils in his neighborhood as would make it worth my while to set up a school. I readily agreed. We soon entered on the business of raising a school. But I quickly discovered that the number of pupils would be far short of what I had been made to expect.

I opened my little school, though the promised income, as might be foreseen, would scarce afford me clothing of the coarsest sort. However, I was content with a little which I could call my own.

Adapted from Devereux Jarratt, The Life of Devereux Jarratt, 1806.

READING REVIEW ★ ★ ★ ★ ★ ★

1. What did Jarratt think was the most important school subject?
2. Why do you think Jarratt was content as a teacher, even though his income was very small?
3. **Expressing an opinion.** Jarratt says he learned more about figures in one month as an adult than he had in years in school. Do you agree with the saying "Education is wasted on the young"? Why or why not?

★ ★ ★ ★ ★ ★ ★ ★ ★ ★ ★ ★ ★ ★ ★ ★ ★

★   6-5   Advice on Entering College

Introduction New Englanders took education seriously, and none more so than the select few who went on to college, often at the age of 13 or 14. This selection is from a letter written by Thomas Shepard, a Massachusetts minister, to his son who was about to enter Harvard College.

Vocabulary Before you read the selection, find the meaning of this word in a dictionary: vanity.

Dear Son,

Remember the end of this turn of your life—your coming into the College. It is to fit you for the most glorious work which God can call you to—the holy ministry.

Remember that though you have spent your time in the vanity of childhood sports and laughter, little minding better things, now, when it is time to enter the College, God and man expect you should put away childish things. So you may not be weary in the work God sets you about, remember these rules.

1. Single out two or three scholars who are most godly, learned, and studious to help you in your studies. Get into the acquaintance of some of your equals, to spend some time with them often discussing the things you hear and read and learn; and also grow acquainted with some that are your superiors, of whom you may often ask questions and from whom you may learn more than by your equals only.

2. Let not your studies be pursued in a disorderly way; but keep a fixed order of studies suited to your own genius and circumstances of things. Fix your course and the season for each kind of study, and allow no other matters or persons to interrupt you.

3. Let difficult studies have the strength and flower of your time and thoughts; and therein allow no difficulty to pass unresolved. But either by your own labor or by asking others, or by both, master it before you pass from it.

4. Choose to confess your ignorance in any matter so that you may be instructed by your tutor or another rather than continue in your ignorance.

5. Suffer not too much to be spent and broken away in visits. Let them be such as may be for your profit in learning some way or other.

Your father,
T. Shepard

Adapted from letter from the Reverend Mr. Thomas Shepard to his son, 1672, in *Publications of the Colonial Society of Massachusetts*, 1913.

READING REVIEW ★ ★ ★ ★ ★ ★ ★

1. What was the purpose of a college education, according to the letter?
2. According to Shepard, what is the chief purpose of friends in college?
3. **Summarizing.** Rewrite in your own words the five instructions Shepard gives to his son.

★ ★ ★ ★ ★ ★ ★ ★ ★ ★ ★ ★ ★ ★ ★ ★ ★ ★ ★

★　6-6　The Wisdom of Benjamin Franklin　★

Introduction Benjamin Franklin was one of the first of this country's many self-made men. Although poor as a boy and lacking much formal schooling, Franklin became one of the most respected men in the world. Franklin learned much in the course of his life about what makes for success. He summed up many of his ideas in brief sayings that people could remember easily. Some are printed here.

Vocabulary Before you read the selection, find the meaning of these words in a dictionary: bestir, industry, hinder, frugality, saucy, suppress.

God helps them that help themselves.

But dost thou love life, then do not waste time, for that is the stuff life is made of.

How much more than is necessary do we spend in sleep, forgetting that the sleeping fox catches no poultry, and that there will be sleeping enough in the grave.

Early to bed and early to rise, makes a man healthy, wealthy, and wise.

So what means wishing and hoping for better times? We may make these times better if we bestir ourselves.

At the working man's house, hunger looks in but dares not enter, for industry pays debts.

God gives all things to industry.

Work while it is called today, for you know not how much you may be hindered tomorrow.

Never leave that till tomorrow which you can do today.

So much for industry, my friends, and attention to one's own business; but to this we must add frugality, if we would make our industry more certainly successful. A man may, if he knows not how to save as he gets, keep his nose all his life to the grindstone and die not worth a penny at last.

If you would be wealthy, think of saving as well as of getting.

Away, then, with your expensive follies, and you will not then have so much cause to complain of hard times, heavy taxes, and chargeable families.

You may think, perhaps, that a little tea, or a little punch now and then, diet a little more costly, clothes a little finer, and a little entertainment now and then can be no great matter; but remember, a small leak will sink a great ship.

Many a one, for the sake of finery on the back, have gone with a hungry belly, and half starved their families.

Pride is as loud a beggar as want, and a great deal more saucy.

When you have bought one fine thing, you must buy ten more that your appearance may be all of a piece. It is easier to suppress the first desire than to satisfy all that follow it.

For age and want save while you may; no morning sun lasts a whole day.

Get what you can, and what you get hold; tis the stone that will turn all your lead into gold.

Adapted from Benjamin Franklin, "The Way to Wealth," 1758.

READING REVIEW ★ ★ ★ ★ ★ ★ ★

1. What is Franklin's policy on spending money on extravagances? Do you agree with him?
2. What reasons does Franklin give for avoiding even one small fine or extravagant item?
3. **Understanding the economy.** What are the two main principles that Franklin says will lead to wealth?

★ ★ ★ ★ ★ ★ ★ ★ ★ ★ ★ ★ ★ ★ ★ ★ ★

Benjamin Franklin made many lasting contributions to American life. For example, he started the colonies' first fire department in Philadelphia.

Introduction By the mid–1700s, the colonists had begun to develop a culture of their own. How did life in this new land transform Europeans into a new breed of men and women called Americans? One of the first people to try to answer this question was a Frenchman named Michel–Guillaume Jean de Crèvecoeur. Crèvecoeur had settled in New York and traveled extensively in the colonies in the 1760s. This selection is from his impressions of what he saw.

Vocabulary Before you read the selection, find the meaning of these words in a dictionary: servile, haughty, resurrection, epoch, freeholder, vagrant.

The American is a new man, who acts upon new principles. From servile dependence, poverty, and useless labor, he has passed to work of a very different nature, rewarded by an ample living. This is an American.

A European, when he arrives, very suddenly alters his scale. Two hundred miles used to appear a very great distance; it is now but a trifle. He no sooner breathes our air than he forms schemes and begins projects he never would have thought of in his own country. Thus Europeans become Americans.

Let me select one as an example of the rest. He is hired. He goes to work and works moderately. Instead of being employed by a haughty person, he finds himself with his equal. His wages are high. If he behaves with decency and is faithful, he is cared for, and becomes, as it were, a member of the family. He begins to feel the effects of a sort of resurrection. Until now he had not lived, but simply vegetated. He now feels himself a man because he is treated as such.

Judge what a change must arise in the mind and thoughts of this man. He begins to forget his former servitude and dependence. His heart begins to swell and glow. This first swell inspires him with those new thoughts which make a man an American.

He looks around and sees many a prosperous person who but a few years before was as poor as himself. This encourages him much. He begins to form some little scheme, the first he ever formed in his life.

He is encouraged, he has gained friends. He is advised and directed, he feels bold, he purchases some land.

What an epoch in this man's life! He is become a freeholder, from perhaps a German peasant. He is now an American. Instead of being a vagrant, he has a place of residence. And for the first time in his life, he counts for something. For until now he has been a nothing.

This great change has a double effect. It snuffs out all his old European attitudes. He forgets that servility which poverty had taught him. If he is a good man, he forms schemes of future prosperity. He proposes to educate his children better than he has been educated himself. He feels a desire to labor he never felt before.

Adapted from Michel–Guillaume Jean de Crèvecoeur, *Letters from an American Farmer*, 1782.

READING REVIEW ★ ★ ★ ★ ★ ★

1. According to Crèvecoeur, what had life been like for people in Europe before they came to America?

2. What was it about life in America that caused colonists to work hard and make plans for their future?

3. **Relating past to present.** Today, poverty is a problem in parts of America, especially in some of our larger cities. If Crèvecoeur were alive today, what do you think he might propose as a solution to poverty?

★ ★ ★ ★ ★ ★ ★ ★ ★ ★ ★ ★ ★ ★ ★ ★ ★

Theme 3

The Struggle for Independence

Topic

7 Crisis in the Colonies (1745–1775)

★ 7-1 Friendship With the Mohawks ★

Introduction English settlers often had conflicts with Native Americans. Unlike French fur traders, English settlers cleared and farmed the land. This threatened the Indian way of life. One English trader, William Johnson, won the respect of the Indians. He convinced the Mohawks to support the English in their struggle with the French. This painting shows a meeting between Johnson and the Mohawks.

READING REVIEW ★ ★ ★ ★ ★ ★ ★

1. Does this appear to be a friendly meeting? Explain.
2. What do you suppose the buildings on either side of the house are for?
3. **Using visual evidence.** What can you conclude about relations between the English and the Mohawks from this painting?

★ ★ ★ ★ ★ ★ ★ ★ ★ ★ ★ ★ ★ ★ ★ ★ ★ ★

Introduction In 1753, young George Washington was sent on a mission to warn the French to pull back their forces from the Ohio Valley. Washington's account of the trip reveals much about both French and English attitudes towards the Indians who were caught in the middle of the struggle between the two great European nations. This selection is from Washington's report to the governor of Virginia.

Vocabulary Before you read the selection, find the meaning of these words in a dictionary: dispatch, complaisant.

Wednesday, October 31, 1753 I was appointed by the Honorable Robert Dinwiddie, Governor of Virginia, to visit and deliver a letter to the commandant of the French forces on the Ohio.

November 25 About three o'clock this evening the Half-King Jeskakate came to town. I went up and invited him privately to my tent and asked him to relate some of the particulars of his journey to the French commandant, and reception there, also to give me an account of the ways and distance.

November 26 As I had orders to make all possible dispatch, I told him that my business would not allow delay. He told me that he could not consent to our going without a guard for fear some accident should befall us. Accordingly he gave orders to King Shingiss, who was present, and two men of their nation to be ready to set out with us next morning.

We set out about nine o'clock with the Half-King, White Thunder, and the Hunter.

December 7 At eleven o'clock we set out for the fort. We were prevented from arriving there till the eleventh by excessive rains, snows, and bad traveling through many mires and swamps.

December 12 I prepared early to meet the French commander.

I asked the commander by what authority he had made prisoners of several of our English subjects. He told me that the country belonged to them; that no Englishman had a right to trade upon those waters; and that he had orders to make every person prisoner who tried it.

December 15 The commandant ordered a plentiful store of provisions to be put on board our canoe. He appeared to be extremely complaisant, though he was using every plan which he could invent to set our own Indians against us. He tried to prevent their going till after our departure, using presents, rewards, and everything which could be suggested by him or his officers. I can't say that ever in my life I suffered so much anxiety as I did in this affair.

December 16 The French were not slack in their inventions to keep the Indians this day also, but I urged and insisted that the Half-King set off with us as he had promised.

Adapted from *The Writings of George Washington,* ed. Worthington C. Ford, 1889.

READING REVIEW ★ ★ ★ ★ ★ ★ ★

1. What gesture did the Half-King make to Washington that showed his concern?
2. How did the French commander justify the arrest of several Englishman?
3. **Analyzing a primary source.** What evidence is there in Washington's report that both the French and the British used the Indians for their own purposes?

★ ★ ★ ★ ★ ★ ★ ★ ★ ★ ★ ★ ★ ★ ★ ★ ★ ★

Introduction The battle on the Plains of Abraham was one of the great battles of history. Not only did its outcome determine whether Canada was to be British or French. It also pitted against each other two great generals——Englishman James Wolfe, just 32 years old, and a French nobleman, the Marquis de Montcalm. This selection about the encounter is from *Montcalm and Wolfe,* written by historian Francis Parkman in 1884.

Vocabulary Before you read the selection, find the meaning of these words in a dictionary: detachment, infantry, ardor, fugitive.

Montcalm had passed a troubled night. At daybreak he heard the sound of cannon above the town. He had sent an officer nearer Quebec, with orders to bring him word at once should anything unusual happen. But no word came, and about six o'clock he mounted and rode there.

Montcalm was amazed at what he saw. He had expected a detachment, and he found an army. Full in sight before him stretched the lines of Wolfe: the close ranks of the English infantry, a silent wall of red. Fight he must, for Wolfe was now in a position to cut off all his supplies. Montcalm's men were full of ardor, and he resolved to attack before their ardor cooled. He spoke a few words to them in his keen, strong way.

"I remember very well how he looked," one of the Canadians, then a boy of eighteen, used to say in his old age. "He rode a black or dark bay horse along the front of our lines, brandishing his sword, as if to excite us to do our duty. He wore a coat with wide sleeves, which fell back as he raised his arm, and showed the white linen of the wristband."

Wolfe himself was everywhere. How cool he was and how his followers loved him. It was toward ten o'clock when, from the high ground on the right of the line, Wolfe saw that the crisis was near. The French came on rapidly, uttering loud shouts, and firing as soon as they were within range. The British advanced a few rods, then halted and stood still.

When the French were within 40 paces, the word of command rang out, and a crash of musketry answered all along the line. When the smoke rose, a miserable sight was revealed: the ground was strewn with dead and wounded. The advancing French stopped short and turned into a frantic mob.

The order was given to charge. Wolfe himself led the charge. A shot shattered his wrist. He wrapped his handkerchief about it and kept on. Another shot struck him, and he still advanced, when a third lodged in his breast. He staggered, and sat on the ground. Lieutenant Brown, of the grenadiers, one Henderson, a volunteer in

The nobility with which General James Wolfe died on the Plains of Abraham quickly became legendary. His last moments were celebrated by artists as well as historians. This painting, Benjamin West's *Death of General Wolfe,* was done in 1770.

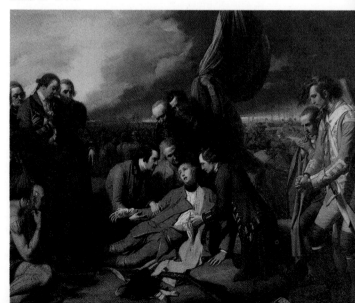

the same company, and a private soldier carried him in their arms to the rear. He begged them to lay him down. They did so, and asked if he would have a surgeon. "There's no need," he answered. "It's all over with me. Go, one of you, to Colonel Burton," ordered the dying man. "Tell him to march Webb's regiment down to Charles River, to cut off their retreat from the bridge." Then, turning on his side, he murmured, "Now, God be praised, I will die in peace!" and in a few moments his gallant soul had fled.

Montcalm, still on horseback, was carried with the tide of fugitives towards the town. As he approached the walls a shot passed through his body. He kept his seat; two soldiers supported him, one on each side, and led his horse through the St. Louis gate. On the open space within, among the excited crowd, were several women, drawn, no doubt, by eagerness to know the result of the fight. One of them recognized him, saw the streaming blood, and shrieked, "Oh my God! my God! The Marquis is killed!" "It's nothing, it's nothing," replied the dying man. "Don't be troubled for me, my good friends."

Adapted from Francis Parkman, *Montcalm and Wolfe*, 1884.

READING REVIEW ★ ★ ★ ★ ★ ★ ★

1. Why was Montcalm surprised when he arrived at Quebec?
2. According to Parkman, why did Montcalm decide he had to fight Wolfe?
3. **Supporting generalizations.** (a) Based on this account, how would you describe each of the two men? (b) Support your generalization with specific examples.

★ ★ ★ ★ ★ ★ ★ ★ ★ ★ ★ ★ ★ ★ ★ ★ ★ ★

★ 7-4 Indians Treat Captives With Kindness ★

Introduction English colonists did much to provoke the anger of Native Americans. Many, such as Pontiac and those he led, eventually fought back. Yet even in the midst of open hostility, many Indians remained friendly towards the colonists. In this selection, William Smith reports that the Indians he fought against in Pontiac's War treated the English prisoners they had taken more like guests than like enemy captives.

Vocabulary Before you read the selection, find the meaning of these words in a dictionary: torrents, provisions, persisted.

They delivered up their beloved captives with the utmost reluctance. They shed torrents of tears over them, recommending them to the care and protection of the French commanding officer. Their regard for the prisoners continued all the time they remained in camp. They visited from day to day and brought them corn, skins, and horses, accompanied with other presents and all the marks of the most sincere and tender affection.

Nay, they did not stop there. When the army marched, some of the Indians asked for and obtained leave to accompany their former captives all the way to Fort Pitt, and employed themselves in hunting and bringing provisions for them on the road.

A young Mingo carried this still further. A young woman of Virginia was among the captives, to whom he had formed so strong an attachment as to call her his wife. He ignored all warnings of the great danger to which he exposed himself by approaching the frontiers. He followed her, at the risk of being killed by the surviving relations of many unfortunate persons who had been captured or scalped by those of his nation.

Among the children who had been carried off young and had long lived with the Indians, it is not to be expected that any marks of joy would appear on being restored to their parents or relatives. They had been accustomed to look upon the Indians as the only connections they had. And they had been tenderly treated by them and spoke their language. Therefore, it is no wonder that they parted from the savages with tears. But it must not be denied that there were even some grown persons who showed an unwillingness to return.

Adapted from William Smith, *An Historical Account of an Expedition Against the Ohio Indians, in the Year 1764, Under the Command of Henry Bouquet, Esq.*

READING REVIEW ★ ★ ★ ★ ★ ★ ★

1. What did the Indians do that showed their affection for their prisoners?
2. How did the children react to being united with their parents? Why?
3. **Relating cause and effect.** What effect did the Indians' treatment have on the colonists who were their prisoners?

★ ★ ★ ★ ★ ★ ★ ★ ★ ★ ★ ★ ★ ★ ★ ★ ★

★ 7-5 Paul Revere on the Boston Massacre ★

Introduction Copies of Paul Revere's engraving of the Boston Massacre, shown here, did much to arouse colonists' anger toward the British. One reason for its powerful effect was a poem Revere wrote to accompany his illustration. Both the poem and the picture presented the massacre in a way that emphasized the gruesomeness of what the British had done. Revere's poem follows on page 498. The words P--n and C---st are thinly disguised names of two of the British involved in the incident.

Vocabulary Before you read the selection, find the meaning of these words in a dictionary: hallowed, aught, appease, venal, execrations.

Unhappy Boston!

Unhappy Boston! see thy sons deplore
Thy hallowed walks besmeared with
    guiltless gore:
While faithless P--n and his savage
    bands
With murderous hatred stretch their
    bloody hands;
Like fierce barbarians grinning o'er
    their prey
Approve the slaughter and enjoy the
    day.
If scalding drops, from rage, from an-
    guish wrung,
If speechless sorrow laboring for a
    tongue,
Or if a weeping world can aught ap-
    pease
The weeping ghosts of victims such as
    these;
The patriots' flowing tears for each are
    shed,
A glorious tribute which embalms the
    dead.
But know, Fate summons to that awful
    goal,

Where justice strips the murderer of
    his soul:
Should venal C---st, the scandal of the
    land,
Snatch the relentless villain from her
    hand,
Keen execrations on this plate in-
    scribed
Shall reach a judge who never can be
    bribed.

Adapted from Paul Revere, "Bloody Boston," in Burton Stevenson, *Poems of American History*, 1908.

READING REVIEW ★ ★ ★ ★ ★ ★ ★

1. What feelings and attitudes does the poem say the British had at the time of the Boston Massacre?
2. According to this poem, what role did the colonists play in the massacre?
3. **Recognizing propaganda.** Propaganda is the promotion or distortion of information in favor of a particular cause. What about the way Revere describes the Boston Massacre makes his poem qualify as propaganda?

★ ★ ★ ★ ★ ★ ★ ★ ★ ★ ★ ★ ★ ★ ★ ★ ★ ★ ★

★   7-6   Philadelphia's Tea Protest   ★

Introduction The Boston Tea Party is well known. Yet other colonial cities also took bold measures against the Tea Act of 1773. This letter was sent by angry colonists in Philadelphia to the captain of a British tea ship. In it they threatened, among other things, to tar and feather* the captain if he should land his cargo.

Vocabulary Before you read the selection, find the meaning of these words in a dictionary: combustible, pitch, diabolical, gauntlet, decant.

---

*Tarring and feathering was a measure frequently used by colonists to strike back at British officials. Hot tar was poured over the victim, often burning him badly. Then feathers were stuck in the tar to give him the appearance of a giant chicken, and so humiliate him.

Sir:

We are informed that you have unwisely taken charge of a quantity of tea which has been sent out by the East India Company as a trial of American virtue and resolution.

Now, your cargo, on your arrival here, will most assuredly bring you into hot water. As you are perhaps a stranger to these parts, we have concluded to advise you of the present situation of affairs in Philadelphia. Thus, you may stop short in your dangerous errand. You can secure your ship against the rafts of combustible matter which may be set on fire and turned loose against her. And more than all this, you may preserve your own person from the pitch and feathers that are prepared for you.

In the first place, we must tell you that the Pennsylvanians are, to a man, passionately fond of freedom, the birthright of Americans, and at all events are determined to enjoy it.

That they sincerely believe no power on the face of the earth has a right to tax them without their consent.

That, in their opinion, the tea in your custody is designed by the ministry to enforce such a tax, which they will undoubtedly oppose.

You are sent out on a diabolical service. And if you are so foolish and stubborn as to complete your voyage by bringing your ship to anchor in this port, you may run such a gauntlet as will cause you in your last moments most heartily to curse those who have made you the dupe of their greed and ambition.

What think you, Captain, of a halter around your neck—ten gallons of liquid tar decanted on your head—with the feathers of a dozen wild geese laid over that to enliven your appearance?

Only think seriously of this—and fly to the place from whence you came—fly without hesitation—without the formality of a protest—and above all, Captain Ayres, let us advise you to fly without the wild geese features.

Your friends to serve,
The Committee of Tarring and Feathering

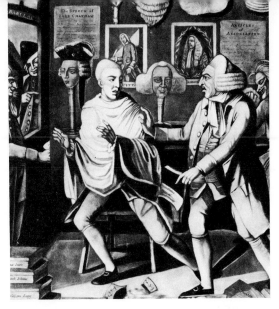

Colonists enjoyed a chance to see the British humiliated. This cartoon shows a surprised British officer being thrown out of a barber shop, wigless and half-shaven. The barber had refused to finish the shave when he discovered that his customer was a British official.

Adapted from Frederick D. Stone in *Pennsylvania Magazine of History and Biography,* 1891.

READING REVIEW ★ ★ ★ ★ ★ ★ ★

1. What did the Philadelphians threaten to do to the captain's ship?
2. Why did they oppose the importation of the captain's tea?
3. **Drawing conclusions.** (a) What does this letter tell you about colonial feelings toward the British? (b) Do you think Captain Ayres brought his tea into Philadelphia?

★ ★ ★ ★ ★ ★ ★ ★ ★ ★ ★ ★ ★ ★ ★ ★ ★ ★

Topic 8
The American Revolution (1775–1783)

★ 8-1 Glory on Bunker Hill ★

Introduction American troops were proud of the showing they made in the Battle of Bunker Hill. Although they lost, they had shown that they could hold their own against the British. The glory soldiers found on Bunker Hill became the subject of this popular Revolutionary War song.

Vocabulary Before you read the selection, find the meaning of these words in a dictionary: veteran, sire.

The Sword of Bunker Hill

He lay upon his dying bed;
His eye was growing dim,
When with a feeble voice he call'd
His weeping son to him:
"Weep not, my boy!" the veteran said,
"I bow to Heaven's high will,—
But quickly from yon antlers bring
The Sword of Bunker Hill;
But quickly from yon antlers bring
The Sword of Bunker Hill."

The sword was brought, the soldier's
        eye
Lit with a sudden flame;
And as he grasped the ancient blade,
He murmured Warren's name:
Then said, "My boy, I leave you gold,—
But what is richer still,
I leave you, mark me, mark me now—
The Sword of Bunker Hill;
I leave you, mark me, mark me now—
The Sword of Bunker Hill.

"'Twas on that dread, immortal day,
I dared the Briton's band,
A captain raised this blade on me—
I tore it from his hand;
And while the glorious battle raged,
It lightened freedom's will—
For boy, the God of freedom blessed
The Sword of Bunker Hill;

For, boy, the God of freedom blessed
The Sword of Bunker Hill.

"Oh, keep the sword!"—his accents
        broke—
A smile—and he was dead!
His wrinkled hand still grasped the
        blade
Upon that dying bed.
The son remains; the sword remains—
Its glory growing still—
And twenty millions bless the sire,
The Sword of Bunker Hill;
And twenty millions bless the sire,
The Sword of Bunker Hill.

A Revolutionary War song.

READING REVIEW ★ ★ ★ ★ ★ ★ ★

1. How did the dying soldier come to own the sword of Bunker Hill?
2. What did the soldier mean when he said to his son that the sword of Bunker Hill was "richer than gold"?
3. **Using a song as historical evidence.** The songwriter says "the God of freedom blessed the Sword of Bunker Hill." What attitudes about the war can you infer from this statement?

★ ★ ★ ★ ★ ★ ★ ★ ★ ★ ★ ★ ★ ★ ★ ★ ★ ★

★ 8-2 How the Declaration Was Written ★

Introduction The Declaration of Independence is one of the most important documents in our country's history. Americans celebrate its signing yearly, on July 4. Yet its origins are humble, little different from those of many other papers written by committees. In this letter written later in his life, Boston patriot John Adams gives us an insider's view of how the Declaration came to be.

Vocabulary Before you read the selection, find the meaning of these words in a dictionary: felicity, explicit, oratory, philippic, hackneyed.

You inquire why so young a man as Mr. Jefferson was placed at the head of the committee for preparing a Declaration of Independence? I answer: Mr. Jefferson came into Congress in June

1775 and brought with him a reputation for literature, science, and a happy talent of composition. Writings of his were handed about, remarkable for the peculiar felicity of expression. Though a silent member in Congress, he was so prompt, frank, explicit, and decisive upon committees and in conversation—not even Samuel Adams was more so—that he soon seized upon my heart. And upon this occasion I gave him my vote and did all in my power to convince the others.

The subcommittee met. Jefferson proposed to me to make the draft. I said, "I will not." "You should do it." "Oh! no." "Why will you not? You ought to do it." "I will not," I replied. "Why?" "Reasons enough." "What can be your reasons?" "Reason first, you are a Virginian, and a Virginian ought to appear at the head of this business. Reason second, I am obnoxious, suspected, and unpopular. You are very much otherwise. Reason third, you can write ten times better than I can." "Well," said Jefferson, "if you are decided, I will do as well as I can." "Very well. When you have drawn it up, we will have a meeting."

A meeting we accordingly had, and looked the paper over. I was delighted with its high tone and the flights of oratory with which it abounded, especially that concerning Negro slavery, which, though I knew his Southern brethren would never allow to pass in Congress, I certainly never would oppose. There were other expressions which I would not have inserted if I had drawn it up, particularly that which called the king a tyrant. I thought this too personal, for I never believed George to be a tyrant in disposition and in nature. I always believed him to be deceived by his advisers on both sides of the Atlantic, and cruel in his official capacity only. I thought the expression too passionate, and too much like a scolding, for so grave and solemn a document. But I do

After debating Jefferson's proposed Declaration of Independence for two days, Congress voted to accept it. This painting shows that historic occasion.

not now remember that I made or suggested a single alteration.

We reported it to the committee of five. It was read, and I do not remember that Franklin or Sherman criticized anything. We were all in haste. Congress was impatient and the document was reported, as I believe, in Jefferson's handwriting, as he first drew it. Congress cut off about a quarter of it, as I expected they would. But they cut some of the best of it, and left all that was objectionable, if anything in it was. I have long wondered that the original draft had not been published. I suppose the reason is the vehement philippic against Negro slavery.

As you justly observe, there is not an idea in it but what had been hackneyed in Congress for two years before. The substance of it is contained in the declaration of rights and the violation of those rights in the Journals of Congress in 1774. Indeed, the essence of it is contained in a pamphlet, voted and printed by the town of Boston, before the first Congress met, composed by James Otis, as I suppose, in one of his lucid intervals, and pruned and polished by Samuel Adams.

Adapted from *The Works of John Adams*, 1850.

1. According to Adams, where did Jefferson get the ideas in the Declaration of Independence?
2. Why did Adams want Jefferson to write the draft of the Declaration of Independence?

3. **Drawing conclusions.** Adams does not say explicitly what was cut from Jefferson's first version of the Declaration. Yet he gives enough clues that you should be able to figure out one of the cut sections. What was this?

★ ★ ★ ★ ★ ★ ★ ★ ★ ★ ★ ★ ★ ★ ★ ★ ★

★　8-3　A Loyalist Is Tarred and Feathered　★

Introduction The treatment suffered by Loyalists at the hands of their fellow colonists was often harsh. One popular means of harrassment was tarring and feathering. The letter below, written by Ann Hulton, a Loyalist woman from Boston, gives a particularly graphic account of a tarring and feathering.

Vocabulary Before you read the selection, find the meaning of this word in a dictionary: magistrate.

The most shocking cruelty was exercised a few nights ago upon a poor old man, one Malcolm. A quarrel was picked with him. He was afterward taken and tarred and feathered. There's no law that knows a punishment for the greatest crimes beyond what this is, of cruel torture. And this instance exceeds any other before it. He was stripped naked on one of the severest cold nights this winter. His body was covered all over with tar, then with feathers. His arms were dislocated in tearing off his clothes. He was dragged in a cart, with thousands attending, some beating him with clubs and knocking him out of the cart, then in again. They gave him several severe whippings, at different parts of the town. This spectacle of horror and sportive cruelty went on for about five hours.

The unhappy wretch they say behaved with the greatest bravery. When under torture they demanded of him to curse his masters, the king, governors, etc., which they could not make him

do. He still cried, "Curse all traitors." They brought him to the gallows and put a rope about his neck saying they would hang him. He said he wished they would, but that they could not for God was above the Devil.

They owe him a grudge for some things, particularly, he was with Governor Tryon in the Battle with the Regulators. The Governor has declared that he was of great service to him in that affair, by his courageous spirit encountering the greatest dangers.

Governor Tryon had sent him a gift of ten guineas just before this inhuman treatment. He has a wife and family and an aged father and mother who, they say, saw the spectacle which no indifferent person can mention without horror.

These few instances among many serve to show the wretched state of government and the barbarisms of the times. There's no magistrate that dare stop the outrages. No person is secure.

Adapted from Ann Hulton, *Letters of a Loyalist: Lady Ann Hulton* (Cambridge, Mass.: Harvard University Press, 1927).

READING REVIEW★ ★ ★ ★ ★ ★ ★

1. What did the Patriots hope to achieve by this tarring and feathering?
2. Why was Malcolm in particular singled out to be a victim?
3. **Supporting generalizations.** (a) What attitude does Ann Hulton express toward the Patriot movement? (b) Do you think the evidence she cites is strong enough to support her conclusion?

★ ★ ★ ★ ★ ★ ★ ★ ★ ★ ★ ★ ★ ★ ★ ★ ★

Introduction Without the help of the Marquis de Lafayette and the French, the colonists might not have won their fight for freedom. The young Marquis who led the French troops was an extraordinary man—enthusiastic, idealistic, warm, and brave. He was just 20 years old when he came over to help Washington in 1777. This letter, written to his wife shortly after his arrival in the colonies, gives much insight into American life as well as into Lafayette's character.

Vocabulary Before you read the selection find the meaning of these words in a dictionary: prevail, higgling, adieu.

Charleston, June 19, 1777

My last letter to you, my dear love, has informed you that I arrived safely in this country, after having suffered a little from seasickness during the first weeks of the voyage.

I will now tell you about the country and its inhabitants. They are as agreeable as my enthusiasm had painted them. Simplicity of manners, kindness, love of country and of liberty, and a delightful equality everywhere prevail. The wealthiest man and the poorest are on a level. Although there are some large fortunes, I challenge anyone to discover the slightest difference between the manners of these two classes respectively toward each other.

I first saw the country life at the house of Major Benjamin Huger. I am now in the city, where everything is very much after the English fashion, except that there is more simplicity, equality, friendliness, and courtesy here than in England. The city of Charleston is one of the handsomest and best built, and its inhabitants among the most agreeable, that I have ever seen. The American women are very pretty, simple in their manners, and exhibit a neatness which is everywhere cultivated even more studiously than in England.

What most charms me is that all the citizens are like brothers. In America there are no poor, nor even what we call peasantry. Each individual has his own honest property and the same rights as the most wealthy landowner. The inns are very different from those of Europe. The host and hostess sit at table with you and do the honors of a comfortable meal. And on going away you pay your bill without higgling.

Considering the pleasant life I lead in this country, my sympathy with the people, which makes me feel as much at ease in their society as if I had known them for 20 years, the similarity between their mode of thinking and my own, and my love of liberty and of glory, one might suppose that I am very happy. But you are not with me; my friends are not with me; and there is no happiness for me far from you and them. I am impatient beyond measure to hear from you.

The night is far advanced, and the heat dreadful. I am devoured by insects; so, you see, the best countries have their disadvantages. Adieu.

Lafayette

Adapted from Marquis de Lafayette, "Letter to his Wife," June 19, 1777, in *America Visited*, ed. Edith I. Coombs (New York: Book League of America, 1946).

READING REVIEW ★ ★ ★ ★ ★ ★ ★

1. How does Lafayette describe American women?

2. What does Lafayette like most about life in the colonies?

3. **Analyzing a primary source.** What clues are there in this letter about why Lafayette decided to support the colonists' cause?

★ ★ ★ ★ ★ ★ ★ ★ ★ ★ ★ ★ ★ ★ ★ ★ ★

Introduction Many Native Americans may have wanted to stay neutral in the conflict between Britain and the colonies. But this was not always easy to do. Both sides pressured the Indians to support them. George Washington wrote this letter to the Passamaquoddy Indians of Maine, urging them to support the colonial cause.

Vocabulary Before you read the selection, find the meaning of these words in a dictionary: allies, covenant, councilor.

Brothers of Passamaquodai:

I am glad to hear by Major Shaw that you accepted the chain of friendship which I sent you last February at Cambridge and that you are determined to keep it bright and unbroken. When I first heard that you refused to send any of your warriors to my assistance when called upon by our brother of St. Johns, I did not know what to think. I was afraid some enemy had turned your hearts against me. But I am since informed that all your young men were hunting, which was the reason of their not coming. This has made my mind easy. And I hope you will always in future join with your brothers of St. Johns and Penobscott when required.

Brothers, I have a piece of news to tell you which I hope you will attend to. Our enemy the King of Great Britain tried to stir up all the Indians from Canada to South Carolina against us. But our brothers of the six nations and their allies the Shawanese and Delawares would not listen to the advice of the messengers sent among them. They kept fast hold of our covenant chain. The Cherokees and the southern tribes were foolish enough to listen to them and to take up the hatchet against us. Upon this our warriors went into their country and burnt their houses, destroyed their corn, and forced them to sue for peace.

Now brothers, never let the king's wicked councilor turn your hearts against me and your brothers of this country, but bear in mind what I told you last February and what I told you now.

In token of my friendship I send you this from my army on the banks of the great River Delaware this 24th day of December, 1776.

George Washington

Adapted from George Washington, "Letter to the Passamaquoddy," December 24, 1776.

READING REVIEW ★ ★ ★ ★ ★ ★ ★

1. What was Washington worried about?
2. Why did colonists burn Cherokee homes and destroy their crops?
3. **Relating cause and effect.** What do you think Washington's motive was for telling the story of the Cherokees in this letter?

★ ★ ★ ★ ★ ★ ★ ★ ★ ★ ★ ★ ★ ★ ★ ★ ★ ★

★ 8-6 A Slave's Support for the Patriots ★

Introduction The brilliant young slave Phillis Wheatley was widely known for her fine poems, many of which supported the colonists' struggle against Britain. Wheatley had been brought from Africa as a child. She had long supported the demand for liberty, as this poem written in 1773 shows.

Vocabulary   Before you read the selection, find the meaning of these
words in a dictionary: grievance, unre-
dressed, wanton, tyranny, sway.

Most blacks, both slave and free, supported the
Patriots in their revolt against Britain. During the
course of the war, about 5,000 blacks fought for
the Patriot cause. This portrait of a free black
sailor was done in 1779.

To the Right Honourable William, Earl
of Dartmouth, His Majesty's Principal
Secretary of State for North America,
and company.

No more America in mournful strain
Of wrongs, and grievance unredress'd
    complain,
No longer shall thou dread the iron
    chain,
Which wanton Tyranny with lawless
    hand Has made,
And which it meant to enslave the
    land.

Should you, my lord, while you pursue
    my song,
Wonder from when my love of Freedom
    sprung,
Whence flow these wishes for the com-
    mon good,
By feeling hearts alone best under-
    stood,
I, young in life, by seeming cruel fate
Was snatched from Afric's fancied
    happy seat:
What pangs excruciating must molest,
What sorrows labour in my parent's
    breast?
Steeled was the soul and by no misery
    moved
That from a father seized his babe be-
    loved.

Such, such my case. And can I then
    but pray
Others may never feel tyrannic sway?

Adapted from Phillis Wheatley, *Poems on Various
Subjects*, 1773.

READING REVIEW ★ ★ ★ ★ ★ ★ ★

1. What do you think the poet means when
she talks of "the iron chain" which is
"meant to enslave the land"?

2. What experience is she referring to when
she talks of being "snatched from Afric's
. . . happy seat"?

3. **Using a poem as a primary source.**
What reason does Wheatley give here for
supporting the Patriots' cause?

★ ★ ★ ★ ★ ★ ★ ★ ★ ★ ★ ★ ★ ★ ★ ★ ★ ★ ★ ★

★   8-7   An Eyewitness at Yorktown   ★

Introduction The surrender of General Cornwallis at Yorktown, Virginia,
did not actually end the Revolution. It
would be a while before the British
would agree to negotiate terms for
peace. Yet both sides were keenly
aware of the significance of the event.
British pride and morale had been dealt
a severe blow—perhaps a mortal one.

This account of the surrender is from
the diary of Dr. James Thacher, a Massachusetts doctor who served as a
surgeon in the colonial army.

Vocabulary Before you read the selection, find the meaning of these
words in a dictionary: chagrin, mortification, sullen, divested.

This print gives a sense of the festive air with which colonists greeted Cornwallis's surrender at Yorktown. American troops are shown in green, French forces in blue, and the British in red. The yellow piles represent the weapons of the British.

October 19, 1781

This is to us a most glorious day; but to the English, one of bitter chagrin and disappointment.

At about twelve o'clock, the combined army was arranged and drawn up in two lines extending more than a mile in length. The Americans were drawn up in a line on the right side of the road, and the French occupied the left.

The Americans were not all in uniform, nor was their dress so neat. Yet they exhibited an erect, soldierly air, and every face beamed with satisfaction and joy. The crowd of spectators from the country was enormous—in point of numbers probably equal to the military—but universal silence and order prevailed.

It was about two o'clock when the captive army advanced through the line formed for their reception. Every eye was prepared to gaze on Lord Cornwallis, the object of peculiar interest. But he disappointed our anxious expectations. Pretending illness, he made General O'Hara his substitute as the leader of his army.

The British army was conducted into a large field, where it was intended they should ground their arms. The royal troops, while marching through the line formed by our army, exhibited a decent and neat appearance as respects arms and clothing. Their commander had opened his store and directed every soldier to be furnished with a new suit prior to the surrender.

But in their line of march we remarked a disorderly and unsoldierly conduct. Their step was irregular and their ranks frequently broken. But it was in the field, when they came to the last act of the drama, that the spirit and pride of the British soldier was put to the severest test. Here their mortification could not be concealed. Some of the platoon officers appeared to be exceedingly chagrined when given the word, "Ground arms." And I am a witness that they performed this duty in a very unofficerlike manner, and that many of the soldiers showed a sullen temper, throwing their arms on the pile with violence, as if determined to render them useless.

After having grounded their arms and divested themselves of their equipment, the captive troops were conducted back to Yorktown.

Adapted from James Thacher, *Military Journal During the American Revolution*, 1854.

READING REVIEW ★ ★ ★ ★ ★ ★

1. How did the American and French troops look at the surrender ceremonies?
2. What in the appearance or behavior of the British showed their feelings.?
3. **Making inferences.** (a) What was the official reason for Cornwallis's absence from the ceremonies? (b) What does Thacher think of this reason? (c) Why do you think Cornwallis was absent?

★ ★

Topic 9 Creating a Government (1776–1790)

★ 9-1 The Articles of Confederation ★

Introduction After declaring their independence, the new states were wary of a strong national government. The first constitution they approved, the Articles of Confederation, guaranteed certain powers to the states and restricted those granted to the new national government. Selections from the articles appear here.

Vocabulary Before reading the selection, find the meaning of these words in a dictionary: sovereignty, confederation.

Article I. The style of this confederacy shall be "The United States of America."

Article II. Each state retains its sovereignty, freedom, and independence. Every power and right which is

In the days of the Articles of Confederation, settlers headed west in large numbers. Indians grew alarmed as settlers occupied land that had been theirs. The Iroquois chief called Cornplanter, shown here, wrote several letters to General Washington protesting the situation.

not expressly delegated to the United States in Congress assembled.

Article III. The said states hereby enter into a firm league of friendship with each other, for their common defense, the security of their liberties, and their mutual and general welfare. They agree to bind themselves to assist each other against all attacks made upon them, or any of them, on account of religion, trade, or any other pretense whatever.

Adapted from *Articles of Confederation*, 1781.

1. What powers and rights did the articles grant to the states?
2. What were the purposes for which the new confederation was formed?
3. **Ranking.** (a) What reason for forming a confederation seems to have been most important to those who wrote the Articles? (b) What in the recent history of the states might account for this?

★ ★ ★ ★ ★ ★ ★ ★ ★ ★ ★ ★ ★ ★ ★ ★ ★ ★ ★

★ 9-2 No Taxation Without Representation ★

Introduction Southern delegates to the Constitutional Convention wanted to include slaves in their population count so that the South could have more representatives in Congress. Yet slaves had no political rights. Many northerners felt that this was unfair. But some northern governments had exploited blacks in a similar fashion. In Massachusetts, for example, blacks could not vote, but free blacks had to pay taxes. This situation was corrected in 1783, largely as a result of a petition written by Paul Cuffe, a free black. This selection is from Cuffe's petition.

Vocabulary Before you read the selection, find the meaning of these words in a dictionary: petition, estate, depressed.

The petition of several poor Negroes and mulattoes who live in the town of Dartmouth humbly shows that, being chiefly of the African race and by reason of long bondage and hard slavery, we have been deprived of the profits of our labor or the advantage of inheriting estates from our parents as our neighbors the white people do. And some of us have not long enjoyed our own freedom. Yet of late, we have been and now are taxed.

We understand that, if continued, this will reduce us to a state of beggary whereby we shall become a burden to others if this is not stopped by the intervention of your justice and power.

Your petitioners further show that we believe ourselves to be wronged, in that while we are not allowed the privilege of freemen of the state, having no vote or influence in the election of those that tax us, yet many of our color (as is well known) have cheerfully entered the field of battle in the defense of the common cause.

We most humbly request therefore that you would take our unhappy case into your serious consideration and in your wisdom and power grant us relief from taxation while under our present depressed circumstances.

Adapted from a manuscript in the Archives Division, Massachusetts Historical Society.

READING REVIEW ★ ★ ★ ★ ★ ★ ★

1. Why did Cuffe feel that it was unjust to tax blacks?
2. What does Cuffe say will eventually happen if blacks are forced to pay taxes?
3. **Understanding economic ideas.** Why, according to Cuffe's petition, did blacks suffer more severe financial hardship than whites after the Revolution?

★ ★ ★ ★ ★ ★ ★ ★ ★ ★ ★ ★ ★ ★ ★ ★ ★ ★ ★

Introduction Some of the great strengths of our Constitution came out of the compromises made. As a result, however, few delegates were happy with all parts of the document. In an attempt to stir up enthusiasm, Benjamin Franklin made this speech to convention delegates on the day they gathered to sign the Constitution.

Vocabulary Before you read the selection, find the meaning of these words in a dictionary: constituents, integrity, unanimously.

Mr. President, I confess that there are several parts of this Constitution which I do not at present approve. But I am not sure I shall never approve them. For, having lived long, I have experienced many instances of being obliged, by better information or fuller consideration, to change my opinions. The older I grow, the more apt I am to doubt my own judgment, and to pay more respect to the judgment of others.

In these sentiments, sir, I agree to this Consitution, with all its faults, if they are such, because I think a general government is necessary for us.

I doubt, too, whether any other convention would be able to make a better constitution. For, when you assemble a number of men to have the advantage of their joint wisdom, you inevitably assemble with those men all their prejudices, their passions, their errors of opinion, their local interests, and their selfish views. From such an assembly can a perfect production be expected? It therefore astonishes me, sir, to find this Constitution approaching so near to perfection as it does. Thus I consent, sir, to this Constitution, because I expect no better, and because I am not sure that it is not the best.

The opinions I have of its errors I sacrifice to the public good. I have never whispered a syllable of them abroad. If every one of us, in returning to our constituents, were to report the objections he has to it, and try to gain partisans in support of them, we might prevent its being generally received. Much of the strength and efficiency of any government, in securing happiness for the people, depends on the general opinion of the goodness of the government, as well as of the wisdom and integrity of its governors.

I hope, therefore, that for our own sakes, as a part of the people, and for the sake of future generations, we shall act heartily and unanimously in recommending this Constitution wherever our influence may extend.

Adapted from James Madison, *Debates in the Federal Convention, 1840.*

READING REVIEW ★ ★ ★ ★ ★ ★

1. Why did Franklin think that this was the best possible Constitution?
2. Did Franklin think the delegates should tell the public of their doubts? Why or why not?
3. **Learning about citizenship.** (a) Why did Franklin say that it was important for delegates to unite in supporting the Constitution? (b) How might the principle Franklin puts forth here apply to our country today?

★ ★ ★ ★ ★ ★ ★ ★ ★ ★ ★ ★ ★ ★ ★ ★

The framers of the Constitution hoped that the document would help strengthen and unify the new country. Another measure they took to help achieve this goal was adopting a national symbol—the powerful bald eagle.

Introduction The Constitutional Convention met just a year after Daniel Shays led a revolt of Massachusetts farmers. When Massachusetts called its convention to vote on ratifying the new Constitution, many farmers opposed it. Some, however, such as Jonathan Smith, favored the new Constitution. This selection is from the speech Smith made at the state convention.

Vocabulary Before you read the selection, find the meaning of these words in a dictionary: anarchy, tyranny, standard, reap.

Mr. President, I am a plain man, and get my living by the plow. I am not used to speak in public, but I beg your leave to say a few words to my brother plow-joggers in this house.

I have lived in a part of the country where I have known the worth of good government by the want of it. There was a black cloud that rose in the east last winter, and spread over the west. It brought on a state of anarchy and that led to tyranny. People

When the last votes needed for ratification finally came in, New York City celebrated with a huge parade. This is the banner that was carried by the Society of Pewterers.

that used to live peaceably, and were before good neighbors, got distracted, and took up arms against government. People took up arms. And if you went to speak to them, you had the musket of death presented to your breast. They would rob you of your property, threaten to burn your houses, oblige you to be on your guard night and day. Alarms spread from town to town, families were broken up, the tender mother would cry, O my son is among them!

Our distress was so great that we should have been glad to snatch at anything that looked like a government. Had any person that was able to protect us come and set up his standard, we should all have flocked to it, even if it had been a monarch, and that monarch might have proved a tyrant. So that you see that anarchy leads to tyranny.

Now, Mr. President, when I saw this Constitution, I found that it was a cure for these disorders. It was just such a thing as we wanted. I got a copy of it and read it over and over. I had been a member of the convention to form our own state constitution, and had learnt something of the checks and balances of power; and I found them all here. I formed my own opinion, and was pleased with this Constitution.

Some gentlemen say, don't be in a hurry, take time to consider, and don't take a leap in the dark. I say, take things in time—gather fruit when it is ripe. There is a time to sow, and a time to reap. We sowed our seed when we sent men to the federal convention. Now is the harvest. Now is the time to reap the fruit of our labor. And if we don't do it now, I am afraid we never shall have another opportunity.

Adapted from Jonathan Elliot, *The Debates on the Federal Constitution*, 1836.

1. According to Smith, how would anarchy lead to tyranny?
2. What reason does Smith give for adopting the Constitution now?

3. **Making inferences.** Why did Smith believe that the present Constitution would be a "cure" for disorders such as Shays' Rebellion?

★ ★ ★ ★ ★ ★ ★ ★ ★ ★ ★ ★ ★ ★ ★ ★ ★

★ 9-5 An Antifederalist Argues His Case ★

Introduction People opposed adoption of the Constitution for many reasons. Some were simply wary of adopting such an important document too quickly without giving it enough thought. The following statement of this objection is from an anonymous contribution to a New York newspaper.

Vocabulary Before you read the selection, find the meaning of these words in a dictionary: illustrious, anarchy, frugality.

As far as I am able to determine, these are the main arguments in favor of the new Constitution.

1. That the men who formed it were wise and experienced; that they were an illustrious band of patriots and had the happiness of their country at heart; that they were four months deliberating on the subject; and therefore it must be a perfect system.

2. That if the system be not received, this country will be without any government, and, as a result, will be reduced to a state of anarchy and confusion; and in the end a government will be imposed upon us, not the result of reason and reflection, but the result of force.

With respect to the first, it will be readily seen that it leaves no room for any investigation of the merits of the proposed Constitution. For if we are to infer the perfection of this system from the characters and abilities of the men who formed it, we may as well accept it without any questions.

In answer to the second argument, I deny that we are in immediate danger of anarchy. Those who are anxious to bring about a measure will always tell us that the present is the critical moment. Tyrants have always made use of this plea, and nothing in our circumstances can justify it.

The country is in profound peace, and we are not threatened by invasion from any quarter.

It is true, the regulation of trade and a provision for the payment of the interest of the public debt is wanting; but no immediate commotion will rise from these. Time may be taken for calm discussion.

Individuals are just recovering from the losses sustained by the late war. Industry and frugality are taking their station and banishing idleness and wastefulness. Individuals are lessening their private debts, and several millions of the public debt is paid off by the sale of western territory.

There is no reason, therefore, why we should hastily and rashly adopt a system which is imperfect or insecure.

Adapted from *New York Journal and Weekly Register,* November 8, 1787.

READING REVIEW ★ ★ ★ ★ ★ ★ ★

1. According to the author, what are the two main reasons for support of the Constitution? State them in your own words.
2. How does the author answer the argument that anarchy would result if the Constitution is not ratified?
3. **Comparing points of view.** (a) How does this author's view of the need to act quickly differ from Jonathan Smith's? (b) What might explain the difference?

★ ★ ★ ★ ★ ★ ★ ★ ★ ★ ★ ★ ★ ★ ★ ★ ★

Strengthening the New Nation

Topic

10 The First Presidents (1789–1800)

★ **10-1 The First President Becomes a Legend** ★

Introduction George Washington was a legend in his own time. The plain, unadorned facts of his life were themselves the stuff of legend. Yet, early on, people began to tell stories about Washington that colored the truth in order to glorify him still further. One of the books that did most to transform the real-life George Washington into a national folk hero was the biography written by Mason Weems, a parson and bookseller. This well-known story comes from Weems's book.

Vocabulary Before you read the selection, find the meaning of these words in a dictionary: vile, barbarously, anecdote, immoderately.

Never did the wise Ulysses take more pains with his beloved son Telemachus, than did Mr. Washington with George, to inspire him with an early love of truth. "Truth, George," said he, "is the loveliest quality of youth. I would ride 50 miles, my son, to see the little boy whose heart is so honest and his lips so pure that we may depend on every word he says. O how lovely does such a child appear in the eyes of everybody!"

"Pa," said George very seriously, "do I ever tell lies?"

"No, George, I thank God you do not, my son; and I rejoice in the hope you never will. At least, you shall never, from me, have cause to be guilty of so shameful a thing. Many parents, indeed, even force their children to this vile practice, by barbarously beating them for every little fault. Hence, on the next offense, the little terrified creature slips out a lie just to escape the rod! But as to yourself, George, you know I have always told you and now tell you again that, whenever by accident you do anything wrong, which must often be the case as you are but a poor little boy yet, without experience or knowledge, never tell a falsehood to conceal it. But come bravely up, my son, like a little man, and tell me of it. And instead of beating you, George, I will but the more honor and love you for it, my dear."

The following anecdote is a case in point. It is too valuable to be lost and too true to be doubted.

When George was about six years old, he was made the wealthy owner of a hatchet! Like most little boys, he was immoderately fond of it and was constantly going out chopping everything that came in his way.

One day, in the garden, he unluckily tried the edge of his hatchet on the body of a beautiful young English cherry tree, which he barked so terribly that I don't believe the tree ever got the better of it.

The next morning, the old gentleman, finding out what had happened to his tree—which, by the by, was a great favorite—came into the house and, with much warmth, asked for the mischievous one responsible. Presently, George and his hatchet made their appearance.

"George," said his father, "do you know who killed that beautiful little cherry tree yonder in the garden?"

This was a tough question, and George staggered under it for a moment. But he quickly recovered himself, and looking at his father, he bravely cried out, "I can't tell a lie, Pa; you know I can't tell a lie. I did cut it with my hatchet."

"Run to my arms, you dearest boy," cried his father with joy, "run to my arms. Glad am I, George, that you killed my tree, for you have paid me for it a thousandfold. Such an act of heroism in my son is worth more than a thousand trees."

Adapted from Mason L. Weems, *The Life of Washington*, 1800.

READING REVIEW ★ ★ ★ ★ ★ ★ ★

1. According to Weem's story, why are many children forced to begin to lie?
2. What moral lesson is Weems trying to teach with this story?
3. **Using fiction as historical evidence.** (a) Historians agree that Parson Weems made up this story. What evidence can you find to support this conclusion? (b) What can you learn from Weem's story about people's feelings toward George Washington in 1800?

★ ★ ★ ★ ★ ★ ★ ★ ★ ★ ★ ★ ★ ★ ★ ★ ★ ★ ★

★ 10-2 Washington Advises Neutrality ★

Introduction George Washington's term as President established many precedents for the new nation. One of the most important was the policy of neutrality in foreign affairs. Washington set this precedent by keeping the United States out of wars among the countries of Europe. In this selection from his Farewell Address, he makes it clear that he believes future generations of Americans should continue to remain neutral.

Vocabulary Before you read the selection, find the meaning of these words in a dictionary: habitual, disposes, illusion, deluded.

Observe good faith and justice towards all nations. Cultivate peace and harmony with all.

In carrying out such a plan, nothing is more essential than that permanent, habitual hatred against particular nations and passionate attachments for others should be excluded. In place of them, just and friendly feelings towards all should be cultivated. Hatred of one nation for another disposes each more readily to offer insult and injury, to lay hold of slight causes of anger, and to be haughty and headstrong when accidental or minor occasions of dispute occur.

So likewise a passionate attachment of one nation for another produces a variety of evils. Sympathy for the favorite nation helps create the illusion of an imaginary common interest in cases where no real common interest exists. It introduces into one the hatreds of the other. And it betrays the former into a participation in the quarrels and wars of the latter, without adequate cause. And it gives to ambitious, corrupted, or deluded citizens (who devote themselves to the favorite nation) an easy chance to betray, or sacrifice the interests of, their own country without hatred, sometimes even with popularity.

Europe has a set of primary interests which to us have no or a very remote relation. Hence she must be engaged in frequent controversies, the causes of which are essentially foreign to our concerns. Therefore, it must be unwise for us to involve ourselves by artificial ties in the ordinary combinations and collisions of her friendships or hatreds.

Adapted from George Washington, "Farewell Address," September 17, 1796.

Americans were eager to find patriotic symbols for their new nation. George Washington soon came to be one such symbol. This painting shows several others: the flag, the American eagle, and Miss Liberty.

READING REVIEW ★ ★ ★ ★ ★ ★ ★

1. What does Washington say are the dangers of too strong an attachment to another nation?
2. What does he say are the dangers of too strong a dislike of another nation?
3. **Relating past to present.** To what degree do you think Washington's advice on foreign policy is still valid?

★ ★ ★ ★ ★ ★ ★ ★ ★ ★ ★ ★ ★ ★ ★ ★ ★ ★ ★

★   10-3   Jefferson Opposes the National Bank   ★

Introduction Early on, the leaders of the new nation began separating into the two camps that would soon become the Federalist and Republican parties. One of the first issues to separate them was that of the national bank. The two men who became leaders of the rival parties, Alexander Hamilton and Thomas Jefferson, locked horns in legendary dispute over the bank. To help him make up his own mind about the bank proposal, President Washington asked Hamilton and Jefferson to give him written defenses of their positions. This selection is from Jefferson's paper.

Vocabulary Before you read the selection, find the meaning of these words in a dictionary: delegate, enumerate, proprietors, commerce, welfare, execution.

I consider the foundation of the Constitution to be laid on this ground— that all powers not delegated to the United States by the Constitution nor prohibited by it to the states are reserved to the states, or to the people. To take a single step beyond the boundaries thus specially drawn around the powers of Congress is to take possession of a boundless field of power no longer capable of being defined.

The incorporation of a bank and the powers assumed by this bill have not, in my opinion, been delegated to the United States by the Constitution.

I. They are not among the powers specially enumerated in the Constitution. For these are:

1. "A power to lay taxes for the purpose of paying the debts of the United States." But no debt is paid by this bill nor any tax laid.

2. "To borrow money." But this bill neither borrows money nor insures the borrowing of it. The proprietors of the bank will be just as free as any other money-holders to lend or not to lend their money to the public.

3. "To regulate commerce with foreign nations and among the states and with the Indian tribes." To erect a bank and to regulate commerce are very different acts.

II. Nor are they within either of the general phrases, which are the two following:

1. "To lay taxes to provide for the general welfare of the United States." They are not to do anything they please to provide for the general welfare, but only to lay taxes for that purpose.

2. "To make all laws necessary and proper for carrying into execution the enumerated powers." But they can all be carried into execution without a bank. A bank, therefore, is not necessary and consequently not authorized by this phrase.

It has been much urged that a bank will give great ease or convenience in the collection of taxes. Suppose this were true. Yet the Constitution allows only the means which are "necessary," not those which are merely "convenient," for effecting the enumerated powers. If such a freedom of construction is allowed to this phrase as to give any nonenumerated power, it will go to every one. Therefore it was that the Constitution restrained them to the necessary means—that is to say, to those means without which the grant of the power would be worthless.

Adapted from Thomas Jefferson, "Opinion on the Constitutionality of the Bank," February 15, 1791.

READING REVIEW ★ ★ ★ ★ ★ ★ ★

1. Explain in your own words Jefferson's idea of a necessary law.
2. (a) What does Jefferson think of as the foundation, or basic principle, of the Constitution? (b) What does he think will happen if the basic principle is not held to?
3. **Making inferences.** Based on Jefferson's paper, list two arguments that were probably being made in favor of the constitutionality of a national bank.

★ ★ ★ ★ ★ ★ ★ ★ ★ ★ ★ ★ ★ ★ ★ ★ ★ ★ ★

With the growth of political parties, election day became an important public event. In this painting, the whole town has turned out for an election.

★ 10-4 Hamilton Supports the Bank ★

Introduction Alexander Hamilton was widely respected for his gifts as a writer as well as for his creative political thinking. This defense of a national bank, which Hamilton wrote for Washington, is regarded as one of his most brilliant works. His plan for a national bank to help solve the financial problems of the new nation was a bold and original one.

Vocabulary Before you read the selection, find the meaning of these words in a dictionary: liberal, latitude, criterion.

Through this manner of reasoning about the right to use all the means required for the exercise of the specified powers of the government, it is objected that none but necessary and proper means are to be used. And Jefferson maintains that no means are to be considered as necessary but those without which the grant of the power would be worthless.

It is essential to the being of the national government that so mistaken an idea of the meaning of the word "necessary" should be exploded.

Necessary often means no more than needful, useful, or helpful to. And this is the true sense in which it is to be understood as used in the Constitution. It was the intent of the Convention to give a liberal latitude to the exercise of the specified powers.

To understand the word as the Secretary of State does would be to depart from its obvious and popular sense and to give it a restrictive function, an idea never before entertained.

It would be to give it the same force as if the word "absolutely" or "indispensably" had been used before it.

The degree in which a measure is necessary can never be a test of the legal right to adopt it. That must be a matter of opinion. The relation between the measure and the end must be the criterion of constitutionality, not the more or less of necessity or usefulness.

If the end be clearly included within any of the specified powers, and if the measure have an obvious relation to that end and is not forbidden by any particular provision of the Constitution, it may safely be said to come within the scope of the national government.

Adapted from *The Works of Alexander Hamilton*, ed. J.C. Hamilton, 1864.

READING REVIEW ★ ★ ★ ★ ★ ★ ★

1. What does Hamilton say the Constitutional Convention intended when it specified the powers it gave to Congress? Explain in your own words.
2. How could Hamilton use the argument in this selection to support a national bank?
3. **Analyzing conflicting opinions.** (a) How does Hamilton's interpretation of the word "necessary" differ from Jefferson's? (b) Give an example of a means one man would consider necessary, the other not necessary, to accomplish a certain end. You may use situations from everyday life.

★ ★ ★ ★ ★ ★ ★ ★ ★ ★ ★ ★ ★ ★ ★ ★ ★

★ 10-5   A Song to Unite Americans ★

Introduction Party rivalry between Republicans and Federalists reached a peak with the passing of the Alien and Sedition acts. Many people were worried that the disputes between the two parties would undermine the strength of the new nation. Joseph Hopkinson, a Philadelphia lawyer, decided to do what he could to reunite his squabbling fellow citizens. He wrote a song for a friend who was a singer. The song, "Hail Columbia," was designed to stir patriotic feelings. It was an immediate hit. President John Adams rose and applauded the first night he heard it.

Vocabulary Before you read the selection, find the meaning of these words in a dictionary: valor, altar.

Hail Columbia, happy land
Hail ye heroes, heav'n-born band
Who fought and bled in freedom's cause
Who fought and bled in freedom's cause
And when the storm of war was gone

Enjoyed the peace your valor won.
Let independence be your boast
Ever mindful what it cost
Ever grateful for the prize
Let its altar reach the skies.

    Chorus
Firm united let us stand
Rallying round our liberty
As a band of brothers joined
Peace and safety we shall find.

Joseph Hopkinson, "Hail Columbia," 1798.

READING REVIEW ★ ★ ★ ★ ★ ★ ★

1. What is Hopkinson referring to with the words "freedom's cause"?
2. Why do you think the songwriter makes such extensive references to America's wartime experiences?
3. **Using a song as historical evidence.** What is the message of the chorus of the song?

★ ★ ★ ★ ★ ★ ★ ★ ★ ★ ★ ★ ★ ★ ★ ★ ★

Topic 10

★ 11-1 The First Republican President ★

Introduction Thomas Jefferson's first inaugural address gave Americans a clear idea of what they could expect from their first Republican President. In this selection from his speech, he spells out what he believed to be the essential principles of the government of the United States. Another key message of Jefferson's speech was his wish to make peace with the Federalists.

Vocabulary Before you read the selection, find the meaning of these words in a dictionary: social intercourse, domestic, pretensions.

Friends and Fellow Citizens:

During the contest of opinion through which we have passed, the liveliness of discussions has sometimes worn an aspect which might make a strong impression on strangers unused to thinking freely and to speaking and writing what they think. But this being now decided by the voice of the nation, all will, of course, unite in common efforts for the common good. All, too, will bear in mind this sacred principle, that though the will of the majority is in all cases to prevail, the minority possesses their equal rights, which equal law must protect, and to violate would be oppression. Let us, then, fellow citizens, unite with one heart and one mind. Let us restore to social intercourse that harmony and affection without which liberty and even life itself are but dreary things.

We have called by different names brothers of the same principle. We are all Republicans, we are all Federalists.

As I am about to enter, fellow citizens, on the exercise of duties which involve everything dear and valuable to you, it is proper you should understand what I think are the essential principles of our government: equal and exact justice to all men, of whatever state or persuasion, religious or political; peace, trade, and honest friendship with all nations, entangling alliances with none; the support of the state governments in all their rights, as the most able administrations for our domestic concerns; absolute willingness to abide by the decisions of the majority; encouragement of agriculture, and of trade as its handmaid; freedom of religion; freedom of the press; trial by juries impartially selected.

I go, then, fellow citizens, to the post you have assigned me. I have no pretensions to that high confidence you placed in our first and greatest revolutionary character, whose outstanding services had entitled him to the first place in his country's love and destined for him the fairest page in the volume of faithful history. I ask so much confidence only as may give firmness and effectiveness to the legal administration of your affairs. I shall often go wrong through defect of judgment. When right, I shall often be thought wrong by those whose positions will not command a view of the whole ground. I ask your indulgence for my own errors and your support against the errors of others.

Adapted from Thomas Jefferson, "First Inaugural Address," 1801.

READING REVIEW ★ ★ ★ ★ ★ ★ ★

1. Why does Jefferson think the Federalists should be treated with respect?
2. With which of the essential principles of government listed by Jefferson might Federalists have disagreed?

3. **Drawing conclusions.** In the last paragraph, Jefferson refers at length to someone whom he does not name. (a) Who is he talking about? (b) What is his attitude toward this person?

★ ★ ★ ★ ★ ★ ★ ★ ★ ★ ★ ★ ★ ★ ★ ★ ★ ★ ★

★ 11-2 The Shoshones Meet Lewis and Clark ★

Introduction Although relations between white Americans and western Indians quickly became hostile, they began with a spirit of friendship and trust on both sides. When Meriwether Lewis and William Clark journeyed west in 1804, they relied heavily on the help of the Shoshone Indians. This selection is an account by a Shoshone of the Indians' first impressions of Lewis and Clark and their party.

Vocabulary Before you read the selection, find the meaning of these words in a dictionary: tranquil, doleful, forebodings, pilfering.

The Shoshones had camped in the mountains because of fears of the Blackfeet, who possessed firearms. After several moons, however, this state of tranquil happiness was interrupted by the unexpected arrival of two strangers. They were unlike any people we had seen before, fairer than ourselves, and clothed with skins unknown to us.

They gave us things like solid water, which was sometimes brilliant as the sun and which sometimes showed us our own faces. Nothing could equal our wonder and delight. We thought them the children of the Great Spirit. But we were destined to be again overwhelmed with fear, for we soon discovered that they were in possession of the identical thunder and lightning that had proved in the hands of our foes to be so fatal to our happiness.

Many of our people were now terrified, fearing that they were allied with our enemies the Blackfeet. This opinion was strengthened when they asked us to go and meet their friends. At first this was denied. But a speech from our beloved chief, who told us that it was best to be friendly to people so terribly armed, convinced most of our warriors to follow him to their camp. As they disappeared over a hill in the neighborhood of our village, the women set up a doleful yell, which was equivalent to bidding them farewell forever. This did anything but raise their drooping spirits.

Lewis and Clark were often helped by Native Americans on their trip west. They spent one winter with the Mandans who lived in villages along the Missouri River much like the one shown here. The Mandans' boats were made of buffalo hide stretched over willow frames.

After such dismal forebodings, imagine how agreeably they were disappointed when, upon arriving at the strangers' camp, they found, instead of an overwhelming force of enemies, a few strangers like the two already with them. The strangers treated them with great kindness and gave them many things that had not existed before even in their dreams.

Our eagle-eyed chief discovered from the carelessness of the strangers with regard to their things that they were unacquainted with theft. This led him to caution his followers against pilfering any article whatever. His instructions were strictly obeyed. Mutual confidence was thus established. The strangers accompanied him back to the village, and there was peace and joy in the lodges of our people.

Adapted from W. A. Ferris, *Life in the Rocky Mountains,* ed. Paul C. Phillips (Denver: The Old West Publishing Co., 1940).

READING REVIEW ★ ★ ★ ★ ★ ★ ★

1. What common objects did the author of this account have in mind when he spoke of "solid water"? Of "thunder and lightning"?
2. What was the Shoshone chief's original motive for agreeing to go with the white men?
3. **Relating cause and effect.** (a) Why did the Shoshones come to trust the white men? (b) What did the Shoshones do that helped the white men trust them?

★ ★ ★ ★ ★ ★ ★ ★ ★ ★ ★ ★ ★ ★ ★ ★ ★

★ 11-3 Sympathy for Impressed Americans ★

Introduction One cause of the War of 1812 was the impressment of American sailors by the British. Whether people wanted war or not, most agreed that this practice was an outrage. Even some of the British sympathized with impressed Americans. This description of impressment was written by a British sailor, Captain Basil Hall, who had witnessed impressment firsthand. His ship, the *Leander*, had stopped and searched a number of American vessels for "British" seamen.

Vocabulary Before you read the selection, find the meaning of these words in a dictionary: annoyance, indignation, indignities.

There was another circumstance of still more serious annoyance to the Americans. I need hardly mention that I refer to the impressment of those seamen whom we found serving on board American merchant ships but who were known to be or supposed to be British subjects.

To place the full annoyance of these matters in a light to be viewed fairly by English people, let us suppose that the Americans and French were to go to war and that England for once remained neutral—an odd case, I admit, but one which might happen.

Imagine that the American squadron, employed to blockade the French ships in Liverpool, were short-handed. And expecting action any day, it had become an object of great concern with them to get their ships manned. And suppose, likewise, that it were perfectly well known to all parties that on board every English ship arriving or sailing from the port there were several American citizens. But they called themselves English and had in their possession "protections," or certificates to that effect. These were sworn to in regular form but were well known to be false. Things being in this situation, imagine that the American men-of-war, off the English port, were then to fire at and stop every ship. Then, besides overhauling her papers and cargo, they were to take out any seaman whom they had reason or said they had reason to consider an American citizen, or whose country they guessed from dialect or appearance. I wish to know with what degree of patience this would be submitted to in England.

I merely wish to put the general case broadly before our own eyes so that we may bring it distinctly home to ourselves and then see whether or not the Americans had reason for their indignation. The truth is that they had very good reason to be annoyed. Now, let us be frank with our rivals and ask ourselves whether the Americans would have been worthy of our friendship, or even of our hostility, had they tamely submitted to indignities which, if passed upon ourselves, would have roused the whole country into a towering passion of nationality.

Adapted from Captain Basil Hall, *Fragments of Voyages and Travels*, 1831.

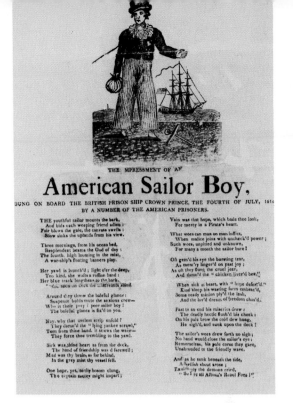

The impressment of American sailors by the British made people furious. This song was written to give a vivid picture of the plight of an impressed sailor.

READING REVIEW ★ ★ ★ ★ ★ ★ ★

1. What methods were used to determine a sailor's nationality?

2. What would Hall have thought of Americans if they had gone along with impressment?

3. **Making inferences.** (a) From Hall's account, what can you infer about the legal status of many British sailors who worked on American ships? (b) How did this affect his opinion of the practice of impressment?

★ ★ ★ ★ ★ ★ ★ ★ ★ ★ ★ ★ ★ ★ ★ ★ ★ ★

★ 11-4 Tecumseh Protests Land Sale ★

Introduction Tecumseh was one of the Native Americans' greatest leaders. He was loved by people of many Indian nations and respected by many white Americans as well. Tecumseh cared passionately about the welfare of his people. Yet, although he was willing to fight on behalf of his fellow Indians, Tecumseh was not a warlike man. He tried first to secure their rights by peaceful means. This selection is from a speech Tecumseh made to Governor William Henry Harrison of Indiana Territory. Harrison had recently tricked several Indians into selling much of their land.

Vocabulary Before you read the selection, find the meaning of these words in a dictionary: obliterate, traverse, encroaching.

81   **Topic 11**

I would not then come to Governor Harrison to ask him to tear the treaty and to obliterate the landmark. But I would say to him: Sir, you have liberty to return to your own country.

The being within, communing with past ages, tells me that until lately there was no white man on this continent. It then all belonged to red men, children of the same parents, placed on it by the Great Spirit that made them to keep it, to traverse it, to enjoy its productions, and to fill it with the same race—once a happy race, since made miserable by the white people, who are never contented but always encroaching.

The way—and the only way—to check and to stop this evil is for all the red men to unite in claiming a common equal right in the land as it was at first and should be yet. For it never was divided but belongs to all for the use of each. That no part has a right to sell even to each other much less to strangers—those who want all and will not do with less.

The white people have no right to take the land from the Indians, because they had it first. It is theirs. They may sell, but all must join. Any sale not made by all is not valid. The late sale is bad. It was made by a part only. Part do not know how to sell. It requires all to make a bargain for all.

All red men have equal rights to the unoccupied land. There cannot be two occupants in the same place. The first excludes all others. It is not so in hunting or traveling, for there the same ground will serve many, as they may follow each other all day. But the camp is stationary, and that is occupancy. It belongs to the first who sits down on his blanket or skins which he has thrown upon the ground. Till he leaves it, no other has a right.

Adapted from *The Library of Oratory*, ed. C. M. Depew, 1902.

READING REVIEW ★ ★ ★ ★ ★ ★ ★

1. How does Tecumseh describe white people?
2. Tecumseh would not completely exclude white settlers from Indian land. Under what circumstances would he allow them?
3. **Finding the main idea.** (a) What is the main reason Tecumseh opposes the recent sale? (b) What other reason does he have for opposing it?

★ ★ ★ ★ ★ ★ ★ ★ ★ ★ ★ ★ ★ ★ ★ ★ ★

★ 11-5 Henry Clay Defends War With Britain ★

Introduction Even after the War of 1812 had begun, many Americans continued to oppose it. Easterners especially objected to the attempt to conquer Canada. Congressman Henry Clay worked hard to win support for the war. In 1813, Clay made this speech to Congress defending the war and the contest in Canada.

Vocabulary Before you read the selection, find the meaning of these words in a dictionary: instigated, judicious, humane, maxim.

What cause, Mr. Chairman, which existed for declaring the war has been removed? Indian hostilities, which were before secretly instigated, are now openly encouraged. The practice of impressment is unceasingly insisted upon. Yet the administration has given the strongest demonstration of its love of peace. An honorable peace is attainable only by an efficient war. My plan would be to call out the ample resources of the country, give them a judicious direction, prosecute the war with the utmost vigor, strike wherever we can reach the enemy, at sea or on land, and negotiate the terms of a peace.

The gentleman from Delaware sees in Canada no object worthy of conquest. Other gentlemen consider the invasion of that country as wicked and unjustifiable. Its inhabitants are represented as unoffending, connected with those of the bordering states by a thousand tender ties, interchanging acts of kindness and all the rituals of good neighborhood. Canada innocent! Canada unoffending! Is it not in Canada that the tomahawk of the savage has been molded into its deathlike form? Is it not from Canadian storehouses that those supplies have been issued which nourish and sustain the Indian hostilities?

The gentlemen would not touch the continental provinces of the enemy nor, I presume, for the same reason, her possessions in the West Indies. The same humane spirit would spare the seamen and soldiers of the enemy. The sacred person of His Majesty must not be attacked, for the learned gentlemen on the other side are quite familiar with the maxim that the king can do no wrong.

Indeed, sir, I know of no person on whom we may make war upon the principles of the honorable gentlemen, except Mr. Stephen, the celebrated author of the Orders in Council, or the Board of Admiralty, who authorize and regulate the practice of impressment.

Adapted from *Annals of Congress*, 12 Cong., 2 sess. 1811–1813.

READING REVIEW ★ ★ ★ ★ ★ ★ ★

1. What does Clay say is the best way to achieve peace?
2. Why, according to Clay, are some people reluctant to pursue a war against Canada?
3. **Summarizing.** Clay uses two arguments to prove that opposition to the war is wrong. Summarize the second of his arguments in your own words.

★ ★ ★ ★ ★ ★ ★ ★ ★ ★ ★ ★ ★ ★ ★ ★ ★ ★ ★

Topic

12 The Nation Prospers (1790–1825)

★ 12-1 Pros and Cons of Factory Life ★

Introduction Working conditions in early factories were a subject of much debate. This imaginary conversation is from an issue of *The Lowell Offering*, a journal published by the young women who worked in the Lowell mills. In it, the workers themselves discuss some of the pros and cons of factory life.

Vocabulary Before you read the selection, find the meaning of these words in a dictionary: degrading, contemptuously, derogatory.

Miss S: I am very happy to see you this evening, Miss Bartlett, for I have something particular to say to you. Now do tell me if you still hold to your decision to return to your factory employment.

Miss B: I do. I have no objection, neither have I heard any sufficiently strong to stop me.

Miss S: The idea that it is degrading, in the opinion of many, would be objection enough for me.

Miss B: By whom is factory labor considered degrading? It is by those

One common complaint about the early factories was of cramped, crowded working conditions. This drawing shows conditions in a book bindery.

who believe all labor degrading—by those who contemptuously speak of the farmer, the mechanic, the printer, the seamstress, and all who are obliged to toil—by those who seem to think the condition of labor excludes all the capacities of the mind and the virtues of humanity.

Miss S: There are objections to factory labor which serve to render it degrading. For instance, to be called and to be dismissed by the ringing of a bell savors of slavery and cannot help but be destructive to self-respect.

Miss B: In almost all kinds of employment it is necessary to keep regular established hours. Because we are reminded of those hours by the ringing of a bell, it is no argument against our employment. Our engagements are voluntarily entered into with our employers. However derogatory to our dignity and liberty you may consider factory labor, there is not a tinge of slavery existing in it.

Miss S: It cannot be denied that some females guilty of immoralities find their way into the factories and boardinghouses. The example and influence of such must be harmful and result in the increase of vice.

Miss B: We know that some objectionable characters occasionally find a place among those employed in factories. But, my dear Miss S, did you ever know or hear of a class of people among whom wrong of any description was never known?

Miss S: O, no!

Miss B: Then, if in one case the guilt of a few has not corrupted the whole, why should it in the other?

Miss S: You will not acknowledge that factory labor is degrading or that it is productive of vice, but you must admit that it fosters ignorance. When there are so many hours out of each day devoted to labor, there can be no time for study and improvement.

Miss B: It is true that too large a portion of our time is confined to labor. But a factory girl's work is neither hard nor complicated. She can go on with perfect regularity in her duties while her mind may be actively employed on any other subject. Our well-worn libraries, evening schools, crowded churches, and sabbath schools prove that factory workers find leisure to use the means of improvement.

Adapted from *The Lowell Offering*, 1833.

READING REVIEW ✶ ✶ ✶ ✶ ✶ ✶ ✶

1. What three objections does Miss S make about factory life?
2. How does Miss B answer the claim that factory work fosters ignorance?
3. **Expressing an opinion.** Do you think the arguments made by Miss B or Miss S are more convincing? Why?

✶ ✶ ✶ ✶ ✶ ✶ ✶ ✶ ✶ ✶ ✶ ✶ ✶ ✶ ✶ ✶ ✶

Introduction Many of the new forms of transportation developed in the 1800s were more than fast and efficient. They often had an air of excitement and glamor about them as well. Certainly the steamboats that traveled the Mississippi did. In this selection from *Life of the Mississippi*, Mark Twain describes the fascination steamboats held for him and his neighbors in the town where he grew up.

Vocabulary Before you read the selection, find the meaning of these words in a dictionary: packet, transpired, drayman, gilded, gingerbread.

When I was a boy, there was but one permanent ambition among my comrades in our village on the west bank of the Mississippi River. That was to be a steamboatman.

One day, a cheap, gaudy packet arrived upward from St. Louis and another downward from Keokuk. Before these events, the day was glorious with expectancy; after they had transpired, the day was a dead and empty thing. Not only the boys but the whole village felt this.

After all these years, I can picture that old time to myself now, just as it was then. A film of dark smoke appears. Instantly a Negro drayman lifts up the cry, "S-t-e-a-m-boat acomin'!" and the scene changes! All in a twinkling, the dead town is alive and moving. Drays, carts, men, boys, all go hurrying from many quarters to a common center, the wharf. Assembled there, the people fasten their eyes upon the coming boat as upon a wonder they are seeing for the first time.

And the boat is rather a handsome sight, too. She is long and sharp and trim and pretty. She has two tall, fancy-topped chimneys, with a gilded device of some kind swung between them, and a fanciful pilothouse, all glass and "gingerbread." The paddle boxes are gorgeous with a picture or with gilded rays above the boat's name. There is a flag gallantly flying from the jackstaff. The pent steam is screaming through the gauge cocks.

The captain lifts his hand, a bell rings, the wheels stop. Then they turn back, churning the water to foam, and the steamer is at rest. Then such a scramble as there is to get aboard and to get ashore, and to take in freight and to discharge freight, all at one and the same time. And such yelling and cursing as the mates accompany it all with!

Ten minutes later the steamer is under way again, with no flag on the jackstaff and no black smoke spewing from the chimneys. After ten more minutes the town is dead again.

Adapted from Mark Twain, *Life on the Mississippi*, 1874.

READING REVIEW ★ ★ ★ ★ ★ ★ ★

1. What effect did the arrival of a steamboat have on a small river town?

2. What details in this passage would support the statement that Mississippi steamboats had a glamorous and romantic air about them?

3. **Understanding geography.** Using a map of the United States and the clues in this selection, find the approximate location of the town Twain grew up in.

★ ★ ★ ★ ★ ★ ★ ★ ★ ★ ★ ★ ★ ★ ★ ★ ★

Steamboats played a key role in the economic growth of the South. Planters used them to ship cotton and other goods to market easily. By the mid-1800's, steamboats were an important feature of life in the bustling port of New Orleans, shown here.

★ 12-3 A Southerner Objects to the Tariff ★

Introduction Many farmers objected to the protective tariffs of 1816 and 1818. They resented the fact that the government was helping industry and not helping agriculture. They also resented having to pay more for manufactured goods. The tariff issue added to the growing distrust between the nation's industrialists, located mainly in the North, and its farmers in the South and West. This selection is from a speech made by Virginia congressman John Randolph against the Tariff of 1816. Randolph was known for his fiery language.

Vocabulary Before you read the selection, find the meaning of these words in a dictionary: cultivators, exotic, speculator, opulence.

It comes down to this: whether you, as a planter, will consent to be taxed in order to hire another man to go to work in a shoemaker's shop or to set up a spinning jenny. For my part I will not agree to it. No, I will buy where I can get products cheapest. I will not agree to lay a duty on the cultivators of the soil to encourage exotic products. After all, we should only get much worse things at a much higher price. Why pay a man much more than the value for it to work up our own cotton into clothing, when, by selling my raw material, I can get my clothing much better and cheaper from Dacca? How does the honorable gentleman have a right to be supported by the earnings of the others?

The cultivators bear the whole brunt of the war and taxation and remain poor, while the others run in the ring of pleasure and fatten upon them. The cultivators not only pay all but fight all, while the others run. The manufacturer is the citizen of no place or any place. The cultivator has his property, his lands, his all, his household goods to defend. The commercial speculators live in opulence, whirling in coaches, and indulging in palaces. Even without your aid, the cultivators are no match for them. Alert, vigilant, enterprising, and active, the manufacturing interest are collected in masses, ready to associate at a moment's warning for any purpose of general interest to their body. Do but ring the fire bell, and you can assemble all the manufacturing interest of Philadelphia in 15 minutes.

The cultivators, the patient drudges of the other orders of society, are now waiting for your resolution. For on you it depends, whether they shall be left further unhurt or be, like those in Europe, reduced and subjected to another squeeze from the hard grasp of power. Sir, I am done.

Adapted from *Annals of Congress*, 14 Cong., 1 sess., 1815–1816.

READING REVIEW ★ ★ ★ ★ ★ ★ ★

1. What specific reasons does Randolph give for objecting to the tariff?
2. (a) What is Randolph's view of manufacturers in general? (b) How does he view farmers?
3. **Distinguishing fact from opinion.** Randolph exaggerates his case to make his point. Name at least two statements he makes that are probably not factual.

★ ★ ★ ★ ★ ★ ★ ★ ★ ★ ★ ★ ★ ★ ★ ★ ★

★ 12-4 Monroe Doctrine Declared ★

Introduction In his Farewell Address, George Washington urged America to stay out of the affairs of other nations. By 1823, however, President James Monroe saw a need to qualify Washington's policy of neutrality. The United States would not stand idly by if European nations tried to interfere in the affairs of North or South America. Monroe made this speech to Congress setting forth the new policy, which soon came to be known as the Monroe Doctrine.

Vocabulary Before you read the selection, find the meaning of these words in a dictionary: comport, impartial, candor, dependencies.

The occasion has been judged proper for asserting, as a principle in which the rights and interests of the United States are involved, that the American continents, by the free and independent condition which they have assumed and maintain, are henceforth not to be considered as subjects for future colonization by any European powers.

Of events in that quarter of the globe with which we have so much intercourse and from which we derive our origin, we have always been anxious and interested spectators. The citizens of the United States cherish sentiments the most friendly in favor of the liberty and happiness of their fellow men on that side of the Atlantic. In the wars of the European powers in matters relating to themselves, we have never taken any part, nor does it comport with our policy so to do. It is only when our rights are invaded or seriously menaced that we resent injuries or make preparation for our defense.

With the movements in this hemisphere, we are of necessity more immediately connected, and by causes which must be obvious to all enlightened and impartial observers. The political system of the European powers is essentially different in this respect from that of America. We owe it, therefore, to candor and to the friendly relations existing between the United States and those powers to declare that we should consider any attempt on their part to extend their system to any portion of this hemisphere as dangerous to our peace and safety. With the existing colonies or dependencies of any European power we have not interfered and shall not interfere. But with the governments who have declared their independence and maintained it, and whose independence we have, on great consideration and on just principles, acknowledged, we could not view any intervention for the purpose of oppressing them, or controlling in any other manner their destiny, by any European power in any other light than as the demonstration of an unfriendly disposition toward the United States.

Adapted from *The Monroe Doctrine*, 1823.

READING REVIEW ★ ★ ★ ★ ★ ★

1. Why, according to Monroe, should the American continents no longer be open to European colonization?

2. Under what circumstances would the United States oppose European involvement in the affairs of South America?

3. **Relating past to present.** Under what circumstances might a President today use the Monroe Doctrine?

★ ★ ★ ★ ★ ★ ★ ★ ★ ★ ★ ★ ★ ★ ★ ★

★ 12-5 Americans Sing Praises of Home ★

Introduction In the early decades of America's growth, singing was one of the main forms of popular entertainment. The songs Americans of this era liked best were often sentimental. They praised the virtues of simple, familiar things. One of the great favorites was "Home, Sweet Home," which appears here. The words were written by Howard Payne, an actor and playwright who never had a home of his own.

Vocabulary Before you read the selection, find the meaning of these words in a dictionary: hallow, exile.

Mid pleasures and palaces though we
    may roam,
Be it ever so humble, there's no place
    like home!
A charm from the skies seems to hal-
    low us there,
Which, seek through the world, is ne'er
    met with elsewhere.
    Chorus
Home! home! sweet, sweet home!
There's no place like home! There's no
    place like home.

I gaze on the moon as I tread the drear
    wild,
And feel that my mother now thinks of
    her child;
As she looks on that moon from our
    own cottage door,
Through the woodbine whose fragrance
    shall cheer me no more.

An exile from home, splendor dazzles
    in vain;
Oh, give me my lowly thatched cottage
    again;
The birds singing gaily, that came at
    my call;
Give me them, and that peace of mind,
    dearer than all.

John Howard Payne, "Home, Sweet Home," 1823.

READING REVIEW ★ ★ ★ ★ ★ ★

1. What sort of home does this song sing the praises of?

2. Which verse of "Home, Sweet Home" would a newcomer to one of America's growing cities probably relate to best?

3. **Using a song as historical evidence.** The decades after the War of 1812 were a time of growth and change for Americans. What does the popularity of a song such as "Home, Sweet Home" tell us about people's reaction to change?

★ ★ ★ ★ ★ ★ ★ ★ ★ ★ ★ ★ ★ ★ ★ ★

A Growing Nation

Topic

13 Age of Jackson (1824–1840)

★ 13-1 The Election of 1824 ★

Introduction The election of 1824 showed the changes that had begun to take place in America. The country was growing and expanding. Its population was growing and becoming more diverse. In 1824, four different Republican candidates ran for President. Each was popular with a different group of Americans. The vote was so close that the House of Representatives had to choose a President from among the top three candidates in the electoral college vote. These circle graphs show how the votes were distributed.

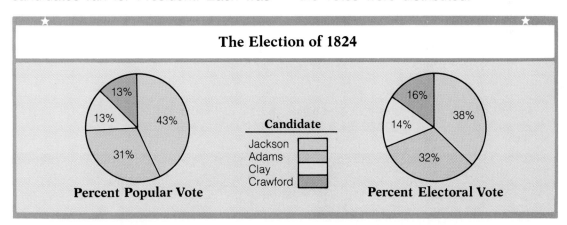

The Election of 1824

| Candidate |
| Jackson |
| Adams |
| Clay |
| Crawford |

Percent Popular Vote — 13%, 13%, 43%, 31%

Percent Electoral Vote — 16%, 14%, 38%, 32%

READING REVIEW ★ ★ ★ ★ ★ ★ ★

1. (a) Which candidates won a greater percentage of electoral votes than popular votes? (b) Which won a smaller percentage?

2. Which three candidates were the ones the House of Representatives had to choose among?

3. **Using graphs.** (a) Who won the largest percentage of electoral votes? (b) Why did he not win the election?

★ ★ ★ ★ ★ ★ ★ ★ ★ ★ ★ ★ ★ ★ ★ ★ ★

Introduction Andrew Jackson owed much of his celebrated strength of character to his mother. Elizabeth Jackson was widowed at a young age. Singlehandedly, she saw her young sons through the horrors of smallpox and the American Revolution. She also nursed imprisoned American soldiers during the Revolution. In the course of this work, she caught a fever and died. In her last hours, she wrote this letter to her young son Andrew.

Vocabulary Before you read the selection, find the meaning of these words in a dictionary: steadfast, obsequious, imposition.

Dear Andrew,

If I should not see you again, I wish you to remember and treasure up some things I have already said to you. In this world, you will have to make your own way. To do that, you must have friends. You can make friends by being honest, and you can keep them by being steadfast. You must keep in mind that friends worth having will in the long run expect as much from you as they give to you.

To forget an obligation or be ungrateful for a kindness is a crime. Men guilty of it sooner or later must suffer the penalty.

In personal conduct, always be polite, but never obsequious. No one will respect you more than you respect yourself. Avoid quarrels as long as you can without yielding to imposition. But sustain your manhood always.

Never wound the feelings of others. If ever you have to defend your feelings or your honor, do it calmly. If angry at first, wait till your anger cools before you proceed.

Love,
Mother

Adapted from *Letters in American History,* by H. Jack Lang. Copyright © 1982 by H. Jack Lang. Used by permission of Harmony Books, a division of Crown Publishers, Inc.

READING REVIEW ★ ★ ★ ★ ★ ★ ★

1. What advice did Elizabeth Jackson give her son about friends?
2. What standard political practice begun by Jackson seems rooted in his mother's advice?
3. **Ranking.** (a) Which parts of his mother's advice seem to have had the greatest effect on Jackson? (b) Which seem to have had the least?

★ ★ ★ ★ ★ ★ ★ ★ ★ ★ ★ ★ ★ ★ ★ ★ ★

Andrew Jackson thought of himself as a friend of the common people. During the Age of Jackson, more people than ever before became involved in the nation's political life. This painting shows a variety of spectators in a country courtroom.

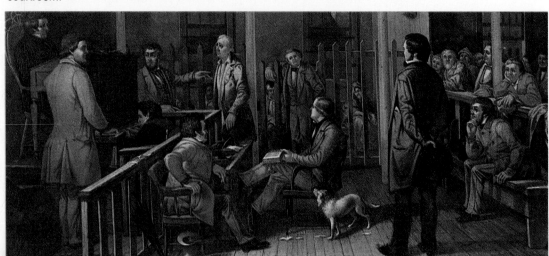

Introduction The debate over the Tariff of Abominations grew into a debate over the right of a state to override the federal government. John C. Calhoun became the leader of those who took the "states' rights" position. This selection is from a speech he gave against a tariff passed in 1832.

Vocabulary Before you read the selection, find the meaning of these words in a dictionary: encroach, revenue, sovereignty, discord, despotism.

We, the people of South Carolina, have declared the act of Congress to alter the tariff on imports to be unconstitutional and therefore null and void.

We hold it to be a very imperfect idea of the duty which each state agreed to in ratifying the Constitution to suppose that a state should simply not exercise the powers delegated to the federal government. This is an important duty. But there is another duty no less important—to resist the government, should it encroach on the reserved powers.

That the protective tariff system included in the act is, in fact, unconstitutional we hold to be certain. And it is under this deep and solemn conviction that we have acted.

It has not been claimed, nor is it now, that there is in the Constitution any positive grant of power to protect manufactures. Nor can it be denied that frequent attempts were made at the Constitutional Convention to obtain the power and that they all failed.

Its advocates claim to derive this power from the right "to lay and collect taxes, duties, imposts, and excises" or from that "to regulate commerce." Yet the claim plainly rests on the assumption that the power to impose duties may be applied not only to raise revenue or regulate commerce but also to protect manufactures.

That such a power is not granted by the Constitution we hold to be certain. It has become an instrument in the hands of the powerful to oppress the weaker. It must, ultimately, concentrate all power in the federal government and abolish the sovereignty of the states. Discord, corruption, and, eventually, despotism must follow, if the system is not resisted.

Adapted from *Works of John C. Calhoun,* ed. Richard K. Crallé, 1856.

READING REVIEW★ ★ ★ ★ ★ ★

1. What major argument does Calhoun use to support the right of a state to declare a federal law null and void?
2. According to Calhoun, why were the tariffs of 1828 and 1832 unconstitutional?
3. **Using diagrams.** Review the diagram of the separation of powers on page 266. (a) Give two examples of delegated powers. (b) Give two examples of reserved powers. (c) Why did Calhoun think the protective tariffs threatened the separation of powers?

★ ★ ★ ★ ★ ★ ★ ★ ★ ★ ★ ★ ★ ★ ★ ★ ★ ★

Introduction Senator Daniel Webster of Massachusetts opposed Calhoun and the South Carolinians. Webster argued that the supreme power of the land lay with the federal government, not with the states. Webster expressed his views in a series of speeches made in response to Senator Robert Hayne of

Vocabulary Before you read the selection, find the meaning of these words in a dictionary: sovereign, agency, discretion, sanctioned, dissevered, fraternal.

This leads us to inquire into the origin of this government and the source of its power. Whose agent is it? Is it the creature of the state legislatures or the creature of the people? It is, sir, the people's Constitution, the people's government. The states are, unquestionably, sovereign, so far as their sovereignty is not affected by this supreme law. But the state legislatures, as political bodies, however sovereign, are yet not sovereign over the people.

The people, then, sir, erected this government. They gave it a Constitution. In that Constitution they have spelled out the powers which they bestow on it. But, sir, they have not stopped here. If they had, they would have accomplished but half their work.

Sir, the very chief end, the main design, for which the whole Constitution was framed and adopted was to establish a government that should not be obliged to act through state agency or depend on state opinion and state discretion. The people had had quite enough of that kind of government under the Confederacy.* Under that system, Congress could only recommend. Their acts were not of binding force till the states had adopted and sanctioned them.

Are we in that condition still? Sir, if we are, then vain will be our attempt to maintain the Constitution under which we sit. But, sir, the people

have wisely provided, in the Constitution itself, a proper, suitable means for settling questions of constitutional law. Congress established, at its very first session, a way to bring all questions of constitutional power to the final decision of the Supreme Court. It then, sir, became a government.

I have thus stated the reasons for my dissent to the doctrines which have been advanced and maintained. This is a subject of which my heart is full. Since it concerns nothing less than the union of the states, it is of most vital and essential importance to the public happiness. It is to that union we owe our safety at home and our dignity abroad. It is to that union that we are chiefly indebted for whatever makes us most proud of our country.

When my eyes shall be turned to behold, for the last time, the sun in heaven, may I not see him shining on the broken and dishonored fragments of a once glorious union. May I not see him shining on states disserved, discordant, belligerent. May I not see him shining on a land torn by civil war or drenched, it may be, in fraternal blood! Let my last feeble and lingering glance, rather, behold the gorgeous flag of the republic, bearing for its motto that sentiment dear to every true American heart—liberty and union, now and forever, one and inseparable!

Adapted from *Congressional Debates*, 21 Cong., 1 sess., 1830.

READING REVIEW ★ ★ ★ ★ ★ ★ ★

1. Who does Webster say is the supreme source of power in the United States?
2. What does Webster imply would happen to the country if states' rights arguments were allowed to hold sway?
3. **Defending a point of view.** Write a paragraph defending either the position of federal sovereignty or that of states' rights. Use Webster's or Calhoun's arguments or your own.

★ ★ ★ ★ ★ ★ ★ ★ ★ ★ ★ ★ ★ ★ ★ ★ ★

---

*Webster is referring to the Articles of Confederation.

Introduction One of Andrew Jackson's goals as President was to move all Native Americans west of the Mississippi River. Jackson was willing to go to great lengths to accomplish this goal. He wrote this letter to the Seminole Indians, advising them to move west voluntarily. In it, Jackson gave a hint of the measures he was prepared to use if the Seminoles refused to leave. The Seminoles did refuse to go. The bloody seven-year-long Seminole War that followed showed that the President meant business.

Vocabulary Before you read the selection, find the meaning of these words in a dictionary: counsel, annuities.

My Children—

I am sorry to have heard that you have been listening to bad counsel. You know me. You know that I would not deceive nor advise you to do anything that was unjust or harmful. Open you ears and attend to what I shall now say to you. They are the words of a friend and the words of truth.

The white people are settling around you. The game has disappeared from your country. Your people are poor and hungry. All this you have known for some time. I tell you that you must go and that you will go. Even if you had a right to stay, how could you live where you now are? You have sold all your country. You have not a piece as large as a blanket to sit down upon. What is to support yourselves, your women, and children?

The tract you have given up will soon be surveyed and sold. Immediately afterwards, it will be occupied by a white population. You will soon be in a state of starvation. You will be forced to rob and plunder the property of our citizens. You will be resisted, punished, perhaps killed.

Now is it not better peaceably to move to a fine, fertile country, occupied by your own kindred, where you can raise all the necessities of life, and where game is yet abundant? The annuities payable to you and the other arrangements made in your favor will make your situation comfortable. They will enable you to increase and improve.

If, therefore, you had a right to stay where you now are, still every true friend would advise you to move. But you have no right to stay, and you must go. I am very desirous that you should go peaceably and voluntarily. You shall be comfortably taken care of and kindly treated on the road. When you arrive in your new country, supplies will be issued to you for a year so that you can have ample time to provide for your future support.

But in case some of your rash young men should forcibly oppose your arrangements for removal, I have ordered a large military force to be sent among you. I have directed that one-third of your people, as provided for in

The Seminole Indians fiercely resisted President Jackson's order to move west. Chief Osceola, shown here, led them in their struggle.

the treaty, be removed during the present season. If you listen to the voice of friendship and truth, you will go quietly and voluntarily. But should you listen to the bad birds that are always flying about you and refuse to move, I have then directed the commanding officer to remove you by force. This will be done. I pray the Great Spirit, therefore, to incline you to do what is right.

Your friend,
A. Jackson

Washington, February 16, 1835

Adapted from "President Andrew Jackson's Letter to the Seminoles," in *History of the Indian Wars*, ed. Henry Trumbull, 1841.

READING REVIEW

1. According to Jackson, why should the Seminoles leave?
2. If the Seminoles refuse to leave, what does Jackson warn them he would do?
3. **Expressing an opinion.** Jackson signs this letter "Your friend." Do you think Jackson was the Seminoles' friend? Why or why not?

★ 13-6   A Campaign Song   ★

Introduction During the Age of Jackson, American politics changed in many ways. New, strong leaders emerged in all sections of the country. New parties were born. Most important, more people began to vote and become involved in politics. As a result, campaigns became more colorful and elaborate, designed to reach more of the new voters. These lyrics are from a song written especially for the election of 1840.

Vocabulary Before you read the selection, find the meaning of these words in a dictionary: faction, fain, swindler, impudent, knavery.

A stands for Adams, whose administration
   Was like a dead weight on the neck of the nation.
B stands for Banks, and also for Biddle,
   Their tune they must alter or hang up their fiddle.
C stands for Clay, for the potter unfit,
   He ne'er can be molded to honor a bit.
D stands for Dollars, half Dollars, and Dimes,

   Then speedily give us good hard-money times.
E stands for Eagle, our country's proud bird,
   He soars where the thunder of battle is heard.
F stands for the Federal faction, who fain
   Would be lords o'er the poor and skin them for gain.
G stands for the Game which the bank swindlers play,
   But the people have called for a reckoning day.

. . . .

I stands for the Impudent lies that are told
   By the aristocratic party, those liars of old.
J stands for Jackson, who never would flinch
   Nor yield to the foes of this country an inch.
K stands for Knavery of every kind;
   Examine the banks and enough of't you'll find.

Adapted from "The Alphabetical Song," 1840.

1. Who does the song imply was responsible for the depression that began in 1837?
2. What is meant by the line "Then speedily give us good hard-money times"?

3. **Drawing conclusions.** (a) What party would you say the writer of this song belonged to? (b) What parts of the song lead you to make this conclusion? Explain your answer.

★ ★ ★ ★ ★ ★ ★ ★ ★ ★ ★ ★ ★ ★ ★ ★ ★ ★ ★

Topic

14 Westward Ho! (1820–1860)

★   14-1   Camp Life in the Rockies   ★

Introduction Life for the Mountain Men who opened the Oregon Country for latter settlers was rough and often difficult. Yet these men's simple ways had an appealing side. This description of life among the Mountain Men was written by Osborne Russell, a trapper and hunter who came to Oregon Country in 1834.

Vocabulary Before you read the selection, find the meaning of this word in a dictionary: comprised.

I joined Mr. Bridger's company, who were passing the winter on Blackfoot Creek. Mr Bridger's men killed plenty of bulls, but they were so poor that their meat was perfectly blue. Yet this was their only article of food, as bread and vegetables were out of the question in the Rocky Mountains.

It would doubtless be amusing to a disinterested spectator to witness the process of cooking poor bull meat. On going through the camp at any time in the day, heaps of ashes might be seen with the fire burning on the summit. An independent-looking individual, who is termed a camp kicker, sits with a "two-year-old club" in his hand watching the pile with much impatience. At

length, he pokes over the ashes with his club to work loose a great mass of meat. When he hits it with his club, it bounds five or six feet from the ground like a huge ball of gum rubber. This operation, frequently repeated, shakes loose the ashes clinging to the meat and prepares it for carving. He then drops his club and draws his butcher knife, calling to his comrades, "Come Major, Judge, Squire, Dollar, Pike, Cotton, and Gabe, won't you take a lunch of Simon?"

Mountain men looked forward to trips to frontier forts where they traded pelts for supplies. They also enjoyed the chance to swap stories with fellow trappers. This painting is of Fort Walla Walla in Oregon Country.

We passed away the time very agreeably. Our only employment was to feed our horses, kill buffalo, and eat—that is to say, the trappers. The camp keepers' business in winter quarters is to guard the horses, cook, and keep fires. We all had snug lodges made of dressed buffalo skins. In the center we built a fire. Each lodge generally comprised about six men.

The long winter evenings were passed away by collecting in some of the most spacious lodges and having debates and arguments or spinning long yarns until midnight, in perfect good humor. I for one will cheerfully confess that I have derived no little benefit from the frequent arguments and debates held in what we termed "The Rocky Mountain College."

At the summer rendezvous at Green River, we found the hunting parties all assembled waiting for the arrival of supplies from the States. Some were gambling at cards, some playing the Indian game of "hand," and others horse racing. Here and there could be seen small groups collected under shady trees relating the events of the past year, all in good spirits and health, for sickness is a stranger seldom met with in these regions.

Adapted from Osborne Russell, *The Journal of a Trapper, or, Nine Years in the Rocky Mountains*, 1914.

READING REVIEW ★ ★ ★ ★ ★ ★

1. Describe the job of a camp kicker.
2. (a) What did the Mountain Men do for entertainment in the winter? (b) At their summer rendezvous?
3. **Supporting generalizations.** What evidence is there in this account that Russell enjoyed life as a trapper?

★ ★ ★ ★ ★ ★ ★ ★ ★ ★ ★ ★ ★ ★ ★ ★ ★ ★

★   14-2   A Defense of the Texas Struggle   ★

Many Texans were ready to go to war with Mexico because they had grown to love their new land. Settlers had poured years of work into building farms such as the one shown here.

Introduction Late in 1835, Texans took up arms against the Mexican Army. In the eyes of Texans such as William Wharton, the struggle against the Mexicans in the Battles of Gonzales and San Antonio was as noble as the Battle of Lexington in the American Revolution. This selection is from a speech Wharton made to urge United States support for the Texan cause.

Vocabulary Before you read the selection, find the meaning of these words in a dictionary: despotism, simultaneously, indignation, smitten.

You have now seen, gentlemen, that our constitution has been violated illegally and totally destroyed. You have seen that, added to this, our governor has been imprisoned and our legislature disbanded. Now, mark the patience of the people of Texas! Even after all these outrages on their rights, they did not rise in arms and make an appeal to the god of battles for justice and righting of their wrongs. They still hoped that the Mexican nation would have the firmness and patriotism to crush this military despotism.

In this hope, they were cruelly deceived. In the month of September last, a Mexican armed schooner appeared off our coast and declared all of our ports in a state of blockade. Simultaneously with this, General Coss invaded our territory by land. About the same time, a military force was sent to the colonial town of Gonzales to demand of the inhabitants a surrender of their arms. This demand was refused with the promptness and indignation of freemen. A battle immediately ensued on the 28th September last, which ended in the defeat and hasty retreat of the Mexican forces.

Gonzales was then the Lexington of our struggle. And the same cry for liberty, which from the blood of the slain at Lexington and Bunker's Hill rose to high Heaven and penetrated every corner of this land, flew with electrical rapidity after the battles of Gonzales and St. Antonio.

The inhabitants promptly responded to its call. They felt now that the rod of oppression had smitten sufficiently severe. They could no longer submit without giving up forever the glorious name of freemen. Accordingly, they rallied around the standard of their country. All were alive with the spirit of "76."

Adapted from an address delivered by William Wharton, April 26, 1836.

READING REVIEW ★ ★ ★ ★ ★ ★ ★

1. How does Wharton show that Mexico was threatening the colony of Texas?
2. Why did the Texans lose patience and take up arms against Mexico?
3. **Making inferences.** How was the struggle of the Texans against Mexico similar to the American Revolution?

★ ★ ★ ★ ★ ★ ★ ★ ★ ★ ★ ★ ★ ★ ★ ★ ★ ★ ★

★ 14-3 Prudencia Higuera's Brass Buttons ★

Introduction By the mid-1800s, the Spanish had been in California for several generations. Some had established large, prosperous ranches. Then, in the early 1800s, settlers from the United States began to arrive. In this selection, Prudencia Higuera, daughter of a Spanish rancher, gives her impressions of the first encounter with these settlers.

Vocabulary Before you read the selection, find the meaning of this word in a dictionary: interpreter.

In the autumn of 1840, my father lived near what is now called Pinole Point in Contra Costa County, California. I was then about 12 years old. I remembered the time because it was then that we saw the first American vessel that traded along the shores of San Pablo Bay.

The captain soon came with a small boat and two sailors. One was a Frenchman who knew Spanish very well and who acted as interpreter. The captain asked my father to get into the boat and go to the vessel. Mother was much afraid to let him go, as we all thought the Americans were not to be trusted unless we knew them well. We feared they would carry my father off and keep him a prisoner. Father said, however, that it was all right. He went and put on his best clothes, gay with silver braid. We all cried and kissed him goodbye, while Mother clung about his neck and said we might never see him again.

Then the captain told her: "If you are afraid, I will have the sailors take him to the vessel while I stay here until he comes back. He ought to see all the goods I have or he will not know what to buy." After a little, my mother let him go with the captain. We stood on the beach to see them off.

He came back the next day bringing four boatloads of cloth, axes, shoes, fish lines, and many new things. My brother had traded some deerskins for a gun and four toothbrushes, the first ones I had ever seen. I remember that we children rubbed them on our teeth till the blood came. We concluded that, after all, we liked best the bits of pounded willow root that we used for brushes before.

After the ship sailed, my mother and sisters began to cut out new dresses, which the Indian women sewed. On one of mine, Mother put some big brass buttons about an inch across with eagles on them. How proud I was! I used to rub them hard every day to make them shine, using the toothbrush.

Then our neighbors, who were 10 or 15 miles away, came to see all the things we had bought. One girl offered me a beautiful black colt she owned for six of the brass buttons. But I continued for a long time to think more of those buttons than of anything else I possessed.

Adapted from *As I Saw It: Women Who Lived the American Adventure,* copyright © 1978 by Cheryl G. Hoople. A Dial Books for Young Readers book. Reprinted by permission of E.P. Dutton, a division of New American Library.

READING REVIEW ★ ★ ★ ★ ★ ★ ★

1. Why was Prudencia's mother afraid to let her father go to the Americans' ship?
2. (a) What American device was new to the Spanish? (b) How did Prudencia finally use it?
3. **Drawing conclusions.** What sort of attitude do you think Prudencia and her family had towards Americans after this first meeting?

★ ★ ★ ★ ★ ★ ★ ★ ★ ★ ★ ★ ★ ★ ★ ★ ★ ★ ★ ★

★ 14-4 America's Manifest Destiny ★

Introduction In the 1840s, more and more Americans looked eagerly toward the rich and beautiful lands of the Southwest. Yet this territory belonged to Mexico. To explain why the United States should own this land, John L. O'Sullivan developed the idea of manifest destiny. This selection is from a newspaper article O'Sullivan wrote in 1845.

Vocabulary Before you read the selection, find the meaning of these words in a dictionary: inevitable, irreversible, preposterous, irresistible, dominion, spontaneous.

It is time now for opposition to the annexation of Texas to cease. It is time for the common duty of patriotism to the country to succeed. Or if this claim will not be recognized, it is at least time for common sense to bow with decent grace to the inevitable and the irreversible.

The pretense that the annexation has been unrightful and unrighteous is wholly untrue and unjust to ourselves. If Texas became peopled with an American population, it was on the express invitation of Mexico herself. The invitation was accompanied with guarantees of state independence and the maintenance of a federal system similar to our own. What, then, can be more preposterous than all this clamor by Mexico against annexation as a violation of any rights of hers, any duties of ours?

Nor is there any just foundation for the charge that annexation is a great proslavery measure calculated to increase and keep alive that institution. Slavery had nothing to do with it. Opinions were and are greatly divided, in both the North and South, as to the influence to be exerted by the annexation on slavery and the slave states.

California will, probably, next fall away. Distracted Mexico never can exert any real governmental authority over such a country. The Anglo-Saxon foot is already on California's borders. Already, the advance guard of the irresistible army of Anglo-Saxon emigration has begun to pour down upon it. It is armed with the plough and the rifle. It marks its trail with schools and colleges, courts and representative halls, mills and meeting houses. A population will soon be in actual occupation of California, over which it will be idle for Mexico to dream of dominion. They will necessarily become independent. All this without interference by our government, without responsibility of our people—in the natural flow of events, the spontaneous working of principles.

Adapted from *United States Magazine and Democratic Review*, 1845.

READING REVIEW ★ ★ ★ ★ ★ ★ ★

1. (a) How does O'Sullivan justify the annexation of Texas? (b) What role does he say slave states had in it?

2. What Mexican territory does O'Sullivan say will be the next to fall to the United States?

3. **Expressing an opinion.** (a) Do you agree that America had a "manifest destiny" to expand across the continent? (b) Why or why not?

★ ★ ★ ★ ★ ★ ★ ★ ★ ★ ★ ★ ★ ★ ★ ★ ★ ★ ★

★　　14-5　　Black Opposition to the Mexican War　　★

Introduction From its beginning, the war with Mexico was controversial. Many Southerners and Westerners supported the war. Many Northerners, both white and black, opposed it. They feared that the acquisition of Mexican territory would lead to the extension of slavery. This editorial, about the news of the American victory in 1848, was written by Frederick Douglass, a black leader of the antislavery movement.

Vocabulary Before you read the selection, find the meaning of these words in a dictionary: barbarous, unoffending, plunder, hypocritical, pretense.

PEACE! PEACE! PEACE!

The shout is on every lip and published in every paper. The joyful news is told in every quarter with enthusiastic delight. We are such an exception to the great mass of our fellow countrymen, in respect to everything else, and we have been so accustomed to

In the final offensive of the Mexican War, Major General Winfield Scott captured Mexico City. This painting shows his army entering the city.

hear them rejoice over the most barbarous outrages committed upon an unoffending people, that we find it difficult to unite with them in their jubilation at this time. We believe that by peace they mean plunder.

In our judgment, those who have all along been loudly in favor of a vigorous prosecution of the war, and announcing its bloody triumphs with apparent delight, have no sincere love of peace and are not now rejoicing over peace, but plunder. They have succeeded in robbing Mexico of her territory. And they are rejoicing over their success under the hypocritical pretense of a regard for peace. Had they not succeeded in robbing Mexico of the most important and most valuable part of her territory, many of those now loudest in their cries of favor for peace would be loudest and wildest for war— war to the knife.

Our soul is sick of such hypocrisy. That an end is put to the wholesale murder in Mexico is truly just cause for rejoicing. But we are not the people to rejoice. We ought rather blush and hang our heads for shame. In the spirit of profound humility, we should beg pardon for our crimes at the hands of a god whose mercy endures forever.

Adapted from Frederick Douglass, editorial in *North Star*, March 17, 1848.

READING REVIEW ★ ★ ★ ★ ★ ★ ★

1. What does Douglass mean when he says Americans are celebrating plunder rather than peace?
2. (a) Who does Douglass blame for the war? (b) How do you know?
3. **Applying information.** Why might a former slave like Douglass have sympathized with the Mexicans?

★ ★ ★ ★ ★ ★ ★ ★ ★ ★ ★ ★ ★ ★ ★ ★ ★ ★

★ 14-6   Louise Clappe Strikes Gold   ★

Introduction After the discovery of gold at Sutter's Mill in January 1848, thousands rushed to the California gold fields. Among this group of eager gold seekers were Louise and Fayette Clappe. They settled in a wild mining town called Rich Bar. Louise Clappe described her new life in letters to her sister, such as this one.

Vocabulary Before you read the selection, find the meaning of these words in a dictionary: erroneous, specimens.

November 25, 1851

Nothing of importance has happened since I last wrote you, except that I have become a miner. I can truly say I am sorry I "learned the trade," for I wet my feet, tore my dress, spoilt a pair of new gloves, nearly froze my fingers, got an awful headache, took cold, and lost a valuable pin in this, my labor of love.

Of lady gold-washers in general—it is a common habit with people residing in towns in the vicinity of the "diggings" to make up parties to those places. Each woman of the company will exhibit on her return at least $20 of ore, which she will gravely inform you she has just "panned out" from a single basinful of the soil. This, of course, gives strangers a very erroneous idea of the average richness of gold-bearing dirt.

I myself thought (now don't laugh) that one had but to stroll gracefully along romantic streamlets on sunny afternoons, with a parasol and white kid gloves perhaps, and to stop now and then to admire the scenery, and carelessly rinse out a small panful of yellow sand in order to fill one's work-bag with the most beautiful and rare specimens of the precious mineral. Since I have been here, I have discovered my mistake—and also the secret of the brilliant success of former gold-washers.

The miners are in the habit of flattering the vanity of their fair visitors by scattering a handful of "salt" (which, strange to say, is exactly the color of gold dust) through the dirt before the dainty fingers touch it. The dear creatures go home with their treasures, firmly believing that mining is the prettiest pastime in the world.

To be sure, there are now and then "lucky strikes." Once a person took $256 out of a single basinful of soil. But such luck is as rare as the winning of a $100,000 prize in a lottery. We are acquainted with many here whose gains have never amounted to much more than "wages"—that is, from $6 to $8 a day. A "claim" which yields a man a steady income of $10 per day is considered very valuable.

Adapted from letter written by Louise Amelia "Dame Shirley" Clappe, November 25, 1851 (published 1854–1855).

READING REVIEW ★ ★ ★ ★ ★ ★ ★

1. According to Louise Clappe, how likely was it that a person could strike it rich panning for gold?
2. (a) What trick played by one miner on another is described in this letter? (b) How common do you suppose such tricks were?
3. **Comparing.** How was the work of mining different from the way Louise Clappe had first imagined it?

★ ★ ★ ★ ★ ★ ★ ★ ★ ★ ★ ★ ★ ★ ★ ★ ★ ★

Topic

15 Two Ways of Life (1820–1860)

★ 15-1 At Work on a Clipper ★

Introduction With the invention of swift clipper ships, American shipping came into its own. To pass the time while they worked, and to keep their movements in rhythm, sailors on board the clippers sang sea chanteys. This chantey was popular not only with sailors but with the many California-bound passengers who sailed the clippers during the Gold Rush.

Vocabulary Before you read the selection, find the meaning of this word in a dictionary: tinker.

Come all ye young fellers that follow the
  sea
With a ho ho, blow the man down
Now just pay attention and listen to me
Give me some time to blow the man down

Speedy clipper ships enabled the United States to become a leader in trade with China. This painting shows the trading posts of six nations at Canton about 1800.

Aboard the *Black Baller* I first served my
time
With a ho ho, blow the man down
But on the *Black Baller* I wasted my time
Give me some time to blow the man down

We'd tinkers and tailors and sailors and
all
With a ho ho, blow the man down
That sailed for good seamen aboard the
Black Ball
Give me some time to blow the man down

Now when the *Black Baller's* preparin'
for sea
With a ho ho, blow the man down
You'd bust your sides laughin' at sights
that you see
Give me some time to blow the man down

But when the *Black Baller* is clear of the
land
With a ho ho, blow the man down
Old kicking Jack Williams gives ev'ry
command
Give me some time to blow the man down

Adapted from the song "Blow the Man Down," 1849.

READING REVIEW ★ ★ ★ ★ ★ ★ ★

1. According to the song, what occupations
   did men leave to go to work at sea?
2. How was life on shipboard different in
   port from the way it was at sea?
3. **Using a song as historical evidence.**
   Life on board ship is often thought to be
   glamorous or romantic. What image of a
   sailor's life does this song present?

★ ★ ★ ★ ★ ★ ★ ★ ★ ★ ★ ★ ★ ★ ★ ★ ★ ★ ★ ★

★   **15-2   Life in a Mill in 1832**

Introduction   In the 1820s, New England textile industries hired many young, unmarried women to work in their factories. As the demand for cheap labor increased, wages dropped and conditions worsened. Some citizens began to protest this growing problem. One of those who spoke out was Seth Luther. The following selection is taken from an address he gave in 1832.

Vocabulary   Before you read the selection, find the meaning of these words in a dictionary: vice, broach, climax.

We see the system of manufacturing praised to the skies. Senators, representatives, owners, and agents of cotton mills use all means to keep out of sight the evils growing up under it. In cotton mills, cruelties are practiced, excessive labor required, and education neglected. Vice is on the increase. Yet they are called "the palaces of the poor."

A member of the United States Senate seems to be extremely pleased with cotton mills. He says, "Who has not been delighted with the clockwork movements of a large cotton manufactory?" He says the women work in large airy apartments, well warmed. They are neatly dressed, with ruddy complexions and happy faces. They mend the broken threads and replace the exhausted balls or broaches. And at stated periods they go to and return from their meals with a light and cheerful step.

While on a visit to that pink of perfection, Waltham, I remarked that the females moved with a very light step. Well they might, for the bell rang for them to return to the mill from their homes 19 minutes after it had rung for them to go to breakfast. Some of these females boarded the largest part of half a mile from the mill.

The grand climax is that, at the end of the week, after working like slaves for 13 or 14 hours every day, according to the Senators, "they enter the temples of God on the Sabbath and thank him for all his benefits. The

Part One

American System above all, he says, requires a peculiar outpouring of gratitude. We do not believe there can be a single person who ever thanked God for permission to work in a cotton mill.

Adapted from Seth Luther, *Address,* 1836.

READING REVIEW ★ ★ ★ ★ ★ ★ ★

1. What specific practices does Luther mention as examples of the hardship of factory life?

2. Luther scoffed at the term "palaces of the poor," used to describe factories. What did people mean by this term?

3. **Relating cause and effect.** Why do you think a senator would give such a glowing report on life in factories?

★ ★ ★ ★ ★ ★ ★ ★ ★ ★ ★ ★ ★ ★ ★ ★

Iron works, as well as textile mills, were important to northern industry in the mid-1800s. The Excelsior Iron Works, shown here, was located in New York State.

★ 15-3   A Violent Reaction to Foreign-Born Voters ★

Introduction As more and more immigrants arrived in the United States, prejudice against them grew. In 1855, some citizens of Louisville, Kentucky, who opposed the right of foreign-born Americans to vote, used violence to keep them from the polls. These nativist Americans worked through the Know-Nothing Party. This description of the election day events is from the *Louisville Courier.*

Vocabulary Before you read the selection, find the meaning of these words in a dictionary: farce, intimidation, pursuance, gauntlet, pillaged.

We passed, yesterday, through the forms of an election. Never, perhaps, was a greater farce, or as we should term it tragedy, enacted. Hundreds and thousands were prevented from voting by direct acts of intimidation. The city, indeed, was, during the day, in possession of an armed mob. The base passions of the mob were aroused to the highest pitch by the fiery appeals of the newspaper and the popular leaders of the Know-Nothing Party.

On Sunday night, large detachments of men were sent to the First and Second Wards to see that the polls were properly opened. These men discharged the important trusts committed to them in such manner as to commend them forever to the admiration of outlaws. They opened the polls. They provided ways and means for their own party to vote. They buffed and bullied all who could not show the sign. They in fact converted the election into a perfect farce, without one redeeming feature.

By daybreak, the polls were taken possession of by the Know-Nothing Party. In pursuance of their planned game, they used every strategy to hinder the vote of every man who could not show to the "guardians of the polls" his soundness on the K. N. question. In the Sixth Ward a party of bullies were masters of the polls. We saw two foreigners driven from the polls, forced to run a gauntlet, beaten unmercifully, stoned, and stabbed.

In the afternoon, a number of houses, chiefly German coffee houses, were broken into and pillaged. After dusk, a row of frame houses on Main Street between Tenth and Eleventh was set on fire. These houses were chiefly tenanted by Irish. When any of the tenants ventured out to escape the flames, they were immediately shot down.

We are sickened with the very thought of the men murdered and houses burned and pillaged that signaled the victory yesterday. No fewer than 20 corpses form the trophies of this wonderful achievement.

Adapted from an article in the *Louisville Courier*, August 6, 1855.

READING REVIEW ★ ★ ★ ★ ★ ★ ★

1. What means did the Know-Nothings use to intimidate foreign-born voters?
2. According to the article, what ethnic groups were the chief victims of the Know-Nothings' violence?
3. **Distinguishing fact from opinion.** (a) Which parts of the article are statements of opinion? (b) Give two examples of facts in the article.

★ ★ ★ ★ ★ ★ ★ ★ ★ ★ ★ ★ ★ ★ ★ ★ ★ ★ ★

★ 15-4 Inventing the Cotton Gin ★

Introduction The invention of the cotton gin revolutionized the cotton industry of the South. The machine was eventually able to clean as much cotton a day as 1,000 slaves could clean by hand. Eli Whitney invented the cotton gin shortly after he graduated from college. In this letter written to his parents, Whitney tells how he came to build the first gin.

Vocabulary Before you read the selection, find the meaning of these words in a dictionary: advantageous, enjoining.

New Haven
Sept. 11th, 1793

Dear Parent,

I presume, sir, you want to hear how I have spent my time since I left college. It is my duty to inform you, and I should have done it before this time.

I went from New York with the family of the late Major General Greene to Georgia. I went immediately with the family to their plantation. I expected to spend four or five days and then proceed into Carolina to take the school, as I have mentioned in former letters.

During this time I heard much said of the extreme difficulty of ginning cotton, that is, separating it from its seeds. There were a number of very respectable gentlemen at Mrs. Greene's who all agreed that if a machine could be invented which would clean the cotton more efficiently, it would be a great thing both to the country and to the inventor.

I involuntarily happened to be thinking on the subject and struck out a plan of a machine in my mind. In about ten days I made a little model. I was offered 100 guineas for it if I would give up all right and title to it. I decided to give up my school and turn my attention to perfecting the machine. I made one with which one man will clean ten times as much cotton as he can in any other way before known.

How advantageous this business will eventually prove to me, I cannot say, but think I had better pursue it rather than any other business into which I can enter.

I wish you, sir, not to show this letter nor communicate anything of its contents to anybody except my brothers and sister, enjoining it on them to keep the whole a profound secret.

With respect to Mama, I am, kind Parent,

Your most obedient Son,
Eli Whitney, Junior

Adapted from a letter of Eli Whitney, Jr., to his father, September 11, 1793.

READING REVIEW ★ ★ ★ ★ ★ ★ ★

1. (a) What had Eli Whitney planned to do after college? (b) What effect did the invention of the cotton gin have on his plans?

2. Why do you think Whitney wanted his family to keep this letter a secret?

3. **Relating past to present.** (a) What recent invention has had as profound an effect on people's lives as the cotton gin had on the lives of Southern planters? (b) In what way or ways has this invention changed our lives?

★ ★ ★ ★ ★ ★ ★ ★ ★ ★ ★ ★ ★ ★ ★ ★ ★ ★

Here, several slaves use an early cotton gin to clean cotton. In the front of the machine, you can see the row of teeth that pulled the cotton from the seeds.

★ 15-5 Memories of a Slave Auction ★

Introduction One of the most degrading events in the lives of slaves was the slave auction. At an auction, the slaves were paraded and poked as though they were horses or cattle. Many were separated from husband, wife, children, or other loved ones. In this selection, Solomon Northrup, an ex-slave, describes an auction that took place in New Orleans in 1841.

Vocabulary Before you read the selection, find the meaning of these words in a dictionary: barter, paroxysm, afflicted, beseeching.

In the first place, we were required to wash thoroughly and those with beards to shave. We were then conducted into a large room in the front part of the building to which the yard was attached, in order to be properly trained before the admission of customers.

The men were arranged on one side of the room, the women at the other. The tallest was placed at the head of the row, then the next tallest, and so on in the order of their respective heights. Freeman, owner of the slave-pen, charged us to remember our places. He ordered us to appear smart and lively, sometimes threatening us. During the day, he exercised us in the art of "looking smart" and of moving to our places with exact precision.

Topic 15

Next day many customers called to examine Freeman's "new lot." The latter gentleman was very talkative, dwelling at much length upon our several good points and qualities. He would make us hold up our heads and walk briskly back and forth, while customers would feel of our hands and arms and bodies, turn us about, ask us what we could do, make us open our mouths and show our teeth, precisely as a jockey examines a horse which he is about to barter for or purchase. Scars upon a slave's back were considered evidence of a rebellious or unruly spirit and hurt his sale.

During the day, a number of sales were made. All the time the trade was going on, Eliza was crying aloud, and wringing her hands. She begged the man not to buy her son Randall unless he also bought herself and her daughter Emily. She promised, in that case, to be the most faithful slave that ever lived. The man answered that he could not afford it. Then Eliza burst in a paroxysm of grief, weeping mournfully. Freeman turned round to her, savagely, with his whip in his uplifted hand, ordering her to stop her noise or he would flog her. All the frowns and threats of Freeman could not wholly silence the afflicted mother. She kept on begging and beseeching them not to separate the three. But it was of no avail. The man could not afford it. The bargain was agreed upon, and Randall must go alone. Then Eliza ran to him, embraced him passionately, kissed him again and again, and told him to remember her—all the while her tears falling in the boy's face like rain.

"Don't cry, mama. I will be a good boy. Don't cry," said Randall, looking back, as they passed out of the door.

It was a mournful scene indeed. I would have cried myself if I had dared.

Adapted from Solomon Northrup, *Twelve Years a Slave*, 1853.

READING REVIEW ★ ★ ★ ★ ★ ★ ★

1. Why were the slaves examined for scars by prospective buyers?
2. Why were Eliza and Randall separated?
3. **Comparing.** How, according to Northrup, was a slave auction like an animal auction?

★ ★ ★ ★ ★ ★ ★ ★ ★ ★ ★ ★ ★ ★ ★ ★ ★ ★

Topic 16 The Reforming Spirit (1820–1860)

★ 16-1 A Daring Escape to Freedom ★

Introduction The history of the Underground Railroad abounds in dramatic stories. The slaves who escaped to freedom and the people who helped them risked their lives. One story was that of the escape from Georgia of Ellen and William Craft, a young slave couple. This letter by a fellow fugitive slave, abolitionist William Wells Brown, tells their story.

Vocabulary Before you read the selection, find the meaning of these words in a dictionary: precedent, advocate.

One of the most interesting cases of the escape of fugitives from American slavery that has ever come before the American people has just occurred, under the following circumstances. William and Ellen Craft, man and wife, lived with different masters in the state of Georgia. Ellen is so near white that she can pass without suspicion for a white woman. Her husband is much darker. He is a mechanic. By working nights and Sundays, he laid up money enough to bring himself and his wife out of slavery.

Their plan was without precedent. But though unusual, it was the means of getting them their freedom. Ellen dressed in man's clothing and passed as the master, while her husband passed as the servant. In this way they traveled from Georgia to Philadelphia. On their journey, they put up at the best hotels where they stopped. Neither of them can read or write. And Ellen, knowing that she would be called upon to write her name at the hotels, tied her right hand up as though it was lame, which proved of some service to her.

In Charleston, South Carolina, they put up at the hotel which Governor McDuffie and John C. Calhoun generally make their home. Yet these distinguished advocates of the "peculiar institution" say that the slaves cannot take care of themselves. They arrived in Philadelphia in four days from the time they started.

They are very intelligent. They are young, Ellen 22 and William 24 years of age. Ellen is truly a heroine.

Yours truly,
William W. Brown

Adapted from *The Liberator*, January 12, 1849.

READING REVIEW ★ ★ ★ ★ ★ ★ ★

1. What did the Crafts have to do before they could even try to escape to freedom?
2. (a) How did Ellen cover up the fact that she could not write? (b) Why would it have been dangerous for people to discover that she could not write?
3. **Analyzing a primary source.** Wells states that both McDuffie and Calhoun believed that slaves cannot take care of themselves. Why do you think Wells mentions this fact?

★ ★ ★ ★ ★ ★ ★ ★ ★ ★ ★ ★ ★ ★ ★ ★ ★ ★

An attempted escape was extremely risky for slaves. Yet to many the chance of freedom made the risk worthwhile. The faces of these runaway slaves who realize they may be free at last show how much freedom could mean.

Introduction As the campaign against slavery heated up, more Southerners began to defend the institution. This selection contains two arguments made by Southerners. Thomas Dew was a professor at William and Mary College in Virginia, and George McDuffie was governor of South Carolina.

Vocabulary Before you read the selection, find the meaning of these words in a dictionary: inevitably, conductive, sanction, servile, attributes.

Thomas Dew

Let us now look a moment to the slave, and consider his position. Mr. Jefferson has described him as hating rather than loving his master. We assert again that Mr. Jefferson is not borne out by the fact. We are well convinced that there is nothing but the relations of husband and wife, parent and child, or brother and sister which produces a closer tie than the relation of master and servant. We do not hesitate to affirm that, throughout the whole slave-holding country, the slaves of a good master are his warmest, most constant, and most devoted friends. They have been accustomed to look up to him as their supporter, director, and defender. Everyone acquainted with southern slaves knows that the slave rejoices in the prosperity of his master.

A merrier being does not exist on the face of the globe than the Negro slave of the United States. They are happy and contented, and the master is much less cruel than is generally imagined. Why then, since the slave is happy and happiness is the great object of all animated creation, should we attempt to disturb his contentment by planting in his mind a vain and indefinite desire for liberty—a something which he cannot understand and which must inevitably dry up the very sources of his happiness?

George McDuffie

No human institution, in my opinion, is more clearly consistent with the will of God than slavery. And no one of his laws is written in more legible characters than that which consigns the African race to this condition as more conducive to their own happiness than any other with which they might meet. Whether we consult the sacred Scriptures or the lights of nature and reason, we shall find these truths as abundantly apparent as if written with a sunbeam in the heavens. Under both the Jewish and Christian branches of our religion, slavery existed with the wholehearted sanction of its prophets, its apostles, and finally its great Author. The ancient Hebrew fathers themselves, those chosen men of God, were slaveholders.

That the African Negro is destined by God to occupy this condition of servile dependence is not less clear. They have all the qualities that fit them for slaves and not one of those that would fit them to be freemen. Until the "African can change his skin," it will be in vain to attempt, by any human power, to make freemen of those whom God has doomed to be slaves.

Adapted from Thomas R. Dew, *Review of the Debate in the Virginia Legislature of 1831 and 1832*, 1832, and George McDuffie, message to the Legislature of South Carolina, *Journal of the General Assembly of the State of South Carolina*, 1835.

READING REVIEW ★ ★ ★ ★ ★ ★ ★

1. What is the main argument Thomas Dew makes in defense of slavery?
2. George McDuffie argues that it is the will of God that the American institution of slavery exists. What are the two principal reasons he gives for believing this?
3. **Comparing points of view.** Compare the attitudes toward slavery expressed here with the attitude expressed by Solomon Northrup in Reading 15-5.

★ ★ ★ ★ ★ ★ ★ ★ ★ ★ ★ ★ ★ ★ ★ ★ ★

Introduction In the 1800s, women began not only to demand equal rights with men under the law. They also began to question the attitudes that kept the sexes unequal. Elizabeth Cady Stanton traced much of women's dependence on men to the way in which young girls were raised. Stanton herself had raised seven children. In this speech to a woman's convention held in Akron, Ohio, she proposes a very different approach to raising girls.

Vocabulary Before you read the selection, find the meaning of these words in a dictionary: self-reliance, drone.

Dear Friends: The great work before us is the education of those just coming on the stage of action. Begin with the girls of today, and in 20 years we can revolutionize this nation. The childhood of woman must be free and unrestrained.

The girl must be allowed to romp and play, climb, skate, and swim. Her clothes must be more like those of the boy—strong, loose-fitting garments, thick boots, etc.—so that she may be out at all times and enter freely into all kinds of sports. Teach her to go alone, by night and day, if need be, on the lonely highway or through the busy streets of the crowded city.

The manner in which all courage and self-reliance is educated out of the girl, her path portrayed with dangers and difficulties that never exist, is sad indeed. Better, far, suffer occasional insults or die outright than live the life of a coward or never move without a protector. The best protector any woman can have, one that will serve her at all times and in all places, is courage. This she must get by her own experience.

The girl must early be impressed with the idea that she is to be "a hand,

not a mouth"—a worker, not a drone—in the great hive of human activity. Like the boy, she must be taught to look forward to a life of self-dependence and to prepare herself early for some trade or profession.

Do you think women thus educated would long remain the weak, dependent beings we now find them? By no means. Depend upon it, as educated capitalists and skilled laborers, they would not be long in finding their true level in political and social life.

Adapted from Elizabeth C. Stanton, Susan B. Anthony, and Matilda J. Gage, *History of Woman Suffrage,* 1881-1922.

READING REVIEW ★ ★ ★ ★ ★ ★

1. How did Elizabeth Cady Stanton propose to develop courage in young girls?
2. Why did she think it important for women to have courage?
3. **Relating past to present.** (a) To what degree have Stanton's proposals for the education of girls been put into practice today? (b) To what degree do today's young women have the attitudes toward life Stanton proposed?

★ ★ ★ ★ ★ ★ ★ ★ ★ ★ ★ ★ ★ ★ ★ ★ ★

Elizabeth Cady Stanton devoted much of her life to working for greater equality for women. She was also a busy wife and mother. Here she is shown with one of her seven children.

Introduction Americans on the frontier shared the nation's growing concern with education. Although poor and struggling, the settlers in a new area often worked hard to scrape together the money and materials needed to build a school and hire a teacher for their children. One-room country schoolhouses, such as the one shown in this painting by Winslow Homer, soon became commonplace.

READING REVIEW ★ ★ ★ ★ ★ ★ ★ ★ ★ ★ ★ ★ ★ ★ ★ ★ ★ ★ ★

1. Judging by this painting, what kind of equipment did teachers and students in country schools have to work with?

2. What would you say is the age range of the children in this classroom?

3. **Using visual evidence.** Based on the painting, how would you describe education in a one-room school?

★ ★

Part One

Introduction Some writers of the 1800s celebrated their country's past and its way of life. Others warned their fellow citizens of potential dangers they saw in American habits and attitudes. Henry David Thoreau was a writer of the second type. In *Walden*, a book he wrote about a year he spent living in the woods, Thoreau urged Americans not to get too caught up in the growing complexity of life.

Vocabulary Before you read the selection, find the meaning of these words in a dictionary: marrow, Spartan, superficial, unwieldy, elevation.

I went to the woods because I wished to live deliberately, to face only the essential facts of life, and to see if I could not learn what it had to teach, and not, when I came to die, discover that I had not lived. I did not wish to live what was not life. Living is so dear. I wanted to live deep and suck out all the marrow of life, to live sturdily and Spartanlike.

Our life is frittered away by detail. An honest man has hardly need to count more than his ten fingers, or in extreme cases he may add his ten toes, and lump the rest. Simplicity, simplicity, simplicity! I say, let your affairs be as two or three, and not a hundred or a thousand. Instead of a million, count half a dozen, and keep your accounts on your thumbnail. Simplify, simplify. Instead of three meals a day, if it be necessary eat but one, and instead of a hundred dishes, five. And reduce other things in proportion.

The nation itself, with all its so-called internal improvements, which, by the way, are all external and superficial, is just such an unwieldy and overgrown establishment. It is cluttered with furniture and tripped up by its own traps, ruined by luxury and heedless expense, by lack of calculation and a worthy aim. And the only cure for it, as for them, is in a stern and more than Spartan simplicity of life and elevation of purpose.

It lives too fast. Men think that it is essential that the nation have commerce, and export ice, and talk through a telegraph, and ride 30 miles an hour. But whether we should live like baboons or like men is a little uncertain. If we do not forge rails and devote days and nights to the work, but go to tinkering upon our lives to improve them, who will build railroads? And if railroads are not built, how shall we get to heaven in season? But if we stay at home and mind our business, who will want railroads?

Adapted from Henry David Thoreau, *Walden*, 1849.

READING REVIEW ★ ★ ★ ★ ★ ★ ★

1. (a) What are two examples Thoreau gives of how to simplify life? (b) What others can you think of?
2. What is Thoreau's opinion of the industrial culture growing up around him?
3. **Making generalizations.** What would Thoreau say is the purpose of life?

★ ★ ★ ★ ★ ★ ★ ★ ★ ★ ★ ★ ★ ★ ★ ★ ★ ★

In the 1800s, writers and painters portrayed both the simplicity and the grandeur of the American landscape. This view of Mt. Whitney was painted by Albert Bierstadt.

The Nation Divided

Topic 17 The Coming of the War (1820–1860)

★ 17-1 A Question of Slavery in the West ★

Introduction In 1846, Pennsylvania Congressman David Wilmot proposed that Congress prohibit slavery in any territory won from Mexico. His proposal touched off a great debate. This selection is from Wilmot's proposal, called the Wilmot Proviso.

Vocabulary Before you read the selection, find the meaning of these words in a dictionary: unmolested, integrity, concession.

Sir, the issue now presented is not whether slavery shall exist unmolested where it now is, but whether it shall be carried to new and distant regions, now free, where the footprint of a slave cannot be found. This, sir, is the issue. Upon it I take my stand, and from it I cannot be frightened or driven by idle charges of abolitionism. I ask not that slavery be abolished. I demand that this government preserve the integrity of free territory against the aggressions of slavery.

Sir, I was in favor of the annexation of Texas. The democracy of the North, almost to a man, went for annexation. Yes, sir, here was an empire larger than France given up to slavery. Shall further concessions be made by the North? Shall we give up free territory? Never, sir, never, until we ourselves are fit to be slaves.

But, sir, we are told that the joint blood and treasure of the whole country being spent in this acquisition,* therefore it should be divided and slavery allowed to take its share. Sir, the South has her share already.

Adapted from *Appendix to the Congressional Globe*, 1847.

READING REVIEW ★ ★ ★ ★ ★ ★ ★

1. What is Wilmot's attitude toward slavery in the states where it already exists?
2. (a) According to Wilmot, why do some people favor allowing slavery in the newly acquired Mexican territory? (b) How does he counter their argument?
3. **Finding the main idea.** State the main idea of the first paragraph.

★ ★ ★ ★ ★ ★ ★ ★ ★ ★ ★ ★ ★ ★ ★ ★ ★

*He is referring to the Mexican War.

Introduction The 1850 Senate debate over Henry Clay's proposed compromise on slavery was one of the most tense in American history. Senator John C. Calhoun, long a champion of the South, warned that the Union was in terrible danger. Because Calhoun was gravely ill, his speech was read by Senator James Mason of Virginia. This selection is from Calhoun's speech.

Vocabulary Before you read the selection, find the meaning of these words in a dictionary: indispensable, consistently, concession, submission.

How can the Union be preserved? To give a satisfactory answer to this mighty question, it is indispensable to have an accurate and thorough knowledge of the nature and the character of the cause by which the Union is endangered.

It is a great mistake to suppose that disunion can be effected by a single blow. The cords which bound these states together in one common union are far too numerous and powerful for that.

Disunion must be the work of time. It is only through a long process that the cords can be snapped, until the whole fabric falls asunder. Already the agitation of the slavery question has snapped some of the most important and has greatly weakened all the others.

If the agitation goes on, the same force, acting with increased intensity, will finally snap every cord. Then nothing will be left to hold the states together except force.

So the question again recurs—how can the Union be saved? To this I answer, there is but one way by which it can be—and that is by adopting such measures as will satisfy the states belonging to the southern section so that they can remain in the Union consistently with their honor and their safety.

The South asks for justice, simple justice, and less she ought not to take. She has no compromise to offer but the Constitution and no concession or surrender to make. She has alreay surrendered so much that she has little left to surrender.

For over a quarter of a century, John C. Calhoun and Daniel Webster had been powerful figures in the United States Senate. The debate over slavery in 1850 was their last. Compare these photographs with those of the younger Calhoun and Webster on pages 277 and 300.

But can this be done? Yes, easily. The North has only to will it to accomplish it—to do justice by conceding to the South an equal right in the acquired territory. The North has to do her duty by causing the laws relative to fugitive slaves to be faithfully fulfilled. It has to cease agitation on the slave question. And it has to provide for the insertion of a provision in the Constitution which will restore to the South, in substance, the power she possessed of protecting herself.

But will the North agree to this? It is for her to answer the question. But, I will say, she cannot refuse, if she has half the love of the Union which she professes to have. At all events, the responsibility of saving the Union rests on the North, and not on the South.

If you, who represent the stronger portion, cannot agree to settle these questions on the broad principle of justice and duty, say so. Let the states we both represent agree to separate and part in peace. If you are unwilling that we should part in peace, tell us so. We shall know what to do when you reduce the question to submission or resistance.

Adapted from *Works of John C. Calhoun*, ed. Richard K. Cralle, 1856.

READING REVIEW ★ ★ ★ ★ ★ ★ ★

1. (a) What does Calhoun believe is the only way to save the Union? (b) Whose responsibility is it?
2. Why, according to Calhoun, should the South not compromise with the North?
3. **Making inferences.** What do you think Calhoun is hinting at when he says that if the North is unwilling to let the South part in peace "we shall know what to do"?

★ ★ ★ ★ ★ ★ ★ ★ ★ ★ ★ ★ ★ ★ ★ ★ ★ ★ ★

★ 17-3 A Plea to Preserve the Union ★

Introduction Probably the best-known speech of the great Senate debate of 1850 was made by Daniel Webster of Massachusetts. Webster had been known for decades as one of the most powerful speakers in the Senate. For much of that time he had used his public speaking talents to win support for the North. However, after hearing Calhoun's address to the Senate, Webster was determined to do what he could to preserve the Union. Webster spoke for over three hours, with hardly a glance at his notes. This selection is from his speech.

Vocabulary Before you read the selection, find the meaning of these words in a dictionary: crimination, recrimination, grievances, injunction, dissolution, eminently.

Mr. President, I wish to speak today not as a Massachusetts man, nor as a northern man, but as an American. I shall speak today for the preservation of the Union. Hear me for my cause. Mr. President, in the excited times in which we live, there is found to exist a state of crimination and recrimination between the North and the South. There are lists of grievances produced by each. Those grievances, real or supposed, alienate the minds of one portion of the country from the other. I see no solid grievance—no grievance presented by the South—but the want of a proper regard to the injunction of the Constitution for the delivery of fugitive slaves.

There are also complaints of the North against the South. The first and gravest is that the North adopted the Constitution recognizing the existence of slavery in the states and recognizing the right, to a certain extent, of representation of the slaves in Congress, under circumstances which do not now exist. The North complains that, instead of slavery being regarded as an evil, as it was then—an evil which all hoped would be extinguished gradually—it is now regarded by the South as an institution to be cherished and preserved and extended—an institution which the South has already extended to the utmost of her power by the acquisition of new territory.

Mr. President, I should much prefer to have heard, from every member of this floor, declarations of opinion that this Union should never be dissolved than the declaration of opinion that, under the pressure of any circumstances, such a dissolution was possible. I hear with pain and anguish and distress the word secession, especially when it falls from the lips of those who are eminently patriotic.

Secession! Peaceable secession! Sir, your eyes and mine are never destined to see that miracle. Peaceable secession is an utter impossibility.

Is the great Constitution under which we live here—covering this whole country—is it to be thawed and melted away by secession, as the snows on the mountain melt under the influence of a vernal sun—disappear almost unobserved, and die off? No, sir! No, sir! I will not state what might produce the disruption of the states, but, Sir, I see it as plainly as I see the sun in heaven—I see that disruption must produce such a war as I will not describe.

Adapted from *Congressional Globe*, 31 Cong., 1 sess., 1849–1850.

READING REVIEW ★ ★ ★ ★ ★ ★ ★

1. What grievance of the South does Webster feel is a solid one?
2. What grievance of the North does he mention?
3. **Analyzing a primary source.** Why is Webster upset by talk of secession?

★ ★ ★ ★ ★ ★ ★ ★ ★ ★ ★ ★ ★ ★ ★ ★ ★ ★

★ 17-4 The Suffering of Uncle Tom ★

Introduction Harriet Beecher Stowe's novel *Uncle Tom's Cabin* led many people to question the morality of slavery and roused others to call for its abolition. In fact, the book's influence was so great that, when President Lincoln finally met Mrs. Stowe during the Civil War, he is said to have greeted her: "So, you're the little lady who made this big war!" In this selection from the book, Simon Legree tries to make Tom tell him where some fugitive slaves are hiding.

Vocabulary Before you read the selection, find the meaning of these words in a dictionary: despotic, paroxysm, vehemence.

"Now, Quimbo," said Legree, as he stretched himself down in the sitting room, "you jest go and walk that Tom up here, right away! The old cuss is at the bottom of this yer whole matter. I'll have it out of his old black hide, or I'll know the reason why!"

Tom heard the message with a forewarning heart, for he knew all the plans of the fugitives' escape and the place of their present concealment. He knew the deadly character of the man he had to deal with and his despotic power. But he felt strong in God to meet death, rather than betray the helpless.

"Ay, ay!" said Quimbo, as he dragged Tom along. "Ye'll cotch it, now! See how ye'll look, now, helpin' Mas'r's niggers to run away! See what ye'll get!"

"Well, Tom!" said Legree, walking up and seizing him grimly by the collar of his coat. Legree spoke through his teeth in a paroxysm of determined rage. "Do you know I've made up my mind to KILL you?"

"It's very likely, Mas'r," said Tom, calmly.

"I have," said Legree, with grim, terrible calmness, "done—just—that—thing, Tom, unless you'll tell me what you know about these yer gals!"

"I han't got nothing to tell, Mas'r," said Tom, with a slow, firm, deliberate utterance.

"Do you dare to tell me, ye old black Christian, ye don't know?" said Legree.

Tom was silent.

Under the new Fugitive Slave Law, free blacks and runaway slaves in the North could be captured and returned to former masters. Antislavery forces printed posters such as this one to alert northern blacks of this danger.

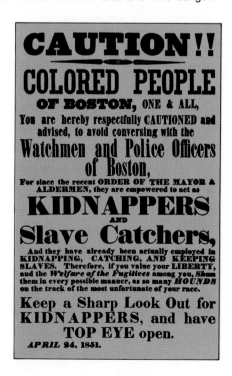

"Speak!" thundered Legree, striking him furiously. "Do you know anything?"

"I know, Mas'r. But I can't tell anything. I can die!"

Legree drew in a long breath. Suppressing his rage, he took Tom by the arm. Approaching his face almost to him, Legree said in a terrible voice, "Hark 'e, Tom! Ye think, 'cause I've let you off before, I don't mean what I say. But this time, I've made up my mind and counted the cost. I'll count every drop of blood there is in you and take 'em, one by one till ye give up!"

Tom looked up to his master and answered, "Mas'r, if you was sick, or in trouble, or dying, and I could save ye, I'd give ye my heart's blood. And if taking every drop of blood in this poor old body would save your precious soul, I'd give 'em freely, as the Lord gave his for me. O, Mas'r! Don't bring this great sin on your soul! It will hurt you more than 'twill me! Do the worst you can. My trouble'll be over soon, but if ye don't repent, yours won't never end!"

Like a strange snatch of heavenly music heard in the lull of a storm, this burst of feeling made a moment's blank pause. Legree stood aghast and looked at Tom.

It was but a moment. There was one hesitating pause, and the spirit of evil came back with sevenfold vehemence. Legree, foaming with rage, smote his victim to the ground.

Adapted from Harriet Beecher Stowe, *Uncle Tom's Cabin*, 1852.

READING REVIEW ★ ★ ★ ★ ★ ★ ★

1. Why was Legree threatening to kill Tom?
2. Why did Tom refuse to answer Legree's questions?
3. **Using fiction as historical evidence.** Tom's final remarks to Legree reflect an argument people often made against slavery. Explain that argument in your own words.

★ ★ ★ ★ ★ ★ ★ ★ ★ ★ ★ ★ ★ ★ ★ ★ ★ ★

Introduction How did blacks react to the Dred Scott decision, which declared that slaves were property and that even free blacks could not be citizens of the United States? Frederick Douglass, a leading black antislavery speaker, responded in this speech made at an abolitionist rally.

Vocabulary Before you read the selection, find the meaning of these words in a dictionary: scandalous, edict.

You will readily ask me how I am affected by this devilish decision. My answer is, and no thanks to the slaveholding wing of the Supreme Court, my hopes were never brighter than now. I have no fear that the national conscience will be put to sleep by such an open, glaring, and scandalous tissue of lies as that decision is and has been over and over shown to be.

The Supreme Court of the United States is not the only power in this world. It is very great, but the Supreme Court of the Almighty is greater. Such a decision cannot stand. We can appeal from man to God. All that is merciful and just, on earth and in heaven, will despise this edict.

If it were at all likely that the people of these free states would tamely submit to this judgment, I might feel gloomy and sad over it. And possibly it might be necessary for my people to look for a home in some other country. But as the case stands, we have nothing to fear. In one point of view, we, the abolitionists and colored people, should meet this decision, unlooked for and monstrous as it appears, in a cheerful spirit. This very attempt to blot out forever the hopes of an enslaved people may be one necessary link in the chain of events leading to the downfall and complete overthrow of the whole slave system.

Adapted from *Two Speeches by Frederick Douglass,* 1857.

READING REVIEW ★ ★ ★ ★ ★ ★ ★

1. With what spirit did Douglass greet the Dred Scott decision?
2. What reason did he give for adopting this attitude?
3. **Making inferences.** What do you think Douglass meant when he said the decision might be "one necessary link in the chain of events leading to the complete overthrow of the slave system"?

★ ★ ★ ★ ★ ★ ★ ★ ★ ★ ★ ★ ★ ★ ★ ★ ★

Introduction One of the events that helped push North and South toward war was John Brown's attempt to start a slave revolt in Harpers Ferry, Virginia. Brown and his raid became the subject of one of the most rousing Union songs to come out of the Civil war. "John Brown's Body" was sung by many Union troops marching to early battles. Later on in the war, the tune was used for the song "Battle Hymn of the Republic."

Vocabulary Before you read the selection, find the meaning of this word in a dictionary: traitor.

John Brown's body lies amold'ring in the grave,
John Brown's body lies amold'ring in the grave,
John Brown's body lies amold'ring in the grave,
His soul goes marching on!

Chorus

Glory, glory! Hallelujah! Glory, glory! Hallelujah!
Glory, glory! Hallelujah! His soul is marching on.

He captured Harpers Ferry with his nineteen men so true,
And he frightened old Virginia till she trembled through and through;
They hung him for a traitor, themselves the traitor crew,
But his soul is marching on!

John Brown died that the slave might be free,
John Brown died that the slave might be free,
John Brown died that the slave might be free,
But his soul goes marching on!

Adapted from a traditional song.

READING REVIEW ★ ★ ★ ★ ★ ★ ★

1. What did John Brown do that "frightened old Virginia"?
2. Why does the song call those who hung Brown traitors?
3. **Using a song as historical evidence.** What do you think the song is referring to when it says Brown's "soul is marching on"?

★ ★

★ 17-7 Mississippi Secedes From the Union ★

Introduction Mississippi was one of the first southern states to secede from the Union. This selection is the formal declaration of secession. In it, the state's political leaders spell out the reasons for their decision to leave the Union.

Vocabulary Before you read the selection, find the meaning of these words in a dictionary: sovereign, compact, enticed, incendiary, insurrection, aggrieved.

The constitutional Union was formed by the several states in their separate sovereign capacity for the purpose of mutual advantage and protection. The several states are distinct sovereignties, whose supremacy is limited only so far as the same has been delegated by voluntary compact to a federal government. When that government fails to accomplish the ends for which it was established, the parties to the compact have the right to resume such delegated powers.

The institution of slavery existed prior to the formation of the federal Constitution and is recognized by its letter. All efforts to reduce its value or lessen its duration by Congress or any of the free states is a violation of the compact of union and is destructive of the ends for which it was established. But in defiance of the principles of the Union thus established, the people of the northern states have assumed a revolutionary position towards the southern states.

They have enticed our slaves from us and by state intervention obstructed and prevented their return under the fugitive slave law.

They declare in every manner in which public opinion is expressed their determination to exclude from admittance into the Union any new state that tolerates slavery in its constitution.

They have sought to create discord in the southern states by incendiary publications.

They encourage a hostile invasion of a southern state to excite insurrection, murder, and plunder.

Therefore, the Legislature of the State of Mississippi resolves that the secession of each aggrieved state is the proper remedy for these injuries.

Adapted from *Laws of Mississippi*, 1860.

READING REVIEW ★ ★ ★ ★ ★ ★

1. According to the declaration, when does a state have the right to take back the powers it has given to the federal government?

2. Why, according to the declaration, is any antislavery action a violation of the national compact of union?

3. **Drawing conclusions.** What event do you think the declaration is referring to when it mentions "a hostile invasion of a southern state to excite insurrection"?

★ ★ ★ ★ ★ ★ ★ ★ ★ ★ ★ ★ ★ ★ ★ ★ ★ ★

When the southern states seceded from the Union, they set up the Confederate States of America. Shown here are Confederate President Jefferson Davis, seated third from left, and his cabinet. General Robert E. Lee is at center.

Topic
18 The Civil War (1860–1865)

★ **18-1   The Bonnie Blue Flag**   ★

Introduction An early Confederate flag showed a white star on a solid blue background. This song was written by Harry McCarty in honor of that flag.

Vocabulary Before you read the selection, find the meaning of these words in a dictionary: treachery, impelled.

We are a band of brothers
　　And native to the soil,
Fighting for the property
　　We gained by honest toil;
And when our rights were threatened,
　　The cry rose near and far —

"Hurrah for the Bonnie Blue Flag
　　That bears the single star!"

　Chorus
Hurrah! hurrah!
For Southern rights, hurrah!
Hurrah for the Bonnie Blue Flag
That bears the single star.

As long as the Union
　　Was faithful to her trust,
Like friends and like brothers
　　Both kind were we and just;
But now, when Northern treachery
　　Attempts our rights to mar,
We hoist on high the Bonnie Blue Flag
　　That bears the single star.

First gallant South Carolina
    Nobly made the stand,
Then came Alabama,
    Who took her by the hand;
Next quickly Mississippi,
    Georgia and Florida,
All raised on high the Bonnie Blue Flag
    That bears the single star.

And here's to old Virginia —
    The Old Dominion State —
With the young Confed'racy,
    At length has linked her fate.
Impelled by her example,
    Now other states prepare
To hoist on high the Bonnie Blue Flag
    That bears the single star.

Then here's to our Confed'racy,
    Strong are we and brave,
Like patriots of old we'll fight
    Our heritage to save.
And rather than submit to shame,
    To die we would prefer;

So cheer for the Bonnie Blue Flag
    That bears the single star.

Then cheer, boys, cheer;
    Raise the joyous shout,
For Arkansas and North Carolina
    Now have both gone out;
And let another rousing cheer
    For Tennessee be given,
The single star of the Bonnie Blue Flag
    Has grown to be eleven.

Adapted from *Rebel Rhymes and Rhapsodies*, 1864.

READING REVIEW

1. What were the first four states to join the Confederacy?
2. According to the song, what was the Confederacy fighting for?
3. **Understanding geography.** Locate the states mentioned in the song on the map on page 394.

★ 18-2   Encouraging Union Soldiers ★

Introduction For many of the Union recruits, army life was a new and often frightening experience. One of their chief sources of encouragement was the support of their mothers, sisters, wives, and sweethearts. This poem shows the passionate patriotism of Phoebe Cary, a Union woman.

Vocabulary Before you read the selection, find the meaning of these words in a dictionary: host, vision, fancy, smite.

Rouse, freeman, the foe has arisen,
    His hosts are abroad on the plain;
And, under the stars of your banner,
    Swear never to strike it again!

O, fathers, who sit with your children,
    Would you leave them a land that is free?

Turn now from their tender caresses,
    And put them away from your knee.

O, brothers, we played with in childhood,
    On hills where the clover bloomed sweet;
See to it that never a traitor
    Shall trample them under his feet.

O, lovers, awake to your duty
    From visions that fancy has nursed;
Look not in the eyes that would keep you;
    Our country has need of you first.

And we, whom your lives have made blessed,
    Will pray for your souls in the fight
That you may be strong to do battle
    For Freedom, for God, and the Right.

We are daughters of men who were heroes;
    We can smile as we bid you depart;

But never a coward or traitor
    Shall have room for a place in our
    heart.

Then quit you like men in the conflict,
    Who fight for their home and their
    hand;
Smite deep, in the name of Jehovah,
    And conquer, or die where you
    stand.

Adapted from *Lyrics of Loyalty*, 1864.

READING REVIEW ★ ★ ★ ★ ★ ★ ★

1. What argument does Cary use to encourage fathers to fight?
2. How do you think Cary would react to reports that her brother had retreated under fire?
3. **Using a poem as a primary source.** According to this poem, what were Union soldiers fighting to defend?

★ ★ ★ ★ ★ ★ ★ ★ ★ ★ ★ ★ ★ ★ ★ ★ ★ ★ ★

★ 18-3 Lee Takes Pity on a Union Soldier ★

Introduction A number of soldiers on both sides were keenly aware that they were fighting against their brothers. Confederate General Robert E. Lee was one of those who always had deep respect for the brave men who fought on both sides, as the following account by a Union soldier shows.

Vocabulary Before you read the selection, find the meaning of these words in a dictionary: exposure, taunted.

I was at the battle of Gettysburg myself, and an incident occurred there which changed my views of the southern people. I had fought and cursed the Confederates desperately. I could see nothing good in any of them. The last day of the fight I was badly wounded. A ball shattered my left leg. I lay on the ground not far from Cemetery Ridge. As General Lee ordered his retreat, he and his officers rode near me. As they came along, I recognized him. Though faint from exposure and loss of blood, I raised up my hands, looked Lee in the face, and shouted as loudly as I could, "Hurrah for the Union!"

The general heard me, looked, stopped his horse, dismounted, and came toward me. I confess that I at first thought he meant to kill me. But as he came up, he looked down at me with such a sad expression upon his face that all fear left me. He extended his hand to me. Looking right into my eyes, he said, "My son, I hope you will soon be well."

If I live a thousand years, I shall never forget the expression on General Lee's face. There he was, defeated, retiring from a field that had cost him

One of the Confederacy's greatest strengths was its generals. In addition to Robert E. Lee, the South had the services of such brave and inspiring leaders as General Stonewall Jackson. Jackson is shown here overseeing manoeuvers at the Battle of Bull Run.

and his cause almost their last hope. And yet he stopped to say words like those to a wounded soldier of the opposition who had taunted him as he passed by! As soon as the General had left me, I cried myself to sleep there upon the bloody ground!

Adapted from *A Civil War Treasury of Tales, Legends and Folklore,* ed. B.A. Bodkin (New York: Random House, Inc., 1960).

READING REVIEW ★ ★ ★ ★ ★ ★ ★

1. What reaction did the Union soldier expect from General Lee?
2. How do you think the Union soldier viewed Southerners after this brief encounter with Lee?
3. **Analyzing a primary source.** What can you learn about Robert E. Lee from accounts such as this?

★ ★ ★ ★ ★ ★ ★ ★ ★ ★ ★ ★ ★ ★ ★ ★ ★ ★

★ 18-4 The Battle of Antietam ★

Introduction People at home learned about the fighting by reading newspaper articles written by reporters who traveled with the armies. Often these reporters risked their lives. This account of the Battle of Antietam was written by George Washburn Smalley, war correspondent for the *New York Tribune*.

Vocabulary Before you read the selection, find the meaning of these words in a dictionary: rapidity, canopied, tumult, flanked, unfaltering.

Battlefield of Sharpsburg
Wednesday evening, Sept. 17, 1862

Fierce and desperate battle between 200,000 men has raged since daylight. Finally, at four o'clock, McClellan sent simultaneous orders to Burnside and Franklin. McClellan was to advance and carry the batteries in his front at all hazards and any cost. Burnside was to carry the woods next in front of him to the right, which the Rebels still held.

Burnside obeyed most gallantly. Getting his troops well in hand, he sent a portion of his artillery to the front. He advanced them with rapidity and the most determined vigor, straight up the hill in front, where the Rebels had maintained their most dangerous battery.

The next moment the road in which the Rebel battery was planted was canopied with clouds of dust swiftly descending into the valley. Underneath was a tumult of wagons, guns, horses, and men flying at speed down the road. The hill was carried, but could it be held?

There is a halt. The Rebel left gives way and scatters over the field. The rest stand fast and fire. More infantry comes up. Burnside is outnumbered, flanked, compelled to yield the hill he took so bravely. His position is no longer one of attack. He defends himself with unfaltering firmness, but he sends to McClellan for help.

Looking down into the valley where 15,000 troops are lying, McClellan turns a half-questioning look on Fitz John Porter, who stands by his side, gravely scanning the field. They are Porter's troops below, fresh and impatient to share in this fight. But the same thought is passing through the minds of both generals: "They are the only reserves of the army. They cannot be spared."

Burnside's messenger rides up. His message is "I want troops and guns. If you do not send them I cannot hold my position for half an hour." McClellan turns and speaks very slowly: "Tell General Burnside that this is the battle of the war. He must hold his ground till dark at any cost."

Part One   122

The sun is already down. Not half an hour of daylight is left. None suspected how near was the peril of defeat. But the Rebels halted instead of pushing on. Before it was quite dark, the battle was over. Only a solitary gun of Burnside's thundered against the enemy. Presently this also ceased, and the field was still.

Adapted from *New York Daily Tribune*, September 20, 1862.

READING REVIEW ★ ★ ★ ★ ★ ★ ★ ★

1. Why did General McClellan refuse to send Porter's troops to help Burnside?
2. How was Burnside able to carry out the order to "hold his ground at any cost"?
3. **Building vocabulary.** General Burnside was famous for his dashing side whiskers, which were named "sideburns" after him. Find out who these styles are named for: pompadour, cardigan, bowler.

★ ★ ★ ★ ★ ★ ★ ★ ★ ★ ★ ★ ★ ★ ★ ★ ★ ★ ★

★ **18-5   Issuing the Emancipation Proclamation** ★

Introduction When the Emancipation Proclamation was issued, the North was fighting for the abolition of slavery as well as for preserving the Union. This new goal won the North much support, especially from free blacks, abolitionists, and many Europeans. This painting by A. A. Lamb shows the mood of many Northerners at the time.

READING REVIEW ★

1. (a) What group of people is at the left? (b) Who is carrying the proclamation?
2. What symbols of the Union does the artist use?
3. **Using visual evidence.** (a) Why do you think Lamb painted this picture? (b) How would his purpose have affected what he painted?

★ ★

Introduction Southern women had an especially hard time during the war. Nearly every able-bodied man enlisted in the army, leaving the women to manage farms and plantations. Women in the South also had to deal with the serious troubles of the Confederate economy—the severe shortages of clothing and food. This selection is from an account of the war years by Victoria Clayton, who was married to a wealthy Alabama planter and lawyer.

Vocabulary Before you read the selection, find the meaning of these words in a dictionary: ingenuity, laborious.

While my husband was at the front doing active service, I was at home struggling to keep the family comfortable. We were blockaded on every side. We could get nothing from without, so we had to make everything at home.

It became necessary for every home to be supplied with spinning wheels and the old-fashioned loom, in order to manufacture clothing for the members of the family. This was no small undertaking. I knew nothing about spinning and weaving cloth. I had to learn myself and then to teach the Negroes. Fortunately for me, most of the Negroes knew how to spin thread, the first step towards cloth-making. Our work was hard and continuous.

Our ladies would attend services in the church of God dressed in their homespun goods. They felt well pleased with their appearances—indeed, better pleased than if they had been dressed in silk of the finest fabric.

We made good warm flannels and other articles of apparel for our soldiers. Every woman learned to knit socks and stockings for her household, and many of the former were sent to the army.

Being blockaded, we were obliged to put our ingenuity to work to meet the demands on us as heads of families. Some things we could not raise—for instance, the accustomed necessary luxury of every home: coffee. So we went to work to hunt up a substitute. Various articles were tried, but the best of all was the sweet potato.

I entrusted the planting and cultivation of the various crops to old Joe. He had been my husband's nurse in infancy, and we always loved and trusted him. I kept a gentle saddle horse, and occasionally, accompanied by Joe, would ride over the entire plantation on a tour of inspection.

We were required to give one-tenth of all that was raised to the government. There being no educated white person on the plantation except myself, it was necessary that I attend to the gathering and measuring of every crop and the delivery of the tenth to the government authorities. This tenth we gave cheerfully, and we often wished we had more to give.

My duties were numerous and often laborious. And this was the case with the typical southern woman.

Adapted from Victoria V. Clayton, *White and Black Under the Old Regime*, 1899.

READING REVIEW ★ ★ ★ ★ ★ ★ ★

1. What new skills did Victoria Clayton learn in order to cope with the shortages created by the war?
2. Clayton says her duties were numerous. What new duties did she have to take on in her husband's absence?
3. **Making inferences.** (a) What sort of relationship did there seem to be between Victoria Clayton and the slaves her family owned? (b) How can you tell? (c) Can you get a complete picture of life at home in the South during the war from this account? Explain.

★ ★ ★ ★ ★ ★ ★ ★ ★ ★ ★ ★ ★ ★ ★ ★ ★ ★

Introduction On April 9, 1865, Robert E. Lee and Ulysses S. Grant met at Appomattox Courthouse to arrange for the surrender of Confederate troops. The day was one of deep feeling and high drama. It brought together two of the greatest leaders to emerge from the war. This selection is from Grant's *Personal Memoirs*.

Vocabulary Before you read the selection, find the meaning of these words in a dictionary: foe, valiantly, humiliation, cavalry, artillery, paroles.

What General Lee's feelings were I do not know. It was impossible to say whether he felt inwardly glad that the end had finally come, or felt sad over the results and was too manly to show it. Whatever his feelings, they were entirely concealed from my observation. But my own feelings, which had been quite jubilant on the receipt of his letter, were sad and depressed. I felt like anything rather than rejoicing at the downfall of a foe who had fought so long and valiantly.

General Lee was dressed in a full uniform which was entirely new. He was wearing a sword of considerable value. In my rough traveling suit, the uniform of a private with the straps of a lieutenant-general, I must have contrasted very strangely with a man so handsomely dressed.

We soon fell into a conversation about old army times. He remarked that he remembered me very well in the old army. I told him that of course I remembered him perfectly. After the conversation had run on in this style for some time, General Lee called my attention to the object of our meeting.

When I put my pen to the paper, the thought occurred to me that the officers had their own private horses and effects, which were important to them but of no value to us. I also thought it would be an unnecessary humiliation to ask them to deliver their sidearms.

General Lee appeared to have no objections to the terms first proposed. When he read over that part of the terms about sidearms, horses, and private property of the officers, he remarked, with some feeling, I thought, that this would have a happy effect upon his army.

Then, General Lee remarked to me that in their army, the men of the cavalry and artillery owned their own horses. Would these men be permitted to keep their horses? I told him that, as the terms were written, they would not.

I then said to him that I took it that most of the men in the ranks were small farmers. The whole country had been so raided by the two armies that it was doubtful whether they would be able to put in a crop to carry themselves and their families through the next winter without the aid of the horses they were then riding. I would, therefore, instruct the officers I left behind to receive the paroles of his troops to let every man of the Confederate army who claimed to own a horse or mule take the animal to his home. Lee remarked again that this would have a happy effect.

Adapted from Ulysses S. Grant, *Personal Memoirs*, 1886.

READING REVIEW ★ ★ ★ ★ ★ ★ ★

1. How did General Grant feel about the surrender?
2. Why did Grant decide to allow the confederate soldiers to keep their horses?
3. **Defending an opinion.** (a) How would you describe the attitudes of Grant and Lee at this meeting? (b) What evidence supports your opinion? (c) What other information would be useful?

★ ★ ★ ★ ★ ★ ★ ★ ★ ★ ★ ★ ★ ★ ★ ★ ★

19 The Road to Reunion (1864–1877)

★ 19-1   A Planter Faces the Future   ★

Introduction After the Civil War, many Southerners returned home to devastation. Many of the planters who had dominated southern society found their homes and crops in ruins. In this selection, Susan Dabney Smedes tells how her father coped with life after the war.

Vocabulary Before you read the selection, find the meaning of these words in a dictionary: contrivances, desolate, chivalrous.

My father, Thomas Dabney, was at Burleigh when he heard of General Lee's surrender. On the day the news reached him, he called his son to him. They rode together to the field where the Negroes were at work. He informed them of the news that had reached him and that they were now free. His advice was that they should continue to work the crop as they had been doing. At the end of the year they should receive such pay for their labor as he thought just.

From this time till January 1, 1866, no apparent change took place among the Burleigh Negroes. Those who worked in the fields went out as usual and cultivated and gathered in the crops. In the house, they went about their customary duties. We expected them to go away or to demand wages or at least to give some sign that they knew they were free. But except that they were very quiet and serious, we saw no change in them. At Christmas such compensation was made them for their services as seemed just. Afterward fixed wages were offered and accepted.

My father had come home to a house stripped of nearly every article of furniture and to a plantation stripped of the means of cultivating any but a small proportion of it. A few mules and one cow were all that was left of the stock. We had brought a few pieces of common furniture from Georgia, and a very few necessary articles were bought. In the course of time, some homemade contrivances and comforts relieved the desolate appearances of the rooms. But no attempt was ever made to refurnish the house.

He owned nothing that could be turned into money without great sacrifice but five bales of cotton. There were yet two sons and two daughters to be educated. He decided to get a tutor for them and to receive several other pupils in his house in order to make up the salary. The household was put on an economical footing. The plantation Negroes were hired to work in the fields, and things seemed to promise more prosperous days.

His chivalrous nature had always revolted from the sight of a woman doing hard work. He determined to spare his daughters all such labor as he could perform. General Sherman had said that he would like to bring every southern woman to the washtub. "He shall never bring my daughters to the washtub," Thomas Dabney said. "I will do the washing myself." And he did it for two years. He was in his seventieth year when he began to do it.

When he was 70 years of age, he decided to learn to grow a garden. He had never performed manual labor, but he now applied himself to learn to hoe as a way of supplying his family with vegetables. With the labor of those aged hands, he made a garden that was the best ordered that we had ever seen at Burleigh. He made his garden, as he did everything that he undertook, in the most painstaking manner, neglecting nothing that could insure success. The rows in that garden were models of exactness and neatness.

The garden was on the top of a long, high hill. In a time of drought or if he had set out anything that needed watering, he toiled up that long, steep hill with bucket after bucket of water. That garden supplied the daily food of his family nearly all the year round. He planted vegetables in such quantities that it was impossible to eat them all. So he sold barrels of vegetables in New Orleans.

He showed with pride what he had done by his personal labor in gardening and in washing. He placed the clothes on the lines as carefully as if they were meant to hang there always. He said that he had never seen snowier ones. And it was true.

At the end of the hard day's work he would say sometimes: "General Sherman has not brought my daughters to the washtub. I could not stand that."

Southerners on the home front had endured great hardships. When General Sherman marched through Georgia, his men looted and burned everything in their path. Many Southerners, like those shown here, left ruined homes and fled in terror.

Adapted from Susan Dabney Smedes, *Memorials of a Southern Planter*, 1887.

READING REVIEW ✶ ✶ ✶ ✶ ✶ ✶ ✶

1. How did Thomas Dabney's former slaves react to the news that they were free?
2. Why did Dabney wash clothes rather than allow his daughters to do it?
3. **Drawing conclusions.** In what ways was Thomas Dabney's life after the Civil War different from his life before the war?

✶ ✶ ✶ ✶ ✶ ✶ ✶ ✶ ✶ ✶ ✶ ✶ ✶ ✶ ✶ ✶ ✶

★ 19-2 From the Black Codes ★

Introduction The black codes passed by southern states in order to control the activity of newly freed slaves were the cause of great controversy. The codes guaranteed freedmen certain rights. Yet, at the same time, these laws undermined many new and hard-won freedoms. These are several articles from the black codes.

Vocabulary Before you read the selection, find the meaning of these words in a dictionary: probate, apprentice, minor, corporeal, vagrant.

It shall be the duty of all sheriffs, justices of the peace, and other civil officers of the several counties in this state, to report to the probate courts of their respective counties semiannually all freedmen, free negroes, and mulattoes under the age of 18 who are orphans, or whose parent or parents have not the means or who refuse to provide for and support them. It shall be the duty of the probate court to apprentice the minors to some competent and suitable person on terms the court may direct. The former owner of the minors shall be preferred when, in the opinion of the court, he or she is a suitable person for that purpose.

In the management and control of the apprentices, the master or mistress shall have the power to inflict such moderate corporeal punishment as a father or guardian is allowed to inflict on his or her child.

All freedmen, free Negroes, and mulattoes in this state over the age of 18 years found with no lawful employment or business, or found unlawfully assembling themselves together, in either the day or the night, and all white persons assembling with freedmen, free Negroes or mulattoes, or usually associating with them on terms of equality, shall be deemed vagrants. On conviction of vagrancy, they shall be fined.

All freedmen, free Negroes, and mulattoes may sue and be sued in all the courts of law of this state. They may acquire personal property by descent or purchase and may dispose of the property in the same manner and to the same extent that white persons may.

Adapted from *Laws of the State of Mississippi, Passed at a Regular Session of the Mississippi Legislature*, 1865.

READING REVIEW ★ ★ ★ ★ ★ ★

1. What rights did the Mississippi black codes grant to the newly freed slaves?
2. Why might the black code law on vagrants be considered harsh?
3. **Summarizing.** Describe in your own words the black code policy on apprenticing young blacks.

★ ★ ★ ★ ★ ★ ★ ★ ★ ★ ★ ★ ★ ★ ★ ★ ★ ★ ★

★ 19-3 A Former Slave on Reconstruction ★

Introduction Freedmen responded to their new freedom in many ways. Some left their old plantations immediately. Others, however, remained on close terms with their former owners. This account is ex-slave Katie Rowe's memory of the first years after the Civil War.

Vocabulary Before you read the selection, find the meaning of these words in a dictionary: pestering, ruction.

When we git back to Monroe to the old place, we git a big surprise. Old Master cut it up in chunks and put us out on it on the halves. But he had to sell part of it to git the money to git us mules and tools and food to run on. Then after a while he had to sell some more. He seem like he git old mighty fast.

About that time they was a lot of people coming into that country from the North. They kept telling us that the thing for us to do was to be free,

and come and go where and when we please.

They try to git us to go and vote. But none of us folks took much stock by what they say. Old Master tell us plenty times to mix in the politics when the young-uns git educated and know what to do.

Some of the blacks who work for the white folks from the North act pretty uppity and big. They come pestering round the dance places and try to talk up ructions amongst us, but it don't last long.

The Ku Kluckers start riding round at night, and they pass the word that the blacks got to have a pass to go and come and to stay at the dances. They have to git the pass from the white folks they work for. Passes writ from the northern people wouldn't do no good. That the way the Kluckers keep the blacks in line.

They wasn't very bad 'cause the blacks round here wasn't bad. But I hear plenty git whupped in other places 'cause they act up and say they don't have to take off their hats in the white stores and such.

Any black who behave hisself and don't go running round late a night and drinking never had no trouble with the Kluckers.

Adapted from "Recollections of Katie Rowe of Arkansas," in B. A. Botkin, *Lay My Burden Down* (Chicago: University of Chicago Press, 1945).

READING REVIEW ★ ★ ★ ★ ★ ★ ★ ★

1. How did Katie Rowe's owner treat his slaves after the war?
2. How did Rowe seem to feel toward her owner?
3. **Using oral history.** Rowe says any black who behaved himself did not have trouble with the Ku Klux Klan. What was her idea of a former slave behaving himself or herself?

★ ★ ★ ★ ★ ★ ★ ★ ★ ★ ★ ★ ★ ★ ★ ★ ★ ★

★ 19-4 Winning and Losing the Right to Vote ★

Introduction During Reconstruction, freedmen voted in large numbers. By the 1880s, however, threats of violence from groups like the Ku Klux Klan, as well as new laws, stopped most blacks from voting in the South. These two drawings illustrate the change.

READING REVIEW ★

1. (a) Which of the drawings represents the situation in the late 1880s? (b) What evidence supports your answer?
2. The caption for the drawing on the right says, "Everything points to a Democratic victory this fall." What do you think the artist meant by that?
3. **Using visual evidence.** What can you learn about the voting rights of blacks by studying these two drawings?

★ ★

Part Two

Transforming a Nation

Topic

1 The Western Frontier (1865–1914)

★ 1-1 Family Life Among the Sioux ★

Introduction Home life was very important to Plains Indians such as the Sioux. The family was the center of Sioux society. At home, children learned the values of their people as well as the skills they would need in life. Each family member had important roles to play in the home. In this selection Chief Standing Bear describes home life among the Lakota, a Sioux nation.

Vocabulary Before you read the selection, find the meaning of these words in a dictionary: sinew, frugality, ceremonial, recipient, plait.

The home was the center of Lakota society—the place where good social members were formed and the place whence flowed the strength of the tribe. Here it was that offspring learned duty to parents, to lodge, to band, to tribe, and to self.

Woman's work, generally, was to cook for the family, keep the tipi in order, and sew the clothing of the household members. The good wife never allowed one of the family to run low in clothing. There were garments to be made, and moccasins, robes and blankets, and sometimes gloves, caps, and scarfs. Buttonholes were never made, probably never thought of, but very pretty buttons were fashioned of rawhide and either painted or covered with porcupine quills. Sinew was split for thread, coarse strands for heavy work and medium fine or very fine strands for decorative work, then folded into little bundles and placed in a sewing kit.

When the men came home from the hunt there were skins to be cleaned and tanned. New tipis were made and old ones, for the sake of frugality, made into clothing for children. From rawhide were made moccasin soles, bags and trunks for holding ceremonial garments, headdresses, and other articles to be kept in neatness and order.

The good wife always kept plenty of food stored and cooked so that it could be served at any moment. The thought was not only to meet the food requirements of the family, but to be able to serve anyone who came to the tipi, strangers or relatives, children who came in from other tipis, or any old people whom the children might bring in.

Many of the courtesies of Indian social life included the preparation and serving of food. The serving of a family meal was a quiet and orderly affair. Mother placed the food in front of her while we children all sat quietly about, neither commenting on the food nor asking for any favors. Father, if at home, sat in his accustomed place at the side of the tipi. He, too, remained perfectly quiet and respectful, accepting the food that mother offered to him without comment. The serving was done on wooden plates, the soup being passed in horn spoons of different sizes, some of them holding as much as a large bowl. The food was portioned to each one of us as mother saw fit, her judgment being unquestioned, for we never asked for more. Before serving us, mother put a small portion of the food in the fire as a blessing for the meal.

Grandmother, next to mother, was the most important person in the home. Her place, in fact, could be filled by no one else. Parental devotion was very strong and the old were objects of care and devotion to the last. They were never given cause to feel useless and unwanted, for there were duties performed only by the old and because it was a rigidly kept custom for the young to treat their elders with respect. Grandmother filled a place that mother did not fill, and the older she got the more, it seemed, we children depended upon her for attention. I can never forget one of my grandmothers and what wonderful care she took of me. As a storyteller, she was a delight not only to me but to other little folks of the village. Her sense of humor was keen and she laughed as readily as we.

The men, when at home, were shown a good deal of attention by the women. This was but natural, as it was the hunters, scouts, and warriors who bore the greatest dangers and consequently were the recipients of much care and consideration.

Women and children were the objects of care among the Lakotas, and as far as their environment permitted they lived sheltered lives. Life was softened by a great equality. All the tasks of women—cooking, caring for children, tanning, and sewing—were considered dignified and worthwhile. No work was looked upon as menial.

The first thing a dutiful husband did in the morning, after breakfasting, was to arrange his wife's hair and to paint her face. The brush was a tail of the porcupine attached to a decorated handle, and in place of a comb a hair parter was used—a slender pointed stick, also with a decorated handle. The husband parted his wife's hair, then carefully brushed and plaited it into two braids which were tied at the ends with strings of painted buckskin. These hairstrings were sometimes works of art, being wrapped with brightly colored porcupine quills and tipped either with ball tassels of porcupine quills or fluffs of eagle feathers. When the hairdressing was finished, the part in the hair was sometimes marked with a stripe of red or yellow paint.

Next, the husband applied red paint to his wife's face, sometimes just to the cheeks, sometimes covering the entire face. If the woman was to be exposed to the wind and sun all day, she usually had her face covered with a protective coat of paint mixed with grease. It was "style"

The tipi, shown here in a drawing by Carl Bodmer, was a home for all seasons for the Plains Indians. With flaps for ventilation, it was cool in summer. About November the fire was brought inside. Buffalo robes provided extra warmth.

for the Lakota woman to use much red paint, but the custom was very likely a necessary and comfortable one before it became a mere matter of style. Many Lakota women had skins quite fine in texture and in childhood were light in color. Such skins, of course, burned easily in the hot wind and sun.

If the man of the family was to be home for several days, he busied himself in many ways, lightening the work of the woman. He cut down trees for wood, made and repaired saddles, cut up meat conveniently for drying, and, when there was nothing else to be done, gladly amused the baby of the family. A man who unduly scolded his wife or who beat her or his children was not considered a good man. A man who would inflict punishment upon the women and children was considered a weakling and a coward. Whenever it was said about a man, "He ought not to have a wife," that was expressing strong disapproval of him.

From *Cry of the Thunderbird: The American Indian's Own Story*. Edited and with an Introduction and Commentary by Charles Hamilton. New edition copyright 1972 by the University of Oklahoma Press.

READING REVIEW

1. What were the main activities of the mother in a Lakota family?
2. How did each adult in the Lakota family contribute to home life?
3. **Relating Past to Present** (a) In what ways is family life today similar to family life among the Lakota Sioux? (b) How is it different?

★ 1-2 Lizzie Miles of Superior, Montana ★

Introduction Old movies often show the saloons, rugged miners, and wild times of old mining towns. This selection gives you a woman's view of a gold rush town. Lizzie Miles lived in Superior, a gold mining town in Montana.

Vocabulary Before you read the selection, find the meaning of this word in a dictionary: catered.

I came to Superior from Kansas in 1891. My husband, Adrian Miles, had gone on ahead a month earlier. Superior was located at the mouth of Johnston Creek. There were just three or four homes but seven saloons. A. P. Johnston's store was in the old Shamrock building, where the Corner Service Station now stands. Johnston ran a combination of store, saloon, and dance hall that catered to the miners. After celebrating there on paydays, the miners would get together a sleighload and go ripping and tearing about the country, having a high old time.

The first day we came here, Old Man Lozeau got Miles and me to work for him at his ranch. He was a Frenchman, but his wife was part Indian. She was fat and jolly, and I liked to hear her talk. I'd often hear her call, "Lozeau, come build fire, Lozeau; that all you good for." They had a whole brood of young ones: Louis, Joe, Dolphe, Puss, Phonzine, and Mary. Dolphe used to fiddle for the dances. He'd play with his eyes shut, all night the same tune. "There'll Be a Hot Time in the Old Town To-Night" was the most popular tune, and usually it was a hot time.

The stub of the Northern Pacific was just completed in 1891. There were no passenger cars, just a common boxcar, with homemade seats of the sort they used in the old schoolhouse. It was rough, like riding on a lumber wagon.

I came through on the railroad from Kansas, about the next week after the stub was laid. The Missoula agent didn't want to sell me a ticket at first. He didn't know if the road was put through here yet. When he found out Iron Mountain was where I was headed for, he said he was sure the track had been laid that far.

I was the first woman to walk across the first bridge across the Missoula River at Superior. There was just the thickness of two boards to walk on, with a space between the planks. I was afraid to look down, for it seemed that any minute I must go through, into the river. Jimmy Harmon was ahead of me, packing my girl Laura, who was a baby then.

I remember a Christmas tree we had once at the Thomas Hotel. Johnston had fixed himself up as a Santa Claus, rigged out with a cotton beard. He came in by a ladder, on the third floor. In those days we didn't have electric lights, only coal-oil lamps and the colored candles on the tree. Johnston got too close to the candles, and his whiskers caught fire. Grandma Riefflin grabbed her plaid shawl, one she had brought from Berlin, Germany, and smothered the blaze with it. By that time, there was a regular stampede, everybody hitting the stairs. A bunch of big men held them back, or some would have been trampled to death.

Soon after we came here, Bill Beach wanted to hire Miles to work in the mine and me to do the cooking, but he'd only pay next to nothing, so I wouldn't hear it. He was a big-bodied man with short legs. He wore his straight, black hair short around the neck and long everyplace else, with big whiskers tucked into his bib overall. I told him: "I'd like to take you by the whiskers and lead you around the country." He laughed and answered, "You're the first woman I ever heard complain about a man's whiskers."

Adapted from *First Person America*, ed. Ann Banks (New York: Alfred A. Knopf, 1980).

READING REVIEW

1. What in Lizzie Miles's story shows that she was tough enough to be successful in the West?

2. Does anything about life in Superior, Montana, appeal to you? Explain.

3. **Analyzing a Primary Source** (a) What part of Lizzie Miles's account gives you the most vivid impression of life in a mining town? Explain. (b) Do you think her recollections are accurate? Why or why not?

★ 1-3 Building the Union Pacific ★

Introduction During the Civil War, General Grenville M. Dodge was Union General Sherman's engineer in the Atlantic campaign. After the war, Dodge was made chief engineer for construction of the Union Pacific Railroad in the westward push across the continent. Starting from Council Bluffs, Iowa, efficient crews led by Dodge rapidly graded land and put down track. The difficulty of the job is made vivid in Dodge's description, which follows. While the problems that came up among workers could be settled, the movement of white people across the continent marked the beginning of the end for the Plains Indians.

Vocabulary Before you read the selection, find the meaning of these words in a dictionary: prominent, grade, sledge.

The organization for work on the plains was as follows. Each of our surveying parties consisted of a chief, who was an experienced engineer, two assistants, also civil

Immigrants, especially Chinese and Irish, played a key role in the race between the Central Pacific and Union Pacific. Here a work crew poses with the first engine that rode on the track they put down.

engineers, rodmen, flagmen, and chainmen, generally graduated civil engineers but without personal experience in the field, besides ax men, teamsters, and herders. When the party was expected to live upon the game of the country, a hunter was added.

Each party would thus consist of from 18 to 22 men, all armed. Each party entering a country occupied by hostile Indians was generally furnished with a military escort of from 10 men to a company under a competent officer. The duty of this escort was to protect the party when in camp. In the field the escort usually occupied prominent hills commanding the territory in which the work was to be done, so as to head off sudden attacks by the Indians. Notwithstanding this protection the parties were often attacked, their chief or some of their men killed or wounded, and their stock run off.

The location part of our work was followed by the construction corps, which graded about 100 miles at a time. That distance was graded in about 30 days on the plains, as a rule. But in the mountains we sometimes had to open our grading several hundred miles ahead of our track in order to complete the grading by the time the track should reach it.

All the supplies for this work had to be hauled from the end of the track, and the wagon transportation was enormous. At one time we were using at least 10,000 animals, and most of the time from 8,000 to 10,000 laborers. To supply one mile of track with material and supplies required about 40 cars. Everything—rails, ties, bridging, fastenings, all railway supplies, fuel for locomotives and trains, and supplies for men and animals on the entire work—had to be transported from the Missouri River. Therefore, as we moved westward, every hundred miles added vastly to our transportation.

The Union Pacific and Central Pacific were allowed to build, one east and the other west, until they met. We were pressed to as speedy a completion of the railroad as possible, although 10 years had been allowed by Congress. The officers of the Union Pacific urged me to plan to build as much road as possible in 1868.

We made our plans to build to Salt Lake, 408 miles, in 1868 and to try to meet the Central Pacific west of Ogden in the spring of 1869. I remember that the parties going to Salt Lake crossed the Wasatch Mountains on sledges and that the snow covered the tops of the telegraph poles. Winter caught us in the Wasatch Mountains, but we kept on grading our road and laying our track in the snow and ice, at a tremendous cost. The instructions I received were to go on, no matter what the cost. Spring found us with the track at Ogden.

The Central Pacific had made wonderful progress coming east. Between Ogden and Promontory each company graded a line, running side by side, and in some places one line was right above the other.

The workers upon the Central Pacific were Chinese, while ours were Irishmen, and there was much ill feeling between them. Our Irishmen were in the habit of firing their blasts in the cuts without giving warning to the Chinese on the Central Pacific working right above them. As a result, several Chinese were severely hurt. Complaint was made to me by the Central Pacific people, and I tried to have the contractors bring all hostilities to a close; but for some reason or other they failed to do so. One day the Chinese put in what is called a "grave" on their work. When the Irishmen right under them were all at work, they let go their blast and buried several of our men. This brought about a truce at once. From that time the Irish laborers showed due respect for the Chinese, and there was no further trouble.

Adapted from Grenville M. Dodge, "How We Built the Union Pacific Railway, and Other Railway Papers and Addresses," n.d.

READING REVIEW

1. What group conflicts made building the transcontinental railroad more difficult?

2. What is your opinion of how these problems were solved? Explain.

3. **Making Inferences** Based on the selection, what was General Dodge's view of Indians?

Introduction As white settlers moved west, many of the Plains Indians refused to give up their land and move to reservations without a fight. Chief Joseph and the Nez Percé Indians were finally defeated at the end of a strategic retreat from Oregon to Montana. The remaining members of the tribe were sent to Oklahoma Territory, where many of them became ill and died. Chief Joseph appealed directly to the President for help. His appeal, printed here, was written in 1879. As a result of his plea, the Nez Percé were allowed to return to the Northwest.

Vocabulary Before you read the selection, find the meaning of these words in a dictionary: misinterpretation, compel.

At last I was granted permission to come to Washington and bring my friend Yellow Bull and our interpreter with me. I am glad I came. I have shaken hands with a good many friends, but there are some things I want to know which no one seems able to explain. I cannot understand how the government sends a man out to fight us, as it did General Miles, and then breaks his word. Such a government has something wrong about it.

I have heard talk and talk, but nothing is done. Good words do not last long unless they amount to something. Words do not pay for my dead people. They do not pay for my country, now overrun by white men. They do not protect my father's grave. They do not pay for my horses and cattle.

Good words do not give me back my children. Good words will not make good the promise of your war chief, General Miles. Good words will not give my people good health and stop them from dying. Good words will not get my people a home where they can live in peace and take care of themselves.

I am tired of talk that comes to nothing. It makes my heart sick when I remember all the good words and all the broken promises. There has been too much talking by men who had no right to talk. Too many misinterpretations have been made; too many misunderstandings

have come up between the white men and the Indians.

If the white man wants to live in peace with the Indian, he can live in peace. There need be no trouble. Treat all men alike. Give them the same laws. Give them all an even chance to live and grow.

All men are made by the same Great Spirit Chief. They are all brothers. The earth is the mother of all people, and all people should have equal rights upon it. You might as well expect all rivers to run backward as that any man who was born a free man should be contented penned up and denied liberty to go where he pleases. If you tie a horse to a stake, do you expect he will grow fat? If you pen an Indian up on a small spot of earth and compel him to stay there, he will not be contented nor will he grow and prosper.

I have asked some of the Great White Chiefs where they get their authority to say to the Indian that he shall stay in one place, while he sees white men going where they please. They cannot tell me.

I only ask of the government to be treated as all other men are treated. If I cannot go to my own home, let me have a home in a country where my people will

---

For many years after his people moved back to Oregon, Chief Joseph continued to work for the welfare of the Nez Percés. He was generous and forgiving toward former enemies. Near the end of his life he said, "I have no grievance against any of the white people."

not die so fast. I would like to go to Bitter Root Valley [western Montana]. There my people would be healthy; where they are now, they are dying. Three have died since I left my camp to come to Washington. When I think of our condition, my heart is heavy. I see men of my own race treated as outlaws and driven from country to country, or shot down like animals.

I know that my race must change. We cannot hold our own with the white men as we are. We only ask an even chance to live as other men live. We ask to be recognized as men. We ask that the same law shall work alike on all men. If an Indian breaks the law, punish him by the law. If a white man breaks the law, punish him also.

Let me be a free man—free to travel, free to stop, free to work, free to trade where I choose, free to choose my own teachers, free to follow the religion of my fathers, free to think and talk and act for myself—and I will obey every law or submit to the penalty.

Whenever white men treat Indians as they treat each other, then we shall have no more wars. We shall all be alike—brothers of one father and mother, with one sky above us and one country around us and one government for all. Then the Great Spirit Chief who rules above will smile upon this land and send rain to wash out the bloody spots made by brothers' hands upon the face of the earth. For this time the Indian race was waiting and praying. I hope no more groans of wounded men and women will ever go to the ear of the Great Spirit Chief above, and that all people may be one people.

Adapted from the *North American Review*, April 1879.

READING REVIEW

1. Where did Chief Joseph want to go with his people?
2. How did he think his people should be treated?
3. **Finding the Main Idea** Write a paragraph describing the main points of Chief Joseph's request to the President.

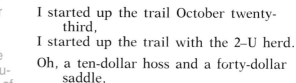

★ 1-5 The Old Chisholm Trail ★

Introduction Perhaps you have heard or sung this cowboy song, for it and others like it have become part of American culture. Some songs the cowboys sang were work songs. Others were stories set to music to relieve the boredom and loneliness of the trail. Songs were also used to soothe the cattle. Few of the melodies were original. The cowboys made up new lyrics to old English tunes brought to America by early immigrants.

Vocabulary Before reading the selection, find the meaning of these words in a dictionary: slicker, commence.

Come along, boys, and listen to my tale,
I'll tell you of my troubles on the old
   Chisholm trail.

   Chorus
   Coma ti yi yippy, yippy yay, yippy
      yay,
   coma ti yi yippy, yippy yay.

I started up the trail October twenty-
   third,
I started up the trail with the 2–U herd.

Oh, a ten-dollar hoss and a forty-dollar
   saddle,
And I'm going' to punchin' Texas cattle.

I woke up one morning on the old
   Chisholm trail,
Rope in my hand and a cow by the tail.

I'm up in the mornin' afore daylight
And afore I sleep the moon shines
   bright.

My hoss throwed me off at the creek
   called Mud,
My hoss throwed me off round the 2–U
   herd.

Last time I saw him he was going 'cross
   the level
A-kicking up his heels and a-running like
   the devil.

It's cloudy in the west, a-looking like rain,
And my darned old slicker's in the wagon
    again.

No chaps, no slicker, and it's pouring
    down rain,
And I swear, by God, I'll never night-
    herd again.

Last night I was on guard and the
    leader broke the ranks,
I hit my horse down the shoulders and I
    spurred him in the flanks.

The wind commenced to blow, and the
    rain began to fall,
Hit looked, by grab, like we was goin' to
    lose 'em all.

My slicker's in the wagon and I'm gittin'
    mighty cold,
And these longhorn sons-o'-guns are
    gittin' hard to hold.

With my blanket and my gun and my
    rawhide rope,
I'm a slidin' down the trail in a long, keen
    lope.

I don't give a darn if they never do stop;
I'll ride as long as an eight-day clock.

We rounded 'em up and put 'em on the
    cars,
And that was the last of the old Two Bars.

Oh, it's bacon and beans 'most every
    day—
I'd as soon be a-eatin' prairie hay.

I went to the boss to draw my roll,
He had it figgered out I was nine dollars
    in the hole.

I'll sell my outfit just as soon as I can,
I won't punch cattle for no darn man.

With my knees in the saddle and my seat
    in the sky,
I'll quit punching cows in the sweet
    by-and-by.

Fare you well, old trail boss, I don't wish
    you any harm,
I'm quittin' this business to go on the
    farm.

Adapted from a traditional cowboy song.

READING REVIEW

1. What do you think was the purpose of this song?
2. Can you think of any songs that have special purposes today? Explain.
3. **Analyzing a Song as a Primary Source** (a) What does the song show about the character of the cowboy? (b) What can you learn from a song like this that you would not learn from a textbook?

★ 1-6 Deadwood Dick ★

Introduction Many of the cowboys herding cattle on the long drives from ranches to railroad depots were blacks or Mexican Americans. Nat Love, a former slave, wrote a book about his adventures in the West. In this selection Love tells how he became known as "Deadwood Dick."

Vocabulary Before reading the selection, find the meaning of the following words in a dictionary: mustang, quirt.

Our trail boss was chosen to pick out the mustangs from a herd of wild horses just off the range, and he picked out 12 of the most vicious horses he could find.

The conditions of the contest were that each of us who were mounted was to rope, throw, tie, bridle and saddle, and mount the particular horse picked for us in the shortest time possible. The man accomplishing the feat in the quickest time was to be declared the winner.

It seems to me that the horse chosen for me was the most vicious of the lot. Eveything being in readiness, the "45" cracked and we all sprang forward together, each of us making for our particular mustang.

I roped, threw, tied, bridled, saddled, and mounted my mustang in exactly 9 minutes from the crack of the gun. The

No figure represents the West in the popular imagination as much as the cowboy. Clara McDonald Williamson painted this picture, "Old Chisholm Trail," from memory. It shows a cattle drive from Texas to Kansas.

time of the next nearest competitor was 12 minutes and 30 seconds. This gave me the record and championship of the West, which I held up to the time I quit the business in 1890, and my record has never been beaten.

It is worthy of passing remark that I never had a horse pitch with me so much as that mustang, but I never stopped sticking my spurs in him and using my quirt on his flanks until I proved master. Right there the crowd named me Deadwood Dick and proclaimed me champion roper of the western cattle country.

Adapted from Nat Love, *The Life and Adventures of Nat Love*, 1907.

READING REVIEW

1. What did Nat Love do to earn the name "Deadwood Dick"?
2. Do you think his account is accurate? Why or why not?
3. **Analyzing a Primary Source** Why is a book like Love's a valuable source even if he exaggerates what happened?

★ 1-7 The Winter of '86–'87 ★

Introduction In the heyday of the cattle boom after the Civil War, beef was in great demand in growing cities, and new railroads made delivery possible. But the cattle boom ended quickly. Overgrazing depleted the grassland, and there were range wars between cattlemen and sheep ranchers. Also, farmers began to fence the land. But the final blow came from nature when first a dry summer and then a severe winter killed cattle by the hundreds of thousands.

Vocabulary Before reading the selection, find the meaning of the following words in a dictionary: morrow, catastrophe, debacle.

May was dry, June did not bring the usual rains, and by July 4 it looked so bad that we finally decided to do nothing. By August it was hot, dry, and dusty, and the grass was closely cropped. Every day made it clear that even with the best of winters, cattle would have a hard time. But our neighbors kept piling cattle onto the bone-dry range.

The Continental Cattle Co. drove up 32,000 head of steers. The Worsham Cattle Co., with no former holdings, turned loose 5,000 head or thereabouts. Major Smith, who had failed to sell 5,500 southern three-year-old steers, was forced to drive them to his range on Willow Creek near to Stoneville, now Alzada, Montana. The Dickey Cattle Co. had brought up 6,000 mixed cattle from the Cheyenne and Arapaho country. Thousands of other cattle were spread over the western and northwestern country in the most reckless way, no thought for the morrow. Even with the best of winters it would have been a case of suicide.

As things turned out it was simple murder, at least for the Texas cattle. Winter came early and it stayed long. The owners were mostly absent and even those who remained could not move about or size up the situation.

It was not till the spring roundups that the real truth was discovered and then it was only mentioned in a whisper. It turned out to be a total loss of from 30 to 60 percent. From southern Colorado to the Canadian line, from the 100th meridian almost to the Pacific slope, it was a catastrophe which the cowmen of today who did not go through it can never understand. The buffalo had probably gone through similar winters with enormous losses and thus natural conditions were evened up in the countless years they had grazed the prairie. And in the survival of the fittest their constitutions had been built up to stand the rigors of winter and the drought of summer.

Adapted from John Clay, *My Life on the Range*, Chicago, 1924.

READING REVIEW

1. Why did the summer weather make conditions difficult for cattle on the plains?
2. How does the author think the cattlemen made conditions worse?
3. **Understanding Geography** How did the climate of the Great Plains contribute to the end of the cattle boom?

★ 1-8 Starting A New Life in Kansas ★

Introduction Among the people seeking new lives in the West were many black settlers. Although life on the plains was hard, the desire to escape discrimination in the South led thousands to migrate to Kansas. This move was called an Exodus after the Bible's description of the flight of the Jews from Egypt. The description of the "Exodusters" that follows is from an article published in 1880.

Vocabulary Before you read the selection, find the meaning of these words in a dictionary: picturesque, fortnight, creditable.

One morning in April 1879, a Missouri steamboat arrived at Wyandotte, Kansas, and discharged a load of colored men, women, and children with barrels, boxes, and bundles of household effects. It was a novel, pathetic sight. They were of all ages and sizes; their garments were incredibly patched and tattered, stretched, and uncertain; and there was not probably a dollar in money in the pockets of the entire party. The wind was cold, and they stood upon the wharf shivering. They looked like persons coming out of a dream. And, indeed, such they were, for this was the advance guard of the Exodus.

Soon other and similar parties came by the same route, and still others, until, within a fortnight, a thousand or more of them were gathered there at the gateway of Kansas—all poor, some sick, and none with a plan of future action.

The case was one to appeal with force to popular sympathy. So temporary shelter was speedily provided for them; food and facilities for cooking it were furnished them in ample measure. Then came more of them. The tide swelled daily.

The closing autumn found at least 15,000 of these colored immigrants in Kansas. Such of them as had arrived early in the spring had been able to do something toward getting a start. The thriftier ones had made homestead entries and contrived, with timely aid, to build cabins. In some cases, small crops of corn and garden vegetables were raised.

Numerous cabins of stone and sod were constructed while the cold season lasted. In many cases, the women went to the towns and took in washing or worked as house servants while the men were doing the building. Those who could find employment on the farms about their "claims" worked willingly and for small wages and in this way supported their families and bought now and then a calf, a pig, or a little poultry. Others found jobs on the railroads, in the coal mines, and on the public works of Topeka. Such as got work at any price did not ask assistance. Those who were compelled to apply

Topic 1

for aid did it slowly, as a rule, and rarely came a second time.

Their savings are not large, to be sure, but they are creditable and not to be lightly passed over. The wonder is that they have anything whatever to show for twelve months of hand-to-mouth hardship and embarrassment.

Adapted from Henry King, "A Year of the Exodus in Kansas," *Scribner's Monthly*, June 1880.

READING REVIEW

1. How did the settlers support themselves while they were setting up their claims?
2. Does the author conclude that the black settlers were successful? Explain.
3. **Drawing Conclusions** What characteristics do you think sodbusters needed to be successful?

★ 1-9 The Homestead Act ★

Introduction Farming on the plains took hard work. In 1862 Congress passed the Homestead Act to encourage people to move West. After the Civil War, thousands of people went west to "stake their claim." Portions of the Homestead Act follow.

Vocabulary Before reading the selection, find the meaning of the following words in a dictionary: enact, affidavit.

Be it enacted by the Senate and House of Representatives of the United States of America in Congress assembled, That any person who is the head of a family, or who is twenty-one, and a citizen of the United States, or who has filed to become a citizen, and who has never born arms against the United States Government or given aid and comfort to its enemies, shall, from January 1, 1863, be entitled to enter one quarter section of public lands, upon which said person may have filed a claim, for one dollar and twenty-five cents, or less, per acre.

And be it further enacted, That the application must be made for his or her exclusive use and benefit, for the purpose of actual settlement and cultivation.

And be it further enacted, That if, at any time after the filing of the affidavit, it shall be proven that the person having filed such affidavit shall have abandoned the said land for more than six months at any time, then and in that event the land so entered shall revert to the government.

Adapted from "An Act to secure Homesteads to Actual Settlers on the Public Domain," *Statutes at Large*, 1862.

READING REVIEW

1. According to the act, who could file a claim for a homestead?
2. Could women file a claim? Explain.
3. **Summarizing** Write a paragraph that summarizes the main points of the Homestead Act in your own words.

This pioneer family proudly sits in front of their sod house with their livestock. The roof of such houses was often 16 inches thick and able to support a cow. The blocks of sod were called "Nebraska marble." The house served until its owners could import enough wood for a frame house.

Topic 2

An Age of Industry (1865–1914)

★ 2-1 A Cable Across the Atlantic ★

Introduction During the age of industry there seemed to be no limit to what could be accomplished. People were thrilled by advances in communication and transportation. Instant contact between nations became possible when Cyrus Field laid a telegraph cable under the Atlantic connecting North America and Europe. It was an incredible engineering feat and one that did not go smoothly. Financial problems and technical difficulties dogged the enterprise. In this selection Field describes some of the problems he faced.

Vocabulary Before you read the selection, find the meaning of these words in a dictionary: hoax, odium, galvanize, grapple.

With the history of the expedition of 1857–1858 you are familiar. On the third trial we gained a brief success. The cable was laid, and for four weeks it worked, though never very brilliantly, never giving forth such rapid and distinct flashes as the cables of today. It spoke, though only in broken sentences. But while it lasted, no less than 400 messages were sent across the Atlantic.

You all remember the enthusiasm which it excited. It was a new thing under the sun, and for a few weeks the public went wild over it. Of course, when it stopped, the reaction was very great. People grew dumb and suspicious. Some thought it was all a hoax, and many were quite sure that it never worked at all. That kind of odium we have had to endure for eight years, till now, I trust, we have at last silenced the unbelievers.

After the failure of 1858 came our darkest days. When a thing is dead, it is hard to galvanize it into life. It is more difficult to revive an old enterprise than to start a new one. The freshness and novelty are gone, and the feeling of disappointment discourages further effort.

When the scientific and engineering problems were solved, we took heart again and began to prepare for a fresh attempt. This was in 1863. In this country—though the war was still raging—I went from city to city, holding meetings and trying to raise capital, but with poor success. Men came and listened and said it was all very fine and hoped I would succeed, but did nothing. Many had lost before and were not willing to throw more money into the sea.

It was at this time I was introduced to a gentleman whom I would hold up to the American public as a specimen of a great-hearted Englishman, Mr. Thomas Brassey. In London he is known as one of the men who have made British enterprise and British capital felt in all parts of the earth. I went to see him, though with fear and trembling. He asked me every possible question, but my answers satisfied him, and he ended by saying it was an enterprise which ought to be carried out and that he would be one of ten men to furnish the money to do it.

A few days after, half a dozen gentlemen joined together and bought the *Great Eastern* to lay the cable.

I will not stop to tell the story of that expedition. For a week all went well. We had laid out 1,200 miles of cable and had only 600 miles farther to go, when, hauling in the cable to fix a fault, it parted and went to the bottom. That day I can never forget—how men paced the deck in despair, looking out on the broad sea that had swallowed up their hopes; and then how the brave Canning for nine days and nights dragged the bottom of the ocean for our lost treasure. Though he grappled it three times, he failed to bring it to the surface. We returned to England defeated, yet full of resolution to begin the battle anew. It was finally concluded that the best course was to organize a new company, which should assume the work. So began the Anglo-American Telegraph Company.

Then the work began again and went on with speed. Never was greater energy put into any enterprise. It was only the first day of March that the new company was formed and was registered as a company the next day. Yet such was the vigor and dispatch that in five months from that day the cable had been manufactured, shipped on the *Great Eastern*, stretched across the Atlantic, and was sending messages, literally swift as lightning, from continent to continent.

But our work was not over. After landing the cable safely at Newfoundland, we had another task—to return to midocean and recover that lost in the expedition of last year. This achievement has perhaps excited more surpise than the other. Many even now "don't understand it," and every day I am asked how it was done. Well, it does seem rather difficult to fish for a jewel at the bottom of the ocean two and half miles deep. But it is not so very difficult when you know how.

At length it was brought to the surface. All who were allowed to approach crowded forward to see it. Yet not a word was spoken—only the voices of the officers in command were heard giving orders. All felt as if life and death hung on the issue. It was only when it was brought over the bow and onto the deck that men dared to breathe. Even then they hardly believed their eyes. Some crept toward it to feel of it, to be sure it was there.

Then we carried it along to the electricians' room, to see if our long-sought treasure was alive or dead. A few minutes of suspense, and a flash told of the lightning current again set free. Then did the feeling long pent up burst forth. Some turned away their heads and wept. Others broke into cheers, and the cry ran from man to man and was heard down in the engine rooms, deck below deck, and from the boats on the water and the other ships, while rockets lighted up the darkness of the sea. Then with thankful hearts we turned our faces again to the west.

The *Great Eastern* bore herself proudly through the storm, as if she knew that the vital cord which was to join two hemispheres hung at her stern; and so, on Saturday, the seventh of September, we brought our second cable safely to the shore.

Adapted from Cyrus Field, Speech, 1866.

READING REVIEW

1. What was the public's reaction when the first cable failed?
2. Why does Field call the years after 1858 their "darkest days"?
3. **Understanding Economic Ideas** How did Field raise capital to pay for the cable?

★ 2-2 The Remarkable Mr. Woods ★

Introduction Many of the great inventions of the industrial age created new businesses and products that changed people's lives. The patent office was kept busy, for no sooner was a product invented than someone would devise a way to improve it. Granville T. Woods was a black inventor whose inspiration never seemed to lag. This account from *Cosmopolitan Magazine* describes some of his accomplishments.

Vocabulary Before you read the selection, find the meaning of these words in a dictionary: ingenious, resistances, interference, dynamotor, prior, intricate.

Mr. Woods has taken out some 35 patents in various countries and has many still pending. He is the inventor of a telephone, which he sold the Bell Telephone Company, and of a system of telegraphing from moving railway trains, which was fully tried on the New Rochelle branch of the New Haven road in 1885. Three years ago, an electric railway system of his in-

New inventions helped to propel industry to great advances following the Civil War. This Currier and Ives print of 1876 shows some of the technology that changed American life: the steamboat, the locomotive, the electric telegraph, and the steam printing press.

vention was operated at Coney Island, New York. It had neither exposed wires, secondary batteries, nor a slotted way. The current was taken from iron blocks placed at intervals of twelve feet between the rails, in which, by an ingenious arrangement of magnets and switches, the current was turned on to the blocks only as they were covered by the cars.

The most remarkable invention of Mr. Woods is for the regulation of electric motors. In almost all applications of electric power it is necessary at times to control the speed of the motors without changing the loads or disturbing the voltage at the source of supply. This has usually been done by introducing large dead resistances in series with the motors. These quickly become hot and are ex-

tremely wasteful of electricity. Mr. Woods has, by his improvements, reduced the size of these resistances so as to materially lessen the losses by them and to remove other objectionable features.

Certain features of this invention are now involved in interference proceedings in the United States Patent Office with five rival inventors. Of these, only one had the invention perfected to the extent of using a dynamotor. The proceedings, however, showed that Woods completely developed his invention when there was no prior model to guide him and when the others were at most only taking the preliminary steps which led them years later in the same direction.

When a boy of ten, Mr. Woods was set to work at bellows blowing in an Aus-

Topic 2

tralian railroad repair shop. He soon made himself familiar with all its departments, and with his spare earnings paid for private instruction from the master mechanic. At the age of sixteen, Woods was brought by his parents to America, and he became a locomotive engineer on the Iron Mountain road, in Missouri. Later, he secured a position as engineer on the British steamer *Ironsides*. And in 1880 he established a repair shop of his own in Cincinnati.

Mr. Woods has a remarkably thorough knowledge of the intricate mathematics of electricity and of legal practice respecting inventions.

Adapted from S. W. Balch, *Cosmopolitan Magazine*, April 1895.

READING REVIEW

1. How did Woods's background lead to his success as an inventor?
2. Why did Woods win the patent dispute?
3. **Supporting Generalizations** Why would Granville Woods be considered an "American success story"?

★ 2-3 The Talent for Wealth ★

Introduction During the late 1800s the leaders of industry believed that the theory of the survival of the fittest should be applied to the growth of business. Economic failure was seen as evidence of nature's plan to allow the more able to flourish. In his article "Wealth," published in 1889, Andrew Carnegie discussed the improvements in life as a result of the industrial age. To Carnegie, the basis for all these good changes was competition. And wealth, the product of successful competition, resulted in better conditions for the entire human race. Portions of the article follow.

Vocabulary Before you read the selection, find the meaning of these words in a dictionary: deplored, beneficial, squalor, prominently.

The problem of our age is the proper administration of wealth so that the ties of brotherhood may still bind together the rich and poor in harmony. The conditions of human life have been revolutionized within the past few hundred years. The contrast between the palace of the millionaire and the cottage of the laborer with us today measures the change which has come with civilization.

This change, however, is not to be deplored, but welcomed as highly beneficial. It is essential for the progress of the race that the houses of some should be homes for all that is highest and best in literature and the arts, rather than that none should be so. Much better this great inequity than universal squalor.

In the manufacture of products we have the whole story. Today the world has goods of excellent quality at such low prices that the poor enjoy what the rich could not before afford. What were the luxuries have become the necessaries of life. The laborer has now more comforts than the farmer had a few generations ago. The farmer has more luxuries than the landlord had and is more richly clothed and better housed. The landlord has books and pictures rarer and more artistic than the king then had.

The price we pay for this change is, no doubt, great. Under the law of competition, the employer of thousands is forced into the strictest economies, among which the rates paid to labor figure prominently. Often there is friction between the employer and the employed, between capital and labor, between rich and poor.

The price which society pays for the law of competition, like the price it pays for cheap comforts and luxuries, is also great; but the advantages of this law are greater still. For it is to this law that we owe our wonderful material development, which brings improved conditions. While the law may be sometimes hard for the individual, it is best for the race, because it ensures the survival of the fittest in every department. We welcome, therefore, as conditions to which we must accept, the concentration of business, industrial and commercial, in the hands of a few. And we accept the law of competition as being essential for the future progress of the race.

One who studies this subject will soon be brought face to face with the conclusion that upon the sacredness of property civilization itself depends—the right of the laborer to his hundred dollars in the savings bank, and equally the legal right of the millionaire to his millions. Not evil, but good, has come to the race from the accumulation of wealth by those who have the ability and energy that produce it.

Private Property, the Law of Accumulation of Wealth, and the Law of Competition are the highest results of human experience, the soil in which society so far has produced the best fruit. Unequally or unjustly, perhaps, as these laws sometimes operate, and imperfect as they may appear to the idealist, they are, nevertheless, like the highest type of man, the best and most valuable of all that humanity has yet accomplished.

Adapted from Andrew Carnegie, "Wealth," *North American Review*, June 1889.

READING REVIEW

1. How does Carnegie think competition made life better for all people?
2. What three laws does he say are humanity's highest accomplishments?
3. **Relating Cause and Effect** What negative effects of competition does Carnegie identify?

Millionaire steel mill owner Andrew Carnegie was a firm supporter of the right to get rich. He believed that the wealthy, such as the Hatch family shown here, preserved and advanced the best in American culture. Having achieved riches, such families were then obligated to aid the poor.

Topic 2

Introduction John D. Rockefeller was the genius behind the organization of the Standard Oil Company. After the 1859 oil strike in western Pennsylvania, many people from all walks of life went into the oil business. However, it took a person with vision to plan beyond the quick and easy profits to the formation of the industry that transformed America. Soon after the first wild flush of the oil boom, overproduction caused prices to fall sharply. In this selection, Rockefeller describes his methods for overcoming the crisis and moving strongly ahead.

Vocabulary Before you read the selection, find the meaning of these words in a dictionary: chaos, constituted, availing, speculative, ascribe.

John D. Rockefeller, shown here, founded the Standard Oil Company in 1870. Only 3.2 million barrels of oil had been produced the previous year. By 1890, over 22 million barrels came out of the oil refineries, most of which belonged to Standard Oil.

It seemed absolutely necessary to extend the market for oil by exporting to foreign countries. It was also necessary to greatly improve the processes of refining so that oil could be made and sold cheaply, yet with a profit. And we wanted to use as by-products all of the materials which in the less efficient plants were lost or thrown away.

These were the problems which confronted us almost at the outset, and this great depression led to consultations with our neighbors and friends in the business in the effort to bring some order out of what was rapidly becoming a state of chaos. To accomplish all these tasks was beyond the power or ability of any concern as then constituted. It could only be done, we reasoned, by increasing our capital and availing ourselves of the best talent and experience.

It was with this idea that we bought the largest and best refining concerns and centralized the administration of them with a view to greater economy and efficiency. The business grew faster than we expected.

This enterprise, conducted by men of ability working hard together, soon built up unusual talents in manufacture, in transportation, in finance, and in extending markets. We had our troubles and setbacks; we suffered from some severe fires; and the supply of crude oil was most uncertain. Our plans were constantly changed by changed conditions. We developed great facilities in an oil center, built storage tanks, and connected pipelines. Then the oil failed and our work was thrown away. At best it was a speculative trade, and I wonder that we managed to pull through so often, but we were gradually learning how to conduct a most difficult business.

I ascribe the success of the Standard Oil Company to its consistent policy of making the volume of its business large through the merit and cheapness of its products. It has spared no expense in using the best and most efficient method of manufacture. It has sought for the best superintendents and workmen and paid the best wages. It has not hesitated to sacrifice old machinery and old plants for new and better ones. It has placed its factories at the points where they could supply markets at the least expense. It has not only sought markets for its principal products but for all possible byproducts, sparing no expense in introducing them to the public in every nook and corner of the world. It has not hesitated to invest millions of dollars in methods for cheapening the gathering and distribution of oil by pipelines, special cars, tank steamers, and tank wagons. It has built tank stations at railroad centers in every part of the country to cheapen the storage and delivery of oil. It has had faith in American oil and has brought together vast sums of money for the purpose of making it what it is.

Adapted from John D. Rockefeller, *Random Reminiscences of Men and Events*, 1908.

READING REVIEW

1. How did Rockefeller propose to solve the problems facing the oil industry?
2. List five reasons he gives for the success of the Standard Oil Company.
3. **Ranking** (a) What do you think are the three most important reasons? (b) Are those activities still important to business today?

★ 2-5 Traveling Through the New South ★

Introduction A decade or so after the Civil War, many visitors to the New South were impressed by the bustle of factories, mines, and other industries. Cities were growing and changing. And the old upper class was giving way to forward-looking young business people.

Rebecca Harding Davis was a popular reporter and novelist of the time. In 1885 she wrote a novel about the New South, which she based on a visit to study conditions for herself. Through the characters of Mr. Ely, a northern clergyman traveling by train through the South, and assorted people he meets along the way, Davis presents her views in this selection.

Vocabulary Before you read the selection, find the meaning of these words in a dictionary: squabbling, superciliously, indolent, girded, pate, sauntered, ardor, clamoring.

Mr. Ely, the old clergyman, bought apples and tongue from half a dozen peddlars. He watched laughing from the window as the train rolled on, leaving them squabbling and joking over the money.

A young man from Chicago was superciliously calling attention to the lean fields, the forlorn houses.

"Wretchedly poor, sir! Now there is really no excuse for such poverty. Even grant that the state was laid waste by the war. All that was twenty years ago. Twenty years is enough for any man to get upon his legs again."

"It is all due to lack of energy!" decisively said a close-shaven little ironmaster from Pennsylvania. "We all know the South. Some of the best books in American literature are descriptions of these people. Did you ever read *Uncle Tom's Cabin* or *A Fool's Errand*? They show you that a more indolent, incapable, pigheaded race never breathed."

Mr. Ely, with an indignant snort, girded himself to make battle. But at that moment the train stopped in the suburbs of Charlottesville. A crowd of students from the university filled the platform. An elderly man, after much handshaking with them, entered the car. Mr. Ely, smiling, motioned for him to share his seat. "I beg pardon. It is a long time ago. But are you not Wollaston Pogue? I am James Ely. Don't you remember?"

"Bless my soul! Of course I remember. Why, my dear sir, I am glad to see you back in Virginia. And how has the world used you in all these years?"

"Well, well! roughly enough," said Ely, with a sigh. He had, in fact, a comfortable home, and until lately sound health. Yet, as the two men sat side by side, it was the anxious, lean northerner who most looked like the victim of a destructive war. The Virginian was a stout, ruddy, overgrown boy. Prosperity apparently oozed out of every pore, from the red fringe of hair about his shining pate to his beaming spectacled eyes, and the gurgling laugh of pure enjoyment that bubbled out every minute.

"Changes?" he said, rubbing his knees meditatively, as Ely plied him with questions. "Oh, great changes! Necessarily. The houses in which you visited years ago have all passed from the old families. It is the men who were children in '65 that have their hands on the lever now. They make no mistake about issues. Where their fathers dreamed of reopening the slave trade, and of conquering Mexico and annexing Cuba to form a great empire, they talk of new cotton gins and of developing our resources. It is the young men who are the New South. I fancy you northern people know little about the New South."

"Very little indeed," replied Mr. Ely, smiling uneasily. "In fact, I did not know until five months ago that there was such a nation."

"You will see," Pogue said, laughing significantly.

"But what did you do after the surrender? Start afresh, like your New South?"

"Precisely. Got a position as clerk in Atlanta. I have an interest in two or three concerns there now, and I have my home near the town. I have just been up to see my boy at the university."

The two men stopped over for a day in Lynchburg, which reminded Mr. Ely of Pittsburgh. "It is almost as busy and as black," he said, as they sauntered past the towering factories, "and the business men look as if, like ours, they are challenging life at the point of the bayonet. We wear out brain and body in our haste to be rich, in the North, and you are following us, I'm afraid."

Mr. Pogue laughed good-humoredly. "We were forced into the race. The southerner, when he goes into business, throws the same ardor into it that 40 years ago he did into his fun, or courting, or fighting." He pointed out the solid blocks of business houses and tasteful dwellings, "built since the war."

The next day, in Charlotte, the same story was told and retold. Instead of speaking, as he would have done ten years ago, on the ancient glories of the old South lost in the struggle, Pogue was eager to show every sight of the solid foundation which the New South was laying for an enduring, stable prosperity. Spartanburg, Greenville, and other pretty towns followed, each with its wide shaded streets, its new mills in the suburbs, its "cheap stores," its imposing new hotel, its stir of freshly awakened life.

"But who has done all this?" asked Mr. Ely, half annoyed. "Northern men?"

"At first, yes. They were the first to see that money was to be made here. They usually met a cold welcome, as you know. Our old men wanted to run the South in the old tracks—cotton, politics, fighting. But our own young men, as I told you, are getting the reins now in their own hands. Our leading manufacturers, brokers, newspapermen, and even city officials, are as a rule southerners, and under 50."

"Atlanta!" shouted the conductor.

"But this is a northern city!" exclaimed Mr. Ely, as they stepped out into a large station, grimy with smoke, and walled in by blocks of huge warehouses that opened into crowded streets of banks, hotels, and shops.

"Atlanta is the capital of our new nation," said Mr. Pogue. "You have been in Birmingham?"

"No. Is it a typical southern city?"

The planter smiled. "I hope so; but not of the old South. Twelve years ago it was a cotton plantation. Now they are working coal mines with an output of over 4,000 tons a day and iron mines that yield metal which they tell me is as good as the best Swedish. With both, they can put pig iron in the northern market six dollars a ton cheaper than it is done in Pennsylvania.

"The enormous mineral wealth of Alabama is but just opened. It has rich virgin soil, and though you may not believe it, Mr. Ely, a law-abiding, God-fearing population, anxious to work. It has good waterways and one of the best harbors on the whole coast at Mobile. What it wants is capital and skilled labor."

Mr. Ely then spoke of the women of the New South. "I have met women, since we came here, capable, shrewd, and alive with energy. They manage plantations and shops; they raise stock, hold offices, publish newspapers. Indeed, while northern women have been clamoring for their rights, southern women have found their way into more careers than they. They keep up with all the questions of the day. I suppose we Americans have but one blood, after all, and a hard struggle with poverty will produce the same women in Georgia as in Connecticut."

Adapted from Rebecca Harding Davis, "Here and There in the South", *Harpers Magazine*, 1885.

READING REVIEW

1. What evidence of economic growth does Mr. Ely see on his trip through the South?
2. What negative effects of industrialization does he see?
3. **Using Fiction as Historical Evidence** (a) How can a novel be a more effective way of telling about people's lives than a history book? (b) Do you think the author of this selection approved of the changes in the South? Explain.

★ 2-6   A Bombing at Haymarket Square   ★

Introduction In the late 1800s, as the economy rapidly expanded, the demand for workers to run the new machines grew. Often an industry boomed at the expense of laborers working 12 hours a day in dangerous surroundings. The Knights of Labor under Terence V. Powderly was organized to win better wages, hours, and working conditions. All workers, including women, blacks, and immigrants, were welcomed into its "brotherhood."

Although Powderly opposed the use of strikes, several branches of the Knights called strikes. This selection describes the background of the Haymarket riot, an event that had a profound effect on the labor movement.

Vocabulary Before you read the selection, find the meaning of these words in a dictionary: disturbances, anarchist, assemblage, complicity.

In May 1886 the first widespread effort was made to introduce the eight-hour workday in the United States. A great many employers opposed the demand for the shorter day, and strikes followed. There were serious conflicts between the strikers and their sympathizers on the one hand and the authorities on the other hand. The disturbances at Chicago and Milwaukee were especially noteworthy. On the night of May 4 the tragedy of the Chicago Haymarket occurred.

The events of that night have their place in the history of the country. Here it is enough if I recall to the reader's mind the connection between that meeting and the eight-hour movement of the Knights of Labor. In consequence of an eight-hour strike at the McCormick Reaper Works, in Chicago, there was a clash between the police and a crowd of workingmen—some of them being strikers. Several persons were seriously injured by the bullets and clubs of the policemen. A meeting was called for the following night, in the Haymarket Square, to "protest against the brutality of the police." The speakers at the meeting were all members of the anarchist groups, though some of them were also identified with the more conservative branches of the labor movement. The speeches at this meeting were not nearly so violent in tone as had been previous speeches, made by the same men, on the Lake Front and in other parts of Chicago.

Carter Harrison was mayor of the city at the time. He was present at the meeting for nearly an hour—leaving for home a short time before the meeting was to end. He later declared, on the witness stand, that he heard nothing that would warn of lawless acts. But within a few minutes after he had left, several hundred policemen marched out of the Desplaines Street Station, half a block away. They headed for the Haymarket Square crowd.

The captain of the police ordered the meeting to break up. The man who had been speaking said, "Captain, this is an orderly assemblage." The captain repeated his order, and some person—neither court proceedings nor any other record tells us who—threw a bomb into the midst of the policemen. Sixty-six policemen were knocked down by the explosion, seven never to rise again and an eighth to die soon after. It was reported that one man in the crowd was killed by the bullets of the policemen and several were wounded. However, there never was an authentic report of the casualties on that side made public.

Many arrests were made of men charged with complicity in the bomb throwing; eight were indicted. After a long trial, seven were found guilty of murder in the first degree and sentenced to be hanged. One was sentenced to 15 years in the state penitentiary for distributing the handbills announcing the Haymarket meeting.

Adapted from Joseph R. Buchanan, *The Story of a Labor Agitator*, 1903.

READING REVIEW

1. What was the main demand of the workers who gathered at Haymarket Square?
2. Do historians know who threw the bomb? Explain.
3. **Recognizing a Point of View** Do you think the author of the reading sympathized more with the strikers or with the police? Explain.

Topic 3

Politics and Reform (1867–1900)

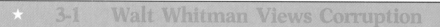

★ 3-1 Walt Whitman Views Corruption ★

Introduction Walt Whitman was an American poet and writer who viewed the country's rapid industrial expansion with deep concern. To Whitman the republic was gaining material success at the expense of its soul. Yet he appreciated the grandeur of new cities and the beauty in their architecture and design. In this selection, he comments on the widespread political corruption of the Gilded Age.

Vocabulary Before you read this selection, find the meaning of these words in a dictionary: diagnosing, hypocrisy, acute, candid, depravity, scoundrelism, flippancy, speculators, vulgarians, farce, endowed.

I say we had best look our times and lands searchingly in the face, like a physician diagnosing some deep disease. Never was there, perhaps, more hollowness at heart than at present here in the United States. Genuine belief seems to have left us. The underlying principles of the States are not honestly believed in nor is humanity itself believed in. What penetrating eye does not everywhere see through the mask?

We live in an atmosphere of hypocrisy throughout. An acute and candid person in the revenue department in Washington, who regularly visits the cities to investigate frauds, has talked much with me about his discoveries. The depravity of the business classes of our country is not less than has been supposed, but infinitely greater. The official services of America, national, state, and municipal, in all their branches and departments are deep in corruption, bribery, and falsehood.

The great cities reek with respectable as much as nonrespectable robbery and scoundrelism. In fashionable life, one finds flippancy and small aims, or no aims at all. In business, the one sole object is monetary gain. The best class we show is but a mob of fashionably dressed speculators and vulgarians. True, indeed, behind this farce, solid things and stupendous labors are to be discovered going on in the background, to advance and show themselves in time. Yet the truths are nonetheless terrible.

I say that our New World democracy, however great a success in uplifting the masses and in developing products, is, so far, an almost complete failure in its social, religious, moral, literary, and esthetic results. It is as if we were somehow being endowed with more and more body, and left with little or no soul.

We question, Are there, indeed, men here worthy the name? Are there athletes? Are there perfect women, to match the generous material luxury? Is there a pervading atmosphere of beautiful manners? Are there crops of fine youths and majestic old persons? Are there arts worthy of freedom and a rich people? Is there a great moral and religious civilization—the only justification of a great material one? Confess that to severe eyes, using the moral microscope upon humanity, a sort of dry and flat Sahara appears.

Adapted from Walt Whitman, *Democratic Vistas in Complete Prose Works*, 1902.

The process of economic concentration reached its peak with the development of the trust. Many senators were thought to be on the payrolls of the trusts, as this cartoon suggests.

READING REVIEW

1. What does Whitman say about the "best class" of society?
2. What does he probably mean by "solid things and stupendous labors . . . going on in the background?"

3. **Distinguishing Fact From Opinion** (a) What is Whitman's opinion of life in the United States about 1900? (b) Does he cite any facts to support his opinion? Explain. (c) Does what you read in Chapter 3 support or refute his opinion?

★   3-2   Standard Oil Uses "Other Ways"   ★

Introduction A small manufacturer had a difficult time surviving the late 1800s, when the railroads were able to switch him out of the market. The experiences of George Rice, an independent oil refiner, reveal some business practices of that era. What happened to Rice provided a test case before state and national investigating committees. This selection was compiled by Henry Demarest Lloyd from testimony before the Ohio legislature. It describes the relationship between the Standard Oil Company and the railroads.

Vocabulary Before you read this selection, find the meaning of these words in a dictionary: exacted, manipulation.

One scandal of the Gilded Age was the ever-growing power of monopolies. In this cartoon from 1900, King Monopoly is shown demanding even more tribute.

George Rice, coming from the Green Mountains of Vermont, entered the oil business 29 years ago, when he and it were young. He was one of the first to develop the new field at Macksburg, Ohio, and to see the advantages of Marietta, on the Ohio River, as a point for refining. The field he entered was unoccupied. He drove no one out but built a new industry in a new place. In 1876 he had risen to the dignity of manufacturer, and had a refinery of a capacity of 500 barrels a week, and later of 2,000 barrels. Owning wells, he produced, himself, a part of the crude which he refined. His position gave him access to all the markets by river and rail. Everything promised him fortune.

Several other refiners, seeing the advantages of Marietta, settled there. They determined that Marietta must be theirs. They bought up some of the refineries. Then they stopped buying. Their representative there, afterwards a member of the trust, told me distinctly that he had bought certain refineries in Marietta, but that he would not buy any more. He had "another way," he said, "of getting rid of them." Of these "other ways" the independents were now to learn.

In January 1879, freight rates on oil were suddenly and without previous notice raised by the railroads leading out of Marietta. Some of the rates were doubled. The increase was only on oil. It was—in Ohio—only on oil shipped from Marietta; it was exacted only from the few refiners who had not been bought out, because there were "other ways of getting rid of them."

This attack on the independent refiners was arranged by their powerful rival and the railroad managers at a secret conference, as the railroad managers admitted.

When the representatives of the combination in this market were accused of manipulation of freight, they laughed. All the railroads took part in the surprise.

Part Two 154

Rice was "got rid of." His successful rival had only to pool the earnings and the control of all its refineries—the essential features of the combination—and its business could be transferred from one point to another without loss.

The demonstration against the independent refiners of Marietta was only part of a wider web spinning, in which those at all points—New York, Boston, Philadelphia, Pittsburg, Oil City, Titusville, Buffalo, Rochester, and Cleveland—were to be forced to "come in" as dependents or sell out, as most of them did.

They were the victims of a competitor who had learned the secret of a more royal road to business supremacy than making a better thing or selling it at a better price. Their better way was not to excel but to exclude.

Adapted from Henry D. Lloyd, *Wealth Against Commonwealth*, 1899.

READING REVIEW

1. Why was Marietta a good place to build an oil refinery?
2. What "other ways" did Standard Oil use to beat the competition in Marietta?
3. **Recognizing a Point of View** (a) Does Lloyd favor the tactics used by Standard Oil? How can you tell? (b) How might a representative of Standard Oil have described these tactics?

★ 3-3 The Need for Practical Skills ★

Introduction Booker T. Washington, founder and head of Tuskegee Institute, was the most influential black American of his time. Born a slave, he worked in coal mines and salt furnaces before attending Hampton Institute. Washington stressed the importance of practical, job-oriented skills for blacks. He believed that greater political and social equality for blacks would come naturally if they first established an economic base. This selection is from the speech Washington made in 1895 at the opening of the Atlanta Cotton States and International Exposition. It is the basis of the Atlanta Compromise.

Vocabulary Before you read this selection, find the meaning of these words in a dictionary: fidelity, treacherous, philanthropists, folly, ostracized.

To those of the white race who look to the incoming of those of foreign birth and strange tongue and habits for the prosperity of the South, I would repeat what I say to my own race—"Cast down your bucket where you are." Cast it down among the 8 million Negroes whose habits you know, whose fidelity and love you have tested in days when to have proved treacherous meant the ruin of your firesides. Cast down your bucket among these people. They have, without strikes and labor wars, tilled your fields, cleared your forests, built your railroads and cities, and brought forth treasures from the earth. They have helped make possible this magnificent showing of the progress of the South.

Cast down your bucket among my people, help and encourage them as you are doing here to education of the head, hand, and heart. You will find that they will buy your surplus land, make blossom the waste places in your fields, and run your factories. While doing this, you can be sure that you and your families will be surrounded by the most patient, faithful, law-abiding, and unresentful people that the world has seen.

We have proved our loyalty to you in the past. In nursing your children, watching by the sickbed of your mothers and fathers, and often following them with tear-dimmed eyes to their graves. So in the future, in our humble way, we shall stand by you with a devotion that no foreigner can approach. We are ready to lay down our lives, if need be, in defense of yours, interlacing our industrial, commercial, civil, and religious life with yours in a way that shall make the interests of both races one. In all things that are purely social we can be as separate as the fingers,

Topic 3

yet one as the hand in all things essential to mutual progress.

Gentlemen of the Exposition, as we present to you our humble effort at an exhibition of our progress, you must not expect overmuch. We started 30 years ago with ownership here and there in a few quilts and pumpkins and chickens. We remember the path that has led from these to the inventions and production of farm tools, buggies, steam engines, newspapers, books, carving, paintings, the management of drug stores and banks. While we take pride in what we exhibit as a result of our own efforts, we do not for a moment forget the constant help that has come to our educational life. It came not only from the southern states, but especially from northern philanthropists, who have made their gifts a constant stream of blessings and encouragement.

The wisest among my race understand that to agitate about questions of social equality is the greatest folly. We know that progress in the enjoyment of all the privileges that will come to us cannot be the result of artificial forcing. No race that has anything to contribute to the markets of the world is long ostracized.

It is important and right that all privileges of the law be ours, but it is vastly more important that we be prepared for the exercises of these privileges. The opportunity to earn a dollar in a factory just now is worth infinitely more than the opportunity to spend a dollar in an opera house.

In conclusion, may I repeat that nothing in 30 years has given us more hope and encouragement, and drawn us so near to you of the white race, as this opportunity offered by the Exposition. I pledge that in your effort to work out the great and intricate problems of the South, you shall have at all times the patient, sympathetic help of my race. From this Exposition showing the products of the field, of forest, of mine, of factory, letters, and art, much good will come. Yet far above and beyond material benefits will be that higher good that, let us pray God, will come to blot out sectional differences and racial hatreds and suspicions. That higher good will create a determination to administer absolute justice, in a willing obedience among all classes to the law. This, coupled with our material prosperity, will bring into our beloved South a new Heaven and a new earth.

Adapted from Booker T. Washington, *Up From Slavery: An Autobiography*, 1901.

READING REVIEW

1. How does Washington describe past relations between blacks and whites?
2. Why did white Americans in 1895 support Washington's views?
3. **Expressing an Opinion** Do you think Washington's ideas were valid in 1895? Why or why not?

Booker T. Washington founded Tuskegee Institute, in Alabama, to educate blacks and thus improve their chances of economic success. This is a chemistry laboratory at the institute.

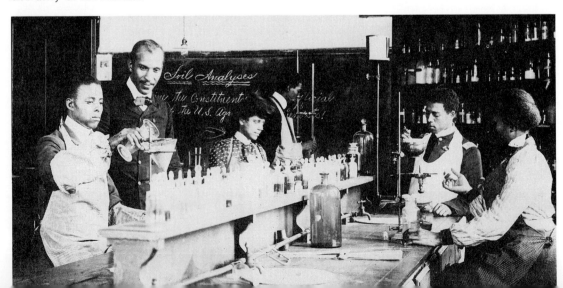

Introduction Black scholar W. E. B. Du-Bois objected strongly to both Booker T. Washington's basic ideas and his suggestions about the proper training for blacks. The first black American to receive a Ph.D. from Harvard, DuBois believed firmly in the goal of higher education for blacks. DuBois was a historian, sociologist, and writer. This selection is from a collection of his essays.

Vocabulary Before you read the selection, find the meaning of these words in a dictionary: conciliation, disenfranchisement, barbarism, unwaveringly.

It has been claimed that the Negro can survive only through submission. Mr. Washington distinctly asks that black people give up, at least for the present,

First, political power,
Second, insistence on civil rights,
Third, higher education of Negro youths,

and concentrate all their energies on industrial education, the accumulation of wealth, and the conciliation of the South. As a result of this tender of the palm-branch, what has been the return? In these years since Booker T. Washington's Atlanta speech there have occurred:

1. The disenfranchisement of the Negro.
2. The legal creation of a distinct status of civil inferiority.
3. The steady withdrawal of aid from institutions for the higher training of the Negro.

These movements are not, to be sure, direct results of Mr. Washington's teachings; but his propaganda has, without a shadow of doubt, helped their speedier accomplishment.

Negroes do not expect that the free right to vote, to enjoy civic rights, and to be educated will come in a moment. They do not expect to see the bias and prejudices of years disappear at the blast of a trumpet; but they are absolutely certain that the way for a people to gain their reasonable rights is not by voluntarily throwing them away and insisting that they do not want them. They know that the way for a people to gain respect is not by continually belittling themselves. They believe, on the contrary, that Negroes must insist continually that voting is necessary to proper manhood, that color discrimination is barbarism, and that black boys need education as well as white boys.

So far as Mr. Washington preaches Thrift, Patience, and Industrial Training for the masses, we must hold up his hands and strive with him. But so far as Mr. Washington apologizes for injustice, North or South, does not rightly value the privilege and duty of voting, and opposes the higher training and ambition of our brighter minds—we must unceasingly and firmly oppose him. By every civilized and peaceful method we must strive for the rights which the world accords to men, clinging unwaveringly to those great words of the Founding Fathers: "We hold these truths to be self-evident: That all men are created equal; that they are endowed by their Creator with certain unalienable rights; that among these are life, liberty, and the pursuit of happiness."

Adapted from W. E. B. DuBois, *The Souls of Black Folks*, 1903.

READING REVIEW

1. What does DuBois say happened to black Americans between 1895 and 1903?
2. How does he think Booker T. Washington's views contributed to these developments?
3. **Analyzing Conflicting Opinions** (a) How do Washington's and DuBois's views differ on civil rights for blacks such as the right to vote? (b) How do their views on education for blacks differ?

Topic 3

Introduction In the late 1880s farmers suffered from falling prices, tight credit, and the unfair practices of railroads who shipped their products to market. Starting as a local movement, a farmer's revolt soon found national expression in a new political party, the Populist party. This selection is from the Populist party platform in 1892.

Vocabulary Before you read the selection, find the meaning of these words in a dictionary: substantial, commodities, impoverishment, temperate.

Beginning as a social organization, the Grange became more and more political. The Populist party eventually emerged out of farmers' groups like the Grange.

The conditions which surround us best justify our cooperation. We meet in the midst of a nation brought to the verge of moral, political, and material ruin. Corruption dominates the ballot box, the legislatures, the Congress, and touches even the Court.

We have witnessed for more than a quarter of a century the struggles of the two great political parties for power and plunder, while grievous wrongs have been inflicted upon the suffering people. We charge that the controlling influences dominating both these parties have permitted the existing dreadful conditions to develop without serious effort to prevent. Neither do they now promise us any substantial reform.

Assembled on the anniversary of the birthday of the nation and filled with the spirit of the grand general and chief who established our independence, we seek to restore the government of the Republic to the hands of the plain people, with which class it began. We assert our purposes to be identical with the purposes of the national Constitution: to form a more perfect union and establish justice, ensure domestic tranquility, provide for the common defense, promote the general welfare, and secure the blessings of liberty for ourselves and our posterity.

We declare that this Republic can only endure as a free government while built upon the love of the people for each other and for the nation; that it cannot be pinned together by bayonets; that the Civil War is over, and that every passion and resentment which grew out of it must die with it, and that we must be in fact, as we are in name, one united brotherhood of free men.

Our country finds itself confronted by conditions for which there is no precedent in the history of the world. Our annual agricultural production amounts to billions of dollars in value, which must, within a few weeks or months, be exchanged for billions of dollars' worth of commodities consumed in their production. The existing currency supply is wholly inadequate to make this exchange; the results are falling prices, the formation of combines, the impoverishment of the producing class. We pledge ourselves that if given power we will labor to correct these evils by wise and reasonable legislation in accordance with the terms of our platform.

We believe that the power of government—in other words, of the people—should be expanded (as in the case of the postal service) as rapidly and as far as the good sense of an intelligent people and the teachings of experience shall justify, to the end that oppression, injustice, and poverty shall eventually cease in the land.

Our sympathies as a party of reform are naturally upon the side of every proposition which will tend to make men intelligent, virtuous, and temperate. Yet we regard these questions as secondary to the great issues now pressing for solution, and upon which not only our individual prosperity but the very existence of free institutions depend. And we ask all men to first help us to determine whether we are to have a republic to administer before we argue about how it is to be administered, believing that the forces of reform this day organized will never cease to move forward until every wrong is righted and equal rights and equal privileges securely established for all the men and women of this country.

Adapted from the Populist Party Platform, 1892.

READING REVIEW

1. List three problems the Populists saw.
2. How does the platform describe the condition of farmers?
3. **Analyzing a Primary Source** (a) What three patriotic symbols does the platform refer to? (b) Why do you think it used these symbols?

★ 3-6 Bryan and the Cross of Gold ★

Introduction William Jennings Bryan was known for many years as the "peerless leader" of the Democratic party. He was noted for his dramatic speeches. As a representative in Congress, he supported the free coinage of silver. However, it was his famous speech to the Democratic National Convention of 1896 that led to his nomination for President. In this selection from that speech, Bryan challenges supporters of the gold standard.

Vocabulary Before you read the selection, find the meaning of these words in a dictionary: zeal, arrayed, magnates, aggressors, calamity.

Never before in the history of this country has there been witnessed such a contest as that through which we have just passed. Never before in the history of American politics has a great issue been fought out as this issue has been, by the voters of a great party.

With zeal our silver Democrats are now assembled, not to discuss, not to debate, but to enter up the judgment already rendered by the plain people of this country. In this contest brother has been arrayed against brother, father against son. The warmest ties of love, acquaintance, and association have been disregarded. Old leaders have been cast aside when they have refused to give expression to the sentiments of those whom they would lead. New leaders have sprung up to give direction to this cause of truth. Thus has the contest been waged, and we have assembled here under binding instructions as representatives of the people.

When you [turning to the gold delegates] come before us and tell us that we are about to disturb your business interests, we reply that you have disturbed our business interests by your course.

We say to you that you have made the definition of a businessman too limited in its application. The man who is employed for wages is as much a businessman as his employer. The attorney in a country town is as much a businessman as the corporation counsel in a great city. The merchant at the crossroads store is as much a businessman as the merchant of New York. The farmer who goes forth in the morning and toils all day, and who by the application of brain and muscle to the natural resources of the country creates wealth, is as much a businessman as the man who goes upon the board of trade and bets upon the price of grain. The miners who go down a thousand feet into the earth and bring forth precious metals are as much businessmen as the few financial magnates who, in a back room, corner the money of the world. We come to speak for this broader class of businessmen.

We do not come as aggressors. Our war is not a war of conquest; we are fighting in the defense of our homes, our families, and our future. We have petitioned, and our petitions have been scorned; we have entreated, and our entreaties have been disregarded; we have begged, and they have mocked when our calamity came. We beg no longer; we petition no more. We defy them.

We say in our platform that we believe that the right to coin and issue money is a function of government. We believe it. We believe that it is a part of sovereignty and can no more with safety be delegated to private individuals than we could afford to delegate to private individuals the power to make laws or levy taxes. Those who are opposed to this proposition tell us that the issue of paper money is a function of the bank, and that the government ought to go out of the banking business. I tell them that the issue of money is a function of government, and that the banks ought to go out of the governing business.

We go forth confident that we shall win. Why? Because upon the paramount issue of this campaign there is not a spot of ground upon which the enemy will dare to challenge battle. If they tell us that the gold standard is the standard of civilization, we reply to them that this, the most enlightened of all the nations of the earth, has never declared for a gold standard and that both the great parties this year are declaring against it. More than that; we can tell them that they will search the pages of history in vain to find a single instance where the common people of any land have ever declared themselves in favor of the gold standard.

Mr. Carlisle said in 1878 that this was a struggle between "the idle holders of idle capital" and "the struggling masses, who produce the wealth and pay the taxes of the country"; and, my friends, the question we are to decide is: Upon which side will the Democratic party fight: upon the side of "the idle holders of idle capital" or upon the side of "the struggling masses"? That is the question which the party must answer first, and then it must be answered by each individual hereafter. The sympathies of the Democratic party, as shown by the platform, are on the side of the struggling masses who have ever been the foundation of the Democratic party. There are two ideas of government. There are those who believe that, if you will only legislate to make the well-to-do prosperous, their prosperity will leak through on those below. The Democratic idea, however, has been that if you legislate to make the masses prosperous, their prosperity will find its way up through every class which rests upon them.

You come to us and tell us that the great cities are in favor of the gold standard. We reply that the great cities rest upon our broad and fertile prairies. Burn down your cities and leave our farms, and your cities will spring up again as if by magic. But destroy our farms, and the grass will grow in the streets of every city in the country.

If the gold delegates dare to defend the gold standard as a good thing, we will fight them to the uttermost. Having behind us the producing masses of this nation and the world, supported by the commercial interests, the laboring interests, and the toilers everywhere, we will answer their demand for a gold standard by saying to them: You shall not press down upon the brow of labor this crown of thorns, you shall not crucify mankind upon a cross of gold!

Adapted from William J. Bryan, *The First Battle*, 1896.

READING REVIEW

1. (a) According to Bryan, who supported the gold standard? (b) Who supported "silver"?

2. What people does Bryan think the Democrats should side with?

3. **Supporting Generalizations** Write two generalizations describing Bryan's view of the Democratic party in 1896. What information in the reading supports the generalizations?

Toward an Urban Age (1865–1914)

★ 4-1 Corrupt Deals in Chicago ★

Introduction Crooked politicians found many sources of graft in growing cities. For example, at the same time that Chicago's Columbian Exposition of 1893 offered visions of a glorious future, a corrupt city council made shady deals with corporations seeking street railway franchises. This selection from a report on franchises describes some of the abuses resulting from such deals.

Vocabulary Before you read the selection, find the meaning of these words in a dictionary: municipal, vested, induce, integrity.

The problem which confronts Chicago is the same that faces every large American city. The evils from which it suffers are not the product of any particular local conditions. To describe the situation in one large American city, with respect to the relation between the municipal government, on the one hand, and the franchise-owning corporations, on the other, is really to describe the situation in all cities rich and active enough to tempt corporate capital.

In a vague and dim way, every intelligent citizen knows that under prevailing arrangements the interests of the people receive no adequate protection at the hands of their municipal rulers. Valuable gifts and franchises are given to corporations. Instead of faithfully serving the public, they defraud and plunder. Consumers of gas and electricity and patrons of street railways are forced to pay unreasonably high rates in order to allow the companies to pay dividends on phony investments. The most modest demands of the public are resisted and fought with extreme bitterness. The cry "attack upon vested rights" is raised by the monopolies whenever an attempt is made to secure some concession in favor of the people.

In theory, nothing can be simpler than the relation between the city and franchise-owning corporations. If these corporations were honest and just, if they were satisfied with a reasonable return on their capital, no mystery would surround the question of the cost of construction, equipment, and operation. What do we find in practice? Confusion, ignorance, mutual suspicion, corrupt scheming on the part of the companies and demands for public ownership on the part of the outraged community.

Why should the managers, officers, and stockholders of such corporations be permitted to enrich themselves at the expense of the community? We generally rely upon the natural laws of trade and the ordinary forces of the market to protect the consumers from the greed of would-be monopolists. Competition, however, is possible only to a very limited extent in franchise-owning corporations. Other safeguards become necessary.

Even worse than the economic consequences are the political and moral consequences. Powerful corporations control city governments and corrupt the people's representatives. Bribery has become common. In our larger cities, primaries, conventions, nominations, and elections are generally managed and dictated by the corporations. Public office is a source of private profit and plunder. The moral tone of the community is lowered, and people cynically regard every man identified with politics as a conspirator against the public.

No one denies the need of an improvement in the quality of Chicago municipal legislators. Of late, its councils have been inefficient, untrustworthy, and not above suspicion of corruption. But it does not appear that the character of the governmental organization needs any important change.

It is true that aldermen are elected by wards instead of on a general ticket, and that the very inadequate pay received by them ensures neither proper attention to duty nor fidelity to public interests. Increasing the salaries of aldermen would induce educated, ambitious, and public-spirited men to seek the office. It would enable them to devote all their time and energy to the business of the city. This would undoubtedly be a step in the right direction. Election on a general ticket would also tend to keep inferior men out and improve the chances of clean, independent, and faithful candidates. Civil service reform has been carried further in Chicago than in any other large American city. It is evident that it is entirely within the power of the citizens to secure honest and faithful municipal government.

But honesty alone can never be enough. Good intentions do not save officials from blunders and the neglect of public interest due to ignorance. Shrewd corporations stand ready to take advantage of the simplicity and inexperience of respectable men elected to municipal office. Skill, intelligence, and experience are as essential in officials as integrity.

Adapted from the *Ninth Biennial Report on Franchises and Taxation, 1896*, Illinois, 1897.

READING REVIEW

1. According to the report, what were the political and moral consequences of the deals between the city government and the corporations?
2. What reforms does the report propose?
3. **Defending a Point of View** Do you think the report's recommendations would have improved city government in Chicago? Why or why not?

★ 4-2 The Ethnic Map of New York ★

Introduction Jacob Riis was a newspaperman whose book *How the Other Half Lives* portrayed the lives of immigrants in city slums. An immigrant himself, Riis came from Denmark at the age of 21. During his 20 years as a reporter he exposed graft, vice, and terrible living conditions in New York City. He took photographs to illustrate his writings. Riis's articles led to housing reforms and the establishment of parks and playgrounds. In this selection Riis describes the jostling of ethnic groups as they settled into neighborhoods and then moved on.

Vocabulary Before you read the selection, find the meaning of these words in a dictionary: scavenger, squalid, influx, rabbinical, somber.

New York's wage earners have no other place to live, more is the pity. The wonder is that they are not all corrupted by their surroundings. If on the contrary there be a steady working up, the fact is a powerful argument for the optimist's belief that the world is after all growing better, not worse. Such an impulse toward better things there certainly is.

The German ragpicker of 30 years ago is the thrifty tradesman or prosperous farmer of today. The Italian scavenger of our time is fast graduating into exclusive control of the corner fruit stands. The Irish hod carrier in the second generation has become a bricklayer, if not the alderman of his wards, while the Chinese is in almost exclusive possession of the laundry business.

The reason is obvious. The poorest immigrant comes here with the purpose and ambition to better himself and, given half a chance, might be reasonably expected to make the most of it. To the false plea that he prefers the squalid homes in which he lives there could be no better answer. The truth is his half chance has too long been wanting, and for the bad result he has been unjustly blamed.

As emigration from east to west follows the latitude, so does the foreign influx in New York distribute itself along certain well-defined lines. A map of the city, colored to designate nationalities, would show more stripes than on the skin of a zebra and more colors than any rainbow. The city on such a map would fall

Immigrants from many countries flocked to American cities in the 1880s and 1890s. This photograph shows a street market on New York City's teeming East Side.

into two great halves, green for the Irish prevailing in the West Side tenement districts and blue for the Germans on the East Side. But intermingled with these ground colors would be an odd variety of tints that would give the whole the appearance of an extraordinary crazy quilt.

From down in the Sixth Ward, the red of the Italian would be seen forcing its way northward along the line of Mulberry Street to the quarter of the French purple on Bleecker Street and south Fifth Avenue, to lose itself and reappear in the Little Italy of Harlem, east of Second Avenue. Dashes of red, sharply defined, would be seen strung through the annexed district northward to the city line. On the West Side the red would be seen overrunning the old Africa of Thompson Street, pushing the black of the Negro rapidly uptown.

Hardly less aggressive than the Italians, the Russian and Polish Jew, having overrun the district between Rivington and Division Streets, east of the Bowery, is filling the tenements of the old Seventh Ward to the river front and disputing with the Italian every foot of available space in the back alleys of Mulberry Street.

Other nationalities that begin at the bottom make a fresh start when crowded up the ladder. Happily both are manageable, the one by rabbinical, the other by the civil law. Between the gray of the Jew and the Italian red would be seen squeezed in on the map a sharp streak of yellow marking the narrow boundaries of Chinatown. Dovetailed with the German population, the poor but thrifty Bohemian might be picked out by the somber hue of his life as of his philosophy, struggling against heavy odds in the big human beehives of the East Side.

Dots and dashes of color here and there would show where the Finnish sailors worship their Djumala [god], the Greek peddlers the ancient name of their race, and the Swiss the goddess of thrift. And so on to the end of the long register, all toiling together in the tenement.

Adapted from Jacob Riis, *How the Other Half Lives*, 1890.

READING REVIEW

1. Why does Riis think immigrants came to the United States?
2. What characteristic is common to all the ethnic groups Riis describes?
3. **Summarizing** Write a paragraph summarizing the main points in Riis's description of ethnic groups in New York City.

★ 4-3   Life in the Promised Land ★

Introduction Although life was difficult and even cruel for many new immigrants, Mary Antin's joy in her new environment is evident in this selection from *The Promised Land*. Antin describes the eagerness with which she and her family greeted new ideas and adopted new customs in Boston.

Vocabulary Before you read the selection, find the meaning of these words in a dictionary: initiation, perpetual, perplexity, deficiencies.

Our initiation into American ways began with the first step on the new soil. My father corrected us even on the way from the pier to Wall Street, which journey we made crowded together in a rickety cab. He told us not to lean out of the windows, not to point, and explained the word greenhorn. We did not want to be greenhorns. So we paid the strictest attention to my father's instructions.

The first meal was an object lesson of much variety. My father produced several kinds of food, ready to eat, without any cooking, from little tin cans that had printing all over them. He tried to introduce us to a queer, slippery kind of fruit which he called banana. But he had to give it up for the time being. After the meal he had better luck with a curious piece of furniture on runners which he called rocking chair. There were five of us newcomers, and we found five different ways of getting into the American machine of perpetual motion and as many ways of getting out of it. We laughed over our various experiments with the novelty, which was a wholesome way of letting off

Many of the immigrants to the United States in the late 1800s spoke no English. Children like these, learning the language and culture of Americans, helped their families bridge the gap between the old and new nations.

steam after the unusual excitement of the day.

In our flat there was no bathtub. So in the evening of the first day my father conducted us to the public baths. As we moved along in a little procession, I was delighted with the lighting of the streets. So many lamps, and they burned until morning, my father said, and so people did not need to carry lanterns. In America, then, everything was free, as we had heard in Russia. Light was free; the streets were as bright as a synagogue on a holy day. Music was free; we had been serenaded, to our delight, by a brass band of many pieces soon after our installation on Union Place.

Education was free. That subject my father had written about repeatedly as comprising his chief hope for us children, the essence of American opportunity, the treasure that no thief could touch, not even misfortune or poverty. On our second day I was thrilled with the realization of what this freedom of education meant.

A little girl from across the alley came and offered to conduct us to school. My father was out, but we five between us had a few words of English by this time. We knew the word school. We understood. This child, who had never seen us till yesterday, who could not pronounce our names, who was not much better dressed than we, was able to offer us the freedom of the schools of Boston! No application made, no questions asked, no examinations, rulings, exclusions; no fees. The doors stood open for every one of us. The smallest child could show us the way. This incident impressed me more than anything I had heard in advance of the freedom of education in America.

Even the interval on Union Place was crowded with lessons and experiences. We had to visit the stores and be dressed from head to foot in American clothing. We had to learn the mysteries of the iron stove, the washboard, and the speaking tube. We had to learn to trade with the fruit peddler through the window and not to be afraid of the policeman. And, above all, we had to learn English.

When I make a long list of my American teachers, I must begin with those who taught us our first steps. To my mother, in her perplexity over the cookstove, the woman who showed her how to make the fire was an angel of deliverance. A fairy godmother to us children was she who led us to a wonderful country called uptown, where, in a dazzlingly beautiful palace called a department store, we exchanged our hateful homemade European costumes, which pointed us out as greenhorns to the children on the street, for real American machine-made garments, and issued forth glorified in each other's eyes.

With our immigrant clothing we shed also our impossible Hebrew names. A committee of our friends, several years ahead of us in American experience, put their heads together and made up American names for us all. My mother, possessing a name that was not easily translated, was punished with the undignified nickname of Annie. Fetchke, Joseph, and Deborah issued as Frieda, Joseph, and Dora, respectively. As for poor me, I was simply cheated. The name they gave me was hardly new. My Hebrew name being Maryashe in full, Mashka for short, Russianized into Marya, my friends said that it would hold good in English as Mary, which was very disappointing, as I longed to possess a strange-sounding American name like the others.

As a family we were so diligent under instruction, so adaptable, and so clever in hiding our deficiencies that when we made the journey to Crescent Beach in the wake of our small wagonload of household goods, my father had very little occasion to admonish us on the way. I am sure he was not ashamed of us. So much we had achieved toward our Americanization during the two weeks since our landing.

Adapted from Mary Antin, *The Promised Land* (Boston: Houghton Mifflin Company, 1912).

READING REVIEW

1. What aspect of American life did Antin consider most valuable?

2. What problem, treated lightly by Mary Antin, could make adjustments to the New World difficult for many immigrants?

3. **Making Inferences** What attitudes held by the Antins probably helped them succeed in the United States?

Introduction The electric trolley was a boon to city dwellers, taking them to work and to play. But another method of transportation also changed their lives: the bicycle. Bicycling became a popular craze in the 1890s as this song chorus and picture demonstrate.

Daisy Bell

Daisy, Daisy,
Give me your answer, do—
I'm half crazy all for the love of you.
It won't be a stylish marriage,
I can't afford a carriage,
But you'll look sweet upon the seat
Of a bicycle built for two.

READING REVIEW

1. (a) Why does the person in the song say he needs a bicycle? (b) Do you think many people had the same problem?
2. **Analyzing a Song as Historical Evidence** What does the song tell you about life in the 1890s?
3. **Using Visual Evidence** (a) How are the people in the picture using the bicycle? (b) Why do you think such activities were especially important to city dwellers?

Introduction Jane Addams was born wealthy, but she developed a social conscience that led her to devote her life to the poor. Addams founded Hull House, the nation's first settlement house, in the midst of the Chicago slums. There immigrants could go with their problems in daily living. There, too, social workers collected statistics on urban conditions and lobbied for regulations of housing and working conditions. In this selection from her book *Twenty Years at Hull House,* Addams describes child labor in Chicago.

Vocabulary Before you read the selection, find the meaning of these words in a dictionary: remorse, recurrence, redress, compunction.

Our very first Christmas at Hull House, when we as yet knew nothing of child labor, a number of little girls refused the candy which was offered them as part of the Christmas good cheer. They said simply that they "worked in a candy factory and could not bear the sight of it." We discovered that for six weeks they had worked from seven in the morning until nine at night, and they were exhausted. The sharp consciousness of stern economic conditions was thus thrust upon us in the midst of the season of good will.

During the same winter three boys from a Hull House club were injured at one machine in a neighboring factory for lack of a guard which would have cost but a few dollars. When the injury of one of these boys resulted in his death, we felt quite sure that the owners of the factory would share our horror and remorse, and that they would do everything possible to prevent the recurrence of such a tragedy. To our surprise they did nothing whatever, and I made my first acquaintance then with those pathetic documents signed by the parents of working children, that they will make no claim for damages resulting from "carelessness."

The visits we made in the neighborhood constantly discovered women sewing upon sweatshop work, and often they were assisted by incredibly small children. I remember a little girl of four who pulled out basting threads hour after hour, sitting on a stool at the feet of her Bohemian mother, a little bunch of human misery. But even for that there was no legal redress. The only child labor law in Illinois with any provision for enforcement had been secured by the coal miners' unions and was confined to children employed in mines.

We found many pathetic victims of the sweatshop system who could not possibly earn enough in the short busy season to support themselves during the rest of the year. However, it became evident that we must add carefully collected information to our general impression of neighborhood conditions if we would make it of any genuine value.

There was at that time no statistical information on Chicago industrial conditions. Mrs. Florence Kelley, an early resident of Hull House, suggested to the Illinois State Bureau of Labor that they investigate the sweatshop system in Chicago with its use of child labor. The head of the bureau adopted this suggestion and hired Mrs. Kelley to make the investigation. When the report was presented to the Illinois Legislature, a special committee was appointed to look into the Chicago conditions.

As a result of its investigations, this committee recommended to the legislature the provisions which afterwards became those of the first factory law of Illinois. This law regulated the sanitary conditions of the sweatshop and fixed 14 as the age at which a child might be employed.

Founded upon some such compunction, the sense that the passage of the child labor law would in many cases work hardship was never far from my mind during the earliest years of its operation. I addressed as many mothers' meetings and clubs among working women as I could,

Many young city children worked in sweatshops or tried their hand at independent labor, like these shoeshine boys.

in order to make clear the object of the law and the ultimate benefit to themselves as well as to their children.

The bitterest opposition to the law came from the large glass companies. They were so accustomed to using the labor of children that they were convinced the manufacturing of glass could not be carried on without it.

Although this first labor legislation was but bringing Illinois into line with the nations in the modern industrial world, it ran counter to the instinct and tradition, almost to the very religion, of the manufacturers of the state, who were for the most part self-made men.

Adapted from Jane Addams, *Twenty Years at Hull House*, copyright 1910 by The Macmillan Company; renewed 1938 by James W. Linn. Reprinted by permission of the publishers.

READING REVIEW

1. How did Addams learn about the conditions under which children were working?
2. What steps did she take to correct the situation?
3. **Relating Cause and Effect** Describe one cause and one effect of the following: (a) Addams's decision to learn more about child labor; (b) the investigation by the legislative committee.

★ 4-6 Tammany Hall ★

Introduction Corrupt city governments were commonplace during the late 1800s. Many were controlled by the bosses of political machines, who had the power to give out jobs and contracts for a fee. Muckrakers stirred up public opinion against scandal and abuse. Lincoln Steffens was a muckraker who assigned reporter Claude Wetmore to investigate government in New York. Part of Wetmore's article, published in *McClure's Magazine,* is printed here.

Vocabulary Before you read the selection, find the meaning of these words in a dictionary: rogues, formidable, intimidate, dispense.

Tammany is Tammany, the embodiment of corruption. All the world knows and all the world may know what it is and what it is after. For hypocrisy is not a Tammany vice. Tammany is for Tammany, and the Tammany men say so. Other rings proclaim lies and make pretensions; other rogues talk about the tariff and imperialism. Tammany is honestly dishonest. Time and time again, in private and in public, the leaders, big and little, have said they are out for themselves and their own; not for the public, but for "me and my friends"; not for New York, but for Tammany.

Foreigners marvel at it and at us, and even Americans—Pennsylvanians, for example—cannot understand why we New Yorkers regard Tammany as so formidable. I think I can explain it. Tammany is corruption with consent. It is bad government founded on the votes of the people. The Philadelphia machine is more powerful. It rules Philadephia by fraud and force and does not require the votes of the people. The Philadelphians do not vote for their machine; their machine votes for them. Tammany used to stuff the ballot boxes and intimidate voters; today there is practically none of that. Tammany rules, when it rules, by right of the votes of the people of New York.

Tammany corruption is democratic corruption. Tammany's democratic corruption rests upon the corruption of the people, the plain people, and there lies its great significance. Its grafting system is one in which more individuals share than any I have studied. The people themselves get very little; they come cheap, but they are interested.

Divided into districts, the organization subdivides them into precincts or neighborhoods, and their sovereign power, in the form of votes, is bought up by kindness and petty privileges. The leader and his captains have their hold because they take care of their own. They speak pleasant words, smile friendly smiles, notice the baby, give picnics up the river or the sound, or a slap on the back; find jobs, most of them at the city's expense.

They have also newsstands, peddling privileges, railroad and other business places to dispense. They permit violations of the law, and, if a man has broken the law without permission, see him through the court. Though a blow in the face is as readily given as a shake of the hand, Tammany kindness is real kindness and will go far, remember long, and take infinite trouble for a friend.

Tammany leaders are usually the natural leaders of the people in these districts, and they are originally good-natured, kindly men. No one has a more sincere liking than I for some of those common but generous fellows; their charity is real, at first. But they sell out their own people. They do give them coal and help them in their private troubles. But, as they grow rich and powerful, the kindness goes out of the charity, and they not only collect at their saloons or in rents—cash for their "goodness." They not only ruin fathers and sons and cause the troubles they relieve; they also sacrifice

the children in the schools. They let the health department neglect the tenements and, worst of all, plant vice in the neighborhood and in the homes of the poor.

This is not only bad; it is bad politics; it has defeated Tammany. Woe to New York when Tammany learns better. Now there is a new boss, a young man, Charles F. Murphy, and unknown to New Yorkers. He looks dense, but he acts with force, decision, and skill. The new mayor will be his man. Charlie Murphy will rule Tammany and, if Tammany is elected, New York also. As a New Yorker, I fear Murphy will prove wise enough to stop the scandal and put all the graft in the hands of a few tried and true men.

Adapted from Claude W. Wetmore, "New York: Good Government to the Test," *McClure's Magazine*, November 1903.

READING REVIEW

1. What does the author mean by "Tammany is honestly dishonest"?
2. Why did ordinary people continue to vote for Tammany?
3. **Drawing Conclusions** What is the end result of a corrupt government like Tammany Hall?

Tammany Hall, the corrupt Democratic political machine in New York, was the target of many of the cartoons of Thomas Nast. Indeed, Nast was largely responsible for creating an angry reform movement against the machine. Here the caption under Nast's Tammany tiger reads, "What are you going to do about it?"

5 Becoming a World Power (1865–1900)

★ 5-1 Looking Outward ★

Introduction Admiral Alfred T. Mahan was an outspoken supporter of a larger United States role in world affairs. The American people, he argued, were ambitious and would see that a powerful fleet was necessary for international trade. In this selection written in 1890, Mahan discusses this need.

Vocabulary Before you read the selection, find the meaning of these words in a dictionary: temperament, alien, sluggish, ominous, prudent, inanition.

For nearly the lifetime of a generation, American industries have been protected* until the practice has assumed the force of a tradition. At bottom, however, the temperament of the American people is essentially alien to such a sluggish attitude. Independently of all bias for or against protection, it is safe to predict that, when the opportunities for gain abroad are understood, American enterprise will try to reach them. The importance of distant markets and their relation to our own production imply the recognition of the link that joins the products and the markets—that is, the carrying trade.† We need not follow far this line of thought before America's unique position becomes clear. Facing the older worlds of the East and West, America's shores are lapped by the oceans which touch the one or the other but which are common to her alone.

Together with these signs of change in our own policy there is a restlessness in the world at large which is deeply significant, if not ominous. There is no sound reason for believing that the world has passed into a period of peace outside the limits of Europe. Unsettled political conditions exist in Haiti, Central America,

and many of the Pacific islands, especially the Hawaiian group. When combined with great military or commercial importance, these conditions contain dangerous germs of quarrel, against which it is at least prudent to be prepared.

Despite a superior geographical location, the United States is woefully unready to assert its influence in the Caribbean and Central America. We have not the navy. And, what is worse, we are not willing to have the navy that will weigh seriously in any disputes with those nations whose interests conflict with our own. We have not, and we are not anxious to provide, the defense of the Atlantic seaboard which will leave the navy free for its work at sea.

Whether they will or not, Americans must now begin to look outward. The growing production of the country demands it. An increasing volume of public sentiment demands it. The position of the United States, between the two Old Worlds and the two great oceans, makes the same claim, which will soon be strengthened by the creation of the new link joining the Atlantic and Pacific. The tendency will be increased by the growth of the European colonies in the Pacific, by the advancing civilization of Japan, and by the rapid peopling of our Pacific states.

The military needs of the Pacific states, as well as their supreme importance to the whole country, are yet a matter of the future. But this future is so near that provision should immediately begin to weigh their importance. To provide this, three things are needed: First, protection of the chief harbors by fortifications and coast-defense ships. Second, naval force, the arm of offensive power, which alone enables a country to extend its influence outward. Third, it should be an unshakeable resolution of our national policy that no European state should henceforth acquire a coaling position

---

*Mahon is referring to protective tariffs that increase the price of imported goods so that American-made goods will be less expensive.

†The carrying trade refers to the fleets of merchant ships that carry products to markets overseas.

within 3,000 miles of San Francisco—a distance which includes the Sandwich and Galapagos islands and the coast of Central America. For fuel is the life of modern naval war. It is the food of the ship. Without it the modern monsters of the deep die of inanition. Around it, therefore, cluster some of the most important considerations of naval strategy.

Adapted from Alfred T. Mahan, "The United States Looking Outward," *Atlantic Monthly*, December 1890.

READING REVIEW

1. Describe two reasons Mahan thinks the United States needs a strong navy.
2. Based on your reading in Chapter 5, what "link joining the Atlantic and Pacific" was Mahon referring to?
3. **Understanding Geography** According to Mahon, how does the geographic location of the United States influence its role in world affairs?

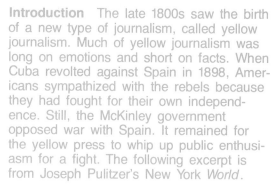

5-2   Yellow Journalism Demands Action

Introduction The late 1800s saw the birth of a new type of journalism, called yellow journalism. Much of yellow journalism was long on emotions and short on facts. When Cuba revolted against Spain in 1898, Americans sympathized with the rebels because they had fought for their own independence. Still, the McKinley government opposed war with Spain. It remained for the yellow press to whip up public enthusiasm for a fight. The following excerpt is from Joseph Pulitzer's New York *World*.

Vocabulary Before you read the selection, find the meaning of these words in a dictionary: arbitrarily, legitimate, immured, rapine.

How long are the peasants of Spain to be drafted away to Cuba to die miserably in a hopeless war, that Spanish nobles and Spanish officers may get medals and honors?

How long shall old Cuban men and women and children be murdered by the score, the innocent victims of Spanish rage against the patriot armies they cannot conquer?

How long shall the sound of rifles in Castle Morro at sunrise proclaim that bound and helpless prisoners of war have been murdered in cold blood?

How long shall Cuban women be the victims of Spanish outrages and lie sobbing and bruised in loathsome prisons?

How long shall American citizens, arbitrarily arrested while on peaceful and legitimate errands, be immured in foul Spanish prisons without trial?

How long shall the navy of the United States be used as the sea police of barbarous Spain?

How long shall the United States sit idle and indifferent within sound and hearing of rapine and murder?

How long?

Adapted from the New York *World*, February 13, 1897.

READING REVIEW

1. What does the article say the Spanish did to American citizens?
2. Describe three Spanish actions that the article condemns.
3. **Recognizing Propaganda** What words in the article would stir readers' emotions? Why?

When the battleship Maine *was blown up in the harbor of Havana, Cuba, an angry public called for war. This headline appeared in the New York* World.

Introduction Yellow journalism was expressed in cartoons as well as in written articles. This cartoon was published in 1898.

Library of Congress

READING REVIEW

1. What does the figure in the cartoon represent?
2. What event does the message on the tombstone refer to?
3. **Analyzing Political Cartoons** (a) How would you describe the artist's attitude toward the figure in the cartoon? Explain. (b) What effect do you think the cartoon probably had on the American public? Why?

Introduction Although the war with Spain began over Spanish rule in Cuba, expansionists in the United States were delighted with the chance to defeat Spain in the Pacific. When Commodore George Dewey scored a triumphant victory at Manila Bay, even antiexpansionists admired his feat. This description of the battle is from Dewey's *Autobiography*.

Vocabulary Before you read the selection, find the meaning of these words in a dictionary: converging, starboard, battery, turret, cessation, sortie, forecastle, mizzenmast, scuttled.

The misty haze of the tropical dawn had hardly risen when at 5:15, at long range, the Cavite forts and Spanish squadron opened fire. Our course was not one leading directly toward the enemy, but a converging one, keeping him on our starboard bow. Our speed was eight knots, and our converging course and ever varying position must have confused the Spanish gunners. My assumption that the Spanish fire would be hasty and inaccurate proved correct.

So far as I could see, none of our ships was suffering any damage. In view of my limited ammunition supply it was my plan not to open fire until we were within effective range and then to fire as rapidly as possible with all of our guns.

At 5:40, when we were within a distance of two and one-half miles, I turned to Captain Gridley and said, "You may fire when you are ready, Gridley."

While I remained on the bridge with Lamberton, Brumby, and Stickney, Gridley took his station in the tower and gave the order to the battery. The very first gun to speak was an eight-inch from the forward turret of the *Olympia*, and this was the signal for the other ships to join the action.

When the flagship neared the five-fathom curve off Cavite, she turned to the westward, bringing her port batteries to bear on the enemy. Followed by the squadron, she passed along the Spanish line until north of the Sangley Point battery, when she again turned and headed back to the eastward.

There had been no cessation in the fire maintained by our whole squadron. The effect of its concentration, owing to the fact that our ships were kept so close together, was smothering, particularly upon the two largest ships, the *Reina Cristina* and *Castilla*. The *Don Juan de Austria* first and then the *Reina Cristina* made brave and desperate attempts to charge the *Olympia*, but becoming the target for all our batteries, they turned and ran back.

In this sortie the *Reina Cristina* was raked by an eight-inch shell which put out of action some twenty men and completely destroyed her steering gear. Another shell in her forecastle killed or wounded all the members of the crews of four rapid-fire guns; another set fire to her; another killed or disabled nine men on her poop deck. Another carried away her mizzenmast, bringing down the ensign and the admiral's flag, both of which were replaced. Another exploded in the ammunition room; and still another exploded in the sick bay, which was already filled with wounded.

The *Castilla* fared little better than the *Reina Cristina*. All except one of her guns were disabled. She was set on fire by our shells and finally abandoned by her crew after they had sustained a loss of twenty-three killed and eighty wounded. The *Don Juan de Austria* was badly damaged and on fire. The *Isla de Luzon* had three guns dismounted, and the *Marques del Duero* was also in a bad way. Admiral Montojo, finding his flagship no longer manageable, half her people dead or wounded, her guns useless, and the ship on fire, gave the order to abandon and sink her. He transferred his flag to the *Isla de Cuba* shortly after 7:00.

There had been such a heavy flight of shells over us that each captain was convinced that no other ship had had such good luck as his own in being missed by the enemy's fire. Each expected the others to have both casualties and damages to report. But fortune was as in our favor at Manila as it was later at Santiago. To my gratification not a single life had been lost. On the *Baltimore* two officers and six men were slightly wounded. None of our ships had been seriously hit, and every one was still ready for immediate action.

At 11:16 we stood in to complete our work. There remained to oppose us, however, only the batteries and the gallant little *Ulloa*. Both opened fire as we advanced. But the contest was too unequal to last more than few minutes. Soon the *Ulloa*, under our concentrated fire, went down valiantly with her colors flying.

At 12:30 the *Petrel* signaled the fact of the surrender and the firing ceased. But the Spanish vessels were not yet fully destroyed. Therefore the executive officer of the *Petrel*, Lieutenant E. M. Hughes, with a whaleboat and a crew of only seven men, boarded and set fire to the *Don Juan de Austria*, *Isla de Cuba*, *Isla de Luzon*, *General Lezo*, *Coreo*, and *Marques del Duero*, all of which had been abandoned in shallow water and left scuttled by their deserting crews. This was a courageous undertaking, as these vessels were not far from the shore, where there were hundreds of Spanish soldiers and sailors, all armed and greatly excited. The little *Petrel* continued her work until 5:20, when she rejoined the squadron, towing a long string of tugs and launches, to be greeted by volleys of cheers from every ship.

The order to capture or destroy the Spanish squadron had been executed to the letter. Not one of its fighting vessels remained afloat.

Adapted from George Dewey, *The Autobiography of George Dewey* (New York: Charles Scribner's Sons, 1913).

READING REVIEW

1. What was the battle plan Dewey followed?
2. What attempts did the Spanish make to defend themselves?
3. **Recognizing a Point of View** (a) Based on this selection, what was Commodore Dewey's opinion of the Spanish? (b) What statements reveal his opinion?

★ 5-5 Under Attack in China ★

Introduction In the late 1800s, several nations carved out spheres of influence in China. In 1900 a group of Chinese nationalists revolted against the presence of foreigners in their country. This Boxer Rebellion was put down by troops from several nations, including the United States. In her diary, Katharine Mullkien Lowry, wife of an embassy employee, describes the Boxers' siege of the mission where she lived.

Vocabulary Before you read the selection, find the meaning of these words in a dictionary: heathen, providentially, antagonizing, torrents.

WEDNESDAY, June 13: Smoke and flame announce that our street chapel is being burned. All night long fires spring up in different parts of the city.

FRIDAY, June 15: Last night for two hours awful sounds of raging heathen filled the air and seemed to surge against the wall in the southern city, opposite our place. Some estimated there were 50,000 voices. "Kill the foreign devil! Kill, kill, kill!" they yelled till it seemed hell was let loose.

WEDNESDAY, June 20: About 9:00 A.M. great excitement was caused by the word that Baron von Ketteler, the German Minister, had been shot on his way to the Tsungli Yamen, and his interpreter wounded. Captain Hall thought as it would be impossible to hold the compound against soldiers. So our only chance would be to abandon it immediately, while it is still possible for women and children to walk on the street.

The nationalities represented here are American, Austrian, Belgian, Boer, British, Chinese, Danish, Dutch, French, Finn, German, Italian, Japanese, Norwegian, Portuguese, Russian, Spanish, Swedish. They are divided into men, 245; women, 149; children, 79; total, 473; not including the marines, of whom there are 409. The

Chinese here number about 700 to 800 Protestants and 2,000 Catholics.

SATURDAY, June 23: Today has been one of great excitement. Five big fires rage close about us, and bucket lines are formed several times. Some of the fires are started by the Chinese; some by our people, to burn out places which are dangerous to us, because the Chinese may burn them or can fire from them.

After burning the Russian Bank the Chinese start a fire in the Han Lin College, with a wind blowing from the north, which makes it very dangerous for us. Hardly is the fire under way, however, when the wind providentially changes and we are saved from that danger, though much hard work is required in passing buckets of water. Sentiment and fear of antagonizing the Chinese caused our people to refrain from firing this Han Lin College, the very foundation of Chinese literature and culture. The intense hatred of the Chinese for us is shown by the fact that they themselves set fire to this relic of the ages.

SUNDAY, June 24: Today the Chinese do their first shelling.

WEDNESDAY, June 27: The usual nervous strain is endured all day from the bullets and shells. We shall forget how it feels to be without their sound. The nights are dreadful with the sound of shattering tiles and falling bricks, and there is so much echo in the courts that at night it is hard to locate where an attack is being made, and harder still to sleep at all. At 11:00 P.M. an alarm is rung at the bell tower for all to assemble there with their firearms. This is the second or third general alarm we have had, and they frighten us almost worse than the attacks.

SATURDAY, July 28: It is estimated that from July 10 to 25, 2,800 cannonballs or shells came into these premises. There have been as many as 400 in one day.

TUESDAY, August 14: Last night was certainly the most frightful we have had. Although they had fired all day yesterday, the Chinese began with renewed vigor about 8:00 P.M., at the very moment that a terrific thunderstorm with lightning and torrents of rain set in. Shells, bullets, and firecrackers vied with the noise of the elements, while our big guns added to the noise. Our men were wild and felt like doing their best, for it was now certain that the foreign troops could not be far distant. In fact, the boom of the distant cannon could easily be heard, and no one felt like sleeping, had it been possible in the din. Our American gunner, Mitchell, is wounded. All morning we have heard the thundering of the foreign troops, and while it seems too good to be true, our hearts rejoice that deliverance is near.

Adapted from K. M. Lowry, "A Woman's Diary of the Siege of Pekin," *McClure's Magazine*, November 1900.

READING REVIEW
1. Why did the foreigners decide not to burn Han Lin College?
2. How did people at the mission react to the shelling by the Boxers? How can you tell?
3. **Making Inferences** How do you think Lowry would have reacted to the scene shown on page 129?

In the late 1800s European nations divided a weak China among themselves, each taking an area to control. However, Chinese nationalists, called Boxers, revolted against all foreigners in their nation. This painting shows violence such as Katharine Lowry witnessed.

Theme 2

Entering a Modern Age

Topic

6 The Progressives (1900–1909)

★ 6-1 Steffens Calls on the Boss of Philadelphia ★

Introduction Muckraking journalist Lincoln Steffens based his book *The Shame of the Cities* on his visits to several cities. When he went to Philadelphia in 1903, he found its citizens—unlike those of the other cities—indifferent to local corruption. As he relates in this selection from his autobiography, he decided to go to the source and pay a call on the boss of the city's political machine.

Vocabulary Before you read the selection, find the meaning of these words in a dictionary: franchise, soliloquy.

In desperation one day I called at the office of the boss, Israel W. Durham. His secretary shook his head. "Don't think Mr. Durham will see you; too busy." He would ask. He came out with his eyes and mouth open in surprise. "Go in," he said, and I went in, and saw a man well worth knowing. He was sitting, a slight figure, relaxed at his desk. "Not well," I thought. Only his eyes were quick; they were kind, inquiring. He did not rise. As I halted on his threshold, he nodded a smiling welcome.

"Close the door," he said quietly. "I want to ask you a couple of questions."

"Oh, no, you don't," I protested. "I came to this town for information, and everybody is asking me questions, like you. I draw the line. You've got to answer me first."

He smiled. "All right," he said. "Your turn first, then mine. What do you want to know?"

There had been a burst, a volcanic eruption, of "steals" and "jobs," all in the administration of Mayor Ashbridge. I asked Durham how they dared do such a wild, wholesale business in such a short time. He did not mind the assumption, in my question, that the franchise grants were steals and that he knew it. He waited a moment; then asked me quietly if I meant to quote him.

No, I said. I was really puzzled and wanted only to understand the politics of the Ashbridge administration. Technically it looked like bad politics, "bad bad politics," I remember saying. He shook his head slowly, thoughtfully, no.

"In the first place," he said, "Ashbridge wished it so. He wanted but one term in office, and having no further ambition, he wanted to crowd as much business as we would let him into that one term. And we—we talked it all over. With

Part Two   176

the mayor known to be for one term only we would have to stay here and take the permanent blame. The responsibility fell upon me. But we reasoned—"

"Well," I urged, when he halted there, "you could put over one of those steals in New York or anywhere else, but one would be enough to strain any machine I know of. And five or—more!" He smiled.

"We reasoned," he resumed, "we agreed among ourselves that it was exactly the five or—more that would save us."

He let me express my bewilderment; then he cleared it as by a lightning flash.

"If we did any one of these things alone, the papers and the public could concentrate on it, get the facts, and fight. But we reasoned that if we poured them all out fast and furious, one, two, three— one after the other—the papers couldn't handle them all and the public would be stunned and—give up."

"Political corruption," I said, "is, then, a process. It is not a temporary evil, not a passing symptom of the youth of a people. If this process goes on, then this American republic of ours will be a government that represents the organized evils of a privileged class." I had forgotten Durham; I wasn't accusing him of wrongdoing. But I remember the awed tone in which he broke into my soliloquy to ask how it could be stopped. I saw that he cared. I said I didn't know, and I rose to go to think over the ideas I had got into my head.

And, then, as he moved with me to the door, he said quite seriously, "I think that I get you now."

The sudden personal turn stalled me. "What do you mean, get me?"

"Well," he said, "we've been looking you over since you came to town, reading your other stuff and wondering how you, a reformer, get on to the game the way you do; you know the way it's done."

"Yes?" I said. "And what is the explanation you say you've got?"

"Oh, I can see that you are a born crook that's gone straight."

Adapted from Lincoln Steffens, *The Autobiography of Lincoln Steffens* (New York: Harcourt, Brace, 1931).

READING REVIEW

1. How does Durham explain the decision to do such "wholesale" business during Ashbridge's administration?

2. How does Steffens describe corruption?

3. **Relating Past to Present** (a) What prediction does Steffens make about the future of the republic? (b) How accurate do you think he was? Explain.

This cartoon from Puck *magazine pictures the power of the party boss, who could dole out special favors in his city.*

Introduction Mary White Ovington, a young woman from a well-to-do New York family, was one of the founders of the National Association for the Advancement of Colored People. Ovington was the first professionally trained American social worker to devote her major energies to the cause of black Americans. Ovington served in the NAACP in various decision-making positions for almost 40 years. When she was over 80, she wrote an account of her life, *The Walls Came Tumbling Down.* This selection from the book describes the earliest days of the NAACP.

Vocabulary Before you read the selection, find the meaning of these words in a dictionary: criminality, lynching.

The average age of the five founders, Du-Bois, Villard, Walter C. Sachs, for a time treasurer, John Haynes Holmes, and myself, was thirty-five. I like to remember this because it is rarely until old age that men are recognized, that their protraits are painted, or their statues placed in parks. I gazed for years at a picture of the Pilgrim Fathers that made each man look at least fifty, and was delighted to learn later that, except for Miles Standish, not one of those men was over thirty. Garrison started *The Liberator* and became the most hated man in America in 1831 at twenty-six years of age. But you see his statue, on the strip of green that runs through Boston's Commonwealth Avenue, as an old man sitting in a large, comfortable chair.

There was no especial courage needed by us as we sat about our council board in New York. Archibald Grimké complained of this once, saying we were not revolutionary. He withdrew this criticism when we pointed out that while it was a small matter to demand that a Negro be served at a public restaurant in New York, it was revolutionary to demand that he vote in Mississippi.

Our first practical job was a case concerned with an arrest at Asbury Park, New Jersey, of a Negro charged with murder. There was no evidence against him, but he was black and had been near the scene of the crime. He was put through the third degree before we learned of the case. Our lawyer went at once to Asbury Park and after some days secured his release. A similar case occurred later at Lakewood, New Jersey. This time we moved more quickly, found that there was no evidence, and freed the man. Imagine our satisfaction when we learned that we had been "rather expected," that there was an organization in New York that was looking into these Negro arrests. Our fame had crossed the North River!

The newspapers usually showed the Negro as a criminal. It made, they thought, interesting reading. We, then, would show the criminality of the white; we would publicize lynching, interpret the story which, in 1911, appeared in the papers on an average of every six days—the story of a colored man taken out of the custody of the law and lynched.

A map of the United States soon appeared in our office with a pin stuck into every spot where there had been a lynching. The lower part of the map was black with pin heads. Our primer was a post card that had been sent to John Haynes Holmes after he had spoken against lynching in Ethnical Cultural Hall. We had tried to get ministers of established positions in New York to speak at this meeting but without success. "We must get young men," Villard then declared, "newcomers who at once will write themselves down as opposed to this shame of America." We did get two such men, the Reverend John Haynes Holmes and Rabbi Stephen S. Wise. Our publicity must soon have reached the South, for shortly after the meeting Holmes came to us with a post card which he had received from a town where a lynching occured. It was a picture post card. In the foreground was the dead Negro, and back of him, and on both sides, were the lynchers, clear-cut photographs that could have been used successfully for identification. The men's confidence that no one would dream of prosecuting them was the most striking thing about the card. We wondered that it had been permitted to go through the United States mail.

We used that post card with accounts of other lynchings as publicity. I remember the morning Mary Maclean and I got the dummy ready for the printer. It was Sunday; our office, in the New York *Evening Post* building, was on Vesey Street and through the open window we heard the singing at the Church of St. John, one of New York's oldest places of worship. While we read "They cut off his fingers for souvenirs" and pasted it at the top of the second page, the voices of the choir sang, "We praise Thee, Oh Lord. We acknowledge Thee to be our God." Were those men who had committed murder in some church singing from the hymnbook?

Slightly adapted excerpts from *The Walls Came Tumbling Down* by Mary White Ovington, copyright 1947 by Harcourt Brace Jovanovitch, Inc.; renewed 1975 by Nicholas N. Kingsbury. Reprinted by permission of the publisher.

READING REVIEW

1. What point does Ovington stress about the five founders of the NAACP?
2. What techniques did the NAACP use to protect the rights of black Americans?
3. **Applying Information** Describe what life was like for blacks based on this selection. Do you think your description "tells the whole story"? Explain.

★ **6-3   After the Triangle Fire** ★

Introduction The tragic fire at the Triangle Shirt Waist Factory in 1911 rallied many progressives to the cause of workers. They especially pressed for the improvement of working conditions. One of those who spoke out was Stephen Wise. Wise, born in Hungary, was rabbi of a New York City synagogue. Here he speaks about the Triangle fire at a citizens' meeting held in the New York Metropolitan Opera House.

Vocabulary Before you read the selection, find these words in a dictionary: contriteness, redeeming, penitence, redress, inexorable, inviolable.

Reformers demanded an end to unsafe working conditions that resulted in tragedies such as the Triangle Fire. They also demanded laws to protect children who worked in factories.

This ought to be a fast day of the citizens of New York, our day of guilt and humiliation. Let it not become a day of unavailing regret, but let it be a day of availing contriteness and redeeming penitence.

It is not the action of God, but the inaction of man that is responsible. I see in this disaster not the deed of God, but the greed of man. For law is divine, and this disaster was brought about by lawlessness and inhumanity. Certain calamities man can do no more than vainly deplore—such calamities as the San Francisco earthquake and the destruction by volcano of Martinque. But this was not an inevitable disaster which man could neither foresee nor control. We might have foreseen it, and some of us did; we might have controlled it, but we chose not to do so. The

179

Topic 6

things that are inevitable we can do no more than vainly regret, but the things that are avoidable we can effectively forestall and prevent.

It is not a question of enforcement of law nor of inadequacy of law. We have the wrong kind of laws and the wrong kind of enforcement. Before insisting upon inspection and enforcement, let us lift up the industrial standards so as to make conditions worth inspecting. And when we go before the Legislature of the State, and demand increased funds in order to ensure a sufficient number of inspectors, we will not forever be put off with the answer: we have no money.

This meeting is not summoned in order to appeal for charity on behalf of the families of the slain. What is needed is the redress of justice and the remedy of prevention. The families of the victims ought to be beyond the reach of the need of charity. They need justice, not charity. It is we who need charity, for dare we face inexorable justice?

We know that we cannot and should not take away property without due process of law. Neither may we take away life with or without due process of law. Alas, for another one of the multitude of proofs that we regard property as sacred, and are ready to suffer a violation of the rights of life.

This consuming fire will have been nothing more than a flash in the pan if other evils are suffered to go unchecked and uncorrected—evils not less terrible because less swift and less sudden. It is just as necessary to protect women workers from the industrial and occupational diseases as it is to protect them from industrial accidents. We need to provide not only for security from accidents but security from the incidents of the industrial regime. I would have women workers safeguarded in every way—safeguarded from the economically, physically, morally, and spiritually disastrous consequences of overwork and underpay and undernourishment.

The hour has come for industrial peace. It must be peace with honor, say some. But it must be more than peace with honor. It must be peace with security as well. We would have no peace with honor for some, and, at the same time, deny security to all.

The lesson of the hour is that while property is good, life is better, that while possessions are valuable, life is priceless. The meaning of the hour is that the life of the lowliest worker in the nation is sacred and inviolable. If that sacred human right be violated, we shall stand condemned before the court of God and of history.

Adapted from Stephen S. Wise, *The Challenging Years* (New York: G. P. Putnam's Sons, 1949).

READING REVIEW

1. What does Wise blame for the Triangle tragedy?

2. What does Wise mean when he calls for "industrial peace"?

3. **Analyzing a Primary Source** Based on Wise's statements, do you think this speech was made soon after the fire? Explain.

★ 6-4 La Follette Uses Scientific Methods ★

Introduction "I am free to confess," Robert La Follette wrote in his autobiography, "that it had been my great ambition to be governor of Wisconsin; not just to be governor—to be a strong factor in securing legislation that should build into the life of the people a new order of things." In achieving his goals, La Follette prided himself on seeking out expert help and presenting Wisconsin citizens with the facts on the issues. Here he describes how the railroad rate commission carried out its job and the results of its work.

Vocabulary Before you read the selection, find the meaning of these words in a dictionary: valuation, prophecies, deteriorate, statisticians.

The commission proceeded with wisdom. Though under great pressure at first, it refused to consider complaints until it had laid a broad foundation of scientific knowledge. Expert engineers and contractors were employed and many months were spent in making a physical valuation of all railroad property in the state. This is the logical first step if you are going to fix rates. It then became necessary to determine the actual cost of maintenance and operation—a very difficult matter in our case—because the railroads of Wisconsin are parts of great systems.

When all this immense work was done, the commission had the wisdom and foresight to submit its findings to the railroad officials, who went over them and approved them. This prevented disputes in the future upon fundamental facts.

All through our fight for railroad control, the lobbyists and the railroad newspapers made the most mournful prophecies of disaster. They predicted that capital would fly from the state, that new construction would stop, that equipment would deteriorate, and so on and so on. What are the facts?

The object of our legislation was not to "smash" corporations, but to drive them out of politics, and then to treat them exactly the same as other people are treated. Equality under the law was our guiding star. It is the special discriminations and unjust rates that are being corrected; the privileges, unfair advantages, and political corruption that have been abolished. Where these do not exist the object has been to foster and encourage business activity. Consequently, no state in the union today offers better security for the savings of its people than Wisconsin. The honest investor, or businessman, or farmer, or laborer, who simply wants equal opportunity with others and security for what he honestly earns, is protected and encouraged by the laws. The mere speculator, or monopolist, or promotor, who wants to take advantage of others under protection of law, is held down or driven out. The result is that instead of falling behind, the state has actually gone forward more rapidly than the rest of the country. This may be shown by facts and figures in practically every direction where there has been progressive legislation affecting business.

The Railroad Commission keeps accurate account of all the business of every railroad and public utility in the state. These accounts show that while during the first five years of its existence the commission reduced rates by more than $2 million a year, the net earnings of the railroads of Wisconsin increased relatively just a little more than the net earnings for all railways in the United States.

How did this come about? Simply from the fact that the decrease in rates for freight and passengers was followed by an enormous increase in the amount of freight and number of passengers carried. So it happened that, notwithstanding the reduction in rates, there was an actual increase of nearly 20 percent in the revenue.

It is not claimed that railroads are both making and keeping more money in Wisconsin than they did before the progressive legislation began. Indeed, they are making more but keeping a smaller proportion of it. They are now paying taxes the same as other people on exactly what their property is worth.

How has it been possible that both the people of Wisconsin and the investors in public utilities have been so greatly benefited by this regulation? Simply because the regulation is scientific. The Railroad Commission has found out through its engineers, accountants, and statisticians what it actually costs to build and operate the road and utilities. On the other hand, since the commission knows the costs, it knows exactly the point below which rates cannot be reduced.

Adapted from Robert M. La Follette, *La Follette's Autobiography* (Madison, Wis.: University of Wisconsin Press, 1911).

READING REVIEW

1. What was the first task undertaken by the Railroad Commission?
2. According to La Follette, what was the aim of the state's railroad legislation?
3. **Distinguishing Fact From Opinion** (a) What is La Follette's opinion of the work of the railroad commissioners? (b) List three facts he gives to support his opinion.

Introduction With his energy, informality, and good humor, Theodore Roosevelt easily captured and held public attention from his earliest days in politics. In fact, "TR's" colorful personality tended to hide his actual accomplishments—and defects. In this selection, a modern historian, William O'Neill, summarizes Roosevelt the man at the time he became President.

Vocabulary Before you read the selection, find the meaning of these words in a dictionary: laissez-faire, impair, equitable, constituency.

Though he tried, Roosevelt did not get along with Tom Platt [New York state's Republican boss] well enough to be certain of renomination. To get him out of New York, Platt arranged his nomination for the vice-presidency in 1900. At the top of his powers, used to command, TR would have been miserable had he been forced to serve for long as the president's shadow. He was spared that by McKinley's assassination, which gave him the power he had always wanted. At the time Roosevelt's views were mostly shallow and conventional. He was against the selfish individualism of laissez-faire, but believed that while government should in-tervene in economic matters it ought not to impair competition. TR wished only to make competition more equitable and humane. He believed in the inferiority of colored peoples and, to a lesser extent, in that of non-Anglo–Saxons. He believed in America's destiny as a great power. To that end he encouraged foreign trade, not for its own sake as businessmen did, but as a means of extending American influence abroad.

Racism, imperialism, and a thirst for martial glory have few admirers today, but they were not barriers to popularity in Roosevelt's time. He became the most loved and admired politician of the age, thanks to his electric personality, gift for dramatization, and keen sense of what people were worrying about. Henry Demarest Lloyd, a radical reformer, said TR had no ear for "the new music of mankind." TR was not responsive to calls for a reconstructed America such as radical humanitarians were making. But he was quick to grasp the concerns of ordinary people—the small businessmen, prosperous farmers, skilled workers, and other middle Americans who made up his natural constituency. He also agreed in part with the less hidebound politicians of his day, who knew that traditional ways of managing—or not managing—national affairs no longer suited the changing times. This understanding, together with his own taste for aggressive leadership, would make him the first modern president.

Pages 23–24 from *The Progressive Years: America Comes of Age*, by William L. O'Neill. Copyright © 1975 by Harper & Row, Publishers, Inc.

Theodore Roosevelt was known as a trust-buster because the government prosecuted several trusts while he was President. Here Roosevelt beams from a window as a giant screw is applied to the trusts.

READING REVIEW

1. O'Neill sees Roosevelt's views in 1901 as being "mostly shallow and conventional." How does he support this opinion?

2. What qualities made TR "the most loved and admired politician of the age"?

3. **Supporting Generalizations** Roosevelt is here called "the first modern president." Why?

Introduction Theodore Roosevelt was a loving father to his six children. This well-educated and well-traveled family exchanged frequent and amusing letters. Every now and then, the President would delight his children with a picture letter. He sent this one to his son Kermit when Kermit was away at boarding school. Though uninterested in politics, Kermit took after his father in his love of adventure.

Department of the Interior
Yellowstone National Park
Office of Superintendent
Mammoth Hot Springs, Wyo.

April 16th, 1903

Blessed Kermit,

All right, here goes for a picture letter! I shall put the pictures on the inside, so as to have more room. I have really enjoyed the trip, though I am homesick. I do not shoot, but I try to get up to things, and to show them to Mr. John Burroughs.*

Father and Mr. Burroughs galloping up on some elk — bulls and cows. The elk are tired and have begun to open their mouths and pant. You can tell Mr. Burroughs by the beard. There are a great many rocks on the ground. The pine tree is small and scraggly.

A small and queer owl (but not as queer as the picture) which perched on the top of a little tree near one of our camps. Two mountain sheep jumping

There! I feel that I shall never try to draw another picture! I have forgotten how—and my pictures are only suited for beloved persons while they are still under seven years old.

Your attached father

Adapted from Will Irwin, ed., *Letters to Kermit from Theodore Roosevelt, 1902–1908* (New York: Charles Scribner's Sons, 1946).

*John Burroughs, with whom the President was traveling, was a noted naturalist of the time.

READING REVIEW

1. What does the letter show about Roosevelt's attitude toward nature?
2. What does the letter show about Roosevelt's feelings toward his son?

3. **Analyzing a Primary Source** (a) How might a historian use a letter like this to learn more about Theodore Roosevelt? (b) In what ways is evidence such as this limited?

Introduction President Taft had a very different personality and approach than Theodore Roosevelt. Few realized this better than Archibald Butt, who served both Presidents as military aide. He wrote about this topic—and many others as well—in letters to his sister-in-law, Clara Butt. Noted for his honesty and personal charm, Butt was widely mourned when he went down with the *Titanic* in 1912. Butt wrote this letter on November 4, 1909, about a trip Taft had made to the West.

Vocabulary Before you read the selection, find the meaning of these words in a dictionary: chicanery, endorse, reproach, discord, repugnant, innuendo, wily, complacency, affiliated.

Taft was unfortunate in starting off his trip with a speech praising Senator Aldrich. This, with a speech in praise of

President William Howard Taft was more formal than the outspoken "Teddy" Roosevelt. Although Roosevelt had chosen Taft to succeed him, the two men had a falling out after Taft took office.

Representative Tawney, had a very bad effect throughout the West. They were both honest, and he believed that both men had been greatly slandered by the press. He soon learned that it was not a popular thing to praise a man even in his own district. In most cases these men had reached Congress through some political chicanery of which the decent element in the state is ashamed. Or they have done something while in Congress which the best-minded people will not endorse. He began by picking out the worst types to endorse. Whether Senator Aldrich is a horse thief or not, the entire West and South so regard him. By the former section, especially, he is regarded as the one man who is against their interests.

President Roosevelt had educated the public to hear the truth about public men. So, when the President began to praise Aldrich and Tawney and Senator Tom Carter of Montana, it hardly knew what to expect. But he soon dropped this crusade. He has been largely won over by Aldrich, and I think he feels grateful to Tawney for doing what he did in the matter of increasing his salary and assisting in passing the bill allowing him traveling expenses. But he has little respect for Tom Carter.

The same thing is true about Speaker Cannon. The President simply hates him and expresses his contempt for him whenever he can do so. Yet, he openly flattered him on the trip down the Mississippi, was photographed with his arms about his neck, and appeared to endorse him whenever they spoke together. At the same time he wrote to Secretary of State Knox that Cannon should be driven out of public life. He felt that was a constant reproach to the decent self-respecting element of the country. He is doing all he can to defeat him, yet he constantly gives him strength by appearing to approve both him and his actions.

I have never known a man to dislike discord as much as the President. He wants every man's approval, and a row of any kind is repugnant to him. If by saying the word publicly that would defeat Cannon, I believe he would say it, so sincere is his dislike of the Speaker. But he does not feel that he is strong enough to say it and so he takes the opposite tact, hoping to aid in his defeat by private innuendo. But the Speaker is too wily for him. He gave several openings which would have afforded President Roosevelt, for instance, many opportunities to kill him politically. But the President let them go by, leaving the impression that he actually endorsed the old vulgarian.

So much in the President's character can be explained by his complacency. He believes that many things left to themselves will bring about the same result as if he took a hand himself in their settlement. He acts with promptness and vigor when he has got to act, but he would rather delay trouble than seek it. Of course that is just the opposite view to the one which would be taken by President Roosevelt. The President everywhere endorsed the Roosevelt policies. Yet, in each state he entered he affiliated with the man whom Roosevelt disliked the most and would call the "Enemy."

Adapted from Archie Butt, *Taft and Roosevelt: The Intimate Letters of Archie Butt* (Garden City, N.Y.: Doubleday, Doran & Company, 1930).

READING REVIEW

1. How, according to Butt, did Taft antagonize the audiences that heard him speak?
2. In what specific ways does Butt contrast Taft and Roosevelt?
3. **Finding the Main Idea** According to Butt, what was the main problem in the way Taft handled the presidency?

★ 7-2 Ringside at the Republican Convention ★

Introduction Theodore Roosevelt's daughter Alice Roosevelt Longworth was a noted Washington figure from the turn of the century until her death in 1980. Longworth enjoyed politics as a spectator sport. Here she recalls some of the events of the Republican convention of 1912, which met in Chicago and nominated Taft.

Vocabulary Before you read the selection, find the meaning of these words in a dictionary: assemblage, sneering, manipulate, buoyancy, raucous, contemptuous.

The bad moments of all the past months seemed nothing in comparison to the strain of that week in Chicago—and particularly that day. At the convention they were voting on the reports of the Credentials Committee on the contests—roll call after roll call. The "razzing" of Mr. Root* that had begun with the opening of the convention became almost continuous. Realistic imitations of the noise made by a steamroller, accomplished by rubbing pieces of sandpaper together—bursts of tooting—shouts of "It's missing, go out and get gasoline."

That night I stopped on the way back to my hotel to see Father. Father was in great fighting form; not the least bitter or angry, perfectly philosophical. The plan at that moment was to insist that they nominate Taft, to "see to it" that all the contests were against us, as they had been so far. We were to demand all or none. Then we should refuse to abide by the proceedings of "such an assemblage." Our men would sit silent and we should not soil our hands by taking part. So our "line of talk" became a sneering "they must nominate Taft." All the same, bravely as we talked, there was an ache in my heart at the thought of Father's great fight and victory coming to this. For victory it was—and clearly and demonstrably stolen from him by those who had it in their power to dictate to the convention, to manipulate this machinery to accomplish their purpose.

By Saturday we knew it was all over. But, nevertheless, we went down to look in at the convention, where the votes on

---

*Senator Elihu Root presided at the convention.

the contest continued—all, of course, going against us. The roar of steamroller noises continued, too—the chugging and whistling kept up almost without pause. We went back in the afternoon. The platform was voted on, 666 voting for it, 343 present and not voting, the rest absent or voting no. That over, nominations were in order. Father's name was not presented. Harding made the nominating speech for Taft—run-of-the-mill stuff. We must have been obstacle-struck not to leave before then. Possibly we stayed, as one sometimes does on those occasions, because it would not be "sporting" to leave.

We left the Coliseum while the seconding was going on, to dine briefly and hurry to join the family to go to the "Rump" convention—and a great and thrilling meeting it was. There was a spirit and buoyancy and enthusiasm that were an odd contrast to what we had left behind—the sullen, shame-faced, obedient regulars—the jeering, raucous, contemptuous galleries.

Hiram Johnson spoke, putting Father in nomination as the candidate of the Progressive Party. Then Father came in. What a meeting it was! We all behaved as if we had suddenly been presented with the one gift that we had always longed to have. Everyone was chockablock with a sort of camp-meeting fervor, cheering, emotional. We were out to "battle for the Lord."

Adapted from Alice Roosevelt Longworth, *Crowded Hours* (New York: Charles Scribner's Sons, 1933).

READING REVIEW

1. What was the strategy of Roosevelt and his followers at the Republican convention?

2. Why do you think the galleries were making noises like a steamroller?

3. **Recognizing a Point of View** (a) What is the author's point of view toward Roosevelt and the "Rump" convention? (b) How can you tell?

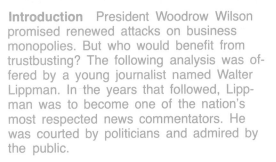

★ 7-3 A Contemporary Looks at Wilson ★

Introduction President Woodrow Wilson promised renewed attacks on business monopolies. But who would benefit from trustbusting? The following analysis was offered by a young journalist named Walter Lippman. In the years that followed, Lippman was to become one of the nation's most respected news commentators. He was courted by politicians and admired by the public.

Vocabulary Before you read the selection, find the meaning of these words in a dictionary: plutocracy, singular, pristine.

Bryan* has never been able to adjust himself to the new world in which he lives. That is why he is so irresistibly funny to sophisticated newspapermen. His virtues, his habits, his ideas, are the simple, direct, shrewd qualities of early America.

—————
*William Jennings Bryan, who ran for President as a Populist, later served as President Wilson's secretary of state.

Yet there has always been great power behind Bryan, the power of those who in one way or another were hurt by the greater organization that America was developing. The Populists were part of the power. La Follette and the insurgent Republicans expressed it. It was easily a political majority of the American people. The Republican Party disintegrated under the pressure of the revolt. The Bull Moose gathered much of its strength from it. But in 1912 it swept the Democratic Party, and by a combination of circumstances, carried the country. The plutocracy was beaten in politics, and the power that Bryan spoke for in 1896, the forces that had made muckraking popular, captured the government. They were led by a man who was no part of the power that he represented.

Woodrow Wilson is an outsider capable of skilled interpretation. He is an historian, and that has helped him to know the older tradition of America. He is a student of theory. Like most theorists of his generation he is deeply attached to the doctrines that swayed the world when America was founded.

But Woodrow Wilson at least knows that there is a new world. He said, "There is one great basic fact which underlies all the questions that are discussed on the political platform at the present moment. That singular fact is that nothing is done in this country as it was done twenty years ago. We are in the presence of a new organization of society. We have changed our economic conditions, absolutely, from top to bottom; and, with our economic society, the organization of our life."

You wait eagerly for some new formula. The new formula is this: "I believe the time has come when the governments of this country, both state and national, have to set the stage, and set it very minutely and carefully, for the doing of justice to men in every relationship of life." Now that is a new formula, because it means a willingness to use the power of government much more extensively.

But for what purpose is this power to be used? There, of course, is the rub. It is to be used to "restore our politics to their full spiritual vigor again, and our national life, whether in trade, in industry, or in what concerns us only as families and individuals, to its purity, its self-respect, and its prestine strength and freedom." The ideal is the old ideal, the ideal of Bryan. The method is the new one of government interference.

That, I believe, is the inner contradiction of Woodrow Wilson. He knows that there is a new world demanding new methods, but he dreams of an older world. He is torn between the two. It is a very deep conflict in him between what he knows and what he feels.

His feeling is, as he says, for "the man on the make." "Just let some of the youngsters I know have a chance and they'll give these gentlemen points. Lend them a little money. They can't get any now. See to it that when they have got a local market they can't be squeezed out of it." Nowhere in his speeches will you find any sense that it may be possible to organize the fundamental industries on some deliberate plan for national service. He is thinking always about somebody's chance to build up a profitable business.

Woodrow Wilson was a professor and historian who brought his ideals to the White House. Here he shakes hands with voters in the 1912 election campaign.

He likes the idea that somebody can beat somebody else, and the small businessman takes on the virtues of David in a battle with Goliath.

Adapted from Walter Lippmann, *Drift and Mastery* (New York: Mitchell Kennerley, 1914).

READING REVIEW

1. What, in Lippman's view, does Bryan represent?
2. How does Wilson differ from Bryan?
3. **Recognizing a Point of View** (a) In Lippman's opinion, what is the "inner contradition" of Wilson? (b) How does he support his opinion?

Topic 7

Introduction No matter how much support a President's programs may have, getting them adopted requires hard work. Enactment of the Federal Reserve system under Wilson was no exception. This selection focuses on the efforts made by the President himself. The author, Joseph Tumulty, first served as an adviser when Wilson was governor of New Jersey. When Wilson was elected President, Tumulty became his private secretary, the first Roman Catholic to hold this post.

Vocabulary Before you read the selection, find the meaning of these words in a dictionary: aptly, autocratic, exasperating, manifest, skirmish.

Never before was Mr. Wilson's open-minded desire to apply in practice the principle of common counsel better illustrated than in his handling of the important work in connection with the establishment of the Federal Reserve Act, the keystone of the great arch of the Democratic administration. It was the first item in his program to set business free in America and to establish it upon a firm and permanent basis. He aptly said to me, when he first discussed the basic reason for the legislation, he wished not only to set business free in America, but he desired also to take away from certain financial interests in the country the power they had unjustly exercised of "hazing" the Democratic party at every presidential election.

Shortly after the presidential election in 1912, he began the preparation of the Federal Reserve Banking and Currency Act. Looking back over the struggle that ensued from the time this measure was introduced into the Senate and House, I often wonder if the people "back home" ever realized the painstaking labor and industry, night and day, which Woodrow Wilson put upon this task.

Mr. Wilson conducted conferences in this matter with friends and foes alike with a great mastery and good temper. This was totally contrary to the reports, circulated for political purposes, that he was autocratic and refused to cooperate with the members of the Senate and House in an effort to pass legislation.

It was in a conference with members of the Banking and Currency Committee that I first saw the President in action with the gentlemen of the Senate and House. He had invited the Democratic members of the Banking and Currency Committee to confer with him in the Cabinet Room in the White House offices. From my desk in an anteroom I heard all the discussions of the bill. There was full, open discussion of the bill in all its phases. Some of the members were openly hostile to the President, even in a personal way, particularly one representative from the South. Some of the questions addressed to the President were ungracious to the verge of open insult. It was an exasperating experience, but Mr. Wilson stood the test with patience, gallantly ignoring the unfriendly tone and manifest unfairness of some of the questions.

It was clear to me as I watched this great man in action on this trying occasion that in the cause he was defending he saw far beyond the little room in which he was conferring. He saw the varied and pressing needs of a great nation laboring now under a currency system that held its resources as if in a straitjacket. He saw in the old monetary system a breeder of panic and financial distress. He saw the farmer of the West and South a plaything of Eastern financial interests. And thus, under the leadership of Woodrow Wilson was begun the first skirmish in the great battle to establish a financial system that would end the danger of financial panic.

Adapted from Joseph P. Tumulty, *Woodrow Wilson As I Know Him* (Garden City, N.Y.; Doubleday, Page & Company, 1921).

READING REVIEW

1. What does Tumulty mean when he writes of reports "circulated for political purposes" that Wilson was "autocratic"?

2. What is his attitude toward Wilson?

3. **Defending a Position** How does the author defend the President against the charge that he was autocratic?

Introduction After decades of struggle, suffragists hoped that the movement for progressive reforms would help them win the vote at last. But not all progressives supported their cause. Theodore Roosevelt did. But he did not "regard it as a very important matter." Woodrow Wilson at first opposed the constitutional amendment granting women the vote. He felt suffrage should be handled at the state level. It was to counteract this opposition that Alice Paul launched her militant program. It appealed especially to younger women—the third generation of American suffragists.

Doris Stevens, the author of this selection, was a colleague of Paul's. Like the woman whose story she tells here, she was arrested for picketing, jailed, and subjected to force-feeding after going on a hunger strike.

Vocabulary Before you read the selection, find the meaning of these words in a dictionary: prone, supine, insubordinate, desolate.

Among the prisoners who with Alice Paul led the hunger strike was a very picturesque figure, Rose Winslow (Rusa Wenclawska) of New York, whose parents had brought her in infancy from Poland to become a citizen of "free" America. At eleven she was put at a loom in a Pennsylvania mill, where she wove hosiery for fourteen hours a day until tuberculosis claimed her at nineteen. A poet by nature, she developed her mind to the full in spite of these disadvantages. When she was forced to abandon her loom she became an organizer for the Consumers' League, and later a vivid and eloquent power in the suffrage movement.

Her group preceded Miss Paul's by about a week in prison. These vivid sketches of Rose Winslow's impressions while in the prison hospital were written on tiny scraps of paper and smuggled out to us and to her husband during her imprisonment.

If this thing is necessary we will naturally go through with it. Force is so stupid a weapon. I feel so happy doing my bit for decency—for our war, which is after all, real and fundamental.

The women are all so magnificent, so beautiful. Alice Paul is as thin as ever, pale and large-eyed. We have been in solitary for five weeks. There is nothing to tell but that the days go by somehow. I have felt quite feeble the last few days—faint, so that I could hardly get my hair brushed, my arms ached so. But today I am well again. Alice Paul and I talked back and forth though we are at opposite ends of the building and a hall door also shuts us apart. But occasionally—thrills—we escape from behind our iron-barred doors and visit. Great laughter and rejoicing!

Women played an active role in the reform movement of the early 1900s. This cartoon shows a temperance leader, Carrie Nation, in a wild attack against alcohol. The temperance movement was victorious in 1917 when Congress passed the Eighteenth Amendment.

These suffragists in New York pose with a banner pointing out that women had won the right to vote in western states. New York granted suffrage in 1917, but women did not win the right to vote in national elections until the Nineteenth Amendment was ratified in 1920.

Alice Paul is in the psychopathic ward. She dreaded forcible feeding frightfully, and I hate to think how she must be feeling. I had a nervous time of it, gasping a long time afterward, and my stomach rejecting during the process. I spent a bad, restless night, but otherwise I am all right. The poor soul who fed me got liberally besprinkled during the process. I heard myself making the most hideous sounds. One feels so forsaken when one lies prone and people shove a pipe down one's stomach.

This morning but for an astounding tiredness, I am all right. I am waiting to see what happens when the President realizes that brutal bullying isn't quite a statesmanlike method for settling a demand for justice at home. At least, if men are supine enough to endure, women—to their eternal glory—are not.

Yesterday was a bad day for me in feeding. I was vomiting continually during the process. The tube has developed an irritation somewhere that is painful.

Never was there a sentence* like ours for such an offense as ours, even in England. No woman ever got it over there even for tearing down buildings. And during all that agitation we were busy saying that never would such things happen in the United States. The men told us they would not endure such frightfulness.

We still get no mail; we are "insubordinate." It's strange, isn't it; if you ask for food fit to eat, as we did, you are "insubordinate"; and if you refuse food you are "insubordinate." Amazing. I am really all right. If this continues very long I perhaps won't be. I am interested to see how long our so-called "splendid American men" will stand for this form of discipline.

All news cheers one marvelously because it is hard to feel anything but a bit desolate and forgotten here in this place.

All the officers here know we are making this hunger strike that women fighting for liberty may be considered political prisoners. We have told them. God knows we don't want other women ever to have to do this over again.

Adapted from Doris Stevens, *Jailed for Freedom* (New York: Boni and Liveright, 1920).

READING REVIEW

1. (a) Why are the women on a hunger strike? (b) Why do you think they are being force-fed?
2. How would you describe Rose Winslow?
3. **Summarizing** What do you think is the main message conveyed by this primary source?

---

*The sentence was seven months for "obstructing traffic."

8 The United States in World Affairs (1900–1916)

Introduction In his annual message to Congress in December 1904, Theodore Roosevelt outlined a policy toward Latin America that came to be known as the Roosevelt Corollary.

Vocabulary Before you read the selection, find the meaning of these words in a dictionary: chronic, impotence, adherence, flagrant.

It is not true that the United States feels any land hunger or entertains any projects as regards the other nations of the Western Hemisphere save such as are for their welfare. All that this country desires is to see the neighboring countries stable, orderly, and prosperous. Any country whose people conduct themselves well can count upon our hearty friendship. If a nation shows that it knows how to act with reasonable efficiency and decency in social and political matters, if it keeps order and pays its obligations, it need fear no interference from the United States. Chronic wrongdoing, or an impotence which results in a general loosening of the ties of civilized society, may in America, as elsewhere, ultimately require intervention by some civilized nation.

In the Western Hemisphere the adherence of the United States to the Monroe Doctrine may force the United States, however reluctantly, in flagrant cases of such wrongdoing or impotence, to the exercise of an international police power. If every country washed by the Caribbean Sea would show the progress Cuba has shown since our troops left the island, all question of interference by this nation would be at an end.

Our interests and those of our southern neighbors are in reality identical. They have great natural riches. If within their borders law and justice reign, prosperity is sure to come to them. While they thus obey the primary laws of civilized society, they may rest assured that they will be treated by us in a spirit of helpful sympathy. We would interfere with them only in the last resort, and then only if their inability to do justice at home had violated the rights of the United States or had invited foreign aggression. Every nation which desires to maintain its independence must realize that such independence cannot be separated from the responsibility of making good use of it.

Adapted from Theodore Roosevelt, "Annual Message to Congress, December 6, 1904," in *Messages and Papers of the Presidents*, Vol. XIV.

READING REVIEW

1. How are Western Hemisphere nations to act in order to "fear no interference from the United States"?
2. What two conditions might require "intervention by some civilized nation"?
3. **Making Inferences** On the basis of this excerpt, how would you describe the relationship between the United States and the countries of Latin America in the early 1800s?

Sugar was the most important crop in much of the Caribbean. But falling prices sometimes led to instability and intervention by the United States. This picture shows a sugar mill in the early 1800s.

Introduction In attacking disease on the Isthmus of Panama, army physician William C. Gorgas had to contend not only with difficult local conditions but also with incompetence on the part of his superiors. This selection gives an idea of how exasperating official attitudes must have been to a trained scientist. It is from a biography of Gorgas written by his wife Marie D. Gorgas and muckraking journalist Burton Hendrick.

Vocabulary Before you read the selection, find the meaning of these words in a dictionary: balderdash, mirth, folly, festering, benevolent, aphoristhms.

Admiral Walker had taken pains to become acquainted with Reed's work and the part played by the Stegomyia mosquito in transmitting yellow fever.* As a result he had reached a definite conviction: that the whole idea was balderdash. And in his gruff and uncompromising naval way he did not hesitate to air his views. Admiral Walker was not famous for a keen sense of humor, but the idea that

---

*Admiral John G. Walker was the first head of the Panama Canal Commission. Walter Reed was the army surgeon who, in Cuba, demonstrated the connection between mosquitoes and yellow fever, thus paving the way for Gorgas's work.

Digging the Culebra Cut, shown here, was the most difficult part of the work on the Panama Canal. When President Roosevelt visited the area, he wrote to his son, "They are eating steadily into the mountain, cutting it down and down."

there was anything dangerous in the bite of a mosquito stirred him to uncontrollable mirth. To spend good American dollars on a group of insane enthusiasts who spent all their time chasing mosquitoes through the Panama jungle seemed to him an extreme form of official folly. The French in their wildest moments had never done anything so bad as that!

On his trip to Washington in the early fall of 1904, Gorgas spent a considerable part of his time haunting Admiral Walker's office. He would talk for hours explaining the part played by mosquitoes in yellow fever and in malaria, and tell over and over again the story of Havana and Rio de Janeiro. His visits were long pleadings for sulphur, pyrethrum powder, wire screening, crude oil, inspectors—all the things and persons needed in fighting the disease. But his arguments and his prayers had no effect.

The Admiral flatly informed Gorgas that he was wrong. Everybody knew, he asserted, what caused yellow fever—and it was not the mosquito. It was filth. The thing to do in Panama and Colon and other towns was to clean things. These ports were reeking with unspeakable smells. Get rid of them, declared the Admiral, and there would be no more disease. Clean the streets, remove the dead cats, whitewash the houses, and yellow fever would vanish as if by magic. Admiral Walker even proposed to draw up a set of regulations for doing this; let Gorgas limit his activities to following these rules!

In vain did the doctor tell how he had scoured and scrubbed Havana and made it almost the cleanest city on the Continent—only to have yellow fever break out more furiously than ever. A dead horse festering in the streets of Colon was not so dangerous to human life, he declared, as a single Stegomyia mosquito! At this Admiral Walker would give an uproarious laugh and stick Gorgas's requisition into his already well-filled pigeonhole.

Gorgas had no better success with General George W. Davis, the first governor of the Canal Zone. Again he had to deal with an engineer of high standing—

the man who had finished the Washington Monument—but likewise a man who had the outlook of another generation. General Davis's attitude toward Gorgas, however, was not severe or intolerant. It was kindly, benevolent, the pose of an older man who wished to keep an enthusiast out of trouble. "What's that got to do with digging the Canal?" he would ask, when Gorgas began talking in his favorite strain. "A dollar spent on sanitation is like throwing it into the bay," was another one of his aphorisms.

Like most of the Commission, General Davis regarded the mosquito notion as beyond the pale. "I'm your friend, Gorgas," he would say pityingly, "and I'm trying to set you right. On the mosquito you are simply wild. All who agree with you are wild. Get the idea out of your head. Yellow fever, as we all know, is caused by filth."

Adapted from Marie D. Gorgas and Burton J. Hendrick, *William Crawford Gorgas: His Life and Work* (Garden City, N.Y.: Doubleday, Page & Company, 1924).

READING REVIEW

1. (a) What, in Walker's view, caused yellow fever? (b) How did he think it could be controlled?
2. How did Davis respond to Gorgas's appeals?
3. **Recognizing a Point of View** (a) What is the authors' point of view toward Walker? (b) Toward Davis? (c) Toward Gorgas?

★ 8-3 The Return of the Great White Fleet ★

Introduction The armada sent around the world by President Roosevelt—called the Battle Fleet at the time—left Hampton Roads, Virginia, in December 1907. When it returned early in 1909, the President was on hand to greet it at its home port. So were a host of other officials, photographers, and reporters. One member of the welcoming party was journalist Harold J. Howland, a staff writer for *The Outlook*, a widely read periodical of the day. He watched the huge ships steam in from his vantage point on a tug in the harbor.

Vocabulary Before you read the selection, find the meaning of these words in a dictionary: inimitable, belated, capacious.

On an instant, out of the dead gray to seaward, leaped one, two, three shapes, bulking huge, inimitable, unlike any other object on the circuit of the waters. One moment the stage was empty, the next the players were there; and one could not say how they came. With the regularity of breathing, the shapes jumped from the mist. There were eight by the time the first neared the *Mayflower* [President Roosevelt's ship], taking its proper form now as a battleship, white of body, buff of upper works, red streaked at the waterline.

At four minutes before the hour, a red flash spurted from under the leader's bridge, a white ball fluffed out around it. After an uncanny interval, seeming more like minutes than seconds, a monster champagne bottle was uncorked in our ears. Ship after ship took up the tale. Flashes and woolly clouds ran down the line, alternately on port and starboard, till each ship was framed in three great clouds, white smoke of powder on either side, black fumes of coal above. The flagship had sighted the President's flag. The American Battle Fleet was saluting the standard of the American navy's commander-in-chief. Twenty-one guns to a ship, five hundred and a quarter to the fleet and its escorts astern—the salutes of the last ships in the column coming only as belated barkings from behind the background curtain.

The column swept on, the ships spaced at exact intervals—200 yards from

Topic 8

stem to stem. Battleship succeeded battleship in saluting the commander-in-chief, who had set them their task and to whom they had come back to render their account. In four divisions the sixteen ships went by.

Behind the Battle Fleet were the escorting squadron, four battleships, two armored cruisers, and three scout cruisers, high of bow and chubby of hull, but ready to do their 26 knots into the enemy's waters at a moment's notice.

As we drew in to our pier, the *Connecticut* had made a turn at the far end of Hampton Roads and was coming to anchor, nose to sea, off the Point. By the time we had reached the luncheon table, by a window overlooking the Roads, the whole fleet was at anchor in two lines reaching out of sight into the capacious harbor. Between the lines at her head rode the *Mayflower*.

So ended the greatest naval event in time of peace in the history of the world. It was appropriate that that event should have its beginning and its end on the spot where modern naval history began. Just over there, beyond the second line of anchored battleships, two fundamental principles of modern naval construction received their baptism—ironclad armor and the revolving turret. There the *Monitor* and the *Merrimac* fought their way into history 47 years ago.

What has the Battle Fleet done? It has steamed more than 42,000 miles in fourteen months and six days. It has crossed the equator four times. It has spent 190 days actually at sea, cruising at a uniform speed of 10 knots an hour, and spent 2,443 days in port and at target practice. It has made the longest run ever made by a fleet without coaling, 3,850 miles from Honolulu to New Zealand. It has strengthened the friendship for our country of several foreign nations. Perhaps it has solved a delicate diplomatic situation, but of that only time can reveal the facts. But, above all, it has taught the American Navy many things.

The Battle Fleet is a fleet that has "found herself." It is no longer a collection of individual ships. It is a unit, an organism, with each ship, each officer, each man performing his own function, not as an end in itself, but as a contribution to the efficiency, the vitality, the life of the whole. The officers and men who took the Battle Fleet once and a half around the world and brought it back, a little worn perhaps, but as a whole immeasurably better than when it went away, can do it again. There are no problems that a war may bring which the Battle Fleet, to the limit of its strength, cannot solve. It has solved them already.

Adapted from Harold J. Howland, "The Return of the Battle Fleet," *The Outlook*, March 6, 1909.

READING REVIEW

1. What did the fleet accomplish in terms of distance and time?

2. Based on your reading in Chapter 8, what was the "delicate diplomatic mission" the fleet may have solved?

3. **Finding the Main Idea** In your opinion, what impressed Howland most about the Great White Fleet?

★ **8-4 War Along the Border** ★

Introduction A progressive New Yorker, Florence Jaffray (Daisy) Harriman was involved in Democratic politics most of her adult life. In 1914, she was a member of the Federal Industrial Relations Commission. She later served as a Democratic National Committeewoman from Washington, D.C., and as minister to Norway.

Harriman had gone to Dallas with other commission members to investigate land problems in the Southwest. In March 1915, she took time off to visit the Texas–Mexico border, where a Mexican civil war was in full swing. The American immigration official in the area traveled with her across the Rio Grande.

Vocabulary Before you read the selection, find the meaning of these words in a dictionary: prudent, mauser, potpourri, phenomenal, morbid, desultory, improvised, stoicism, anaesthetic.

We walked two miles back from the river to Reynosa, a jaunty multicolored Mexican town which had been captured by the Carranzaistas* from the Huertaistas two years before. When the Villaistas marched in the other day they found it deserted. All the Carranza sympathizers had had news of this army of the North down the wind and decided that the American side of the Rio Grande was a prudent move in their civil war.

The "ragged Villa army" was a thing of the past. Every man we saw seemed well equipped with a mauser and ammunition. We asked a good many questions as to what the civil war was all about and what they were fighting for, and we got a strange potpourri of answers. Their voices were so soft and Spanish itself is such a musical speech that their replies seemed even gentler than they were. Several told us that there really wasn't going to be any battle. It was certain that they were going to walk in and take Matamoros without any real trouble at all.

During the night following my visit to Reynosa, after 24 hours' rest the Villaistas broke camp and silently stole away.

Friday night our party arrived in Brownsville. The town was full of news that the Villa troops were 20 miles from Matamoros and were expected to attack at dawn. Their army had made a phenomenal march, 183 miles in five days; women on foot, and all. The artillery of 25 guns had been left at Reynosa awaiting the mending of the railway bridge. Carranzaistas had been ready for this attack for a week and were in trenches about a mile from the town.

Saturday I was awakened at 7:00 A.M. by our own troopers galloping through the streets. I am ashamed now by the thrill I had, aware that the great show, civil war, was about to open. Yet it was

*Carranzaistas were supporters of Carranza; Huertaistas were supporters of Huerta; and Villaistas were supporters of Villa.

The United States became involved in the Mexican civil war when Pancho Villa and his men crossed into New Mexico and killed 19 American citizens. United States troops then pursued Villa back into Mexican territory. This photo shows some of Villa's men.

not only morbid interest that caused me to throw on my clothes so hastily and clamber to the roof, where all the day long, through a powerful fieldglass, I was to watch the "Battle of Matamoros."

At first the shooting was rapid and insistent. After noon it grew more desultory. I could easily see the Villaista cavalry grouped on the hill. Suddenly all the men dropped from their horses' backs and I thought that they must be preparing to make a charge on foot. Only afterwards I learned that what I saw were men falling dead or wounded. Presently a single Red Cross ambulance began to make many trips back and forth from the International Bridge with terrible regularity.

When the sun went down, things grew quiet and news poured in of a crushing defeat for Villa. All that night and all the next day the wounded poured into Brownsville.

Sunday morning I learned that a theater near our hotel was being used as an improvised hospital, and that many wounded there were in need of care. I went to offer my services and found about 50 boys and men lying on the floor. Here a doctor, who had been up all night, and a Christian citizen of Brownsville and his splendid wife, who dropped in by chance, were trying to bring some comfort and help to those poor, brave sufferers. Such stoicism I never expect to witness again, as was shown by these men—these children! One little warrior of 10 was shot clear through the body, but he stood the dressing and probing of the wound without uttering a sound and had no anaesthetic. Throughout that day and the next, not a murmur was heard, although their agony was so intense that at times the tears would pour down their cheeks.

The whole border business is a curious mess. Our cavalry does wonders policing the border and putting down smuggling and illicit trading, but there is something a little ironical in refereeing a civil war. We Americans are so part of the situation and so out of it. So many complicating things happen. Often whole districts get panicky and run to the army officer in command. And before he knows it he finds himself in the role of a military governor. He knows very well, too, that pacific citizens far from the border are worried by what may happen next.

The Carranza Consul here in Brownsville held out for a long time against letting me cross the bridge to Matamoros, giving as excuse that the Villaistas were expected back to attack at any moment. Only just as I was about to leave for the north did he send a member of his staff to guide me to the besieged town. The plaza was quite empty, and we heard no sounds in the long, silent streets or from behind the closely shuttered housefronts. The women and children were refugees seeking a haven on American soil and the men were in the trenches.

We drove to military headquarters, the one corner of the town where there was life, and I was introduced to General Nafarrate, "the man who never smiles, the most fearless general in Carranza's army." He plied me with eager questions, as he did when he discovered that I had watched the engagement a few days before with my own eyes from a Brownsville roof.

On the balcony outside his office he showed me the colors they had captured in Saturday's engagement. Some were shot into ribbons; some were stiff with blood. My sense of adventure vanished. Those were the very colors I had seen on the white ponies at Reynosa. Here by the Rio Grande and over there in Europe war is all the same piteous game.

Adapted from Mrs. J. Borden Harriman, *From Pinafores to Politics* (New York: Henry Holt, 1923).

READING REVIEW

1. What is Daisy Harriman's role in the events she describes?
2. What is the author's attitude toward the troops of Carranza, Huerta, and Villa?
3. **Analyzing a Primary Source** Harriman calls "the whole border business" a "curious mess." What does she mean?

Topic

9 The World at War (1914–1919)

Introduction When World War I broke out in Europe, the American ambassador to Britain was Walter Hines Page, a journalist and publisher. Although he and President Wilson had long been friends, a coolness developed as the war continued. Hines felt that the United States should provide the Allies with more aid. Hines wrote this memorandum as war broke out.

Vocabulary Before you read the selection, find the meaning of these words in a dictionary: consular, registry, primacy, drubbing, flog.

Bachelor's Farm, Ockham, Surrey.
Sunday, August 2, 1914.

The Grand Smash is come. Last night the German Ambassador at St. Petersburg handed the Russian Government a declaration of war. Today the German Government asked the United States to take its diplomatic and consular business in Russia in hand. Herrick, our Ambassador in Paris, has already taken the German interests there.

It is reported in London today that the Germans have invaded Luxemburg and France.

Troops were marching through London at one o'clock this morning. Colonel Squier came out to luncheon. He sees no way for England to keep out of it. There is no way. If she keeps out, Germany will take Belgium and Holland, France would be betrayed, and England would be accused of forsaking her friends. People came to the Embassy all day today to learn how they can get to the United States—a rather hard question to answer. I thought several times of going in, but Greene and Squier said there was no need of it. People merely hoped we might tell them what we can't tell them.

Returned travelers from Paris report indescribable confusion—people unable to obtain beds and fighting for seats in railway carriages.

It's been a hard day here. I have a lot of routine work on my desk which I meant to do. But it has been impossible to get my mind off this Grand Smash. It holds one in spite of oneself. I revolve it and revolve it—of course getting nowhere.

It will revive our shipping. In a jiffy, under stress of a general European war, the United States Senate passed a bill permitting American registry to ships built abroad. Thus a real emergency knocked the old Protectionists out, who had held on four 50 years! Correspondingly, the political parties here have agreed to suspend their Home Rule quarrel till this war is ended. Artificial structures fall when a real wind blows.

The United States is the only great power wholly out of it. The United States, most likely, therefore, will be able to play a helpful and historic part at its end. It will give President Wilson, no doubt, a

The United States entered World War I in 1917 with high ideals. This propaganda poster shows the Allies as heroic defenders of civilization against the evil serpent of Germany.

great opportunity. It will probably help us politically, and it will surely help us economically.

The possible consequences stagger the imagination. Germany has staked everything on her ability to win primacy. England and France (to say nothing of Russia) really ought to give her a drubbing. If they do not, this side of the world will henceforth be German. If they do, Germany will for a long time be in discredit.

I walked out in the night a while ago. The stars are bright, the night is silent, the country quiet—as quiet as peace itself. Millions of men are in camp and on warships. Will they all have to fight and many of them die—to untangle this network of treaties and alliances and to blow off huge debts with gunpowder so that the world may start again?

Adapted from Burton J. Hendrick, *The Life and Letters of Walter H. Page* (Garden City, N.Y.: Doubleday, Page & Company, 1925).

READING REVIEW

1. What does Hines think would happen if England stayed out of the war?
2. According to Hines, how will the war help the United States economically?
3. **Making Inferences** What role do you think Hines foresees for the United States in the war?

Topic 9

Introduction On February 17, 1917, the British liner *Laconia* sailed from New York to Liverpool. On board was newspaperman Floyd Gibbons on his way to the front. When the ship was torpedoed eight days later, thirteen people lost their lives. Most of the ship's crew members and passengers, like Gibbons, spent a miserable night at sea before being picked up by another British vessel in the morning. Gibbons's 4,000-word dispatch on the sinking, parts of which appear here, made him famous.

Vocabulary Before you read the selection, find the meaning of these words in a dictionary: deliberative, solicitor, vitals, davit, murky, silhouetted, guttural.

"What do you think are our chances of being torpedoed?" was the question I put before the circle in front of the fireplace.

The deliberative Mr. Henry Chetham, a London solicitor, was the first to answer.

"Well," he drawled, "I should say about 4,000 to 1."

Lucien J. Jerome of the British Diplomatic Service advanced his opinion.

"Nonsense," he said. "Utter nonsense. Considering the zone that we are in and the class of the ship, I should put the chances down at 250 to 1 that we don't meet a 'sub.'"

At that minute the torpedo hit us.

I looked at my watch; it was 10:30 P.M.

Five sharp blasts sounded on the *Laconia's* whistle. Since that night, I have often marveled at the quick coordination of mind and hand that belonged to the man on the bridge who pulled that whistle rope. Those five blasts constituted the signal to abandon the ship. Everyone recognized them.

We walked hurriedly down the corridor leading from the smoke room in the stern to the lounge which was amidships. We moved fast but there was no crowding and no panic.

Steam began to hiss from some of the pipes leading up from the engine well. It seemed like a dying groan from the very vitals of the stricken ship. Clouds of white and black smoke rolled up from the giant grey funnels that towered above us.

Already boat No. 10 was loading up and men and boys were busy with the ropes. I started to help near a davit that seemed to be giving trouble but was sternly ordered to get out of the way and to get into the boat.

"Lower away," someone gave the order, and we started downward with a jerk toward the seemingly hungry, rising and falling swells.

Many feet and hands pushed the boat from the side of the ship, and we renewed our sagging, scraping, sliding, jerking descent. It ended as the bottom of the lifeboat smacked squarely on the pillowy top of a rising swell.

As we pulled away from the side of the ship, its receding terraces of glowing port-hole and deck lights towered above us. The ship was slowly turning over.

It must have been 20 minutes after that first shot that we heard another dull thud, which was accompanied by a noticeable drop in the hulk. The German submarine had despatched a second torpedo through the engine room and the boat's vitals from a distance of 200 yards.

We watched silently during the next minute as the tiers of lights dimmed slowly from white to yellow, then to red and then nothing was left but the murky mourning of the night which hung over all like a pall.

A mean, cheese-coloured crescent of a moon revealed one horn above a ragged bundle of clouds low in the distance. A rim of blackness settled around our little world, relieved only by a few leering stars in the zenith, and, where the *Laconia's* lights had shown, there remained only the dim outlines of a blacker hulk standing out above the water like a jagged headland, silhouetted against the overcast sky.

The ship sank rapidly at the stern until at last its nose rose out of the water and stood straight up in the air. Then it slid silently down and out of sight like a piece of scenery in a panorama spectacle.

Boat No. 3 stood closest to the place where the ship had gone down. As a result of the aftersuction, the small lifeboat rocked about in a perilous sea of clashing spars and wreckage.

As the boat's crew steadied its head into the wind, a black hulk, glistening wet and standing about eight feet above the surface of the water, approached slowly. It came to a stop opposite the boat and not ten feet from the side of it. It was the submarine.

"Vot ship vass dot?" were the first words of throaty, guttural English that came from a figure which projected from the conning tower.

"The *Laconia*," answered Chief Steward Ballyn, who commanded the lifeboat.

"Vot?"

"The *Laconia*, Cunard Line," responded the steward.

"Vot did she veigh?" was the next question from the submarine.

"Eighteen thousand tons."

"Any passengers?"

"Seventy-three," replied Ballyn, "many of them women and children—some of them in this boat. She had over two hundred in the crew."

"Did she carry cargo?"

"Yes."

"Iss der Captain in dot boat?"

"No," Ballyn answered.

"Well, I guess you'll be all right. A patrol will pick you up some time soon." Without further sound save for the almost silent fixing of the conning tower lid, the submarine moved off.

"I thought it best to make my answers sharp and satisfactory, sir," said Ballyn, when he repeated the conversation to me word for word. "I was thinking of the women and children in the boat. I feared every minute that somebody in our boat might make a hostile move, fire a revolver, or throw something at the submarine. I feared the consequence of such an act."

Adapted from Floyd Gibbons, *"And They Thought We Wouldn't Fight"* (New York: George H. Doran Company, 1918).

READING REVIEW

1. How does Gibbons describe the initial reaction of the *Laconia's* passengers?

2. (a) What words in Gibbons's account dramatize the sinking ship? (b) The water below?

3. **Recognizing a Point of View** (a) How would you describe the attitude of the German submarine captain? (b) The steward of the *Laconia?*

★ 9-3 The Home Front: Changes and Traditions ★

Introduction The entry of the United States into World War I brought many changes. Yet as historian David Kennedy points out here, American history and traditions influenced the way the government mobilized the nation in support of the war effort.

Vocabulary Before you read the selection, find the meaning of these words in a dictionary: collusion, ironic, legacy, impress, salutary, perverse, pluralism, homogeneous, fissures, statutory, coercive.

The most lasting and important economic transformation to come out of the war was an organizational one. With the Department of Justice's Anti-Trust Division conveniently napping for the duration,

Many talented artists made posters urging people to support the war effort. This poster encouraged people to grow war gardens and can their own produce.

and under the active prodding of war administrators, there occurred a marked shift toward corporatism* in the nation's business affairs. Entire industries, even entire economic sectors, were organized and disciplined as never before. They were brought into close and regular relations with congressional committees, cabinet departments, and executive agencies. Under Hoover, trade associations modeled on the Farm Bureau Federation and Chamber of Commerce multiplied. And the flood of special-interest legislation in the postwar decade testified to the influence of the war in raising the art of lobbying to new degrees of effectiveness. From the war can be dated the origins of the modern practice of massive informal collusion between government and organized private enterprise.

It is ironic, perhaps, that the origins of this association can be traced to the progressive era, which witnessed such earnest efforts to redefine the relation of public to private. But the war had distorted that process. It left a legacy of institutions and practices—such as the Federal Reserve Board, the income tax system, and the giant lobbies—that showed the influence of the reform circumstances in which they were conceived. They showed, too, the impress of the crisis into which they were born. Under the lash of war, public authority not only proved responsive to private associations but also actively participated in their formation. For the remainder of the century, government in America would be in large measure an affair conducted of, by, and for special-interest groups. World War I neither began nor perfected that system but gave it powerful momentum.

The First World War marked a distinct and formative moment in the history of American society. But economic mobilization also laid bare some timeless features of that society. "The great object of terror and suspicion to the people of the thirteen provinces," Henry Adams once wrote, "was power; not merely power in the hands of a president or a prince, of one assembly or several, of many citizens or few, but power in the abstract, wher-

ever it existed and under whatever form it was known." That fear has run like an electric current through American life. But in the twentieth century that fear of power, so salutary for the founding fathers, has sometimes had perverse effects.

Eighteenth- and nineteenth-century Americans could indulge their dislike of power and their preference for pluralism because they were in the main a comfortably united and generally equal people, resting securely behind the Atlantic Ocean. But as the twentieth century opened, American society was no longer so homogeneous. The major cities were boiling pots of various ethnic ingredients. Industrialism had everywhere opened the ugly fissures of class. Nor could national security any longer be taken for granted or isolation freely enjoyed.

Yet to a striking degree, Wilson and his administrators tried to base American participation in that war on the old principles. They avoided one-sided exercises of government power. They sought the barest minimum of statutory bodies. They divided administrative responsibility. They relied wherever possible on the time-honored principle of contractual agreement. And they affirmed repeatedly the temporary nature of those few naked instruments of authority they were forced to grasp. Because of distance and history, they were largely successful. But the war crisis touched America hard enough that feats of discipline and organization had somehow to be accomplished. Given the deep-grained reluctance to exercise power in a straightforward, coercive way, Wilson and his war managers turned instead to persuasion, propaganda, and the purposeful fueling of patriotic fires. Americans, prizing the weakness of their ancient institutions, strove to substitute aroused passion for political authority.

The war thus showed that voluntarism has its perils. Reliance on sentiment rather than power compounded the problem of requiring all people to do what but few people wished. That kind of coercion had deep roots in liberal democratic culture. It was to become a notable feature of twentieth-century American life.

*Corporatism refers to a society organized around large corporate interests.

Adapted from David M. Kennedy, *Over Here* (New York: Oxford University Press, 1980).

READING REVIEW

1. In Kennedy's view, what was the most important economic change to result from World War I?

2. (a) How had Americans traditionally felt about power? (b) According to Kennedy, how did this attitude affect President Wilson's actions?

3. **Summarizing** Using your own words, explain the main points of this selection.

★ 9-4 How the Americans Helped ★

Introduction Although the United States fought in World War I only for a few months, it's contribution to the outcome was important. One man who observed at first hand the difference American troops made was Alden Brooks, an American newspaperman in Europe at the outbreak of the war. Brooks volunteered for duty with the French army. When the Germans launched their big offensive—the Second Battle of the Marne—he not only fought but also analyzed the part played by fellow Americans.

Vocabulary Before you read the selection, find the meaning of these words in a dictionary: ravines, avalanche, impregnable, husbanding, ultimate, rejuvenated.

During that night and all next day we heaped shells continually on the Marne, its woods and slopes and ravines, concentrating now our whole fire there. All my own insistence was on this point. I had seen, and still saw, those parts too clearly. What was the use of wasting one shell where a German might not be, when it was certain that there must be many Germans over in that valley, crossing and re-crossing. Further, on the morning of the sixteenth, one of our aviators dropped us a map with positions marked of the half-dozen footbridges thrown across the stream. How we profited by the message!

So heavy did our fire continue that at one moment the Colonel wondered if the American batteries would be able to stand the pace set them. And then the ammunition officer brought in the figures of the gigantic total of shells our American guns alone had fired in the last 24 hours. But figures mean nothing at such moments; hundreds or thousands, what difference does it make? The chief matter was that the supply should never fail.

And so our avalanche of steel continued on that Marne Valley. The enemy might dislodge the light artillery, but he could not reach far enough to dislodge us. Our nervous tension relaxed. Also, from the rest of the battlefield, reports were encouraging.

It is common knowledge, now, how the Tenth Army Mangin, composed largely of Americans—namely of the First and Second U.S. Divisions—suddenly advancing, without artillery preparation, behind 300 tanks, broke into the German flank and turned the Marne attack into disaster.

All the Germans this south side of the Marne were in full retreat. In the mind of each of us, here was the turning point of the war—indeed, the beginning of the end.

There were many factors to contribute to the victory of the Second Battle of

One American who fought in the trenches recalled: "The men slept in mud, washed in mud, ate mud, and dreamed mud." These troops of the Thirtieth and Thirty-eighth U.S. Infantry regiments are fighting in France.

the Marne. In the first place, the German attack was known by the Allies in advance down to its least detail. Secondly, in the counterattack from Villers–Cotterets woods, the German surprise was complete. Further, this was made possible by the effective use for the first time of the new weapon of tanks—multitudes of them, advancing straight on their lines without any preliminary artillery preparation. Again there was General Pétain.* It was his intelligence and constant personal supervision that coordinated an impregnable defense.

The attack seems, in any case, to have been a mad undertaking of Ludendorff's† part. With all these American battalions that he knew to be stiffening the Allied forces, surely his only strategy was a calculated retreat to a smaller line of front and a general husbanding of his own forces in the ultimate hope of wearing out the Allies. The chief reason, after all, for the victory of the Marne must lie in the disproportion in quantity and quality of the forces engaged. On one side were the Germans, worn out by four years of ceaseless warfare. On the other side were the

---

*Henri Pétain was the French commander-in-chief.
†Erich Ludendorff was chief of staff to the German high commander.

French, equally worn out it is true, but equally well primed with knowledge given by long years of experience. They were further possessed of the great material aid of tanks. And their ranks were rejuvenated by seven divisions of sturdy young Americans. Whereas German divisions were only a show of force, with companies reduced to 50 and 60 men, American divisions were at full strength and incomparably larger. In short, then, the Second Battle of the Marne was the turning point of the war because there came at last into the fight important forces of American infantry.

Adapted from Alden Brooks, *As I Saw It* (New York: Alfred A. Knopf, 1930).

READING REVIEW

1. (a) What was the author's role in the battle? (b) How do you think it might have affected his observations?
2. How does the author explain the German offensive?
3. **Ranking** (a) List the factors Brooke thinks account for the Allied victory in the Second Battle of the Marne. (b) Rank the factors from most important to least important.

★   9-5   A Black Perspective on Black Soldiers   ★

Introduction Almost 400,000 black Americans served in the United States Army during World War I. Of these, some 50,000 saw overseas duty, mainly as stevedores and other service workers. Those who took part in combat fought in segregated units. Toward the end of the war, Robert Moton, who had succeeded Booker T. Washington as principal of Tuskegee Institute, traveled to France to visit black soldiers. Albon Holsey, Moton's secretary, here describes how Moton spoke to black—and white—troops.

Vocabulary Before you read the selection, find the meaning of these words in a dictionary: privations, tangible, hindrance.

Just what did Dr. Moton say to the Negro troops in his parting address to them? He said, in part: "The record you have made in this war—of faithfulness, bravery, and loyalty—has deepened my faith in you as men and as soldiers, as well as in my race and my country. You have been tremendously tested. You have suffered hardships and privations. You have been called upon to make many sacrifices. Your record has sent a thrill of joy and satisfaction to the hearts of millions of white and black Americans, rich and poor, high and low. Black mothers and wives, sweethearts, fathers, and friends have rejoiced with you and with our country in your record.

"You will go back to America," he said, "as heroes, as you really are. You will go back as you have carried yourselves over here—in a straightforward, manly, and modest way. If I were you, I would find a job as soon as possible, and get to work. To those who have not already done so, I would suggest that you get hold of a piece of land and a home as soon as possible, and marry and settle down. Save your money and put it into something tangible. I hope no one will do anything in peace to spoil the magnificent record your troops have made in war."

What Dr. Moton said in addresses to white officers and soldiers in France was even more significant. The following were the final paragraphs in one of his speeches.

"These black soldiers—officers and men—have, along with you, placed their lives willingly and gladly at the disposal of their country, not only to make the world safe for democracy, but, what is equally important, to make democracy safe for mankind, black and white. You and they go back to America as heroes, brave and modest, of course, but there is a difference; you go back without hindrance, with every opportunity our beloved country offers open to you. You are the heirs of all the ages. God has never given any race more than He has given you.

"The men of my race who return will have many unnecessary hardships and limitations, along many lines. What a wonderful opportunity you have, therefore, and what a great responsibility, if you go back to America resolved that as far as in your power lies, you are going to see that these black men and the 12 million people whom they represent in our country, who have stood so loyally by you and America in peace and in war, shall have a fair and absolutely equal chance with every other American citizen, along every line—this is your duty and sacred obligation. They ask only fair play and, as loyal American citizens, they should have it."

Adapted from *Robert Russa Moton of Hampton and Tuskegee*, ed. William H. Hughes and Frederick D. Patterson (Chapel Hill, N.C.: University of North Carolina Press, 1956).

READING REVIEW

1. What advice did Moton give the black troops?
2. What was the main point of Moton's address to white officers and soldiers?
3. **Comparing** Do you think Moton made the same basic points in the two speeches? Explain.

★ 9-6 Versailles: An Insider's View ★

Introduction One of President Woodrow Wilson's closest advisers was Colonel Edward House, who served as the President's chief deputy at the Versailles peace conference. Like many others, House was disappointed by the results of the negotiations. The Treaty of Versailles seemed to violate the spirit of Wilson's Fourteen Points, especially those concerned with open treaties and self-determination. Not long after Wilson left the presidency, House published his version of the events of the peace conference. A portion is printed here.

Vocabulary Before you read the selection, find the meaning of these words in a dictionary: stimulus, convenants, conducive.

From the American viewpoint and that of the smaller nations—for the outlook and interests of both were much the same—one of the mistakes at Paris was the lack of publicity. If the American purposes could have been known, a moral backing and stimulus would have been given our representatives which was almost wholly lacking. This sustaining force might have come from the entire world, and would have had a double effect inasmuch as it would have weakened the opposition and strengthened us.

We had taken the position of overthrowing the old order and bringing a new and different diplomacy into play. "Open covenants, openly arrived at," was

Topic 9

one of the popular slogans of the day, and it was clearly to our advantage, as well as our obligation, to carry it through. The failure to do this left us in the attitude of reformers working in the dark. Darkness is conducive to secret covenants secretly arrived at, and what we needed for success was light—all the light which could properly be thrown about the subjects proposed and discussed.

It may be entirely proper to have conferences in groups of two or more in which no one but those vitally interested may appear. But when the meetings begin to be official and take on an aspect of final decision, then the public should be given the text of the entire discussion. In this way, and in this way alone, may the public of every country know and fairly assess the motives of each participant and bring to bear, if need be, the power of public opinion.

The outstanding feature of the Paris congress which made it different from other congresses was the creation of the League of Nations. This noble conception was the product of no single brain, but was the consummation of the thoughts and hopes of the forward-looking men of the past and the present. It was the great dream of the centuries which had at last come true.

While the idea was not President Wilson's, yet the power to make it a real and living thing was his. History will give him the credit of using this power to the utmost to create an instrument to make wars less probable.

In fairness to those who opposed the covenant, as it was made in Paris, let it be said that some were frankly against any such adventure on the part of our government. Others believed our interests were not sufficiently safeguarded. And there was yet another group maintaining that there was even a more vital issue involved—that of the right of the Senate to exercise its constitutional functions.

Adapted from Edward M. House and Charles Seymour, *What Really Happened at Paris* (New York: Charles Scribner's Sons, 1921).

READING REVIEW

1. (a) Why was House opposed to "working in the dark"? (b) What force would have been brought to bear if Versailles had been held in the open?

2. Why did some people oppose the covenant made in Paris?

3. **Recognizing the Main Idea** According to House, what did President Wilson contribute to the conference?

★ 9-7 Versailles: A Novelist's View ★

Introduction One of the most ambitious works about the United States during World War I is John Dos Passos's novel *U.S.A.* Scattered throughout the novel are many brief biographies. Although the biographies are of real people—William Jennings Bryan, Henry Ford, and J. P. Morgan, among others—Dos Passos gives them a special slant. This selection is from a biography of "Meester Veelson"—as Woodrow Wilson was called by the French.

Vocabulary Before you read the selection, find the meaning of this word in a dictionary: epaulettes.

January 18, 1919, in the midst of uniforms, cocked hats and gold braid, decorations, epaulettes, orders of merit and knighthood, the High Contracting Parties, the allied and associated powers met in the Salon de l'Horloge to dictate the peace,

but the grand assembly of the peace conference was too public a place to make peace in

so the High Contracting Parties

formed the Council of Ten, went into the Gobelin Room and

began to dictate the peace.

But the Council of Ten was too public a place to make peace in

so they formed the Council of Four.
Orlando went home in a huff
and then there were three:
Clemenceau,
Lloyd George,
Woodrow Wilson.
Three old men shuffling the pack,
dealing out the cards:
the Rhineland, Danzig, the Polish corridor, the Ruhr, self-determination of small nations, the Saar, League of Nations, mandates, the Mespot, Freedom of the Seas, Transjordania, Shantung, Fiume and the Island of Yap.

On June 28th the Treaty of Versailles was ready
and Wilson had to go back home to explain to the politicians who'd been ganging up on him meanwhile in the Senate and House and to sober public opinion and to his father's God how he'd let himself be trimmed and how far he'd made the world safe
for democracy and the New Freedom.
From the day he landed in Hoboken he had his back to the wall of the White House, talking to save his faith in words, talking to save his faith in the League of Nations, talking to save his faith in himself, in his father's God.
He strained every nerve of his body and brain, every agency of the government he had under his control.

In Pueblo, Colorado, he was a grey man hardly able to stand, one side of his face twitching:
Now that the mists of this great question have cleared away, I believe that men will see the Truth, eye for eye and face to face. There is one thing the American People always rise to and extend their hand to, that is, the truth of justice and of liberty and of peace. We have accepted that truth and we are going to be led by it, and it is going to lead us, and through us the world, out into pastures of quietness and peace such as the world never dreamed of before.
That was his last speech;
on the train to Wichita he had a stroke. He gave up the speaking tour that

was to sweep the country for the League of Nations. After that he was a ruined paralysed man barely able to speak;
the day he gave up the presidency to Harding the joint committee of the Senate and House appointed Henry Cabot Lodge, his lifelong enemy, to make the formal call at the executive office in the Capitol and ask the formal question whether the President had any message for the Congress assembled in joint session;
Wilson managed to get to his feet, lifting himself painfully by the two arms of the chair. "Senator Lodge, I have no further communication to make, thank you. . . . Good morning," he said.
In 1924 on February 3rd he died.

Adapted from John Dos Passos, *U.S.A.* (New York: Modern Library, Random House, 1930).

READING REVIEW

1. How does Dos Passos describe Clemenceau, Lloyd George, and Wilson in their meetings?
2. What does he mean when he talks about them dealing out the cards?
3. **Analyzing Conflicting Sources** (a) How does Dos Passos's description of openness at Versailles differ from House's in Reading 9-6? (b) How might you explain the difference?

The peace treaty that ended World War I was signed in the Hall of Mirrors in the Palace of Versailles outside Paris. President Wilson is shown holding a copy of the treaty.

Introduction The creation of the League of Nations was one of the most important parts of the Versailles Treaty to President Wilson. He thought such a league would help prevent future wars because it would be a forum for discussion between nations. Some Americans, however, opposed the League of Nations. Senator Henry Cabot Lodge, for example, thought the league threatened the independence of the United States. The debate over ratification of the Treaty of Versailles often hinged on the question of the league, as this cartoon shows.

Interrupting the Ceremony

READING REVIEW

1. What figure in the cartoon represents the United States? (b) What does the bride represent?

2. (a) What does the figure jumping through the window represent? (b) What is he trying to do?

3. **Analyzing Cartoons** (a) Do you think the cartoonist favored the League of Nations? (b) What evidence in the cartoon leads you to that conclusion?

Part Two 206

Theme 3

The Roaring Twenties

Topic

10 A Search for Peace and Prosperity (1919–1928)

★ 10-1 The Red Scare ★

Introduction In 1919, after an exhausting trip across the country to promote the League of Nations, President Wilson suffered a stroke that paralyzed him. During the following year, much of the work of the presidency was carried on by the cabinet. In particular, the attorney general, Mitchell A. Palmer, took action against what he considered to be a growing communist threat against the republic. This selection from a history done by *American Heritage* describes public feelings at the time.

Vocabulary Before you read the selection, find the meaning of these words in a dictionary: demobilized, pittance, anarchism, espionage, phantom, perpetual, rebuked, aplomb.

In 1919, as the President lay isolated in the White House and great armies demobilized, Americans stirred uneasily to reports of Red revolts sweeping across Europe. Concern grew as tens of thousands of coal miners and steelworkers, toiling more than 60 hours a week for a pittance—and all infected, so rumor had

it, by Bolshevism and anarchism—went out on strike by the end of the year. As crises and rumors mounted, the nation was on the verge of panic.

It had been in a state of alarm for three years. The wartime assistant to the Attorney General in espionage cases related some of the fantastic stories current during the war: "A phantom ship sailed into our harbors with gold from the Bolsheviks with which to corrupt the country. Another phantom ship was found carrying ammunition from one of our harbors to Germany. Submarine captains landed on our coasts, went to the theater and spread influenza germs. A new species of pigeon, thought to be German, was shot in Michigan."

The armistice did nothing at first to calm the country. Instead, the heightened tension resulted in an ugly rash of race riots. In Washington, D.C., federal troops were called out and 6 persons died. In Chicago, 38 persons died in a week-long riot. In New York, in Omaha, and in a number of parts of the rural South, riots also took place.

Fifteen states in 1919 declared it a criminal offense to teach in any language but English, not merely in public schools but in private schools as well. On November 11, 1919, the first anniversary of the armistice, a disorderly crowd in Centralia, Washington, celebrated victory and saved America by seizing an organizer for the Wobblies, the radical Industrial Workers of the World. They dragged him out of jail, tied a rope around his neck, and flung him from a bridge. That year, too, fourteen states passed antistrike legislation.

To some, the deep fabric of America seemed threatened when steelworkers and coalworkers struck. Worst of all, that autumn the very forces of the law, the Boston police, struck too, and hoodlums looted the city while citizen volunteers tried to restore order.

The witch hunt went on. Five Socialist members of the New York State legislature were expelled on the ground that they represented a "disloyal organization composed exclusively of perpetual traitors." When Theodore Roosevelt's son denounced the action, the Speaker rebuked him harshly, comparing his patriotism unfavorably with that of his father.

Palmer fanned the flames. "By stealing, murder, and lies, Bolshevism has looted Russia not only of its material strength, but of its moral force," he warned the country. The same fact threatened America. Information "showed that communism in this country was an organization of thousands of aliens," "direct allies of Trotzky," "aliens of the same misshapen caste of mind and indecencies

of character." There were, he asserted, 60,000 communists at large—enough, if unchecked, to bring the republic down. They planned to launch an attack on May Day, 1920. The police mobilized, the National Guard stood ready. Yet May Day came and went without incident.

What a decent regard for evidence and the guarantees of constitutional liberty could not accomplish, boredom and a sense of the ridiculous did. The mood of the country began to lift. Palmer was through. When in the fall what appears to have been a genuine anarchist bomb plot did materialize—a huge explosion at the junction of Broad and Wall streets, killing 30 and wounding hundreds more—the country absorbed the news with surprising aplomb.

But it would be many years before the fever entirely ran its course. In 1921 America turned its back on the longstanding rule of opening the doors to the wretched of the earth. It passed laws designed to preserve the Anglo-Saxon nature of the American Population.

Adapted from *The American Heritage History of the 20s and 30s*, by the editors of *American Heritage, The Magazine of History* (New York: Charles Scribner's Sons, 1970).

READING REVIEW

1. What "fantastic stories" helped fuel the flames of anti-Red hysteria?

2. What actual events had taken place to cause alarm?

3. **Relating Past to Present** Do you think attitudes such as those in 1919 could prevail today? Why or why not?

★ 10-2 Vanzetti Addresses the Court ★

Introduction In the early 1920s violence committed by radicals struck terror into many American hearts. However, when Nicola Sacco and Bartolomeo Vanzetti, two anarchists, were convicted of robbery and murder, many people remained unconvinced of their guilt. Sacco and Vanzetti maintained their innocence. Vanzetti gave this speech in the form of a poem to the court. It is included in poetry anthologies as an example of eloquence possible without a knowledge of correct English.

Vocabulary Before you read the selection, find the meaning of these words in a dictionary: verge, mundane, dispersed.

I have talk a great deal of myself
but I even forgot to name Sacco.
Sacco too is a worker,
from his boyhood a skilled worker, lover
    of work,
with a good job and pay,
a bank account, a good and lovely wife,
two beautiful children and a neat little
    home
at the verge of a wood, near a brook.

Sacco is a heart, a faith, a character, a
    man;
a man, lover of nature, and mankind;
a man who gave all, who sacrifice all
to the cause of liberty and to his love for
    mankind:
money, rest, mundane ambition,
his own wife, his children, himself
and his own life.

Sacco has never dreamt to steal, never to
    assassinate.
He and I have never brought a morsel
of bread to our mouths, from our child-
    hood to today
which has not been gained by the sweat of
    our brows.
Never.

Oh, yes, I may be more witful, as some
    have put it;
I am a better babbler than he is, but
    many, many times
in hearing his heartful voice ringing a
    faith sublime,
in considering his supreme sacrifice, re-
    membering his heroism,
I felt small at the presence of his great-
    ness
and found myself compelled to fight back
from my eyes the tears,
and quanch my heart
trobling to my throat to not weep before
    him:
this man called thief and assassin and
    doomed.

But Sacco's name will live in the hearts of
    the people
and in their gratitude when Katzmann's
    bones
and yours will be dispersed by time;
when your name, his name, your laws, in-
    stitutions,

*The conviction of Nicola Sacco (left) and
Bartolomeo Vanzetti (right) created great
controversy. Many people worldwide believed in
their innocence.*

and your false god are but a dim re-
    memoring
of a cursed past in which man was wolf
to the man.

If it had not been for these thing
I might have lived out my life
talking at street corners to scorning men.
I might have die, unmarked, unknown, a
    failure.
Now we are not a failure.
This is our career and our triumph. Never
in our full life could we hope to do such
    work
for tolerance, for justice, for man's under-
    standing
of man, as now we do by accident.

Our words, our lives, our pains—nothing!
The taking of our lives—lives of a good
    shoemaker and a poor fishpeddler—.
all! That last moment belongs to us—
that agony is our triumph.

Adapted from *A New Anthology of Modern Poetry*, ed. Sel-
den Rodman (New York: Random House, 1938).

READING REVIEW

1. (a) What is Vanzetti's opinion of Sacco?
    (b) How can you tell?
2. What does Vanzetti probably mean
    when he speaks of "our triumph"?
3. **Defending a Position** Is Vanzetti's
    speech an effective defense of their in-
    nocence? Why or why not?

Introduction Born in Mississippi, Richard Wright was a black author who gained fame describing black life in the South and in northern urban slums. He was one of many blacks who migrated north to the cities during the 1920s. Unable to accept the traditional role of blacks at the time, his anger at discrimination led him to express his views in several vivid novels. Among them was *Black Boy*, the autobiographical novel from which this selection was taken. In it Wright describes how he left his home to seek a new future.

Vocabulary Before you read the selection, find the meaning of these words in a dictionary: exasperatingly, pondered, transgressions, appropriate, futile.

Out of my salary I had begun to save a few dollars, for my determination to leave had not lessened. But I found the saving exasperatingly slow. I pondered continuously ways of making money, and the only ways that I could think of involved transgressions of the law. No, I must not do that, I told myself. To go to jail would mean the end. And there was the possibility that if I were ever caught I would never reach jail.

This was the first time in my life that I had ever consciously entertained the idea of violating the laws of the land. I had felt that my intelligence and industry could cope with all situations, and, until that time, I had never stolen a penny from anyone. Even hunger had never driven me to appropriate what was not my own. The mere idea of stealing had been repugnant. I had not been honest from deliberate motives, but being dishonest had simply never occurred to me.

My objections to stealing were not moral. I did not approve of it because I knew that, in the long run, it was futile, that it was not an effective way to alter one's relationship to one's environment. Then, how could I change my relationship to my environment? Almost my entire salary went to feed the eternally hungry stomachs at home. If I saved a dollar a week, it would take me two years to amass a hundred dollars, the amount which for some reason I had decided was necessary to stake me in a strange city.

If I stole, I would have a chance to head northward quickly. If I remained barely honest, piddling with pints of bootleg liquor, I merely prolonged my stay, increased my chances of being caught, exposed myself to the possibility of saying the wrong word or doing the wrong thing and paying a penalty that I dared not think of.

I had learned to master a great deal of tension now; I had developed, slowly and painfully, a capacity to contain it within myself without betraying it in any way. Had this not been true, the mere thought of stealing, the risks involved, the inner distress would have so upset me that I would have been in no state of mind to calculate coldly, would have made me so panicky that I would have been afraid to steal at all. But my inner resistance had been blasted. I felt that I had been emotionally cast out of the world, had been made to live outside the normal processes of life, had been conditioned in feeling against something daily, had become accustomed to living on the side of those who watched and waited.

I went through another week. Late one night I resolved to make that week the last. The cans of fruit preserves in the storehouse of the college came to my mind. If I stole them and sold them, I would have enough to tide me over in Memphis until I could get a job, work, save, and go north.

The following night I rounded up two boys whom I knew to be ready for adventure. We broke into the college storehouse and lugged out cans of fruit preserves and sold them to restaurants.

Meanwhile I brought clothes, shoes, a cardboard suitcase, all of which I hid at home. Saturday night came. Uncle Tom was upstairs, Granny and Aunt Addie were at church. My brother was sleeping. My mother sat in her rocking chair, humming to herself. I packed my suitcase and went to her.

"Mama, I'm going away," I whispered.

"Oh, no," she protested.

During the 1920s black Americans left the South in large numbers seeking better jobs in the North and freedom from Jim Crow laws. This painting by black artist Jacob Lawrence shows crowds in a railroad station waiting for trains to northern cities.

"I've got to, mama. I can't live this way."

"You're not running away from something you've done?"

"I'll send for you, mama. I'll be all right."

"Take care of yourself. And send for me quickly. I'm not happy here," she said.

"I'm sorry for all these long years, mama. But I could not have helped it."

I kissed her and she cried.

"Be quiet, mama. I'm all right."

I went out the back way and walked a quarter of a mile to the railroad tracks. It began to rain as I tramped down the crossties toward town. I reached the station soaked to the skin.

An hour later I was sitting in a Jim Crow coach, speeding northward, making the first lap of my journey to a land where I could live with a little less fear. Slowly the burden I had carried for many months lifted somewhat. My cheeks itched and when I scratched them I found tears. In that moment I understood the pain that accompanies crime and I hoped that I would never have to feel it again. I never did feel it again, for I never stole again. What kept me from it was the knowledge that, for me, crime carried its own punishment.

Adapted and abridged pages 174–181 from *Black Boy: A Record of Childhood and Youth*, by Richard Wright. Copyright © 1937, 1942, 1944, 1945 by Richard Wright. Reprinted by permission of Harper & Row, Publishers, Inc.

READING REVIEW

1. How did Wright think he should be able to get the money to move north?

2. Why does he say he felt he had to resort to stealing?

3. **Drawing Conclusions** (a) What punishment does Wright refer to in the last sentence? (b) Why do you think that punishment was enough to stop him from committing a crime again?

★ 10-4 Harding Creates an Image ★

Introduction President Warren G. Harding made some good appointments, such as that of Judge Charles Evans Hughes to the position of Secretary of State, but his administration was known for its corruption. History had judged him as an honest man who was far too agreeable toward conniving cronies. This selection by Evelyn Walsh MacLean, one of Harding's closest friends, provides an inside view of how Harding modified his "image" to fit the views of voters in the election of 1920.

Vocabulary Before you read the selection, find the meaning of these words in a dictionary: compromising, chided, circumspect, infuriate, grimaced, myriads, convolutions.

It was the stage of the 1920 campaign when the Republican candidate was leaving his front porch from time to time to make speeches. He spoke from the rear platform of his train and in auditoriums before vast gatherings of cheering people whom he addressed as his "fellow countrymen." Ned and I were with the Hardings for a while and found out that the Hardings we had known as poker-playing friends were quite unchanged. However, out-of-doors or any place where others might observe us, Mrs. Harding was clutched by a set of the strangest fears that I ever encountered. And so, to a less degree, was her husband.

I stood beside her one day as photographers prepared to take our picture in a group with several others. I was engaged at the time in what for 30 years or more has been one of the least compromising of my habits—I was smoking a cigarette. Suddenly, aware of its smoke, she whirled on me and snatched the cigarette from my lips. She was as much concerned as if its tip had been hovering over a powder barrel.

"Evelyn," she chided me a little later, "you've got to help us by being circumspect. The Lord knows I don't mind your cigarettes, or jewels. You know how much I think of you; but you must give a thought to what we now are doing."

"But the senator smokes cigarettes," I said.

"Not when he is having his picture taken," said Mrs. Harding grimly. "Just let me catch him light a cigarette when any hostile eye might see him! He can't play cards until the campaign is over, either."

"But does he smoke tobacco?"

"A pipe, cigars, yes; but a cigarette is something that seems to infuriate swarms of voters who have a prejudice against cigarettes. He can chew tobacco, though." When she added that bit of information Mrs. Harding grimaced with a twinkle in her cornflower-blue eyes.

I learned that golf was something else that seemed to upset the stomachs of great masses of the voters, of factory laborers, of farmers, and of others who dwelt by myriads in those states where the campaign would be won or lost. Altogether the candidate had to shape himself, or seem to, just to fit the convolutions of the voters' minds.

I began to understand how sincere Warren Harding had been when he told us one time when we played poker that he really did not want to run for President.

"I'm satisfied with being senator," he said. "I'd like to go on living here in Washington and continue to be a member of the world's most exclusive club. I'm sure I can have six years more; I may have twelve or eighteen. If I have to go on and live in the White House I won't be able to call my soul my own. I don't want to be spied on every minute of the day and night. I don't want secret-service men trailing after me." He meant it, and it is my conviction that his wife meant it, too, when she said she preferred that they should be to the end of their days Senator and Mrs. Harding. The one who nagged and coaxed him to change their course was Harry M. Daugherty.

The constant praise of people was beginning to have an effect on Senator Harding. He was more and more inclined to believe in himself. He cherished an idea that when a man was elevated to the presidency his wits by some automatic mental chemistry were increased to fit the stature of his office. We, his friends, could see him, during that vacation, as a young Aladdin testing experimentally the terrific power of the mighty engine called the presidency.

"Hey, Ed," we would hear him call in a loud tone, as a king in olden times called for a jester. He really loved Ed Scobey, and it was fun for Harding to be able to announce to him that he should become the Director of the Mint and to know that what he promised would, by reason of his great power, come to pass.

Ned, before long, was to learn that he had been made chairman of the inaugural committee, which would have full charge of all arrangements for the celebration in connection with the ceremony whereby Woodrow Wilson would give up power and Warren Harding take it. A few other acts of powered graciousness were revealed to us on that trip, or just a few weeks later, as, one by one, all of Harding's well-liked friends received some kind of title. Dick Crissinger, for example, had been Harding's playmate when they were barefoot country boys. He grew up to be a Democrat of consequence in Marion, but it was his old pal Harding who made him governor of the Federal Reserve Board.

These were not bad appointments; as good, no doubt, as needed for the jobs. But it seems significant to me, now, that they were made as they were—because Warren Harding had received the presidency by chance, without having expected until late in life that he had even a chance to win the office. The office of President was hardly a subject that he had studied. I think it was a thing he had merely dreamed about, as we all dream when we wish we had power to fix everything. It is my opinion that Warren Harding, if he could have looked ahead when he was young and seen a vision of the time when he would be selected to go and live in the White House, would have lived quite differently. As it happened, he was a loyal friend who was, unhappily, loyal sometimes to the wrong people.

Adapted from Evelyn Walsh MacLean with Boyden Sparks, *Father Struck It Rich* (Boston: Little, Brown & Co., 1936).

READING REVIEW

1. Which of Harding's habits did Mrs. Harding think should be concealed from the voters?
2. How does MacLean describe Harding's attitude toward the presidency?
3. **Expressing an Opinion** Do you agree with MacLean that Harding was, "unhappily, loyal sometimes to the wrong people"? Explain.

★ 10-5 Will Rogers Gives His Opinions ★

Introduction Will Rogers became a famous figure in the 1920s by making homespun comments about the political scene. While chewing gum and twirling a lariat on stage, ex-cowboy Rogers gently needled the powerful. Part Oklahoma Cherokee, and proud of it, he charmed the public with clever remarks made in an easygoing drawl. During his career he appeared in silent movies and on radio and wrote a daily column published in nearly 400 newspapers. These are some of his comments on the Coolidge years.

Vocabulary Before you read the selection, find the meaning of these words in a dictionary: unique, monotonous, commissions.

I have been in many a country, and they have thousands of problems. But America's problem as to "where to invest my money?" is unique. The whole world would give their right leg to be bothered with that problem.

We are a people that get tired of a thing awful quick and I believe this continual prosperity will begin to get monotonous with us. We can't go through life just eating cake all the time. Of course, we like prosperity, but we are having so much of it that we just can't afford it.

No nation in the history of the world was ever sitting as pretty. If we want anything, all we have to do is go and buy it on credit. So that leaves us without any economic problems whatsoever, except perhaps some day to have to pay for them.

We'll show the world we are prosperous, even if we have to go broke to do it.

We will never get anywhere with our finances till we pass a law saying that every time we appropriate something we got to pass another bill along with it stating where the money is coming from.

I thought I was going to have some farm relief to report to you by this day. But the commissions are just gathering data. They won't take the farmer's word for it that he is poor. They hire men to find out how poor he is. If they took all the money they spend on finding out how poor he is and give it to the farmer he wouldn't need any more relief.

President Coolidge kept his mouth shut. That was such a novelty among politicians that it just swept the country. Originality will be rewarded in any line.

Here comes Coolidge and does nothing and retires a hero, not only because he hadn't done anything, but because he had done it better than anyone.

Adapted from *Will Rogers* by the Will Rogers Company (Claremore, Okla.: Hallmark Editions, 1969).

READING REVIEW

1. According to Rogers, what was America's unique problem?
2. What is his opinion about credit?
3. **Relating Past to Present** (a) Do any humorists today call attention to American behavior and politicians? (b) What purpose does this type of humor serve?

John Stuart Curry painted this mural of popular American entertainers. Will Rogers appears at right.

Topic 11 Life in the 1920s (1920–1929)

★ 11-1 An Experiment in Productivity ★

Introduction Most Americans benefited from the more efficient, greatly increased production of the 1920s. For many workers scientific advances in industry and medicine meant easier labor and less disease. Yet it soon became apparent that industrial progress was producing side effects few people had expected. In the effort to achieve the greatest possible efficiency, many factory managers forgot that workers were not machines. This selection describes a famous experiment in worker efficiency.

Vocabulary Before you read the selection, find the meaning of these words in a dictionary: congestion, ominous, anonymous, productivity, cohesive, banal, manifestations, acquisitiveness.

White-collar workers were the fastest-growing part of the population, for as the factories reared blackly on the skyline and the cities spread out to pave over the farms, the world was swamped with paperwork. But this new middle class, raised with puritanical values of self-dependence, was swallowed up within huge organizations. The man who rose to the top in business was still admired. But the business he rose to the top of was viewed with suspicion.

The factories themselves were distasteful. They created noise, dirt, and population congestion. There was hardly a factory that was not an eyesore. And nearly every factory turned the streets around it into a slum. Factories fouled the air and poisoned the rivers. They displaced fields and turned men into cogs. More ominous still, the factory system—anonymous, ruthless, competitive—was becoming the model for modern society itself.

Middle-aged factory workers knew only too well how things were changing. In the late nineteenth-century factory it was easy for the boss and the workers to establish a personal relationship with one another. When visitors came to the plant they met the men. But as one worker bitterly complained in 1928, these days the men were ignored. Visitors were taken to admire the new machinery. The new work disciplines imposed by the machines could strip men of their humanity. There were presses that punched sheet steel. All that the worker had to do was to insert the steel before the press descended and withdraw his hands quickly. But some men became fatigued, or surrendered to the numbness or monotony, or were simply careless. The machines cut off their hands.

The solution that managers hit on was to handcuff the worker's hands to a lever, which pulled them away as the press came down. "Go to the press rooms today and you will see lines of workers standing before their presses," wrote one visitor, "their hands jerking away each time the presses move. The individual workers do not control the movement of the presses, which are started and stopped by the foreman. Even though they may be out of material, they have to stand before the press, their hands jerking back and forth. There they work, chained to their machines, as galley slaves were chained to their oars."

To get the most out of the machinery that they were so eagerly arranging along the factory floor, managers had to turn the wheel full circle. They had to rediscover the humanity of workers. In 1927 Elton Mayo and his colleagues at the Harvard Business School were hired to study working conditions at the Western Electric Company in Hawthorne, Illinois, where telephones were made. Mayo's team introduced rest breaks, provided free refreshments, and shortened the work day. Worker productivity rose almost at once.

The rest breaks, the free refreshments, and the shorter day were all abruptly withdrawn. Productivity continued to rise! What Mayo had hit on was what might be called the experimentation effect. By taking a personal interest in these workers, Mayo's team had formed them into a cohesive unit in which self-respect and job satisfaction were high. That cohesion continued even after the old work routines were reestablished, because the experiment was still going on. The workers still felt that management was interested in them. Happy workers turned out more than unhappy workers. An obvious lesson, perhaps, but now it had been proved by scientific methods.

What made Western Electric ideal for this experiment was that the company seemed almost faultless by the standards of the time. It offered good wages, a company hospital, paid vacations, a subsidized cafeteria, and a pension plan. The Hawthorne findings would have been banal to the point of uselessness in the case of a bad employer. What Mayo had done was to show how far even the best employer needed to go to create a genuinely happy, highly productive work force.

Mayo's research remains a landmark in American industrial psychology, the starting point of a thousand personnel programs. Yet, he unearthed something that went far beyond the factory walls. Rapid industrialization was disrupting social organization, and one of the manifestations of that disorganization was acquisitiveness. It was not so much greed that was making society sick as a sick society making people greedy. After all, what else was there to justify their work, once they were stripped of their pride in their strength or skill, except money?

Adapted from Geoffrey Perret, *America in the Twenties* (New York: Simon & Schuster, 1982). Copyright © 1982 by Geoffrey Perret. Reprinted by permission of Simon & Schuster, Inc.

READING REVIEW

1. According to Perrett, what were the usual working conditions in the 1920s?
2. Why was the choice of Western Electric ideal for the experiment?
3. **Summarizing** What conclusions did the experimenters reach?

Topic 11

Introduction During the 1920s the automobile helped change the way Americans lived. At a cost of less than $300, Americans rushed to buy new cars. With a car they could visit friends, drive to work, or escape into the countryside. This advertisement shown at right appeared in *Life* magazine.

READING REVIEW
1. What features of the car does the advertisement emphasize?
2. What people does the advertisement try to appeal to?
3. **Using Visual Evidence** (a) Based on the picture, how would you describe people's attitude toward the automobile in the 1920s? (b) How does that attitude compare to the attitude of people today?

Confidence

Wonderful driving simplicity of the Baker and Rauch & Lang Electric inspires utmost confidence on the part of the occupants at all times.

The mother finds comfort in knowing that the safety and pleasure of her little ones are enhanced because of this driving simplicity—this independence from mechanical obtrusion and confusion.

And in full keeping with this is the rich coach work—genuine coach work—the best that can come of over sixty years' leadership in fashionable coach building.

Confidence all 'round—in the knowledge that your Baker and Rauch & Lang represents the best, and that it insures the utmost in safety.

Baker Electrics

The Baker R. & L. Company
Cleveland, Ohio
See our latest models at the New York Show, Dec. 31—Jan. 8

Rauch Lang Electric

Introduction During the Harlem Renaissance, jazz and poetry flourished. Black poets expressed both universal feelings and folklore unique to their people. Poet James Weldon Johnson was a leader of this cultural reawakening. During his many-sided life he was a lawyer at the Florida bar, a public school principal, a diplomat, and the executive secretary of the NAACP. In addition to many volumes of poetry, which included "O Black and Unknown Bards," Johnson wrote the lyrics for several musical shows and served as Professor of Creative Literature at Fisk University.

Georgia Douglas Johnson (no relation) was born in Atlanta, Georgia. After studying at Oberlin Conservatory to become a composer, she later turned to school teaching and then to writing poetry. The poem "Common Dust" is from one of her many volumes of published verse.

Vocabulary Before you read the selections, find the meaning of these words in a dictionary: bards, minstrel, lyre, clod, subtle, elusive, valorous, degraded, servile, paean, empyrean, chromatique.

Part Two   216

O BLACK AND UNKNOWN BARDS
James Weldon Johnson

O black and unknown bards of long ago,
How came your lips to touch the sacred fire?
How, in your darkness, did you come to know
The power and beauty of the minstrel's lyre?
Who first from midst his bonds lifted his eyes?
Who first from out the still watch, lone and long,
Feeling the ancient faith of prophets rise
Within his dark-kept soul, burst into song?

Heart of what slave poured out such melody
As "Steal away to Jesus"? On its strains
His spirit must have nightly floated free,
Though still about his hands he felt his chains.
Who heard great "Jordan roll"? Whose starward eye
Saw chariot "swing low"? And who was he
That breathed that comforting, melodic sigh,
"Nobody know the trouble I see"?

What merely living clod, what captive thing,
Could up toward God through all its darkness grope,
And find within its deadened heart to sing
These songs of sorrow, love and faith, and hope?
How did it catch that subtle undertone,
That note in music heard not with the ears?
How sound the elusive reed so seldom blown,
Which stirs the soul or melts the heart to tears?

Not that great German master in his dream
Of harmonies that thundered amongst the stars
At the creation, ever heard a theme
Nobler than "Go down, Moses." Mark its bars,
How like a mighty trumpet-call they stir
The blood. Such are the notes that men have sung
Going to valorous deeds; such tones there were
That helped make history when Time was young.

There is a wide, wide wonder in it all,
That from degraded rest and servile toil
The fiery spirit of the seer should call
These simple children of the sun and soil.
O black slave singers, gone, forgot, unfamed,
You—you alone, of all the long, long line
Of those who've sung untaught, unknown, unnamed,
Have stretched out upward, seeking the divine.

You sang not deeds of heroes or of kings;
No chant of bloody war, no exulting paean
Of arms-won triumphs; but your humble strings
You touched in chord with music empyrean.
You sang far better than you knew; the songs
That for your listeners' hungry hearts sufficed
Still live—but more than this to you belongs:
You sang a race from wood and stone to Christ.

From *St. Peter Relates an Incident* by James Weldon Johnson. Copyright 1935
by James Weldon Johnson. Copyright renewed © 1963 by Grace Nail Johnson.
Reprinted by permission of Viking Penguin Inc.

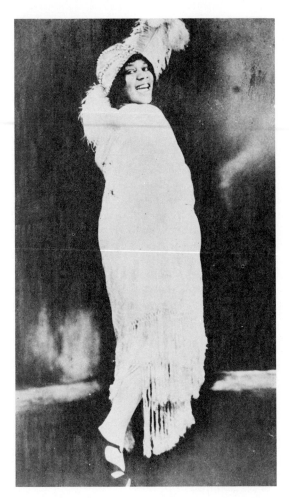

The Harlem Renaissance produced composers and entertainers as well as poets and writers. Bessie Smith was one of the most popular jazz singers of the 1920s.

COMMON DUST
Georgia Douglas Johnson

And who shall separate the dust
Which later we shall be:
Whose keen discerning eye will scan
And solve the mystery?

The high, the low, the rich, the poor,
The black, the white, the red,
And all the chromatique between,
Of whom shall it be said:

Here lies the dust of Africa;
Here are the sons of Rome;
Here lies one unlabeled
The world at large his home!

Can one then separate the dust,
Will mankind lie apart,
When life has settled back again
The same as from the start?

From *3000 Years of Black Poetry*, ed. Alan Lomax and Raoul Abdual (New York: Dodd, Mead & Co., 1970).

READING REVIEW

1. To what "wide, wide wonder" is James Weldon Johnson referring?
2. In James Weldon Johnson's poem, to whom are the bards singing?
3. **Analyzing a Poem as a Primary Source** (a) What aspects of black experience are described in the first poem? (b) What is the basic point of the second poem?

★ **11-4   Lindbergh Conquers the Atlantic** ★

Introduction   The conquest of the air and space has provided America with many heroes. Yet today the country as a whole seems to take the mastery of space for granted. It is difficult, therefore, to imagine the nation's wild joy following Charles A. Lindbergh's first flight across the Atlantic in 1927. In this selection, Lindbergh reveals the matter-of-fact bravery that impressed the world.

Vocabulary   Before you read the selection, find the meaning of these words in a dictionary: throttled, beacons.

I returned to the field before daybreak on the morning of the twentieth. A light rain was falling which continued until almost dawn; consequently the takeoff was delayed from daybreak until nearly eight o'clock. About 7:40 A.M. the motor was started and at 7:52 I took off on the flight for Paris.

The field was a little soft due to the rain during the night and the heavily loaded plane gathered speed very slowly. After passing the halfway mark, however, it was apparent that I would be able to clear the obstructions at the end. I passed over a tractor by about 15 feet and a telephone line by about 20, with a fair reserve of flying speed. I believe that the ship would have taken off from a hard field with at least 500 pounds more weight.

I turned slightly to the right to avoid some high trees on a hill directly ahead, but by the time I had gone a few hundred yards I had sufficient altitude to clear all obstructions and throttled the engine down to 1750 rpm. I took up a compass course at once and soon reached Long Island Sound where the Curtiss Oriole with its photographer, which had been escorting me, turned back.

The haze soon cleared and from Cape Cod through the southern half of Nova Scotia the weather and visibility were excellent. I was flying very low, sometimes as close as 10 feet from the trees and water.

Darkness set in about 8:15, and a thin, low fog formed over the sea through which the white bergs showed up with surprising clearness. This fog became thicker and increased in height until within two hours I was just skimming the top of storm clouds at about 10,000 feet. Even at this altitude there was a thick haze through which only the stars directly overhead could be seen.

There was no moon and it was very dark. The tops of some of the storm clouds were several thousand feet above me and at one time, when I attempted to fly through one of the larger clouds, sleet started to collect on the plane and I was forced to turn around and get back into clear air immediately and then fly around any clouds which I could not get over.

The moon appeared on the horizon after about two hours of darkness; then the flying was much less complicated.

Dawn came at about 1:00 A.M., New York time, and the temperature had risen until there was practically no remaining danger of sleet.

Shortly after sunrise the clouds became more broken, although some of them were far above me and it was often necessary to fly through them, navigating by instruments only.

As the sun became higher, holes appeared in the fog. Through one the open water was visible, and I dropped down until less than 100 feet above the waves.

There is a cushion of air close to the ground or water through which a plane flies with less effort than when at a higher altitude, and for hours at a time I took advantage of this factor.

Also it was less difficult to determine the wind drift near the water. During the entire flight the wind was strong enough to produce white caps on the waves. When one of these formed, the foam would be blown off, showing the wind's direction and approximate velocity. This foam remained on the water long enough for me to obtain a general idea of my drift.

The first indication of my approach to the European coast was a small fishing boat which I first noticed a few miles ahead and slightly to the south of my course. There were several of these fishing boats grouped within a few miles of each other.

I flew over the first boat without seeing any signs of life. As I circled over the second, however, a man's face appeared, looking out of the cabin window.

Less than an hour later a rugged and semimountainous coastline appeared to the northeast. I was flying less than 200 feet from the water when I sighted it. I had very little doubt that it was the southwestern end of Ireland.

In a little over two hours the coast of England appeared. My course passed over southern England and a little south of Plymouth; then across the English Channel, striking France over Cherbourg.

The sun went down shortly after passing Cherbourg and soon the beacons along the Paris–London airway became visible.

I first saw the lights of Paris a little before 10:00 P.M., or 5:00 P.M., New York time, and a few minutes later I was circling the Eiffel Tower at an altitude of about 4,000 feet.

The lights of Le Bourget were plainly visible, but appeared to be very close to Paris. I had understood that the field was farther from the city, so continued out to the northeast into the country for four or five miles to make sure that there was not another field farther out which might be Le Bourget. Then I returned and spiraled down closer to the lights. Presently I could make out long lines of hangars, and the roads appeared to be jammed with cars.

I flew low over the field once, then circled around into the wind and landed.

Adapted from Charles A. Lindbergh, *We* (New York: G.P. Putnam's Sons, 1927).

READING REVIEW

1. What were the field and weather conditions when Lindbergh took off?
2. Why did Lindbergh fly close to the water?
3. **Analyzing a Primary Source** Why is Lindbergh's account an important source?

★ 11-5 One View of Small-Town America ★

Introduction In his novel *Main Street* Sinclair Lewis describes a small midwestern town, Gopher Prairie, in the 1920s. The heroine of the story, Carol Kennicott, has a very negative view of the town. Through Kennicott, Lewis describes the feelings of the "new" woman who wanted to enter the world of work outside the home. Later in the novel, Kennicott comes to appreciate the small-town values of loyalty and helpfulness. But in this selection she is still rebelling against Gopher Prairie.

Vocabulary Before your read the selection, find the meaning of these words in a dictionary: drawl, vaudeville, facetious, silos, chaste, agility, rusticity, sluggishness, negation, canonized, savorless, inane.

In reading popular stories and seeing plays, asserted Carol, she had found only two traditions of the American small town. The first tradition, repeated in scores of magazines every month, is that the American village remains the one sure abode of friendship, honesty, and clean sweet marriageable girls. Therefore all men who succeed in painting in Paris or in finance in New York at last become weary of smart women, return to their native towns, assert that cities are vicious, marry their childhood sweethearts and, presumably, joyously abide in those towns until death.

The other tradition is that the significant features of all villages are whiskers, iron dogs upon lawns, gold bricks, checkers, jars of gilded cat-tails, and shrewd comic old men who are known as "hicks" and who drawl "Waal I swan." This altogether admirable tradition rules the

vaudeville stage, facetious illustrators, and syndicated newspaper humor, but out of actual life it passed forty years ago. Carol's small town thinks not in hoss-swapping but in cheap motor cars, telephones, ready-made clothes, silos, alfalfa,

Novelist Sinclair Lewis criticized so many aspects of American society that Vanity Fair *magazine showed him grasping the American eagle by the neck.*

Part Two

220

Kodaks, phonographs, leather-upholstered Morris chairs, bridge prizes, oil stocks, motion pictures, land deals, unread sets of Mark Twain, and a chaste version of national politics.

With such a small-town life a Kennicott or a Champ Perry is content, but there are also hundreds of thousands, particularly women and young men, who are not at all content. The more intelligent young people (and the fortunate widows!) flee to the cities with agility and, despite the fictional tradition, resolutely stay there, seldom returning even for holidays. The most protesting patriots of the towns leave them in old age, if they can afford it, and go to live in California or in the cities.

The reason, Carol insisted, is not a whiskered rusticity. It is nothing so amusing!

It is an unimaginatively standardized background, a sluggishness of speech and manner, a rigid ruling of the spirit by the desire to appear respectable. It is contentment, the contentment of the quiet dead, who are scornful of the living for their restless walking. It is negation canonized as the one positive virtue. It is the pro-hibition of happiness. It is slavery self-sought and self-defended. It is dullness made God.

A savorless people, gulping tasteless food, and sitting afterward, coatless and thoughtless, in rocking chairs prickly with inane decorations, listening to mechanical music, saying mechanical things about the excellence of Ford automobiles, and viewing themselves as the greatest race in the world.

Slightly adapted from *Main Street* by Sinclair Lewis, copyright 1920 by Harcourt Brace Jovanovich, Inc.; renewed 1948 by Sinclair Lewis. Reprinted by permission of the publisher.

READING REVIEW

1. According to Kennicott, what are the two traditions of the American small town?
2. What does the small-town person value, in Kennicott's opinion?
3. **Using Fiction as Historical Evidence** (a) Do you think Sinclair Lewis gives an accurate picture of small-town life? Why or why not? (b) In what ways is a novel like this a limited view of history?

Topic 12
From Prosperity to Despair (1928–1932)

★ 12-1 A Boom in Florida Real Estate ★

Introduction The 1920s seemed to be a time of endless prosperity. Even people who had never invested money were eager to take part in the boom. Speculating in land was one popular investment. In this selection, economist John Kenneth Galbraith discusses the land boom in Florida.

Vocabulary Before you read the selection, find the meaning of these words in a dictionary: inordinate, manifestation, speculative, indispensable, accessible, indolent, brine, eloquence.

One thing in the twenties should have been visible even to Coolidge. It concerned the American people of whose character he had spoken so well. Along with the sterling qualities he praised, they were also displaying an inordinate desire to get rich quickly with a minimum of physical effort. The first striking manifestation of this personality trait was in Florida. There, in the mid-twenties, Miami, Miami Beach, Coral Gables, the East Coast as far north as Palm Beach, and the cities over on the Gulf had been

During the 1920s, everyone learned about the stock market. In the stock market, bears are investors who think stock prices will fall. Bulls expect prices to rise. This humorous painting shows the bears celebrating a drop in the market.

struck by the great Florida real estate boom.

The Florida boom contained all of the elements of the classic speculative bubble. There was the indispensable element of substance. Florida had a better winter climate than New York, Chicago, or Minneapolis. Higher incomes and better transportation were making it increasingly accessible to the frostbound North. The time indeed was coming when the annual flight to the South would be as regular and impressive as the migrations of the Canada goose.

On that indispensable element of fact, men and women had proceeded to build a world of speculative make-believe. This is a world inhabited not by people who have to be persuaded to believe but by people who want an excuse to believe. In the case of Florida, they wanted to believe that the whole peninsula would soon be populated by the holiday makers and the sun wor-

shippers of a new and remarkably indolent era. So great would be the crush that beaches, bogs, swamps, and common scrubland would all have value. The Florida climate obviously did not insure that this would happen. But it did enable people who wanted to believe it would happen so to believe. . . .

Through 1925 the pursuit of effortless riches brought people to Florida in satisfactorily increasing numbers. . . . As the speculation spread northward, an enterprising Bostonian, Mr. Charles Ponzi, developed a subdivision "near Jacksonville." It was approximately 65 miles west of the city. . . .

However, in the spring of 1926, the supply of new buyers, so essential to the reality of increasing prices, began to fail. . . . For a while in 1926 the increasing eloquence of the promoters offset the diminishing supply of prospects. . . . But this boom was not left to collapse of its own weight. [Two deadly hurricanes then brought an abrupt end to the boom, although some hopeful people believed it would begin again.]

The Florida boom was the first indication of the mood of the twenties and the conviction that God intended the American middle class to be rich. But that this mood survived the Florida collapse is still more remarkable. It was widely understood that things had gone to pieces in Florida. While the number of speculators was almost certainly small compared with the subsequent participation in the stock market, nearly every community contained a man who was known to have taken "quite a beating" in Florida. . . . Even as the Florida boom collapsed, the faith of Americans in quick, effortless enrichment in the stock market was becoming every day more evident.

From *The Great Crash* by John Kenneth Galbraith. Copyright © 1954, 1955, 1961 by John Kenneth Galbraith. Reprinted by permission of Houghton Mifflin Company.

READING REVIEW

1. According to Galbraith, what factors fed the Florida land boom?
2. What methods did some developers use to attract buyers?
3. **Relating Past to Present** Do you think such a land boom could take place today? Why or why not?

Introduction During the depression, thousands of unemployed men "rode the rails," hopping freight trains to almost anywhere that seemed to offer a promise of work. When they failed to find jobs, they might live for a while in shantytowns near the railroad tracks before moving on. Here Upton Sinclair describes a more unusual type of "city of forgotten men," in San Sebastian, California.

Vocabulary Before you read the selection, find the meaning of these words in a dictionary: durable, gondolas, crenelated, bulls, lee, requisite.

As a place of residence for human beings, a piece of concrete sewer pipe, while still above ground and before it has become part of a sewer, has some virtues and some defects. It is durable and requires no repairs. It is rainproof—at least until the rain has gathered on the ground. It provides plenty of ventilation. It will not be blown over by a "santa ana"* nor wrecked by the earthquakes which are common in California. Finally, it is impossible for an automobile to come crashing through the side of it—something which has been known to happen to frame and stucco houses along California highways.

On the other hand, it is rather difficult to close the two entrances to such a residence. You can draw a board cover or a sheet of tin up against the opening; but you cannot pull it closed. Otherwise it will fall over; and a gust of wind may take it away at the very time it is most needed. You cannot drive a nail into concrete—not unless you have money to buy a special kind of nail. The early dwellers in Pipe City suffered much discomfort, until some genius thought of fastening a length of rope to each of the board covers or pieces of tin. When these ropes were drawn together and tied, there you were, safe and snug.

In the city of San Sebastian, California, was a concern which manufactured concrete sewer pipe. This concern had a large quantity of pipe stored on a vacant

tract; rows upon rows of unconnected pipe joints, each five feet in diameter and ten feet in length. They were near the waterfront, and the railroad passed, and the tops of the freights, especially the gondolas, were crenelated with men and boys, riding here and riding there, anywhere that was a different place. The riders would see these pipes, shining in the sunlight, gay and festive with yellow underwear and blue shirts laid out to dry, and groups of men sitting about, smoking pipes and chatting. The riders would descend and make inquiries: "Hey, buddy, do the bulls let you alone here?" The answer being satisfactory, they would unsling their bundles and file a claim.

Only when the sun went down and fog began to creep in from the bay did they discover the defects of five-foot sewer pipe as a residence for grown men. In the first place, you can't stand erect in it. And when you lie down, you discover that concrete is one of the chilliest substances invented.

You might solve the problem by begging, borrowing, or stealing a tiny wood stove and a couple of pieces of rusty pipe. This would establish you among the aristocracy of the settlement. You would set up your stove in the lee end of your home and make it firm and snug. You would gather driftwood along the waterfront and with stones pound or smash it into the right sizes. And then, when the sun went down and the fogs stole in, you could crawl inside and spend a night in lonely solitude—alternately baked when your fire burned and shivering when it didn't.

But in the morning hunger would drive you forth. You would stand in the bread line for the requisite number of hours, and after you had filled your belly with thin soup, thin coffee, and thick bread, you would come back and find your stove and stovepipe gone.

One of the luxuries of life in Pipe City was a dry board to keep your feet away from the concrete. Not all knew this—only those who had become permanents and learned how pleasant it is to take off your shoes and rub one foot against the other to warm them.

---

*A santa ana is a strong, hot wind.

It was difficult to read in such a place, and few men tried it. But on cold nights they had to crawl in early; and then, huddled together, they talked. They talked about the scraps of news they had picked up in papers by the wayside. They talked about baseball scores and, later in the year, football. They talked about bread lines, missions, and other places to get food. They talked about the races, and various kinds of gambling—few of which could be carried on inside a five-foot sewer pipe. They talked about politics, and how rotten it was. They talked about economics—why times had got so bad and the chances of their getting better. More and more they were becoming interested in economics, for the depression was finishing its third year. They had been told that prosperity was just around the corner, but the corner seemed as far away as ever, and they were beginning to ask if it was a roundhouse.

Adapted from Upton Sinclair, Co-op (New York: Farrar & Rinehart, 1936). Copyright 1936 by Upton Sinclair.

READING REVIEW

1. What was the source of Pipe City?
2. (a) What advantages did Pipe City have over other shantytowns? (b) What were its disadvantages?
3. **Making Inferences** (a) In what ways did misery make people in Pipe City cooperative? (b) In what way were they not cooperative?

★ 12-3 Going on Relief in Baltimore ★

Introduction In the years following the crash of 1929, many people who took pride in hard work and economic independence were forced by circumstances to accept charity. Especially hard hit were people like the parents of small children, who could not travel in search of work. They had to accept what aid was offered or go hungry. In this selection from his autobiography Growing Up, Russell Baker describes his family's efforts at survival and how he felt when they had to accept a "handout."

Vocabulary Before you read the selection, find the meaning of these words in a dictionary: dilapidation, cellophane, incriminating, ostentatiously, humiliation.

The paper route earned me three dollars a week, sometimes four, and my mother, in addition to her commissions on magazine sales, also had her monthly check coming from Uncle Willie, but we'd been in Baltimore a year before I knew how desperate things were for her. One Saturday morning she told me she'd need Doris and me to go with her to pick up some food. I had a small wagon she'd bought me to make it easier to move the Sunday papers, and she said I'd better bring it along. The three of us set off eastward, passing the grocery stores we usually shopped at, and kept walking until we came to Fremont Avenue, a grim street of dilapidation and poverty in the heart of East Baltimore.

"This is where we go," she said when we reached the corner of Fremont and Fayette Street. It looked like a grocery, with big plate-glass windows and people lugging out cardboard cartons and bulging bags, but it wasn't. I knew very well what it was.

"Are we going on relief?" I asked her.

"Don't ask questions about things you don't know anything about," she said. "Bring that wagon inside."

I did, and watched with a mixture of shame and greed while men filled it with food. None of it was food I liked. There were huge cans of grapefruit juice, big paper sacks of cornmeal, cellophane bags of rice and prunes. It was hard to believe all this was ours for no money at all, even though none of it was very appetizing. My wonder at this free bounty quickly changed to embarrassment as we headed home with it. Being on relief was a shameful thing. People who accepted the government's handouts were scorned by everyone I knew as idle no-accounts without enough self-respect to pay their own way in the world. I'd often heard my mother say the same thing of families in the neighborhood suspected of being on relief. These, I'd been taught to believe, were people beyond hope. Now we were as low as they were.

Pulling the wagon back toward Lombard Street, with Doris following behind to keep the edible proof of our disgrace from falling off, I knew my mother was far worse off than I'd suspected. She'd never have accepted such shame otherwise. I studied her as she walked along beside me, head high as always, not a bit bowed in disgrace, moving at her usual quick, hurry-up pace. If she'd given up on life, she didn't show it, but on the other hand she was unhappy about something. I dared to mention the dreaded words only once on that trip home.

"Are we on relief now, Mom?"

"Let me worry about that," she said.

What worried me most as we neared home was the possibility we'd be seen with the incriminating food by somebody we knew. There was no mistaking government-surplus food. The grapefruit-juice cans, the prunes and rice, the cornmeal—all were ostentatiously unlabeled, thus advertising themselves as "government handouts." Everybody in the neighborhood could read them easily enough, and our humiliation would be gossiped through every parlor by sundown. I had an inspiration.

"It's hot pulling this wagon," I said. "I'm going to take my sweater off."

It wasn't hot, it was on the cool side, but after removing the sweater I laid it across the groceries in the wagon. It wasn't a very effective cover, but my mother was suddenly affected by the heat too.

"It is warm, isn't it, Buddy?" she said. Removing her topcoat, she draped it over the groceries, providing total concealment.

"You want to take your coat off, Doris?" asked my mother.

"I'm not hot, I'm chilly," Doris said.

It didn't matter. My mother's coat was enough to get us home without being exposed as three of life's failures.

Adapted from Russell Baker, *Growing Up* (New York: Congdon & Weed, Inc., 1982). Copyright © 1982 Russell Baker.

READING REVIEW

1. How did Baker know that his family was going on relief?

2. Why did the young boy think accepting aid was a disgrace?

3. **Expressing an Opinion** Do you think the Bakers' reaction to going on relief was typical? Why or why not?

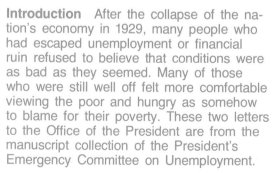

★ 12-4 Letters to the White House ★

Introduction After the collapse of the nation's economy in 1929, many people who had escaped unemployment or financial ruin refused to believe that conditions were as bad as they seemed. Many of those who were still well off felt more comfortable viewing the poor and hungry as somehow to blame for their poverty. These two letters to the Office of the President are from the manuscript collection of the President's Emergency Committee on Unemployment.

Vocabulary Before you read the selection, find the meaning of these words in a dictionary: debauchery, posterity, predicament.

Annapolis, Maryland
September 10, 1931

President Herbert Hoover
Washington, D.C.

My dear Mr. Hoover,

It is my purpose to write you a short letter and to cheer you along with your trying undertakings.

In these days of unrest and general dissatisfaction, it is absolutely impossible for a man in your position to get a clear and impartial view of the general conditions of things in America today. But of this fact I am very positive, that there is not 5 percent of the poverty, distress, and general unemployment that many of your enemies would have us believe. It is true that there is much unrest, but this unrest is largely caused by the excessive prosperity and general debauchery through which the country has traveled since the period of the war. The result being that in three cases out of four, the unemployed is looking for a very light job at a very heavy pay, and with the privilege of being provided with an automobile if he is required to walk more than four or five blocks a day.

National Relief Director Walter S. Gifford and his committee are entirely unnecessary at this time, as it has a tendency to cause communities to neglect any temporary relief to any of their people, with the thought of passing the burden on to the National Committee. I am also of the opinion that the suggested $5-billion loan that the Hearst papers have been agitating for is an impractical, foolish, and unnecessary burden and obligation that they would place upon the shoulders of future posterity to pay off.

One of these days, when I am in Washington, I shall hope to greet you in person for two or three minutes, and during the interval believe me to be one of your well-wishers in this ocean of conflict.

Yours Sincerely,
W.H.H., Contractor and Builder

Minneapolis, Minnesota
November 9, 1931

Hon. Walter Newton
White House, Washington, D.C.

My dear Mr. Newton:
The Sunday papers were full of encouraging information about almost every line of activity. The advance in wheat was particularly stressed, as was the advance in the price of silver. Stocks and bonds, both foreign and domestic, were shown as having enjoyed very substantial advances over the quoted prices of the week previous. Sunday's papers made in the main pleasant reading. Then in the evening, the radio programs brought out a lot of most depressing statements.

If the information contained in the papers is true, and I believe it is, it seems to me we are not justified in broadcasting statements to the effect that 6 million or more people of the United States are actually starving or will starve before the winter is over, unless those who have contribute generously to the needs of those who have not.

I am not opposed to contributions for the benefit of those in need. My thought is that the President has been doing everything humanly possible to promote right thinking by the minds of the American people. The broadcasting of such a program as we listened to last night cannot help but have a depressing effect, or of offsetting some of the things which we claim we have accomplished.

I was impressed last night with the fact that all reference to unemployment emphasized the suffering and deprivations we might expect to experience during the winter months. If conditions are improving, would it not be well to have at least a number of the people on the program speak of the improvement that has been made, the improvement that is being made, and leaving to others the responsibility of telling of the depression that still exists in certain industries and in certain sections of the country?

President Hoover is not responsible for any of our problems. Criticism comes largely from those who are responsible; and his critics will be the first to try to take the credit unto themselves as soon as we get out of our present predicament.

This letter comes from a Democrat who usually votes the Republican ticket, and it may or may not be of interest to you. However that may be, I am, with best regards,

Very truly yours,
J.B.

Adapted from *Down and Out in the Great Depression*, ed. Robert S. McElvaine (Chapel Hill: University of North Carolina Press, 1983).

READING REVIEW

1. What does W.H.H. think is the cause of unrest in the country?
2. Why did J.B. think the radio program was a mistake?
3. **Finding the Main Idea** (a) What is the major point of each letter? (b) On what point would the letter writers agree?

Theme 4

A Time of Trial

Topic

13 A New Deal (1933–1935)

Introduction In 1932 Franklin D. Roosevelt led the Democratic party to an overwhelming election victory. Bringing hope to a depressed country, Roosevelt proposed far-reaching reforms that he promised to carry out as soon as he took office. In this selection from his inaugural address, Roosevelt lists some ways in which he felt government could put the country back on its feet.

Vocabulary Before you read the selection, find the meaning of these words in a dictionary: curtailment, redistribution, foreclosure, unprecedented, reposed, arduous, mandate.

This is the time to speak the truth, the whole truth, frankly and boldly. Nor need we shrink from honestly facing conditions in our country today. This great nation will endure as it has endured, will revive and will prosper.

So first of all let me assert my firm belief that the only thing we have to fear is fear itself—nameless, unreasoning, unjustified terror which paralyzes needed efforts to convert retreat into advance.

In every dark hour of our national life, a leadership of frankness and vigor has met with that understanding and support of the people themselves which is essential to victory. I am convinced that you will again give that support to leadership in these critical days.

In such a spirit on my part and on yours, we face our common difficulties. They concern, thank God, only material things. Values have shrunken to fantastic levels. Taxes have risen, and our ability to pay has fallen. Government of all kinds is faced by serious curtailment of income. The means of exchange are frozen in the currents of trade. The withered leaves of industrial enterprise lie on every side. Farmers find no markets for their produce. The savings of many years in thousands of families are gone.

More important, a host of unemployed citizens faces the grim problem of existence, and an equally great number toils with little return. Only a foolish optimist can deny the dark realities of the moment.

Our greatest primary task is to put people to work. This is no unsolvable

This satirical cover done for Vanity Fair *magazine shows Franklin D. Roosevelt's inauguration as a heroic occasion. The new President is crowned with a laurel wreath while angels with trumpets salute him.*

problem if we face it wisely and courageously.

It can be accomplished in part by direct recruiting by the government itself, treating the task as we would treat the emergency of a war. But at the same time, through this employment we can accomplish greatly needed projects to stimulate and reorganize the use of our natural resources.

Hand in hand with this, we must frankly recognize the overbalance of population in our industrial centers. By engaging on a national scale in a redistribution, we must endeavor to provide a better use of the land for those best fitted for the land.

The task can be helped by definite efforts to raise the values of agricultural products and with this the power to purchase the output of our cities.

It can be helped by preventing realistically the tragedy of the growing loss, through foreclosure, of our small homes and our farms.

It can be helped by insistence that the federal, state, and local governments act forthwith on the demand that their cost be drastically reduced.

It can be helped by the unifying of relief activities which today are often scattered, uneconomical, and unequal.

It can be helped by national planning for and supervision of all forms of transportation and of communications and other utilities which have a definitely public character.

There are many ways in which it can be helped, but it can never be helped merely by talking about it. We must act and act quickly.

It is to be hoped that the normal balance of executive and legislative authority may be wholly adequate to meet the unprecedented task before us. But it may be that an unprecedented demand and need for undelayed action may call for temporary departure from that normal balance of public procedure.

I am prepared under my constitutional duty to recommend the measures that a stricken nation in the midst of a stricken world may require.

These measures, or such other measures as the Congress may build out of its experience and wisdom, I shall seek, within my constitutional authority, to bring to speedy adoption.

But in the event that the Congress shall fail to take one of these two courses, and in the event that the national emergency is still critical, I shall not evade the clear course of duty that will then confront me.

I shall ask the Congress for the one remaining instrument to meet the crisis—that is, broad executive power needed to wage a war against the emergency as great as the power that would be given me if we were in fact invaded by a foreign foe.

For the trust reposed in me I will return the courage and the devotion that befit the time. I can do no less.

We face the arduous days that lie before us in the warm courage of national unity; with the clear consciousness of seeking old and precious moral values; with the clean satisfaction that comes from the stern peformance of duty by old and young alike.

We aim at the assurance of a rounded and permanent national life.

We do not distrust the future of essential democracy. The people of the United States have not failed. In their need they have registered a mandate that they want direct, vigorous action.

They have asked for discipline and direction under leadership. They have made me the present instrument of their wishes. In the spirit of the gift I take it.

In this dedication of a nation we humbly ask the blessing of God. May He protect each and every one of us! May He guide me in the days to come!

Adapted from Franklin D. Roosevelt, "First Inaugural Address," 1933.

READING REVIEW

1. What did Roosevelt see as the primary task of his administration?
2. What step is Roosevelt prepared to take if Congress fails to act?
3. **Summarizing** How does Roosevelt propose "to provide a better use of the land for those best fitted for the land"?

★ 13-2 What Was the New Deal? ★

Introduction Franklin D. Roosevelt was born into a wealthy family. However, he was raised with the belief that wealth brought responsibilities toward the poor. When he became President, he promised a New Deal. In this selection, Frances Perkins, Roosevelt's Secretary of Labor, describes what the New Deal meant in the beginning.

Vocabulary Before you read the selection, find the meaning of these words in a dictionary: potent, humanitarian, invoke, adherence, evoked.

When Franklin Roosevelt and his administration began their work in Washington in March 1933, the New Deal was not a plan with form and content. It was a happy phrase he had coined during the campaign, and its value was psychological. It made people feel better, and in that terrible period of depression they needed to feel better.

As Roosevelt described it, the "new deal" meant that the forgotten man, the little man, the man nobody knew much about, was going to be dealt better cards to play with.

The idea was not specific; it was general, but it was potent. On Roosevelt's part it was truly and profoundly felt. He understood that the suffering of the depression had fallen with terrific impact upon the people least able to bear it. He knew that the rich had been hit hard too, but at least they had something left. But the little merchant, the small householder and home owner, the farmer who worked the soil by himself, the man who worked for wages—these people were desperate. And Roosevelt saw them as principal citizens of the United States, numerically and in their importance to the maintenance of the ideals of American democracy.

That phrase, "new deal," which gave courage to all sorts of people, was merely a statement of policy and emphasis. It expressed a new attitude, not a fixed program. When he got to Washington, he had no fixed program.

The general situation, however, was clear in Roosevelt's mind and in the minds of his supporters and party. He represented the humanitarian trend. The idea was that all the political and practical forces of the community should and could be directed to making life better for ordinary people. This was accepted by most of the dominant elements in the Democratic party in 1933.

He was going to work with the states. He was going to break down the conflict which so often existed between state and federal government. He was going to take the governors into his confidence and invoke their cooperation.

Another procedure Roosevelt had in mind before he went to Washington was regular cooperation with Congress. I suppose every President-elect has gone to Washington with the best of resolutions to cooperate with Congress. Roosevelt had observed the failure in a number of cases, and he had a plan of his own. He told me he would call in the leaders regularly and would invite committees of Congress to the White House. He meant to keep the Congress informed of what was going on in the President's mind before legislation was formulated.

He was clear that the duty of Congress was to legislate and the duty of the President was to execute. He expected to make it clear that he relied on Congress. But he also had solid ideas about the place of the President's office in our American scheme of things. And he felt that the failure of some Presidents to assert the leadership which came to them by right of their election by the entire nation had been a mistake.

He recognized that to assert leadership and to develop a plan for legislation required tact, and that it had to be done slowly. The President, he thought, should be responsible for developing and recommending a program for the good of the whole country.

He had ideas about party responsibility. Keenly aware of the two-party system under which American democracy thrives, he felt that there should be more internal party unity. He believed a party program must be worked out to get the adherence of the rank and file. He often said that we must work out a method whereby the enthusiasm and political intelligence evoked among the voters during campaigns would be kept alive, harnessed, and put to work between campaigns. Then we would have, he said, a democratic, representative way of expressing the will of the people to the Congress.

But these were ideas for procedure, not a total pattern for the New Deal. It is important to repeat, the New Deal was not a plan, not even an agreement, and it was certainly not a plot, as was later charged. Most of the programs later called the New Deal arose out of the emergency which Roosevelt faced when he took office at the low point of the depression.

From *The Roosevelt I Knew* by Frances Perkins. Copyright © 1946 by Frances Perkins. Copyright renewed © 1974 by Susanna W. Coggeshall. Reprinted by permission of Viking Penguin, Inc.

READING REVIEW

1. How did Roosevelt plan to work with Congress?
2. What role did he think the political party should play?
3. **Making Generalizations** How would you describe the New Deal in 1933 based on Perkins' account?

★ 13-3 Millard Ketchum in the CCC ★

Introduction President Roosevelt had set relief of unemployment as a main goal of his administration. In response, Congress created the Civilian Conservation Corps as one of its first major acts. By employing young men in forests and parks, the corps also helped to conserve the nation's resources. This selection is from an interview with one of these young men.

Vocabulary Before you read the selection, find the meaning of these words in a dictionary: flushed, scowled.

Millard Ketchum had just come in from his day's work in the field. He was still in his blue CCC work uniform. "This is better clothes than I ever had at home," he said, "before I got to the CCC. You see, at home there was so many of us, we couldn't have much clothes to wear and in summertime we jist didn't wear no shoes, and no shirts much, nor nothing else much.

"Let me git you somewhere to set if you want to talk a while. Hey, Sarge! Kin I get a few minutes off to talk here to this lady here? Okay, Sarge."

When asked about his family, he said, "Well, my mama she come from Bundy County. She was a Dunlap. My papa, he come from Chester County, over here nigh Henderson. They live at Zama now and been there about two year. I ain't got so big a family to keep up, not so big as lots of the boys has. I jist got five brothers and one sister. I'm the oldest and I ain't but 19 year old.

"My brothers, they's named Winston Gormer, Jim Ables, Luther Crocker, Ray

Slowey, and Jonathan Junior. My sister, she's named Pearlie Jo and she's 13.

"We's farmers and renters. Ain't ever owned no home as yet. We lives at Zama now with a Mr. Lew Truitt. We've got two big houses on each side of us and they's shore pretty, too. We ain't got so big a house to live in—just a small house, but my mother she's a good housekeeper and keeps everything spick and span. Ain't much trouble, you know, with a little house to keep it clean. We ain't got so much in it neither. Jist enough to make it comfortable for us. We got plenty of beds. You know, jist like most any pore farmer's got, but enough to do us all.

"I ain't never been much to school. Jist went to the second grade, that's all, excepting what I learned here in the CCC. I could have gone, I guess, but for some reason didn't keer nothing about it. Jist didn't want to go. I would have went if I wanted to. They didn't make me not go. We jist didn't none of us go. I got one brother that went to the second grade, too, and my sister she went to the first. Then she quit. We jist wasn't a family that like school."

I asked, "Would you go on to school and finish now if you had the chance?"

"Don't know whether I could or not. I would really like to learn." He flushed and scowled. "The boys, they make fun of us when we can't read the funnies nor nothing. I look at pictures in books and things like that in the recreation hall, so they won't laugh at me. I wish I had gone on to school now and would go as far as I could if I git the chance. Guess I couldn't git much learning now though, could I? I'm too old most to learn now."

I asked if he wanted to stay with the CCC.

"Yes'm, as long as I kin, because I git plenty to eat here. I didn't always at home, not the same kind of stuff, anyhow. Guess we had plenty, such as it was, at home, but it jist wasn't good like this, nor enough of it for the kind it was. I git to go more, git to see more. I'm learning too. I watch the others, and then, I have more clothes and can keep cleaner too.

"I git up about five in the morning, eat breakfast, go to morning classes, then go to the field. I don't work nearly so hard in this as I do in the field at home. I git to

The Civilian Conservation Corps provided jobs and training for young men between the ages of 18 and 25. Here a conservation worker has drilled for a soil sample.

be with lots of boys that I wouldn't at home. They help me lots, show me how to do things I wouldn't have never knowed about. I like all my bosses and I like all the fellers. They tease me sometimes, but they like me, too."

Adapted from *These Are Our Lives*, Federal Writers Project of the Works Progress Administration (Chapel Hill, N.C.: University of North Carolina Press, 1939).

READING REVIEW

1. How much schooling did the Ketchum family have?

2. (a) What was the family's attitude toward education? (b) Why do you think they felt this way?

3. **Making Inferences** How did Millard Ketchum think his life was better as a member of the CCC?

Introduction Louise V. Armstrong worked as a relief administrator in a rural county of 18,000 people in northern Michigan. Many times during her first two years on the job, Armstrong interviewed over a hundred people a day. In this selection from her book *We Too Are the People*, she tells what work at the office was like.

Vocabulary Before you read the selection, find the meaning of these words in a dictionary: quavering, surge, mottled, burly, genial, swarthy, puttees, stalwart, mackinaw, trolls, oculist.

The sound of tramping feet in a long hall, the noise of scuffling feet in a big room, the babble of human voices pitched in every key, mingle with other sounds in a ceaseless jazz symphony of human life. A baby cries, a woman's shrill complaints rise above the general theme. The quavering tones of an aged voice become distinct in a sudden lull, to be drowned by the gruff voices of men. Crisp sentences in the brisk tones of busy people cut through at times and are lost again in the surge of angry voices, pleading voices, gentle voices, harsh voices, good-natured voices.

There are at least 50 people in the big room, but the group is constantly changing. Against this mottled background colorful figures stand out, taking the spotlight for a moment, and passing on as others take their places.

An old Ottawa Indian stands at the far end of the room, leaning on a long staff. In spite of his dingy, furry, ragged clothing, he is the most dignified figure in the room. With his white hair hanging to his shoulders, head erect, eyes narrowed, he looks like some ancient prophet. A handsome young Indian stands beside him. As you look at him, his forlorn cap and patched overalls seem to melt away, and you see him with eagle feather warbonnet and blanket, for the glory of the past still lives in that bronze face, a glory which he himself has never known.

A burly truck driver lurches in, slapping his leather-mittened hands together. His genial face, bright red from the stinging cold, breaks into a grin as a swarthy, brown-eyed boy of 20 strides across the room to him with his hands full of papers.

A white-haired, trimly dressed woman doctor has entered. As her keen eyes glance about the crowd, she smiles and nods a greeting here and there. She stops to speak to an old man.

A sergeant of the State Police has come in, his shining black puttees a contrast to the many shabby boots. Keen face, trim uniform, quick, decisive movements make him seem like a high-geared machine, ready to function on the instant. He is all modern, this trooper, in this crowd, where many seem somehow of the past.

A United States Army officer and two CCC boys are talking to a striking-looking dark woman in a brown sport dress. The captain's handsome tan boots put all the other boots in the room to shame.

Is this creature who just shambled in a man? That hairy face, those half-closed, shifty eyes are hardly human. Certainly he is a different species from these stalwart men in boots and mackinaws. But there is another like him, leaning against the wall, scratching his head. That matted hair has never known a comb. Over yonder is another. Were those rags, tied about his middle with a string, ever a coat? These creatures are out of the picture. This scene is set in the present. This is civilization and the age of progress. They must be trolls.

Is this Hollywood? Is the scene set for some feature film? Are these the extras made up from character parts? No, this is the Emergency Relief Office.

The little Golinski boy is worse. Pneumonia.... Yes, certainly we'll O.K. the drugstore order.... Old Mrs. Peterson's chimney has fallen down and she can't build a fire in her stove. That's too bad. No, of course we won't let the poor old lady freeze to death. We'll send a man right over.... Ten more men for the highway project near Housetown. That's good news. Better have Elsie look over the list. That's her territory. Tell her not to forget that poor Collins chap. His wife is sick and his cow died and he's in an awful state of mind.... Yes, what did you want to see me about? Oh, you haven't been here before. Your landlord is going to evict you. Well, you leave your name and address with the young lady at the desk there and fill out a blank. We'll send a case worker over to see you. The Sheriff. Oh, you don't need to worry. They can't put you out for a few days at least. We'll call up the Sheriff. . . . Old Peter needs coal. He had half a ton the fifteenth of last month. That's going pretty well for this weather. Yes. Give it to him. . . . Good morning! A note for me? Oh, from the school nurse. She says his eyes are very bad. Yes, indeed, we'll be very glad to. Margaret, please make out an order for an office call to the oculist for this little boy. . . . Yes, what is it? Everybody gets work but you! Why, we mailed you a work card yesterday. You're to report on the city sidewalk project next Monday. Yes, absolutely sure. You'd better go home and watch for the postman.

What does Myrtle want? Shoes for Nita. Does she need them? Did you look at her shoes? Yes, give them to the poor little soul. . . . Good morning, Sergeant! What's the news today? Goldie's arrested again. Well, I certainly want to hear about that. Can you wait a minute? The doctor's ahead of you. . . . Good morning,

Doctor! We'll go into my office. . . . What is it? A call from out in the county. Is it urgent? All right, I'll take it on this phone. . . . Just a minute please, Doctor. . . . Yes? Talking. Wait a minute. I'll write that down. Give me a pencil, Marie. Yes? Farm family—burned out last night. Father, mother, and six children. Any of them hurt? That's good. No insurance, I suppose. Where do they live? Two miles east of the schoolhouse in Brookdale Township. One of our case workers started up that way about half an hour ago. Maybe we can catch him. Oh, yes. We'll take care of it today.

Adapted from Louise V. Armstrong, *We Too Are the People* (Boston: Little, Brown and Company, 1938). Copyright 1938 by Louise V. Armstrong.

READING REVIEW

1. What kinds of people went to the Emergency Relief Office?
2. What types of problems did the people face?
3. **Recognizing a Point of View** (a) What seems to be Louise Armstrong's attitude toward her work? (b) What does her description of the relief office tell you about life during the Great Depression?

★ 13-5 Father Coughlin Presents His Principles ★

Introduction Radio priest Father Coughlin supported Franklin D. Roosevelt in 1932. However, he later turned against the President. Coughlin accused the New Deal of matching the "puny brains of idealists against the viril viciousness of business and finance." Coughlin saw himself as a champion of the common people. He outlined his goals in these 16 "principles of social justice."

Vocabulary Before you read the selection, find the meaning of these words in a dictionary: avocation, alleviation, sanctity.

1. I believe in liberty of conscience and liberty of education, not permitting the state to dictate either my worship to my God or my chosen avocation in life.

2. I believe that every citizen willing to work shall receive a just, living, annual wage which will enable him to both maintain and educate his family according to the standards of American decency.

3. I believe in nationalizing the public resources which by their very nature are too important to be held in the control of private individuals.

4. I believe in private ownership of all other property.

5. I believe in upholding the right to private property but in controlling it for the public good.

6. I believe in the abolition of the privately owned Federal Reserve banking system and the establishment of a government-owned central bank.

7. I believe in rescuing from the hands of private owners the right to coin and regulate the value of money, which right must be restored to Congress where it belongs.

8. I believe that one of the chief duties of the government-owned central bank is to maintain the cost of living on an even keel and arrange for the repayment of dollar debts with equal-value dollars.

9. I believe in the cost of production plus a fair profit for the farmer.

10. I believe not only in the right of the laboring man to organize in unions but also in the duty of the government, which that laboring man supports, to protect these organizations against the vested interests of wealth and intellect.

11. I believe in the recall of nonproductive bonds and therefore in the alleviation of taxation.

12. I believe in the abolition of tax-exempt bonds.

13. I believe in broadening the base of taxation according to the principles of ownership and the capacity to pay.

14. I believe in the simplification of government and the further lifting of crushing taxation from the slender revenues of the laboring class.

15. I believe that, in the event of a war for the defense of our nation and its liberties, there shall be a conscription of wealth as well as a conscription of men.

16. I believe in preferring the sanctity of property rights; for the chief concern of government shall be for the poor because, as it is witnessed, the rich have ample means of their own to care for themselves.

Adapted from Sheldon Marcus, *Father Coughlin* (Boston: Little, Brown and Company, 1973). Copyright © 1973 by Sheldon Marcus.

READING REVIEW

1. What were Father Coughlin's views about property?
2. What group do Coughlin's "16 principles" seem to be attacking?
3. **Defending an Opinion** (a) Which of Coughlin's "principles" do you think reflect American traditions? Why? (b) Which do you think were at odds with American traditions? Explain.

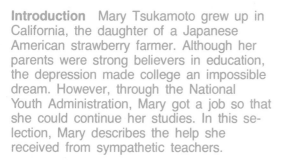

★ 13-6 Getting an Education ★

Introduction Mary Tsukamoto grew up in California, the daughter of a Japanese American strawberry farmer. Although her parents were strong believers in education, the depression made college an impossible dream. However, through the National Youth Administration, Mary got a job so that she could continue her studies. In this selection, Mary describes the help she received from sympathetic teachers.

Vocabulary Before you read the selection, find the meaning of these words in a dictionary: bicultural, segregated, oration, wardrobe, anonymous, interpretive.

In 1925 my father brought us from Fresno to a farm in Florin. I was ten years old. We had always attended school with Caucasian children; Fresno had been more of a melting pot, with Armenians and Italians. I'd never encountered discrimination—oh, there were embarrassing moments when people made unthinking remarks, but somehow, I didn't see it as my personal problem.

All this changed when I went to the Florin grammar school, where I soon found out that everybody had a Japanese face. Of course, I spoke English, but many of my classmates were aliens—their parents spoke only Japanese—and they were growing up in a strange bicultural world.

So you see, in 1929 when I graduated from the segregated school, it was quite a shock to go to the Elk Grove High School, which was mixed with all kinds of people.

At the same time, I was interested in my education. Among Japanese families, education is important. My parents felt

Part Two 234

they had suffered by missing their education in Japan because of poverty. My father felt a powerful need to educate his children and was always willing to give us a lot of time to study although he had to work even harder on our strawberry farm.

To be fair, I think the teachers tried their best to involve us in high school activities. They encouraged us and yet we were shy. I felt inadequate. I tried to go to the class parties and things, but it was hard. I was always aware that I was Japanese.

It's really a long story, but during my last years at Elk Grove I had a wonderful English teacher, Mrs. Mabel Barren. She also taught public speaking. Now, I don't know why I took public speaking, but I did. One time the assignment was to prepare an oration on California history and the best speech was to win a prize. I was told I won. Later, I was called to the principal's office and he told me that because of my background, I'd been refused the prize by the Elk Grove Native Sons and Daughters of the Golden West.

I was innocent. I did my assignment. I had no ambition to win—no plans to be part of an oratorical contest where they didn't want me. My teacher, Mrs. Barren, was upset about all this, more shocked and hurt, I think, than I was.

But there was nothing she could do. I knew then that there would be places where I couldn't go, where doors would be closed to me.

After that, Mrs. Barren made up her mind she was going to get me into college. She went to Stockton and talked about me with Dr. Towlie Knowles at College of the Pacific, and got me a fifty-dollar scholarship for my first semester. And that same spring—during Easter vacation—this wonderful woman begged and borrowed clothes from people, cut them down, and sewed a wardrobe for me. And she did that on her vacation.

Then she came home with me one day and talked with my father and got his permission for me to go to college.

I helped on the farm that summer, in '33, and then went to college. Things I could major in were limited because

The Works Progress Administration (WPA) supported various projects for people in the arts, including writers, photographers, painters, sculptors, and actors. This WPA-sponsored mural by Victor Arnauntoff is in the Coit Tower in San Francisco.

counselors told me I wouldn't be able to find jobs in many fields. I was religious, and so I told them I would be a missionary. They agreed I could minor in that, but that I should major in social work. At that point, I really didn't know what I wanted except a college education. I was sure of that.

The college got me a job working in a home for my room and board. It was the depression, remember, and tuition was high. But now and then there would be an anonymous gift for a worthy student. So, when my tuition was due, I would get a call from the dean's office that a gift had come which I could have. I was able to finish all but the last year of college this way.

Another job at Pacific came as an NYA grant. I worked in the infirmary for 40 cents an hour, dusting furniture and sweeping rooms.

The College of the Pacific was a wonderful learning experience for me. And for the first time I became involved in stu-dent activities. During my sophomore year, I discovered interpretive dancing; and the class really made me feel welcome. I would wear my kimono and interpret Japanese dance for them. I think I contributed to their appreciation of Japanese culture.

There were many warm friends I made there, and my wonderful teachers helped to heal the wounds.

Adapted from Jeane Westin, *Making Do: How Women Survived the Thirties* (Newton, Mass.: Allyn & Bacon, Inc., 1976). © 1976 by Jeane Westin.

READING REVIEW

1. What success alerted Mary Tsukamoto's teacher to her talents?
2. What problems besides financial ones did Mary face?
3. **Relating Past to Present** (a) How did the NYA help Tsukamoto go to college? (b) How can students today get financial help for college?

Topic

14 The New Deal Continues (1936–1939)

★ 14-1 The Election of 1936 ★

Introduction Harold L. Ickes served as Secretary of the Interior from 1933 to 1946. A former lawyer and newspaper columnist, he was known for his acid comments about public officials. Ickes was originally a Republican but later joined the Progressive party. Still later, as a Democrat, he became one of Roosevelt's strongest supporters. This selection from his diary describes the election of 1936, when Republican Alfred Landon challenged Roosevelt for the presidency.

Vocabulary Before you read the selection, find the meaning of these words in a dictionary: lumbago, retrospect, rout, atrocious, barnstormer, denunciations, temporately, mendacious, venomous.

Saturday, November 7, 1936

The campaign continued in high gear until the very end. Landon made a speech in New York at Madison Square Garden Thursday night, October 29, in which he challenged the President bluntly to state his position on a number of national issues and tell what he would do as to these matters if he should be reelected. Then Landon started back, via St. Louis, for Topeka, Kansas, making speeches all along the way, with one particularly big meeting in St. Louis. But I was confident of Wisconsin and Minnesota and all of the western states generally, except South Dakota. I thought that Nebraska was safe, and I had a sneaking hope that the President would carry Kansas. However, this was nothing more than a hope. I also felt reasonably confident of West Virginia.

But, even believing as I did that the President would carry many more states than he needed in order to win, I was not prepared for the surprising results that came over the radio Tuesday night. I had been suffering from a severe attack of lumbago since Sunday afternoon, so that I was content to stay at home and listen to my own radio. It was soon clear that the President had not only won but that he had gone over by a tremendous popular and electoral college vote.

It is all over now, but even in retrospect the result is astonishing. Landon carried only two states—Maine and Vermont—with eight electoral votes between them. Although there are still some precincts missing, the President's popular majority is well over 10 million. There has been nothing like it in the history of American politics. The Democrats gained governors and senators and congressmen where already they had too many congressmen and senators and, with respect to some states, too many governors. The President pulled through to victory men whose defeat would have been better for the country. It was a complete rout of the Republican party and the big financial interests that had hoped through that party to regain control of the federal government.

The Republicans ran a perfectly atrocious campaign, and Landon proved to be even a weaker candidate than I had ever supposed him capable of being. Landon, in my judgment, would have been a stronger candidate if he had sat on his front porch at Topeka throughout. As a barnstromer, he lost votes, and his loss became progressively greater as the campaign continued. Frank Knox [the vice-presidential candidate] lost votes, in my judgment. He talked too much and he talked too recklessly. I doubt if toward the end of the campaign the people listened much to him or gave heed to his explosive denunciations of everything that the New Deal had ever done. Hamilton, as a national chairman, seemed to be a washout.

Landon started off rather temperately, admitting that there were some good things that the New Deal had done, but he allowed himself to be swept along

In 1936 the Republican party nominated Kansas governor Alfred M. Landon for President. Trying to stem Roosevelt's popularity, the party compared Landon to an earlier midwestern Republican, Abraham Lincoln.

with the tide. Then, too, the people pretty generally got the impression that he had neither the character nor the ability that a President of the United States ought to have.

To my view, the outstanding thing about the campaign was the lack of influence of the newspapers. With over 80 percent of the newspapers of the country fighting Roosevelt, it is remarkable that he should have swept everything as he did. Cook County was an outstanding example. There, only the tabloid *Times* supported the President, with the *Tribune*, the *News*, and the Hearst papers in bitter opposition. Nevertheless, the President carried Cook County by over 600,000 votes, and he carried downstate Illinois as well.

Never have the newspapers, in my recollection, conducted a more mendacious and venomous campaign against a candidate for President, and never have they been of so little influence. Apparently the people saw through the whole tissue of deceit and lies and misrepresentation.

They sensed that the great financial interests which were backing Landon and pouring money into his campaign fund had some sinister purpose. In my judgment, they voted for the President because they believed that he had some interest in and concern for the welfare of the common man. The very bitterness of the assault upon the President by the newspaper reacted in his favor.

Adapted from *The Secret Diary of Harold L. Ickes* (New York: Simon & Schuster, 1953). Copyright 1953 by Simon & Schuster, Inc.

READING REVIEW

1. Which states did Alfred Landon and the Republican party carry in the 1936 election?

2. In Ickes's opinion, what errors did the Republicans make in their campaign for the presidency?

3. **Distinguishing Fact From Opinion** List two facts and two opinions from the selection. On what basis did you decide what was fact and what was opinion?

★ 14-2 Evelyn Finn Organizes a Union ★

Introduction Studs Terkel is an interviewer with a talent for getting people to speak freely of their lives and pasts. In his book *Hard Times: An Oral History of the Great Depression*, he asks them to recollect their experiences of the 1930s. Here Evelyn Finn, a seamstress in St. Louis during those years, describes how she helped organize a union at her shop.

Vocabulary Before you read the selection, find the meaning of these words in a dictionary: apt, sweetheart union, menial, dormant, drudgery.

You could upset the shop quite a bit. Even when there was no union. You'd get the girls on your side, one by one, until you had a majority. I remember this one straw boss. He wanted us to speed up. In the morning, the girls'd be tired. He'd go through the shop: "Is everybody happy today?" I'd say, "I'm not happy." He says, "What's the matter with you?" I'd tell him, "I come here to fight."

Another girl sided with me. He fired us. "Troublemakers." He had the nerve to say, "I'll write you a letter of recommendation." This poor little thing, she was crying. I said, "I'd be ashamed to show anything you'd write on paper. I wouldn't want anybody to know I worked for a person like you." Lucky we got another job.

Sometimes you'd have to fight for your moral support against your boss. I've even lost jobs against that. I was still pretty young. I weighed about 115 pounds,

As the depression wore on, hardships and hunger defeated many people. Others, like this man, found inventive ways to resist the blows to their independence and pride.

brown hair. I didn't notice my personality because I had such fight in me. I used to tell 'em off. . . .

One time I was on piecework. You get paid for the amount you do. But the boss wanted us to ring the time clock. If you're a pieceworker and you're very fast and very apt, which I was, you don't want him to know this, that, or the other. I refused to ring the clock. Did they have a time with me! They didn't want to lose me. I was skilled.

"Why won't you please punch it?"

"You want me to work here?"

"Why, yes."

"Then don't bother me. If you stand when I come in in the morning, you punch it. Watch me all day long. And when I get home, you punch it again. O.K.?" (Laughs.)

They put up with it, even during the depression. I had a gift in my fingers. And I wasn't scared. (Laughs.)

One day I took out the whole shop. There never was a shop yet I couldn't take out. This is when we had the union. I was the chairlady. They didn't get us what we wanted. I think they were playin' sweethearts [a sweetheart union] with the boss. So we had a sit-in. I said to the girls, "Just sit, don't do nothin'." We sat and joked about a lot of things and had a lotta fun. The boss was goin' crazy. The union officials came down. They went crazy, too. It was a hilarious day. They called us a bunch of communists. The girls didn't know what it meant. I knew what it meant, but I wasn't. So, if that's the way they behave, I said, "Girls, it's a nice day. Let's all go for a walk." So we did, the whole shop. They got us what we wanted.

After all, I played a big part in organizin' our union in St. Louis. We used to go to the homes of people. It wears you out, but when you're young, you don't think about it. One day, this other girl and me, we're ringin' the bell, and somebody threw buckets of water out on us. Everybody was not in favor of the union. They were just scared to death.

I don't remember ever bein' scared. Even if I didn't have a penny. And I was supporting a little girl. What can we lose? We haven't got that much to lose. But some people are just afraid of every little thing. What was there to be afraid of?

There were no colored girls in our shop. The one next door to us had four or five. They did very menial work. But they didn't work with white girls. Not in St. Louis. Now, three of us work together, these two colored girls and I. The rest of the shop can be dormant, but we've always got something going on in that corner. Not a dull moment. You wouldn't think we're doin' a thing, but we produce more than the rest of 'em. Even when we get mad about something, we laugh about it. When the boss nags us, we just laugh him to death.

I never made my work a drudgery. I always made it a hobby. I enjoy my work today like if I was sitting down reading a book.

From *Hard Times: An Oral History of the Great Depression,* by Studs Terkel. Copyright © 1970 by Studs Terkel. Reprinted by permission of Pantheon Books, a division of Random House, Inc.

READING REVIEW

1. Why were the seamstresses called communists by the officials?

2. (a) What personal qualities of Evelyn Finn helped to make her a leader? (b) What methods of organizing did she use?

3. **Analyzing Oral Evidence** (a) How accurate do you think Evelyn Finn's account is? Why? (b) What historical value do such recollections provide?

★ 14-3   Losing the Farm

Introduction A deadly drought from 1932 to 1936 destroyed crops on land throughout the Great Plains. As the land turned into dust and blew away, men from the banks and land companies came to repossess family farms and remove tenants. John Steinbeck's *The Grapes of Wrath* describes the plight of poor farmers and tenants and their desperate trek west to California in search of work. In this selection, men representing the landowners encourage this migration.

The owners of the land came onto the land, or more often a spokesman for the owners came. They came in closed cars, and they felt the dry earth with their fingers, and sometimes they drove big earth augers into the ground for soil tests. The tenants, from their sun-beaten dooryards, watched uneasily when the closed cars drove along the fields. And at last the owner men drove into the dooryards and sat in their cars to talk out of the windows. The tenant men stood beside the cars for a while, and then squatted on their hams and found sticks with which to mark the dust.

In the open doors the women stood looking out, and behind them the children—corn–headed children, with wide eyes, one bare foot on top of the other bare foot, and the toes working. The women and the children watched their men talking to the owner men. They were silent.

Some of the owner men were kind because they hated what they had to do, and some of them were angry because they hated to be cruel, and some of them were cold because they had long ago found that one could not be an owner unless one were cold. And all of them were caught in something larger than themselves. Some of them hated the mathematics that drove them, and some were afraid, and some worshipped the mathematics because it provided a refuge from thought and from feeling. If a bank or a finance company owned the land, the owner man said, The Bank—or the Company—needs—wants—insists—must have, as though the bank or the company were a monster, with thought and feeling, which had ensnared them. These last would take no responsibility for the banks or the companies because they were men and slaves, while the banks were machines and masters all at the same time. Some of the owner men were a little proud to be slaves to such cold and powerful masters. The owner men sat in the cars and explained. You know the land is poor. You've scrabbled at it long enough, God knows.

The squatting tenant men nodded and wondered and drew figures in the dust, and yes, they knew, God knows. If the dust only wouldn't fly. If the top would stay on the soil, it might not be so bad.

The squatting men looked down again. What do you want us to do? We can't take less share of the crop—we're half starved now. The kids are hungry all the time. We got no clothes, torn an' ragged. If all the neighbors weren't the same, we'd be ashamed to go to meeting.

And at last the owner men came to the point. The tenant system won't work any more. One man on a tractor can take the place of 12 or 14 families. Pay him a wage and take all the crop. We have to do it. We don't like to do it.

The tenant men looked up alarmed. But what'll happen to us? How'll we eat?

You'll have to get off the land. The plows'll go through the dooryard.

And now the squatting men stood up angrily. Grampa took up the land, and he had to kill the Indians and drive them away. And Pa was born here, and he killed weeds and snakes. Then a bad year came and he had to borrow a little money. An' we was born here. There in the door—our children born here. And Pa had to borrow money. The bank owned the land then, but we stayed and we got a little bit of what we raised.

We know that—all that. It's not us, it's the Bank. A bank isn't like a man. Or an owner with 50,000 acres, he isn't like a man either. That's the monster.

Sure, cried the tenant men, but it's our land. We measured it and broke it up. We were born on it, and we got killed on it, died—being born on it, working it, dying on it. That makes ownership, not a paper with numbers on it.

We're sorry. It's not us. It's the monster. The Bank isn't like a man.

Yes, but the Bank is only made of men.

No, you're wrong there—quite wrong there. The Bank is something else than men. It happens that every man in a bank hates what the Bank does, and yet the Bank does it. The Bank is something more than men, I tell you. It's the monster. Men made it, but they can't control it.

But if we go, where'll we go? How'll we go? We got no money.

We're sorry, said the owner men. The Bank, the 50,000-acre owner can't be responsible. You're on land that isn't yours. Once over the line maybe you can pick cotton in the fall. Maybe you can go on relief. Why don't you go on west to California? There's work there, and it never gets cold. Why, you can reach out anywhere and pick an orange. Why, there's always some kind of crop to work in. Why don't you go there? And the owner men started their cars and rolled away.

From *The Grapes of Wrath* by John Steinbeck. Copyright 1939, renewed copyright © 1967 by John Steinbeck. Reprinted by permission of Viking Penguin, Inc.

READING REVIEW

1. What do the men from the bank mean by "the monster"?

2. Do you think the bank had any alternative to repossessing the farms? If so, what?

3. **Using Fiction as Historical Evidence** (a) What was Steinbeck's attitude toward what was happening to the farmer? (b) What can you learn about the farmers' attitude from this reading? (c) Do you think the author gives an accurate description of the feelings on both sides? Why or why not?

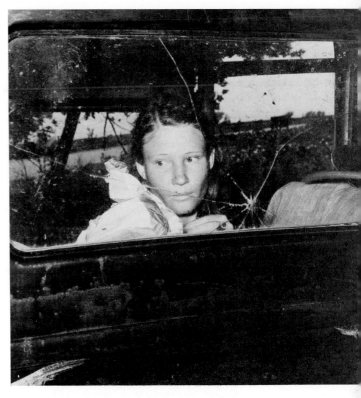

In the 1930s a devastating drought scorched much of the Midwest. As the land turned to dust, bankrupt farmers piled families and belongings into trucks and headed west in search of work. Uncertainty about her future shows in this young migrant's face.

★ 14-4 Sam T. Mayhew Sets It Down ★

Introduction Despite Roosevelt's active promotion of economic aid and reforms, not all poor Americans supported him or his policies. In this selection from an interview he gave in 1939, Sam T. Mayhew tells why he votes Republican. Born in 1890 to former slaves, Mayhew attended college for two years. He lost his leg in a mill accident in 1918. Here he explains his attitude toward the New Deal.

Vocabulary Before you read the selection, find the meaning of this word in a dictionary: amputation.

I've been voting some 15 years, though my vote does little good here in this Democratic section. For county offices I'm forced to vote for a Democrat, since no Republicans run, but I'd rather vote for a man I don't want than not to exercise my voting privilege.

It's true I didn't think Landon would have made a good President. Neither do I think Roosevelt has. All the prosperity he has brought to the country has been legislated and is not real. Nothing he has ever started has been finished. My common way of expressing it is that we are in the middle of the ocean like a ship without an anchor. No good times can come to the country as long as there is so much discrimination practiced.

I can't tell you my real feelings, but I think I can give you an idea of what I mean. Take me: I have applied for work at the welfare office, tried hard to get work. All they had for me, they said, came under the unskilled head. I tried one of these jobs—digging ditches for the sanitary department of the board of health. With my artificial limb, I simply couldn't compete with the other men who were digging ditches. So the inspector said he couldn't use me. It wasn't fair to the other men to pay me what they were getting; as hard as the work was for me, I couldn't take any less. So I didn't last long at that.

Then I applied again for work, for something in the skilled labor line. I had seen men overseeing groups of workers, keeping their time, and so forth, and this I knew I could do as well as anybody. They told me that only white men had these jobs, that I would have to take something in the unskilled classification or none. I'm just as needy—needier, I expect—as the white men, and I can do the job as well. Because of my color, I must ditch or work on the road, in spite of my college training and in spite of physical handicaps from amputaton and high blood pressure. That leaves me helpless, for in this agricultural area there are no jobs open to day labor that I am able to do for a whole day at the time. Besides, there are tenants to do all the odd work on the farms. I asked Mr. Lee the other day to let me come work on his garden for him. He said he had more men idle on his place than he could give work to. There's nothing for me except relief, and what's $14.60 for three months and—seventeen grapefruits? Seventeen grapefruits!

The same thing is true of colored girls. Our high-school graduates need jobs just as much as the white girls. Go over yonder to the county office at the agriculture building. Not a single colored girl has a job there, when they could do the work as well and need it worse than the white girls. I don't think that discrimination is intended at Washington, but here in this county the colored race has no chance to get a job when it's a choice between colors. I don't see much chance for our people to get anywhere when the color line instead of ability determines the opportunities to get ahead economically.

Adapted from *Such As Us*, ed. Tom E. Terrill and Jerrold Hirsch (Chapel Hill, N.C.: University of North Carolina Press, 1978).

READING REVIEW

1. Why does Mayhew think that Roosevelt was not a good President?
2. What does Mayhew see as the main reasons for his difficulties?
3. **Summarizing** In a paragraph, explain why Mr. Mayhew is a Republican.

★ 14-5 That Gentleman in the White House ★

Introduction Many businessmen opposed the New Deal because they felt it presented a threat to the free enterprise system. They also doubted that the country could continue providing programs for the poor without eventually ending up in a state of financial collapse. In this selection, one businessman offers his solution to the economic problems of the time.

Vocabulary Before you read the selection, find the meaning of these words in a dictionary: boondoggling, carte blanche, cleave.

At 105th Street and Riverside Drive, the Hudson River like a railroad track of water separates residential Manhattan from Edgewater, New Jersey. On one side the apartment houses and mansions of the wealthy. West, in the afternoon sun, lies the mainland.

The city's western shore is Riverside Drive Park with its green lawns and ballfields swarming with boys. The new filled-in stretches, not yet sweated into skating rinks, shine raw and coppery in the sun. Laborers are working here.

A stout man of 60 in a blue suit, brown shoes, and brown hat is watching the wheelbarrow men. He looks as if he had just come downstairs from one of the apartment buildings. He stands solidly on his legs, his grayish-blue eyes narrowed against the sun. "It's a nice park they're building," he remarks to me. "And they're not boondoggling. You can say that for them." He grins cautiously.

I nod.

"PWA is all right. But it all has to stop soon. Where's the money coming from? The government's cutting a sewer uptown. Two and a half years and not finished yet! Money won't come out with all this spending. This country will be like Germany was 20 years ago. I was in Stuttgart some time back, and one room in the hotel where I was stopping was called the billion-mark room. It was all plastered up with marks.

"The businessmen got to run this country! We can't depend on that gentleman! He better get out of the White House and give carte blanche to the businessmen. Or else make his peace with us. This PWA, WPA, can't go on forever! There are 11 million men on the government projects or on WPA. We owe 41 billions of dollars and it will soon be 45 billion!" He wipes his brow.

"That gentleman's impractical. He's no businessman. His forebears, his father, his mother, left him his money. He has to surrender the reins to business! It's a businessman's job. I'm connected with a bank over in Hoboken. We're afraid to let the money out!" He stops. He has shown me. There can be no better proof. The bank is afraid to let the money out.

"Were you always a banker?"

"I'm not a banker. I'm connected with a bank, a little bank. We have $5 million in deposits, $2 million in cash. But we can't let that money out!" His lips cleave open, the tip of his tongue poises for a second between his teeth.

"I wasn't always against him. I voted for him in 1932, even donated a little to his campaign. I thought the big evil was prohibition. I thought if we repealed that, things would straighten out in a year or two. I was in the liquor business myself but when prohibition came I couldn't do business any more. That was when I went

Like this cartoonist, Republican businessmen criticized Roosevelt for his spending programs. But neither business nor an expanded federal government could pull the nation from its slump until World War II created new economic demand.

into real estate. Business is afraid. That's why the money won't come out. Because 11 million men depend on the government! Even if they only get a dollar a day, that's $11 million dollars a day, $11 million a day for 11 million men. That's some pay envelope! There's only one solution. Private employment has to take care of the nation's pay envelope."

Adapted from Benjamin Appel, *The People Talk* (New York: E. P. Dutton & Company, Inc., 1940).

READING REVIEW

1. What "gentleman" is the businessman referring to?
2. What steps to revive the economy do you think this businessman would suggest?
3. **Understanding Economic Ideas** (a) Why does the businessman think Roosevelt does not know how to run the economy? (b) Why does he think businessmen should run it?

Introduction Many working-class people felt that Roosevelt was their savior. They regarded him as the first President who took a sincere interest in the welfare of the common people. Interviewing such workers about their lives was one of the programs of the Federal Writers' Project, part of the Works Progress Administration (WPA). In this selection, George Dobbin, a 67-year-old cotton mill worker, tells of his feelings toward Roosevelt.

Vocabulary Before you read the selection, find the meaning of this word in a dictionary: desolation.

I do think that Roosevelt is the biggest-hearted man we ever had in the White House. He undoubtedly is the most fore-sighted and can speak his thoughts the plainest of any man I ever heard speak. He's spoke very few words over the radio that I haven't listened to. It's the first time in my recollection that a President ever got up and said, "I'm interested in and aim to do somethin' for the workin' man." Just knowin' that for once in the time of the country they was a man to stand up and speak for him, a man that could make what he felt so plain nobody could doubt he meant it, has made a lot of us feel a sight better even when they wasn't much to eat in our homes.

Roosevelt picked us up out of the mud and stood us up but whenever he turns us loose I'm afraid we're goin' to fall and go deeper in the mud than we was before. That's because so many of his own party has turned against him and brought defeat to lots of his thinkin' and plannin'. The Bible says, "A house divided against itself cannot stand, a kingdom divided against itself will end in desolation." If they keep abuckin' against him and bigheads get in there that try to make too quick a turn back, desolation will follow in our country.

Roosevelt is the only President we ever had that thought the Constitution belonged to the pore man too. The way they've been areadin' it it seemed like they thought it said, "Him that's got money shall have the rights to life, freedom, and happiness." Is they any freedom to bein' throwed out of yore home and have to watch yore children suffer just because you joined a organization you thought might better you? Does it make you think you've got liberty to be treated like that when the man you're workin' for has always had the right to join the association to multiply his own good livin'? Yessir, it took Roosevelt to read in the Constitution and find out them folks way back yonder that made it was talkin' about the pore man right along with the rich one. I am a Roosevelt man.

Adapted from *These Are Our Lives*, Federal Writers Project of the Works Progress Administration (Chapel Hill, N.C.: University of North Carolina Press, 1939).

During the depression radio broadcasting thrived. President Franklin D. Roosevelt created a new feeling of closeness with the public through his "fireside chats."

READING REVIEW

1. What is George Dobbin afraid will happen if Roosevelt and his programs are defeated?

2. According to Dobbin, how does Roosevelt's view of the Constitution differ from that of earlier Presidents?

3. **Analyzing Conflicting Opinions** (a) How does Dobbin's attitude toward Roosevelt differ from the attitude of the businessman in Reading 14-5? (b) How would you explain the difference?

15 Prelude to Another World Conflict (1920–1941)

Introduction During the Harding administration, the United States surprised the world with its open proposal for a reduction of naval armaments. Britain, France, Italy, and Japan sent delegates to Washington, D.C., to confer about arms limitations. This selection from the memoirs of Eleanor B. Roosevelt describes the occasion. Her husband Ted, Theodore Roosevelt, Jr., was assistant secretary of the Navy at the time.

Vocabulary Before you read the selection, find the meaning of these words in a dictionary: diet, formidable, tumultuous.

The Conference for the Limitation of Armaments began in hope in November 1921 and ended in optimism in February 1922. Its aims were the reduction of naval armaments and settlement of affairs in the Far East. To this end President Harding invited the governments of the British Empire, France, Italy, and Japan to send delegates to Washington to confer on limitation of armaments, in connection with which the Far Eastern questions would be taken up. Belgium, China, the Netherlands, and Portugal were invited to take part in the Far Eastern discussions.

At the time France had the only really big army, but various signs indicated that a race in naval armaments was due to start at any time. Although there had been agitation in the Japanese press for peace and disarmament, her diet had been voting seven to one for a formidable program of military preparedness. About 50 percent of her budget was going for arms and munitions. She had extensive contracts for war materials in Europe. A considerable number of Japanese were emigrating from Hawaii because, it was said, of bad industrial conditions, but they were going to Japan, where conditions were as bad. Many Japanese were leaving California, ostensibly on tours to their land of origin, but selling their homes before going. All this looked dangerous.

The conference opened dramatically. After greetings by the President, Charles Evans Hughes, Secretary of State and chief United States delegate, began to speak. No one had thought this first session would be anything more than addresses of welcome and exchanges of courtesies. But after a few minutes the delegates suddenly realized that this speech was nothing of the kind.

The atmosphere in the hall grew tense as Mr. Hughes described specifically the drastic reduction in naval armaments the United States was prepared to make, and made definite proposals as to what the other nations should do. Foreign delegates were startled and whispered excitedly to their advisers. At certain propositions the galleries broke into applause. It was amid tumultuous cheering that Mr. Hughes finished laying the full American plan before the conference for consideration.

The whole world was surprised. It was the first time in history that a matter of such importance had not been settled behind closed doors before being told to the people. Here was a novel kind of diplomacy, inviting public opinion all over the world to express itself, which it did with enthusiasm and unqualified approval. Mr. Hughes had felt that the success or failure of the conference depended in large measure on the sentiment it aroused among the people of the countries concerned. For this reason he placed the American plan not simply before the foreign delegates but also before our people and all peoples at one and the same time. In order to be fair to all, he confined the circle of those who knew of the plan entirely to the Americans who were intimately concerned in its preparation.

Mr. Hughes was anxious to achieve real, not merely token, reduction. He had consulted members of the General Board of the Navy and got nowhere, because he wanted to cut so much and they so little. Finally he requested Secretary Denby to appoint a committee of three—Ted; Admiral Coontz, Chief of Naval Operations; and Rear Admiral William V. Pratt, member of the Navy General Board. This committee was to draw up a plan acceptable both to Mr. Hughes and to the General Board. Several plans were submitted before one was satisfactory. Mr. Hughes was pleased and took it home to put in his private safe. He wanted no one else to know he intended to read it at the opening of the conference. Two days before this he told Ted he wanted fifty copies for distribution to the delegates, saying it was so important to prevent leakage that he did not want them done in his own office in the State Department, and he asked Ted to have them made in the Navy Department. Ted had them mimeographed by Admiral Pratt. No attempt was made to print any copies until the morning of the day when the plan was to be announced to the general public.

From *Day Before Yesterday* by Eleanor B. Roosevelt. Reprinted by permission of Curtis Brown, Ltd. Copyright © 1959 by Eleanor B. Roosevelt.

READING REVIEW

1. What countries attended the Washington Naval Conference?
2. In what ways does Roosevelt think the conference was unusual?
3. **Relating Past to Present** (a) What arms reduction proposals concern the nations of the world today? (b) What advances in technology have changed the nature of disarmament?

★ 15-2 The Neutrality Act of 1935 ★

Introduction In the 1930s most Americans were concerned with their own economic problems. Few wanted the nation to become involved in European affairs. Despite alarming events in Italy, Germany, and Spain, public sentiment favored a neutral position. Journalist Dorothy Thompson was an outspoken critic of isolationist policy. Here she describes her view of the Neutrality Act of 1935.

Vocabulary Before you read the selection, find the meaning of these words in a dictionary: belligerents, flagrantly, dubious.

It is expected that some time this week the Pittman resolution will be favorably reported out of the Foreign Affairs Committee of the Senate. The bill will extend to the President the very great power of deciding what, anywhere in the world, constitutes a state of war, whether international or civil, thereupon giving him enormous controls over our entire foreign trade. The bill, furthermore, definitely favors, in wartime, that country or those countries which can control the seas, extending to it or to them special privileges which other belligerents cannot enjoy. It also extends special privileges to those nations who hold credits in this country or operate industries or exploit natural resources here. The bill is called a neutrality law and is designed to keep us out of war. I submit that its measures have nothing to do with neutrality and that it is extremely likely to serve exactly the opposite purpose for which it is designed.

Now, what does this bill actually mean in practice? First of all, it means that we are flagrantly reversing the attitude expressed in the Kellogg Pact, which denounces aggression. We, the greatest, strongest single nation on earth, announce by implication that there is no such thing as "right" or "wrong" and no such thing as international morality. We say by implication that morally speaking it is a matter of complete indifference to this country whether a large and strong nation deliberately overruns a weak one. The attacked is a belligerent as well as the attacker, and we shall furnish arms to neither of them and possibly no food or basic raw materials either.

But then we qualify that stand of dubious morality. We say that we will sell goods to anybody who can come and get them. That will mean in practice that we will sell goods to anybody who can control the high seas. That means, in the field of realistic politics, that as matters stand today, we will sell goods to Great Britain. Tomorrow, perhaps, Germany and Russia will make a great combination, build tremendous navies, and set out to conquer the world. Anything at all is possible. And in that case, it will mean that we will sell goods to them. Or it may mean that two warring countries, let us say Great Britain and Germany, are contending for the control of the high seas and both buying goods in our ports. That will mean that they may be blowing up each other's ships just outside our harbors—or inside them!

The President may forbid American nationals to engage in almost any form of trade from this country, but the bill exempts non-Americans doing business in this country. This means that although we may embargo oil to any belligerent, British companies who own oil fields here or cotton plantations can sell oil or cotton to anyone they choose. It will also, in all probability, mean that Germans, French, and others will set about purchasing oil fields here, as well as other sources of necessary raw materials.

Adapted from Dorothy Thompson, *Let The Record Speak* (Boston: Houghton Mifflin Company, 1939). Copyright 1939 by Dorothy Thompson Lewis.

READING REVIEW

1. According to Thompson, which nations were really being favored by the neutrality act?

2. In what way does Thompson think the United States was ignoring "international morality"?

3. **Summarizing** What are Thompson's main objections to the Neutrality Act of 1935?

While the Axis powers lined up and Great Britain and France anxiously waited, isolationists and internationalists fought it out in Congress. Sympathy with the democracies was not strong enough to counteract a longtime policy of United States neutrality.

Introduction The leaders of Germany, Italy, and Japan used many arguments to explain and justify their use of force against other nations. In this 1938 address to the American Academy of Political and Social Science, Chinese scholar Hu Shih challenges the reasons given for using aggressive force.

Vocabulary Before you read the selection, find the meaning of these words in a dictionary: auspices, distinguished, apologists, superimposed, rationalizations, jargon, fallacy, status quo, anarchy.

Almost exactly 18 months ago, in the same hotel and under the same auspices, I had the pleasure of speaking from the same platform with a distinguished Italian scholar. He defended the right of the have-not nations to seek outlets for their population pressure and to control sources of supply for raw materials. He frankly said: "Force is the only solution. The inferior races must be sacrificed for the benefit of the strong."

These words, which still ring in my ears, sum up the philosophy of force as preached by the dictators and apologists of the aggressor nations which choose to call themselves "the have-nots," as if to have not would somehow justify their right to plunder the haves!

What has happened in the world during the last seven years—ever since the first acts of Japanese aggression in China in September 1931—is nothing but this philosophy of force of the so-called have-not nations being ruthlessly but methodically tested out in actual application.

Let us first take up the problem of population pressure. Population pressure is solved by birth control, by voluntary emigration, by increased productivity of the soil, and by industrialization. Military conquest and political domination of territories already densely populated or climatically unsuited to large-scale emigration have never contributed much towards solving the population problem.

Japan, for instance, has possessed Formosa for 43 years, but the Japanese population there is only 264,000 in a total population of 5,000,000—that is, 5.2 percent. She has had Korea for 30 years, but the Japanese population in Korea is 560,000 in a total of 21,000,000—i.e., 2.6 percent.

Next, I wish to point out that it is equally untrue to say that it is necessary for a nation to rely upon force for insuring supplies of raw materials. It is generally accepted that in time of peaceful and normal commerce raw materials of all nations are open to all who can pay for them. A nation like Japan, which imports rubber, oil, iron ore, pig iron, scrap iron, tin, lead, nickel, and aluminum from foreign countries, is always welcomed as a best customer. No force or political domination is necessary to insure the constant supply of all needed materials for her industries.

And, after all, it is physically impossible for any nation, or even for any economic bloc of nations, to secure political control of all possible sources of raw materials. That is to say, strictly speaking, economic self-sufficiency is impossible. Even the United States must depend upon the outside world for rubber, tin, nickel, and manganese. Even the Union of Soviet Socialist Republics is deficient in rubber, tin, bauxite, and nickel. Even the British Empire has to rely upon outside supply of petroleum and cotton.

Apart from its economic absurdities, the force philosophy of the have-nots is politically suicidal. As a matter of historical truth, the philosophy of the have-nots is essentially political in nature and origin, its economic doctrines being largely superimposed rationalizations. It is absurd, for example, to talk about population pressure and at the same time actively encourage population growth!

Behind the economic jargon, the real motivating force is a fantastic dream of unlimited political power. Hitler dreams of his new Germanic Empire; Mussolini, his new Roman Empire; and the Japanese military, their great continental Japanese Empire and their world empire which shall cover the whole world wherever the sun shines.

But this political success of an individual or a class should not blind us to the huge losses which their respective nations have had to sustain in increased national economic burdens, in sacrifices of individual liberty and standards of living, and in the international hatred aroused all around.

Herein lies the basic political fallacy of this philosophy of the have-nots which seeks to destroy the status quo in order that they themselves may have more possessions at the expense of other peoples. It fails to appreciate the political importance of an international order which not merely protects the weak nations, but also guarantees the power and prestige of the strong nations. It fails to understand that law and order, internationally as well as internally, however troublesome and inconvenient they may seem to our selfish desires, are better than anarchy and chaos.

Adapted from Hu Shih, "To Have Not and Want to Have," *The Annals of the American Academy of Political and Social Science*, ed. Ernest Minor Patterson. Copyright 1938 by The American Academy of Political and Social Science.

READING REVIEW

1. According to Hu Shih, how do the aggressors try to justify their actions?
2. What weakness does he find in the argument that have-not nations need to use force to insure a supply of raw materials?
3. **Recognizing a Point of View** (a) How would you describe Hu Shih's attitude toward the aggressor nations? (b) How do you think his nationality might have affected his point of view?

★ 15-4 An Ambulance Station in London ★

Introduction In 1940 and 1941, before the United States entered World War II, England, especially London, suffered terribly from German bombing raids. Many crucial defense jobs at that time were held by women. The writer of this letter worked at an ambulance station. She took calls and directed ambulances to areas that had been hit. Here she describes how she and other Londoners responded to the air raids.

Vocabulary Before you read the selection, find the meaning of these words in a dictionary: debris, replica, uninhabitable, mutilated, commiserated, stoic, gramophone, superficially.

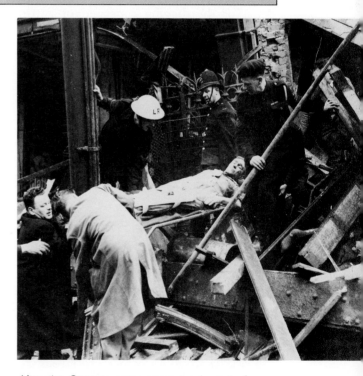

After the German army conquered most of Europe, it concentrated on Great Britain. Daily bombing raids rained on London. Here rescue workers remove a wounded man from a wrecked building.

London
November 21, 1940

Darling J.:

Well, on goes the bombing. London is beginning to show her scars, and there are some heartrending sights. I think St. James's, Piccadilly, moved me more than anything. It stands, but the top of the tower has gone, there is no roof. The beautiful windows are buckled up and broken. The courtyard is full of debris.

249 **Topic 15**

The gateway is crooked and dangerous and it will never be the same again whatever people say about building a replica.

A land mine exploded on [*the name of the place was cut out by a censor*] destroying it utterly—that dignified late Georgian building—but I haven't seen it. Not long ago, one of the biggest explosives known dropped [*censored*] from my house. We were sitting at the top in my room and heard the inevitable whistle and then, for what seemed ages after the explosion, the sound of falling masonry. Our house shook like a leaf and crackled as though it was made of paper.

Nine houses were totally demolished and seventeen made uninhabitable—roofs blown off, etc. The crater [*censored*] and there were at least 20 people killed—mostly buried under the rubble. The rescue squads were days digging them out.

About a week later, another good-sized bomb fell on top of [*censored*] station. A train was there at the time and there were about 50 dead—not only dead but mutilated beyond all recognition. Most of the digging consisted of getting out arms, legs, etc., separately and packing them up in labeled bundles to be sent to the mortuary to be sorted out. Our ambulances were out all that night (and next day with reliefs). I didn't go because I had to be at the telephone sending them out one after another.

There is no doubt the Germans are pretty hard at it and I can't think why they don't send more. But perhaps they prefer the slow agony of pure chance hits. London has settled down to it. I take no more notice at all and never dream of going to a shelter or any longer sleeping anywhere but in my own bed. If I am bombed—all right, but until then I shall be comfortable and as little tired as possible.

Several people at the ambulance station have had bombs on their houses but have escaped in various ways. One man had everything he possessed destroyed, and, when commiserated with, said, "After all, we are both young and strong and can set up a home again. When one door shuts, another always opens." Later he was seen carrying a small suitcase and held it up saying, "I'm just taking my house away."

Jokes are made daily and it is still the main social topic of conversation. The result of it all is that it is very difficult to know where anyone is living—very difficult to see people. Everyone has a stoic cheerfulness and there is a great deal of heartbreaking bravery and moving incidents. The raids have become part of life.

I have just overheard the following. A: "There's a raid on, isn't there?" B: "No, there isn't." C: "Yes, of course there is." B: "Oh. We don't see much of so-and-so these days, do we?" A: "Well, she's got a new job, you know," etc. Evenings are so much changed. No cinemas, theatres, or gaiety of any kind and only people scurrying home, tin hats bobbing past one in the streets and a few A.R.P. cars whizzing by on deserted streets.

People study the weather: "Good night for bombing." "Lovely night, isn't it?" "Yes, I wish it wasn't." "Isn't this rain filthy in the blackout—the bombs don't seem to mind, do they?" etc. Pubs are full all the time. Here at the station we are keeping going fairly well.

We all become more and more separated and out of touch. That I can't bear. One forgets people and they forget one too. But I have got some new friends here.

My health is absolutely bounding except for exhaustion at times. Sometimes I feel very excited, perhaps just because of the times we live in. The National Gallery [concerts] continue in the basement. I play the gramophone more than ever and music means increasingly more to me—so does poetry, but I seldom read it, or read at all. But I am not superficially depressed, only when I think hard, but that applies to everyone.

Adapted from *Women of Britain: Letters from England*, ed. Beatrice Curtis Brown and Jan Struther (New York: Harcourt Brace Jovanovich, Inc., 1941).

READING REVIEW

1. How did the workers at the ambulance station adjust to the nightly air raids?
2. Why do you think parts of her letter were censored?
3. **Relating Cause and Effect** What effect did the bombing of England, as described in the letter, probably have on American public opinion? Why?

Introduction On December 7, 1941, the Japanese launched a surprise attack on the American Fleet at Pearl Harbor, Hawaii. In his call for a declaration of war, President Roosevelt called it "a day which will live in infamy." In this selection, Walter Lord describes the beginning of the attack.

Vocabulary Before you read the selection, find the meaning of these words in a dictionary: buzzing, sabotage, gig.

Thirteen-year-old James B. Mann, Jr., stood with his father, squinting at the planes that circled high above their beach house at Haleiwa on the northwest coast of Oahu. More than 100 planes were orbiting about, gradually breaking up into smaller groups of three, five, and seven. Soon, several fighters dropped down low enough for Junior to observe, "They've changed the color of our planes." Then the fighters sped off to the east, down the road toward Schofield and Wheeler Field. Now the other groups were flying away too, and by 7:45 A.M. they had all disappeared.

Fourteen miles to the southeast, two other young fishermen were trying their luck in Pearl Harbor. Thirteen-year-old Jerry Morton and his kid brother Don, 11, sat on the enlisted men's landing at Pearl City, a peninsula that juts southward into the middle of the anchorage. Like most service children, Jerry and Don regarded Pearl Harbor not as a naval base but as a huge, fascinating play pool.

This morning they set out as usual—barefoot, khaki pants rolled up, T-shirts stuffed in their pockets as soon as their mother wasn't looking. Little gusts of wind stirred the harbor waters, but the sun poked through the clouds often enough to make the day hot and lazy. It was a typical Sunday morning, except for one thing: incredibly, the fish were biting. By 7:45 the boys had used up all their bait, and Don was dispatched to the house for more. Jerry, the senior partner, lolled in the morning sun.

Around him, the ships of the Pacific fleet lay in every direction. The large and the small, the mighty and the meek, they all added up to 96 warships in Pearl Harbor this Sunday morning.

Just down the road from the Pearl Harbor gate—a few hundred yards closer to Honolulu—lay the main entrance to Hickam Field, where the army bombers were based. Normally there was a good deal of practice flying here, including some friendly buzzing of the navy next door. The carrier planes, in turn, would occasionally stage mock raids on Hickam. But this morning all was quiet. The carriers were at sea, and the bombers were lined up in neat rows beside the main concrete runway.

General Short's sabotage alert was in full force, and obviously the best way to guard the planes was to group them together, out in the open. So there they all were—or at least all that mattered, for only 6 of the B-17s could fly, only 6 of the 12 A-20s, and only 17 of the 33 outmoded B-18s.

Out in the harbor, Lieutenant Commander Bill Burford made the best of things as skipper of the ready-duty destroyer *Monaghan*. She was due to be relieved at 8:00, and Burford had planned to go ashore. In fact, the gig was already alongside. Then at 7:51 a message suddenly came in from Fourteenth Naval District Headquarters to "get under way immediately and contact Ward in defensive sea area." The message didn't even say what he should prepare for, but obviously it might be a couple of hours before he would be free again to go ashore.

Whatever was in store for the *Monaghan*, the other ships in Pearl Harbor had only morning colors to worry about. This ceremony was always the same. As the clock ticked toward 7:55, all over the harbor men went to their stations. On the big battleship *Nevada*, the ship's band assembled for a ceremony that would have all the trimmings. While everybody waited around, some of the bandsmen noticed specks in the sky far to the southwest.

Planes were approaching, and from more than one direction. Ensign Donald L. Korn, officer of the deck on the *Raleigh*, noticed a thin line winging in from the northwest. Seaman "Red" Pressler of the *Arizona* saw a string approaching from the mountains to the east. On the destroyer *Helm*, Quartermaster Frank Handler noticed another group coming in low from the south.

As the planes roared nearer, Pharmacist's Mate William Lynch heard a California shipmate call out, "The Russians must have a carrier visiting us. Here come some planes with the red ball showing clearly."

In they hurtled—Lieutenant Commander Takahashi's 27 dive bombers plunging toward Ford Island and Hickam, Lieutenant Commander Murata's 40 torpedo planes swinging into position for their run at the big ships. Commander Fuchida marked time off Barbers Point with the horizontal bombers, watching his men go in. They were all attacking together instead of in stages as originally planned, but it would apparently make no difference—the ships were sitting ducks.

A few minutes earlier, at 7:49 A.M., Fuchida had radioed the signal to attack. Now he was so sure of victory that at 7:53—even before the first bomb fell—he signaled the carriers that the surprise attack was successful: "Tora ... tora ... tora ..."

The men who saw the planes couldn't understand. One of them was Fireman Frank Stock of the repair ship *Vestal*, moored beside the *Arizona* along Battleship Row. Stock and six of his mates had taken the church launch for services ashore. As they reached the Merry's Point landing at the end of the loch, six or eight torpedo planes flew in low from the east,

about 50 feet above the water and heading down the loch toward the battleships.

The men were mildly surprised—they had never seen U.S. planes come in from that direction. They were even more surprised when the rear-seat gunners sprayed them with machine-gun bullets. Then Stock recalled the stories he had read about "battle-condition" maneuvers in the southern states. This must be the same idea—for extra realism they had even painted red circles on the planes. The truth finally dawned when one of his friends caught a slug in the stomach from the fifth plane that passed.

Ship after ship began to catch on. The executive officer of the supply ship *Castor* shouted, "The Japs are bombing us! The Japs are bombing us!" For an instant Seaman Bill Deas drew a blank and wondered whether the man was speaking to him. On the submarine *Tautog*, the topside anchor watch shouted, "The war is on, no fooling!"

Down the corridors, up the ladders, through the hatches the men ran, climbed, milled, and shoved toward their battle stations. And it was high time. The alarm was no sooner given when the *Oklahoma* took the first of five torpedoes, the *West Virginia* the first of six. These were the golden targets—directly across from Southeast Loch. Next the *Arizona* took two, even though a little to the north and partly blocked by the *Vestal*. Then the *California* got two, even though far to the south and a relatively poor target. Only the inboard battleships seemed safe—*Maryland* alongside *Oklahoma* and *Tennessee* beside *West Virginia*.

On Sunday morning, December 7, 1941, the Japanese stunned Americans by attacking Pearl Harbor. This official navy photograph shows some of the damage inflicted on United States ships.

In the navy housing areas around Pearl Harbor, people couldn't imagine what was wrecking Sunday morning. Captain Reynolds Hayden, enjoying breakfast at his home on Hospital Point, thought it was construction blasting—then his young son Billy rushed in shouting, "They're Jap planes!"

As 11-year-old Don Morton scuffed back to his house in Pearl City for more fishing bait, an explosion almost pitched him on his face. Then another, and still another. He scrambled home and asked his mother what was happening. She just told him to go fetch his brother Jerry. He ran out to find several planes now gliding by at house-top level. One was strafing the dirt road, kicking up little puffs of dust. Don was scared to go any further. As he ran back to the house, he saw his next-door neighbor, a navy lieutenant, standing in his pajamas on the grass, crying like a child.

From *Day of Infamy* by Walter Lord. Copyright © 1957 by Walter Lord. Reprinted by permission of Holt, Rinehart and Winston, Publishers.

READING REVIEW

1. How large was the fleet in Pearl Harbor at the time of the attack?
2. What was the initial response of the servicemen stationed at Pearl Harbor?
3. **Understanding Geography** Find Japan and Hawaii on a world map. (a) About how far is Hawaii from Japan? (b) Is any part of the United States closer to Japan? (c) Why did the Japanese choose Hawaii instead?

Topic

16 The Second World War (1941–1945)

★ 16-1 Private Mollie, the Mayor of Broadway ★

Introduction During World War II, news correspondents often traveled with the troops. The dispatches they sent from battlefronts gave people at home a vivid sense of what the war was like. Here A. J. Liebling, a reporter for *The New Yorker* magazine, draws a portrait of one unusual soldier who gave his life in the war in North Africa.

Vocabulary Before you read the selection, find the meaning of these words in a dictionary: surmised, suppression, promenade, beret, reverently, concession.

I saw an American soldier by the side of the road. This one was dead. A soldier nearby said that the dead man had been a private known as Mollie. A blanket covered his face, so I surmised that it had been shattered, but there was no blood on the ground, so I judged that he had been killed in the brush and carried out to the road to wait for transport. A big, wild-looking sergeant was standing alongside him—a hawk-nosed, red-necked man with a couple of front teeth missing—and I asked him if the dead man had been in the patrol with the four wounded ones. "Jeez, no!" the sergeant said, looking at me as if I ought to know about the man with the blanket over his face. "That's Mollie, Comrade Molotov. The Mayor of Broadway. Didn't you ever hear of him? He always liked to do crazy things—go off by himself with a pair of big field glasses he had and watch the enemy put in minefields, or take off and be an artillery spotter for a while, or drive a tank."

"Was his name really Molotov?" I asked.

"No," said the sergeant, "he just called himself that. The boys mostly shortened it to Mollie. I don't even know what his real name was—Warren, I think. Carl Warren. He used to say he was a

Broadway big shot. 'Just ask anybody around 44th Street,' he used to say. 'They all know me.' Me, I'm from White Plains—I never heard of him before he joined up."

It was a month later, aboard the United States War Shipping Administration steamer *Monterey*, a luxury liner that had been converted to war service without any needless suppression of comfort, that I next heard of Molotov, the Mayor of Broadway. The *Monterey* was on her way from Casablanca to New York. On the passenger list were four correspondents besides myself, a thousand German prisoners, five hundred wounded Americans, all of whom would need long hospitalization, and a couple of hundred officers and men who were being transferred or were on various errands.

The hospital orderlies would wheel the legless wounded out on the promenade deck in wheelchairs to see the German boxing bouts, and the other wounded would follow them, some swinging along on crutches or hopping on one foot, some with their arms in slings or casts, some with their broken necks held stiffly in casts and harnesses. They had mixed reactions to the bouts. An arm case named Sanderson, a private who wore the Ninth Division shoulder patch, told me one day that he wished he could be turned loose on the prisoners with a tommygun, because he didn't like to see them jumping about in front of his legless pals. Another arm case named Shapiro, from the same division, always got a lot of amusement out of the show. Shapiro was a rugged-looking boy from the Brownsville part of Brooklyn. He explained how he felt one day after two Afrika Korps heavyweights had gone through a couple of rounds of grunting, posturing, and slapping. "Every time I see them box, I know we can't lose the war," he said. "The Master Race—phooey! Any kid off the street could of took the both of them."

Shapiro and Sanderson, I learned during one ringside conversation with them, had both been in the Sixtieth Infantry, Molotov's old regiment. They had been wounded in the fighting around Maknassy, in southern Tunisia, early in April, the first serious action the regiment had been in. Molotov had been killed late in April, during the drive on Bizerte, and until I told them, the boys hadn't heard he was dead. I asked them if they had known him.

"How could you help it?" Shapiro said. "There will never be anybody in the division as well known as him. In the first place, you couldn't help noticing him on account of his clothes. He looked like a soldier out of some other army, always wearing them twenty-dollar green tailor-made officer's shirts and sometimes riding boots, with a French beret with a long rooster feather that he got off an Italian prisoner's hat, and a long black-and-red cape that he got off another prisoner for a can of C ration."

"And the officers let him get away with it?" I asked.

"Not in the rear areas, they didn't," Shapiro said. "But in combat, Mollie was an asset. Major Kauffman, his battalion commander, knew it, so he would kind of go along with him. But he would never have him made even a Pfc. Mollie couldn't of stood the responsibility. He was the greatest natural-born foul-up in the Army," Shapiro added reverently. "He was court-martialed 20 or 30 times, but the major always got him out of it. He had the biggest blanket roll in the Ninth Division, with a wall tent inside it and some Arabian carpets and bronze lamps and a folding washstand and about five changes of uniform, none of them regulation, and he would always manage to get it on a truck when we moved. When he pitched his tent, it looked like a concession at Coney Island. I can hardly think of him being dead."

"Well, what was so good about him?" I asked.

Sanderson, who was a thin, sharp-faced boy from Michigan, answered me with the embarrassed frankness of a modern mother explaining the facts of life to her offspring. "Sir," he said, "it may not sound nice to say it, and I do not want to knock anyone, but in battle almost everybody is frightened, especially the first couple of times. Once in a while you find a fellow who isn't frightened at all. He goes forward and the other fellows go along with him. So he is very important. Some fellows get brave with experience, I guess, but Mollie never had any fear anyway.

"Like one time on the road to Maknassy, the battalion was trying to take some hills and we were getting no place. Mollie stands right up, wearing the cape and the beret with the feather, and he says, 'I bet those Italians would surrender if somebody asked them to. What do they want to fight for?' he says. So he walks across the minefield and up the hill to the Italians, waving his arms and making funny motions, and they shoot at him for a while and then stop, thinking he is crazy.

"He goes up there yelling, 'Veni qua!' which he says afterward is New York Italian for 'Come here!' and 'feeneesh la guerree!' which is French. And when he gets to the Italians he finds a soldier who was a barber in Astoria but went home on a visit and got drafted in the Italian Army, so the barber translates for him. And the Italians say sure, they would like to surrender, and Mollie comes back to the lines with 568 prisoners. He had about 10 Italian automatics strapped to his belt and 15 field glasses hung over his shoulders. So instead of being stopped, we took the position and cleaned up on the enemy.

"That was good for the morale of the battalion. The next time we got in a fight, we said to ourselves, 'Those guys are just looking for an easy out,' so we got up and chased them away from there.

"A disciplined soldier would never have did what Mollie done. He was a very unusual guy. He gave the battalion confidence and the battalion gave the regiment confidence, because the other battalions said, 'If the Second can take all those prisoners, we can, too.' And the Thirty-ninth and the Forty-seventh Regiments probably said to themselves, 'If the Sixtieth is winning all them fights, we can, also.' So you might say that Mollie made the whole division."

Reprinted by permission of the Putnam Publishing Group from *Liebling Abroad*, by A. J. Liebling. Copyright © 1981 by P.E.I. Books, Inc.

READING REVIEW

1. What reactions did the wounded Americans have to the German prisoners sharing the ship with them?
2. What was unusual about Private Mollie, according to Sanderson?
3. **Finding the Main Idea** How did Private Mollie influence his fellow soldiers?

★ 16-2 Running a Norton OD Grinder ★

Introduction After the United States entered World War II, many young men volunteered for the armed services. Many young women also joined the war effort by working in war production plants. Patricia Megargee was just out of high school when the war began. Here she recalls her work in an airplane engine factory.

Vocabulary Before you read the selection, find the meaning of these words in a dictionary: calipers, micrometers, niche, flanges, adjacent, zealous, paternalistic.

Gradually everyone started going off. All the boys who had been going to Lawrenceville and Choate and the various schools were graduating and instead of going on to college were taken into the army. I had a brother, two years younger; later on, he was in the navy. He was on a ship that went to Anzio; he was very uncommunicative, like kids are today. He didn't finish high school, ran off and joined the navy before the proper age. My parents were very upset about that. They were also upset about the fact that I didn't go on to college.

It was a strange time; there didn't seem to be any point in going to college. Everything was out of kilter. We went to visit a very good friend of my mother's up in Connecticut. Her husband was an officer in the navy, and she had gone to stay on a farm. She had just decided to leave her apartment in New York and sort of hole up there for a couple of years. It was strange. People were going into things like that. I went up to stay with her.

When young men left their jobs to join the armed forces in World War II, women took their places. Here artist Norman Rockwell portrays "Rosie the Riveter." She became a symbol of women who worked in war production.

I heard that they were looking for help at Pratt & Whitney, in East Hartford. We were in a little town called Winsted, Connecticut. I drove in one day with some neighbors and was interviewed. I was either just 18 or not quite 18. Anyway, they said, "Fine."

They were desperate for people to work. They put me into a training program for about two months, every day, eight hours or whatever. Oh, I was so pleased with myself. Mother was furious. I just kept telling her it was for the war effort. I got this certified machinist certificate, and I remember I was so proud. They put you through this thing about how to run these machines, how to read calipers and micrometers and various testing devices.

We were in a separate building for the training. Then we went into this big factory; it covered miles. You'd check in,

and then you'd walk and walk and walk and walk until you got to your own little niche. It was very exciting. As a matter of fact, I really wouldn't mind doing it again.

I ran a Norton OD grinder, OD being "outside diameter." We would put parts under this thing and then grind various portions of the flanges and what have you. These were parts that would go into the Pratt & Whitney engines. Pratt & Whitney made the engine, and I think Republic made the airplane itself. I was in the engine section, and Hamilton Propeller was right adjacent to it.

It was nifty! Great fun—if you were 18, anything was fun. In my particular area there were mostly men working, but it was so vast, it's hard to explain. There were trucks that drove right down the aisles where people would walk. Small, sort of Jeeplike things. Or if there was a fire, a sort of minifiretruck would come. It was so vast that you couldn't see from one end to the other. It was like a small town all under this one roof.

I was very unsophisticated at the time, but I was very zealous, probably overzealous. I remember some of the older guys who had been there for years used to say, "Hey, kid, don't be in such a hurry!" But I'd get into the thing and geared up for it and I'd just keep plugging away, measuring and grinding, measuring and grinding, and they'd say, "Hey, kid, take it easy." They'd been doing it for 15 or 20 years, and they didn't want me approaching what they had done at the end of the day because then they didn't look good, and of course they could do it with one hand tied behind their backs.

I got into the night shift because it paid more money and it worked out better as far as my getting a ride in a car pool. We had maybe a 40-minute drive into East Hartford, and it got a little complicated with the driving business. I didn't have a car and so I was in a car pool, and you paid so much a week to drive with these guys, nice country-type of guys, who had been doing this kind of thing all their lives and were either too old or for some reason or another didn't go in the service. The ones I rode with were kind of paternalistic about the whole thing. They thought it was funny that I would want to do that rather than go into the hairdressing business or something. We'd work from midnight to seven, only seven hours instead of eight hours. You got the benefit of the extra hour because you were on the night shift.

It was always an exciting thing to drive up there at eleven-thirty at night. From a distance you could see the plant, all the antiaircraft lights on the roof, and you just felt like you were involved in it, so that when you got letters from your friends overseas, you weren't as cut off as you would have been if you weren't doing anything.

Adapted from *Americans Remember the Home Front, An Oral Narrative*, ed. Roy Hoopes (New York: Hawthorn Books, 1977). Copyright © 1977 by Roy Hoopes.

READING REVIEW

1. How did Megargee's family react to her working at the plant?
2. How did Megargee feel about her work? Why?
3. **Analyzing Oral Evidence** What can you learn about life on the home front from Megargee's account?

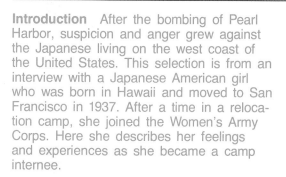

★ 16-3 The Detention of Japanese Americans ★

Introduction After the bombing of Pearl Harbor, suspicion and anger grew against the Japanese living on the west coast of the United States. This selection is from an interview with a Japanese American girl who was born in Hawaii and moved to San Francisco in 1937. After a time in a relocation camp, she joined the Women's Army Corps. Here she describes her feelings and experiences as she became a camp internee.

Vocabulary Before you read the selection, find the meaning of this word in a dictionary: evacuation.

How well I remember December 7 because that started a whole lot of changes in my life. Sunday was my usual day off and I was supposed to go see my nisei* girl friend to have lunch with her. She was working in a domestic job also. I was over there about 10:30 in the morning and we were just talking. The radio was not on. About 11 o'clock the nursemaid came dashing downstairs. She was very excited because she said that Pearl Harbor was being bombed.

The first thing I thought of during the numbness which came over me was about

---

*Nisei refers to a native United States citizen whose parents were Japanese immigrants. Issei refers to a Japanese person who emigrated to the United States after the exclusion act of 1907. An issei could not become a citizen until 1952.

my family back in Honolulu. I wanted to get word from them or to them immediately. However, the radio said for nobody to use the phone, so that I didn't try to get a radiogram through. I was so excited that I forgot about lunch.

The next day I had a cablegram from my mother in Hawaii so that my mind immediately became more settled. It was such a relief after the tension of the preceding day. I did not give any thought as to what would happen to the Japanese in the United States. I did not conceive of anything like evacuation. I did not know what my plans were going to be as everything was so indefinite. I had certain fears when the waterfront areas of San Francisco were closed to enemy aliens and the FBI started to round up Japanese in earnest. I heard so many rumors but I did not know what to think. However, I thought that the FBI must have had good reasons for the roundup because many of the issei had connections with pro-Japan organizations. This was a justified action because of the war. And the government had to remove the aliens from strategic places right away for the public safety.

Soon the talk started about the general evacuation of the issei. More and more reports appeared in the newspapers about this possibility. The papers were generally sympathetic until about February. The governor had made favorable statements in regard to the nisei loyalty so that it never occurred to me that anything could possibly affect us. Then around February the sentiment in the newspaper and radio got more and more anti-Japanese due to the battles that Japan was winning. Even though I did not think it was fair to evacuate all the issei from strategic areas, I thought it had to be done because of the danger of invasion.

Soon the Japanese started to say that if the issei went, the nisei would also have to go because there were so many young children involved. I could not believe that all of the nisei would ever be moved because I said that we were Americans and that such actions were against the laws of this country.

I was amazed when all of the restrictions began to be applied to all of the nisei. I was a little angry but I felt helpless about it. Then the news came out saying that we had to register and all go to a camp.

It was finally announced that the Japanese in our suburb were going to be sent to Santa Anita and I tried to get to Tanforan but the army would not let me go. On May 26 I was sent to Santa Anita with the rest of the people. By that time most of the Japanese in California had already been evacuated.

Finally after a most miserable trip we got to Santa Anita. I saw the barbed-wire fences immediately and I thought to myself, "This is the end." I realized then and there that it was not going to be a very easy matter to get out. Somebody on the train said that we were going to be in there for the duration and that made me feel almost ill. I think I even got a little panicky. I had some sort of a wild idea to make my escape and lose myself in Los Angeles but this was only a thought as I would never have the courage to do that. I felt that I had been cheated but I did not know why.

After we were registered, I was put into a room with another nisei single girl. The first few days in camp were very confused for me and I went around in a sort of dreamlike daze. It still did not seem true to me. There were quite a few nisei wandering around who had a bewildered look on their faces. However, people are adjustable and most of the Japanese in camp immediately began to make the best

of it and make their homes as comfortable as possible.

I was in Santa Anita from May 1942 to September 1942. During that time I did not work at all as I thought I would be able to get out almost any day. We had to stand in line for everything and I spent most of my time in Santa Anita this way. I stood in line for meals, for showers, and even for the women's latrine. About the only constructive thing I did was knitting.

While in Santa Anita I still managed to keep up my contacts with the outside. I could not get over the feeling that I was in a jail. We had a special visitor's house for our friends to come to. There was a long table running down the center and we had to stay on the other side of the table, five feet across from our friends. We couldn't even reach over to shake hands

The Japanese attack on Pearl Harbor created hostility toward Japanese Americans. Afraid that Japanese Americans would be disloyal if Japan tried to invade the mainland, the United States government shipped thousands from the west coast to inland internment camps. Note the identification tags worn by this mother and child.

or pass anything across. There were guards there to enforce the rules. Then another thing, we could only visit with our friends for a half hour even if they had come from a long distance. I resented this more than anything in Santa Anita as I felt that it was an insult. I just did not feel like having any visitor at all to let them go through this awful experience.

However, I did not become bitter against this country but I did blame it on Japan. I hated Japan worse than ever and I blamed it for our predicament in camp. I hated Japan more than Germany and Italy and I even feel the same way now because what Japan has done has touched me more. I realized in camp that the Japanese had brought this upon themselves to a certain degree, and yet I saw that it was something that they had to go through before they are completely integrated. We were born at the wrong time, that's all.

Adapted from Dorothy Swaine Thomas, *The Salvage* (Berkeley, Calif.: University of California Press, 1952). Copyright 1952 by the Regents of the University of California.

READING REVIEW

1. (a) How did this Japanese American girl react when she heard about the evacuation of the issei? (b) How was her reaction different when she heard that the nisei were also being sent to a camp?
2. What did she feel about life in the camp?
3. **Making Inferences** Who did the girl blame for the detention of Japanese Americans? Why?

★ 16-4 Life Aboard a United States Destroyer ★

Introduction These letters were written by Meyer Davis, Jr., Petty Officer Second Class aboard the destroyer *Buck*. The *Buck* accompanied convoys of merchant ships transporting supplies to fighting forces in Europe. Its job was to sink the submarines that preyed on ships in the convoy. Here Officer Davis writes home about shipboard life and how he felt during his first action. At age 24, Davis went down with his torpedoed ship off the coast of Salerno, Italy.

Vocabulary Before you read the selection, find the meaning of these words in a dictionary: intermittent, annunciator, navigator, ferocious, rationalization.

Sunday We had a devil of a time getting in here. The weather was quite cold with intermittent snowstorms, and the ship is quite badly caked with ice. We had a great deal of trouble getting the anchor out when we first came in because it was frozen fast. Finally they had to resort to live steam before it would come free.

I was on the bridge while this was all going on—as a member of the "Special Sea Detail" which takes over the ship when we come in and out of an anchorage. I am in charge of the annunciator which signals the engines which speed to go. The Captain says "Starboard, two-thirds ahead," and I repeat the command and pull a lever which moves another lever in the engine room and the starboard engine goes two-thirds ahead. A very simple job as you can see, but you have the advantage of being on the bridge where everything is happening right before you. Radio messages are coming in all the time, the navigator is getting bearings, telephone messages are coming in from all over the ship—quite exciting.

Monday The food is getting progressively bad as the trip goes on, and since it started out on a low level you can imagine where it is now. What I would give for a good hamburger with lots of onions on it, or a steak, any size! It's funny how you get to appreciate little things when you can't have them such as drinking out of a glass again, eating a piece of fresh bread (the mold is plainly visible on a good deal of the stuff we brought from port), and sleeping in a bed that doesn't rock.

You may be wondering about the feeling of danger which constantly surrounds us, and may perhaps be curious as to whether we are frightened or scared. Well, frankly, the whole thing is so boring that you welcome any danger that might come your way with open arms.

Thursday It is hard for me to describe just how things are out here, for there is really nothing to compare it with. The waves are the most ferocious things imaginable, and you can stand on deck and see them tower over you—well, it scares you silly. It is impossible to walk from the sleeping compartments which are aft (back) to the forward mess hall without getting wet. At least it must be impossible because nobody has done it yet. Consequently a lot of the crew are sleeping in the mess hall, including yours truly.

The convoy is still hanging around out there, but in the last couple of days we have lost about [censored] of them—not from torpedoes; they just couldn't stand the pace of the rest so they dropped back. That is the only good thing about this weather. It is much too rough for submarines to operate, and all we have to worry about is keeping the convoy together.

Friday I was wrong about submarines not operating in this weather. We got a report last night of a ship being sunk just a hundred miles or so from our present position. Sharks are always hungry, I guess.

1942 At last, after all these days, I have some real news to give you.

We got a submarine today! There is almost no chance that we missed, and the crew is already cutting notches in their belts. Here is a blow-by-blow description by one who had not only a ringside seat, but felt a good deal of the time as if he were in the ring.

At 9:40 General Quarters were sounded—but upon reaching the bridge I found that someone had tripped the alarm by mistake and there wasn't to be any. Then at 11:10 General Quarters sounded again, and I started swearing to myself, "Why the x?!x* can't they make up their *?!x?* minds," when BLOOIE! Before I could get on deck two depth charges went off at the stern followed by five more in short order.

The first charge went off at 11:14. Soon after that I got on the bridge and took over the phones. All this time the sound operators were giving the range and bearing of the submarine, and we were circling for another attack.

At 11:29 we dropped seven more depth charges, and at 11:31 two more or sixteen altogether.

It was reported to me, via my phones, that after the first seven were released, a great deal of oil came to the surface, and one of the lookouts reported seeing some wreckage come to the surface with the bubbles of the first charge. So it is pretty definitely established, at least to our satisfaction if not to yours, that there are widows and orphans in Germany tonight. I'm sorry that I have to be so hard-boiled about it, but this is no Girl Scout outing or Rotary Club picnic, and if we hadn't gotten them, they would have had us.

So there you are—a firsthand account of what took place during a submarine attack and death. Perhaps I could have made it more exciting, but frankly that is an element that doesn't enter the picture. With us it is strictly a business. The fact that men die down below us doesn't really come into the mind. They just happened to have the misfortune to be inside the sub when it went down. Essentially, we are killing submarines, not men. If they want to have the bad judgment to be in the vicinity, that's their hard luck.

Perhaps the foregoing is only a rationalization of an uncomfortable feeling that today I helped kill some men that had wives and sweethearts, mothers and children, back in Germany, but I have to try to be quite ruthless or I won't be much use in this war.

Adapted from *Letters Home*, ed. Mina Curtiss. (Boston: Little, Brown and Company, 1944). Copyright 1944 by Mina Curtiss.

READING REVIEW

1. What is Davis's job on the *Buck*?
2. (a) How does the crew feel about the possibility of action? (b) How does Davis feel when it occurs?
3. **Drawing Conclusions** (a) What does Davis say about the Germans on the submarine? (b) Why do you think he reacts this way?

Introduction One of history's most epic invasions took place on D-Day, when the Allies won their beachhead in Axis-held France. The Germans were dug deep into positions, and the waters were heavily mined. But offshore, big guns of the United States Navy supported the men as they swarmed ashore. War correspondent Ernie Pyle went in with troops of the First and Twenty-ninth Divisions. On the second day, when the coast was secured, Pyle walked along the beach of Normandy. This selection is from his description of what he saw.

Vocabulary Before you read the selection, find the meaning of these words in a dictionary: infinite, expendable, equipage, carnage, ironic.

On D-Day, June 6, 1944, the Allies established a long-awaited beachhead in Nazi-occupied France. This photograph shows American troops landing on the beach.

I walked for a mile and a half along the water's edge of our many-miled invasion beach. I walked slowly, for the detail on that beach was infinite.

The wreckage was vast and startling. The awful waste and destruction of war, even aside from the loss of human life, has always been one of its outstanding features to those who are in it. Anything and everything is expendable. And we did expend on our beachhead in Normandy during those first few hours.

For a mile out from the beach there were scores of tanks and trucks and boats that were not visible, for they were at the bottom of the water—swamped by overloading, or hit by shells, or sunk by mines. Most of their crews were lost.

There were trucks tipped half over and swamped, partly sunken barges, the angled-up corners of jeeps, and small landing craft half submerged. And at low tide you could still see those vicious six-pronged iron snares that helped snag and wreck them.

On the beach itself, high and dry, were all kinds of wrecked vehicles. There were tanks that had only just made the beach before being knocked out. There were jeeps that had burned to a dull gray. There were big derricks on caterpillar treads that didn't quite make it. There were half-tracks carrying office equipment that had been made into a shambles by a single shell hit, their interiors still holding the useless equipage of smashed typewriters, telephones, office files.

In this shoreline museum of carnage there were abandoned rolls of barbed wire and smashed bulldozers and big stacks of thrown-away life belts and piles of shells still waiting to be moved. In the water floated empty life rafts and soldiers' packs and ration boxes and mysterious oranges. On the beach lay snarled rolls of telephone wire and big rolls of steel matting and stacks of broken, rusting rifles.

On the beach lay, expended, sufficient men and mechanism for a small war. They were gone forever now. And yet we could afford it.

We could afford it because we were on, we had our toehold, and behind us there were such enormous replacements for this wreckage on the beach that you could hardly conceive of the sum total. Men and equipment were flowing from England in such a gigantic stream that it made the waste on the beachhead seem like nothing at all, really nothing at all.

But there was another and more human litter. It extended in a thin little line, just like a high-water mark, for miles along the beach. This was the strewn personal gear, gear that would never be needed again by those who fought and died to give us our entrance into Europe.

There in a jumbled row for mile on mile were soldiers' packs. There were socks and shoe polish, sewing kits, diaries, Bibles, hand grenades. There were the latest letters from home, with the address on each one neatly razored out—one of the security precautions enforced before the boys embarked.

There were toothbrushes and razors and snapshots of families back home staring up at you from the sand. There were pocketbooks, metal mirrors, extra trousers, and bloody, abandoned shoes. There were broken-handled shovels, and portable radios smashed almost beyond recognition, and mine detectors twisted and ruined.

There were torn pistol belts and canvas water buckets, first-aid kits, and jumbled heaps of life belts. I picked up a pocket Bible with a soldier's name in it and put it in my jacket. I carried it half a mile or so and then put it back down on the beach. I don't know why I picked it up or why I put it down again.

Soldiers carry strange things ashore with them. In every invasion there is at least one soldier hitting the beach at H-hour with a banjo slung over his shoulder. The most ironic piece of equipment marking our beach—this beach first of despair, then of victory—was a tennis racket that some soldier had brought along. It lay lonesomely on the sand, clamped in its press, not a string broken.

Adapted from Ernie Pyle, *Brave Men* (New York: Grosset & Dunlap, 1943). Copyright 1943 by Ernie Pyle.

READING REVIEW

1. What did Pyle mean when he wrote that we could afford the losses of D-Day?
2. Why might soldiers carry such items as banjos into battle?
3. **Recognizing a Point of View** (a) Does Pyle seem to think the victory of D-Day was worth the cost? (b) How can you tell?

★ 16-6 The Big Three at Teheran ★

Introduction At the time of the Teheran conference in November 1943, Russia was under heavy pressure from German forces. Thus Soviet Premier Joseph Stalin pressed for Operation Overlord, the planned invasion of Normandy. British Prime Minister Winston Churchill favored a delay, while President Roosevelt backed Marshal Stalin. Fleet Admiral William D. Leahy, President Roosevelt's Chief of Staff, attended the meeting. In this selection Leahy gives his impressions.

Vocabulary Before you read the selection, find the meaning of these words in a dictionary: plenary, induced, dispersing, flank, exasperated, brusquely.

The first plenary session of EUREKA, code for the Teheran meeting, opened at 4:00 P.M. Roosevelt presided and was the first to speak.

Briefly, the strategy that had been worked out at previous Anglo-American conferences was reviewed by our President. He said that the United States shared equally with the Soviets and the United Kingdom a desire to hurry the day of victory in Europe. In the Pacific, our country was carrying the greatest burden with some help from the British. Our strategy was to destroy enemy forces while advancing through the Pacific islands and keeping the Japanese away from American territory. It was proving successful to date, Roosevelt emphasized.

Turning to China, the President stressed that keeping our eastern ally in the war was considered essential. This would be assisted shortly by a vigorous campaign led by Admiral Lord Mountbatten to recapture Burma.

In Europe, Roosevelt continued, the United States strategy for more than a year had been to relieve German pressure on the Russian front. Final plans to achieve this had not been possible until the conference in Quebec had agreed upon May 1944 as the date for a cross-channel invasion of Normandy. Roosevelt added that many were in favor of further operations in the Mediterranean, but he was convinced that the vital thrust into France in May should not be delayed by any such secondary operations.

Stalin then spoke briefly, but in detail, to show that Italy was not a suitable place from which to launch an attack on Germany. However, he held that the Mediterranean Sea should be kept free for Allied shipping. Every American and British eye and ear were fixed on the Soviet leader. Most of us were hearing and seeing him for the first time. The marshal spoke quietly, without gestures, and, as translated by Interpreter Pavlov, expressed himself in a convincing manner.

Prime Minister Churchill began to talk about possible areas of operations against the Nazis from all parts of Europe. He urged that Turkey be induced to enter the war. Churchill then asked if any of the possible operations in the Mediterranean were of sufficient interest to delay for two or three months the projected cross-channel project.

Stalin answered quickly by questioning the wisdom of dispersing Allied forces. He did not believe the Turks could be persuaded to declare war. He said that all additional Allied strength that would be available could be used to the best advantage in a flank attack in southern France to be timed to support the Normandy attack. The meeting adjourned without any major decisions being made.

The initial session had been pleasant, polite, and agreeable. The three principals stated their respective views and sounded out each other. The Soviets and Americans seemed to be nearly in agreement as to the fundamental strategic principles

This stylized Persian miniature commemorates the Teheran Conference. Stalin, Churchill, Roosevelt, and Chiang Kai-shek hunt down Mussolini, Hitler, and Tojo. The artist, Musavirel Mulk, created one miniature for Churchill and one for Roosevelt.

that should be followed. In the hands of the three men gathered around a table in the Russian Legation in Teheran rested the fate of millions of men organized into the largest armies and navies ever assembled in any war up to that time. Yet the atmosphere in this first session probably was more calm than that which might prevail at a staff meeting aboard a single ship or at some army base.

At noon on November 29 the Prime Minister, acting for King George of England, presented a sword of honor to Marshal Stalin for the city of Stalingrad. It was a token of the appreciation of the British people for the city's heroic and successful defense against the German invaders of Russia.

That afternoon, at another plenary session, the dispute over timing of the invasion of Normandy was again brought up. Stalin was insisting on fixing an early date. Churchill was asking for delay. The President was favorably inclined toward the Soviet view. Becoming exasperated with Churchill's tactics, Stalin said bluntly, "Do you really believe in Overlord, or are you stalling on it to make us feel better?" The sense of Churchill's reply was that he did endorse the cross-channel operation. However, he believed sincerely that the other operations he was proposing would help ensure the eventual success of the invasion of France. In order to delay a final decision on the date of Overlord, Churchill proposed that the political aspects of his Mediterranean proposals be referred to the foreign ministers present at Teheran for their advice.

Stalin retorted quickly and brusquely. "Why do that? We are the chiefs of government. We know what we want to do. Why turn the matter over to some subordinates to advise us?"

The heat of argument taxed the well-known skill and diplomacy of Roosevelt, who was presiding. At this same meeting, Stalin also confronted the President with an uncomfortable question. The Soviet leader asked bluntly who was going to command Overlord. Roosevelt said frankly he had not made up his mind. I was sitting next to the President, and he leaned over to me and whispered, "That old Bolshevik is trying to force me to give him the name of our Supreme Commander. I just can't tell him because I have not yet made up my mind." The President was absolutely honest in his reply.

Like the one of the day before, this session ended with no final decision as to the date of the cross-channel operation, and, as a result of Stalin's frank question, the problem of who would command that operation had again been thrust to the forefront.

The British finally fell into line at the forenoon meeting of the British–American chiefs of staff on November 30. They agreed to launch the attack on Germany in France during the month of May 1944 and to support the southern France invasion with such force as could be handled by the landing craft available in the Mediterranean at that time.

I never asked Brooke, Portal, or any of our British colleagues what caused their change of heart, but the American argument was so logical that I cannot but believe that as professional soldiers they knew Overlord was the most sensible move to bring to an end the war with Germany in the shortest possible time. We had to come to grips with a German army that would be defending its homeland as soon as we should have the force available. If we could break that army, the road to Berlin and victory in Europe would be in sight.

Adapted from William D. Leahy, *I Was There* (New York: McGraw-Hill Book Company, 1950). Copyright © 1950 by William D. Leahy.

READING REVIEW

1. What was Allied strategy in regard to China?

2. (a) What was the atmosphere at the Teheran conference? (b) Why might this have been so?

3. **Comparing Points of View** (a) What reasons did Stalin give for invading Normandy as planned? (b) Why might Churchill have wanted to delay Overlord? (c) Why did the United States support Overlord as planned?

Introduction Nothing had prepared the Allied troops for what they found as they liberated prisoners from the Nazi concentration camps of Europe. Starvation, slave labor, and murder had left but a tragic few survivors out of the millions of people who had been forced to leave their homes. Marika Frank Abrams was a Hungarian Jew who survived. In this selection she described her experiences.

Vocabulary Before you read the selection, find the meaning of these words in a dictionary: devastating, contingent.

We were at a summer resort near Budapest in September 1939 when the war broke out. It did not break out in Hungary until June 17, 1941. In those two years my personal life hardly changed. My parents were so Hungarian that they couldn't believe they would be harmed by Hungarians. They recognized the dangers but couldn't really accept them. It was not foresighted and not intelligent but that was the way it was.

And then the Germans came into Hungary, and this was the end of everything for us. All the Jews in Debrecin had to leave their homes and move into a certain part of the city they called the ghetto. This was a great circus. You can imagine: all the people living there who were not Jewish had to move out and all the Jews had to move in. It was actually accomplished by the end of May.

My father was full of life and hope, very positive in his thinking. We had a number of air raids and he volunteered to help clean up the rubble. This was in May and June of 1944 when the Russian army was in the Carpathian Mountains, about four hours away by car, and the American army was in France. So we thought we were just waiting the war out and adjusted to the situation. We were in a house with our Christian aunt, her son, two of my girl friends and their families. We got our food together and distributed the work and everybody was willing to do their share.

About four weeks after we came to the ghetto the whole population was taken to the brick factory and deported in three transports. The first included the political people—the Zionists, the socialists—and also people with large families. There were many children in that group. The second transport included the hospital, with all the doctors and nurses. We were in the third transport. Each had about 5,000 people.

The first transport was very lucky. The tracks to Auschwitz had been bombed and they were sent to Vienna instead. My girl friend was on that one and she said they were treated as prisoners of war, housed in school buildings and assigned jobs in the city. The second transport with the hospital went straight to Vienna. All the people on it came back to Hungary unharmed. The third transport went straight to Auschwitz. The tracks, by then, had been repaired.

When we arrived we were asked to come out of the boxcars and the men and women were immediately separated. This is a scene as clear in my brain as if it happened today. I wish I could describe it but I really can't. My father said goodbye to us in a very positive way. I was in a row

The Allies had heard reports of Nazi concentration camps during the war. But they were horrified at what they found when they reached the camps. At this camp in Austria, 2,000 prisoners per week starved to death.

with my mother. She was 52 years old. I'm almost that old now. She looked 75. And there was my beautiful aunt, who must have been about 38, and her son, who was 8 years old. I was holding the little boy's hand and my arm was in the arm of my mother. We had to form rows of five. That was the rule. And as we were walking by the selection officer, he asked me how old I was and I said 19. He put his hand on my shoulder and pushed me off to the left. I looked back and couldn't see the others any more. And that was that.

Between May 1 and July 31, 1944, 140,000 were gassed in Auschwitz immediately upon arrival. I, however, was sent to Birkenau, which was a section of Auschwitz not yet finished. I was in a barrack with about 500 other women. There were just empty rooms, no bunks, just the floor to sleep on. And we could not lie down until we lined up in a Z on the floor, one woman next to the other, very, very close. No latrines, only a few buckets between the barracks. I'm sure it has been described many times how we were taken into a room in which we undressed and left our clothes. Our heads were shaved. After the showers we were given a piece of rag to cover ourselves with. This was all we had. This first time we were allowed to keep our shoes, which was a blessing, because the camp roads were covered with sharp pebbles. There was of course no running water, no water to drink and no water to wash with. The only drink we had was some so-called coffee in the morning.

In the beginning I couldn't eat the food. Six months later I would eat anything. All they gave us was a thin slice of bread and a thin slice of sausage. Everybody started losing weight and because of the poor sanitary conditions we began to get typhoid fever, diphtheria, scarlet fever, and dysentery. I came down with scarlet fever but just three days before they had set up a barrack for people with contagious diseases. They put me in there and I survived the scarlet fever. While I was in the hospital barrack everyone from my city was taken to West Germany.

I was taken from Auschwitz to Bergen–Belsen. This trip across Germany in a boxcar was nightmarish. We were given some food and water and locked in for three days. There were tiny windows and I looked out at this beautiful landscape. There were hills with little houses and forests and all the beautiful colors. In Auschwitz everything was gray; it was nothing but clay and gray barracks and gray sky and the devastating mass of miserable women. And all of a sudden I looked out and I saw there was the world. That was life. It was touching and disturbing. It filled me with great pain and longing. How nice it would be to be in one of those little shacks with my mother.

Let me explain that even though I had been in Auschwitz I did not know about the gas chambers. Can you imagine that? We thought, when we were there, that our parents and the children were taken to camps which were much better. We assumed that they couldn't live through the camp we were in. It was not until a large contingent from Auschwitz came to Bergen–Belsen that I had to give up that idea that they were safe. I met two women in their thirties who spoke Hungarian and they asked if it was true that the Hungarian transports were so severely selected—people to the camps and the others to be gassed. I said, "What are you saying?" And they looked at me as if I were foolish, but they didn't want to destroy my hope and so didn't try to explain.

I ran back to the tent and collapsed. I think I cried for weeks. I finally realized that everybody was killed. And this little girl with me couldn't believe it either. But I knew it was true and I really didn't want to live then anymore. It's very easy not to live, you know, in a camp, very easy to lose that bit of thing in you that makes you want to go on.

Then I met another older Hungarian woman who had been deported from Paris. She told me about her life in France. She was a painter and also a designer of clothes.

I didn't mention when I talked about my childhood that I painted when I was growing up. Art education in the Hungarian schools was very bad, but I was painting and drawing nonetheless. In Bergen–Belsen I realized that I would like to draw and paint and this helped me to go on living.

Early in December I was taken out of Bergen–Belsen with my girl friend. We were sent to a camp in Magdeburg. There were many factories in Magdeburg and about 100,000 POWs working in the area. I was in a barrack with 300 Jewish women. We went on foot to the factory every morning. I leave to your imagination how we looked. We were starved, we had no hair and hardly any clothes, and we marched in rows of five with the German citizens watching us, as many as 1,200 coming together from different barracks.

There was not too much time. We worked 12 hours a day at the factory. They manufactured shells for bombs, and I measured the circumference of the shells, which had to fit a special pattern if they were to work. There were two girls and a man at each machine and our small contribution was that we sometimes let the machine run for a long time after we knew the shells were faulty.

We preferred the factory to the barracks. In the barracks there were lice and there was no water, no way of keeping clean, no way to wash clothes. We would steal the rags they gave us to wipe the machines and make things out of them.

And this is how we lived and worked while we waited for the Russians and the Americans to meet on the Elbe River. In March there were lots of bombardments and I could see the Germans were scared. I was not a bit scared. I felt that if I had to die it was a good time because I had had such a marvelous life before. I had been so happy and had lived with marvelous people. We had had a beautiful life together and it was all over. It was all gone. So I wasn't afraid of dying and I was very happy when the planes came. It meant that justice would be done.

From *Voices From the Holocaust* edited by Sylvia Rothchild. Copyright © 1981 by the William E. Weiner Oral History Library of the American Jewish Committee. Reprinted by arrangement with New American Library, New York, New York.

READING REVIEW

1. How did Abrams and the other slave laborers try to help the Allies?
2. Was Abrams afraid of the allied bombardment? Why or why not?
3. **Making Generalizations** What might make people want to go on living even under conditions such as Abrams describes?

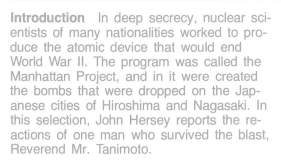

★ 16-8 A "Sheet of Sun" at Hiroshima ★

Introduction In deep secrecy, nuclear scientists of many nationalities worked to produce the atomic device that would end World War II. The program was called the Manhattan Project, and in it were created the bombs that were dropped on the Japanese cities of Hiroshima and Nagasaki. In this selection, John Hersey reports the reactions of one man who survived the blast, Reverend Mr. Tanimoto.

Vocabulary Before you read the selection, find the meaning of these words in a dictionary: rendezvous, abstinence, evacuate, maneuvered, finicky, designated, solicitous, compassion.

The Reverend Mr. Tanimoto got up at five o'clock that morning. He was alone in the parsonage, because for some time his wife had been commuting with their year-old baby to spend nights with a friend in Ushida, a suburb to the north. Of all the important cities of Japan only two, Kyoto and Hiroshima, had not been visited in strength by B-san, or Mr. B, as the Japanese, with a mixture of respect and unhappy familiarity, called the B-29. And Mr. Tanimoto, like all his neighbors and friends, was almost sick with anxiety. He had heard uncomfortably detailed accounts of mass raids on Kure, Iwakuni, Tokuyama, and other nearby towns. He was sure Hiroshima's turn would come soon.

He had slept badly the night before, because there had been several air-raid warnings. Hiroshima had been getting such warnings almost every night for weeks, for at that time the B-29s were

Topic 16

using Lake Biwa, northeast of Hiroshima, as a rendezvous point. No matter what city the Americans planned to hit, the Superfortresses streamed in over the coast near Hiroshima. The frequency of the warnings and the continued abstinence of Mr. B with respect to Hiroshima had made its citizens jittery. A rumor was going around that the Americans were saving something special for the city.

Besides having his wife spend the nights in Ushida, Mr. Tanimoto had been carrying all the portable things from his church, in the close-packed residential district called Nagaragawa, to a house that belonged to a rayon manufacturer in Loi, two miles from the center of town. The rayon man, a Mr. Matsui, had opened his then unoccupied estate to a large number of his friends and acquaintances, so that they might evacuate whatever they wished to a safe distance from the probable target area. A friend of his named Matsuo had, the day before, helped him get the piano out to Koi. In return, he had promised this day to assist Mr. Matsuo in hauling out a daughter's belongings. That is why he had risen so early.

Before six o'clock that morning, Mr. Tanimoto started for Mr. Matsuo's house. There he found that their burden was to be a tansu, a large Japanese cabinet, full of clothing and household goods. The two men set out. The morning was perfectly clear and so warm that the day promised to be uncomfortable. A few minutes after they started, the air-raid siren went off—a minute-long blast that warned of approaching planes but indicated to the people of Hiroshima only a slight degree of danger, since it sounded every morning at this time, when an American weather plane came over. The two men pulled and pushed the handcart through the city streets.

Pushing the handcart up to the rayon man's house was tiring, and the men, after they had maneuvered their load into the driveway and to the front steps, paused to rest awhile. They stood with a wing of the house between them and the city. Like most homes in this part of Japan, the house consisted of a wooden frame and wooden walls supporting a heavy tile roof. Its front hall, packed with rolls of bedding and clothing, looked like a cool cave full of fat cushions. Opposite the house, to the right of the front door, there was a large, finicky rock garden. There was no sound of planes. The morning was still; the place was cool and pleasant.

Then a tremendous flash of light cut across the sky. Mr. Tanimoto has a distinct recollection that it traveled from east to west, from the city toward the hills. It seemed a sheet of sun. Both he and Mr. Matsuo reacted in terror—and both had time to react (for they were 3,500 yards, or two miles, from the center of the explosion). Mr. Matsuo dashed up the front steps into the house and dived among the bedrolls and buried himself there. Mr. Tanimoto took four or five steps and threw himself between two big rocks in the garden. He bellied up very hard against one of them. As his face was against the stone, he did not see what happened. He felt a sudden pressure, and then splinters and pieces of board and fragments of tile fell on him. He heard no roar.

When he dared, Mr. Tanimoto raised his head and saw that the rayon man's house had collapsed. He thought a bomb had fallen directly on it. Such clouds of dust had risen that there was a sort of twilight around. In panic, not thinking for the moment of Mr. Matsuo under the ruins, he dashed out into the street. He noticed as he ran that the concrete wall of the estate had fallen over—toward the house rather than away from it.

In the streets, the first thing he saw was a squad of soldiers who had been burrowing into the hillside opposite, making one of the thousands of dugouts in which the Japanese apparently intended to resist invasion, hill by hill, life for life. The soldiers were coming out of the hole, where they should have been safe.

Mr. Tanimoto attached himself sympathetically to an old lady who was walking along in a daze, holding her head with her left hand, supporting a small boy of three or four on her back with her right, and crying, "I'm hurt! I'm hurt!" Mr. Tanimoto transferred the child to his own back and led the woman by the hand down the street, which was darkened by what seemed to be a local column of dust. He took the woman to a grammar school

The first atomic bomb was dropped on Hiroshima, Japan, on August 6, 1945. This photograph shows Hiroshima on the following day.

not far away that had previously been designated for use as a temporary hospital in case of emergency. By this solicitous behavior, Mr. Tanimoto at once got rid of his terror.

At the school, he was much surprised to see glass all over the floor and 50 or 60 injured people already waiting to be treated. He reflected that, although the all-clear had sounded and he had heard no planes, several bombs must have been dropped.

Mr. Tanimoto ran along Koi Highway. He was the only person making his way into the city. He met hundreds and hundreds who were fleeing, and every one of them seemed to be hurt in some way. The eyebrows of some were burned off and skin hung from their faces and hands. Others, because of pain, held their arms up as if carrying something in both hands. Some were vomiting as they walked. Many were naked or in shreds of clothing. On some undressed bodies, the burns had made patterns of undershirt straps and suspenders and, on the skin of some women (since white repelled the heat from the bomb and dark clothes absorbed it and conducted it to the skin), the shapes of flowers they had had on their kimonos. Many, although injured themselves, supported relatives who were worse off. Almost all had their heads bowed, looked straight ahead, were silent, and showed no expression whatever.

After crossing Koi Bridge and Kannon Bridge, having run the whole way, Mr.

Tanimoto saw, as he approached the center, that all the houses had been crushed and many were afire. Here the trees were bare and their trunks were charred. He tried at several points to penetrate the ruins, but the flames always stopped him. Under many houses, people screamed for help, but no one helped.

In general, survivors that day assisted only their relatives or immediate neighbors, for they could not comprehend or tolerate a wider circle of misery. The wounded limped past the screams, and Mr. Tanimoto ran past them. As a Christian he was filled with compassion for those who were trapped, and as a Japanese he was overwhelmed by the shame of being unhurt, and he prayed as he ran, "God help them and take them out of the fire."

Adapted from John Hersey, Hiroshima (New York: Alfred A. Knopf, 1946). Copyright 1946 by John Hersey.

READING REVIEW

1. Why was Mr. Tanimoto on the street so early on the day the bomb was dropped?
2. (a) How did he react when he saw the "sheet of sun"? (b) What action did Mr. Tanimoto take that helped rid him of his terror?
3. **Supporting Generalizations** (a) Based on this selection, how would you say people react to sudden terrible disaster? (b) List two facts from the reading that support your generalization.

The United States in a Changing World

17 The Postwar International Scene (1945–1960)

★   17-1   Ralph Bunche, Diplomat for Peace   ★

Introduction In 1947 Ralph Bunche went to Israel as secretary to the United Nations Special Committee on Palestine. When the official mediator between Arabs and Jews, Count Bernadotte of Sweden, was killed, Bunche took over the negotiations. But the warring sides refused to discuss an armistice. Finally, in January 1949 they agreed to sit down together at the Hotel del Roses in Rhodes. This selection from a biography of Bunche illustrates his diplomatic skills.

Vocabulary Before you read the selection, find the meaning of these words in a dictionary: dossiers, partisans, impassive, anthropologist, stolidly, imprecations, belligerent, contrite, concessions, reprimanded, affront, chagrined.

For months, daily and Sunday, Bunche had been going from one floor to another in the hotel, talking, pleading, shouting himself hoarse. But it was difficult, for every day Arab and Jewish negotiators received reports of the fighting in Palestine and grew more and more bitter. Although they cut each other in the dining room of

the hotel and there were several fist fights among them, Bunche cooly continued to report back progress to the United Nations Security Council. "This war will end, but whether I will be responsible for ending it, I don't know," he cabled.

The war grew more ferocious. There were thousands of dead on each side and hundreds of thousands were displaced and homeless. Many other tens of thousands died of disease or starvation. No longer was it a "two-bit war" as weapons from many Arabian factions and nations poured in and vast supplies also reached the Israelis. Too, Arab and Jewish negotiators were divided and quarreled incessantly. There was not only no hope of peace in Palestine but no promise of it among the peace negotiators themselves.

There came a day when Bunche smiled at his assistants and said: "Here's the beginning. I think we'll get somewhere today. They've agreed to meet." He had been up since dawn, going back and forth between the leaders, assured, stern, smiling, and furious by turns as it served his purpose.

At two o'clock that afternoon Bunche roamed anxiously about the conference room to see whether pads and pencils were placed before each chair and whether the proper brands of cigarettes had been placed.

He also made sure that the guards before the door had received their instructions, and that they were not biased but would properly salute each man of each side as he came in. He also looked over the dossiers of the interpreters to make sure that there were no partisans among them who would translate improperly and with motive.

The hour arrived. Bunche, at the door, anxious but impassive, greeted the Arab delegation as it filed in. He shook each hand, spoke easily, then ranged them on one side of the table. It was a bad moment—and there was no assurance that the Israelis would arrive.

Then there was a knock at the door, and a soldier, bearing a bayonet, flung it wide and announced the Israelis.

Bunche, the anthropologist and social scientist who knew the ways of the East, was thunderstruck when the Arabs remained seated as the Jews, led by their chairman, walked in. He immediately sensed trouble and tried to cover it by pumping the hand of the Jewish chairman.

The Arabs, blank faced, remained stolidly seated. The Jewish chairman stepped around Bunche and extended his hand to the Arab chairman who still remained seated.

Seif ed-Din, the Arab also known as the Sword of God, turned about in his chair and ignored the offered hand of Walter Eytan, the Israeli chairman. Deliberately, he turned his back and faced the wall. The Arabs murmured among themselves approvingly. The Israeli delegation, behind Eytan, was stunned and then several voices among them shouted imprecations. Eytan withdrew his hand and turned angrily to Bunche. The Sword of God turned and smiled at Bunche and stroked his whiskers.

Bunche said diplomatically: "I'm glad both sides have met for this preliminary meeting. Suppose we adjourn." As the Arabs began to rise, Bunche waved them down. "Keep seated, please. There will be refreshments." He counted heavily on Arab politeness, which could not permit them to refuse an offer of food from a host.

Then he followed the Israelis out into the corridor. Eytan was furious and belligerent. "What kind of nonsense is this? I'm flying back to Palestine this afternoon."

"You don't know the Arabs," Bunche said severely. "They're very formal at a meeting like this. You should have nodded instead of holding out your hand. Arabs place great store in formality."

Eytan looked at Bunche in disbelief. "I know Arab customs well. The chairman was deliberately rude and offensive. I am sorry, but we are flying back today."

"In some respects you may be right," Bunche said shrewdly. "But now that the Arab has been guilty of offensive conduct, he'll be more contrite. Consider that and think of the concessions you may be able to get. Arabs hate to be rude and I am sure Seif ed-Din knows he was rude. Consider. After all, what's a handshake? Just a gesture."

Then he asked Eytan to wait.

He walked back into the conference room and reprimanded the Sword for his unmannerly conduct. "Why did you do that?" he stormed. "That was an affront to me as well."

The Sword admitted that the Arab council the night before had instructed him, after a vote, to behave so. "We wanted to show the Jews that we are independent and that we are not seeking a cease-fire."

"It was wrong, rude and an insult to the United Nations," Bunche said. Then he added: "The United Nations Security Council, many nations of which are on your side, will hold you responsible."

The Arabs talked among themselves and shook their heads. The Sword glared about, chagrined and ashamed. "You stupids have made a mock with your counsels. I am humiliated," he shouted.

Bunche again went to the corridor where Eytan was waiting. "The chairman of the Arab delegation is sorry. He meant no harm, he says, and is willing to meet you personally and talk with you. It would be rude for you not to agree, would it not?" he asked.

Eytan shrugged and discussed this with several of his committee members.

"I agree," he said angrily, "but no more insults."

"After all," he added smilingly, "we are winning this war. We can demand the terms."

"Only the United Nations will set the terms," Bunche said. "No one wins a war," he added. Eytan thought that over for a moment, then nodded. "We'll meet with the Sword again."

From J. Alvin Kugelmass, *Ralph Bunche: Fighter for Peace*. Copyright © 1952, 1962 by J. Alvin Kugelmass, renewed © 1980 by Elizabeth Kugelmass. Reprinted by permission of Julian Messner, a division of Simon & Schuster, Inc.

READING REVIEW

1. What was going on in Palestine while the Arabs and Israelis were meeting in the hotel?

2. What happened that made the Israeli delegation determined to leave the conference?

3. **Relating Cause and Effect** How did Bunche get the two opposing sides back to the negotiating table?

★ 17-2 Marshall's Mission to China ★

Introduction During the civil war in China, some nationalists and communists were willing to try to achieve peace by negotiation. Others on both sides were intent on victory through armed conflict. President Harry Truman and General George Marshall, Truman's envoy to China, faced a difficult task: trying to bring peace to a nation where anti-American feeling was strong. In this selection from his memoirs, Truman describes what happened to Marshall's mission and why.

Vocabulary Before you read the selection, find the meaning of these words in a dictionary: coalition, disintegrating, remnants, conciliatory, agrarian, proletariat.

I had sent General Marshall to China to try to end the fighting and to help put into effect the agreement between the nationalists and the communists to form a coalition government. He set up an executive headquarters, and the fighting stopped, temporarily. The Chinese began these endless, oriental negotiations between themselves, and only an expert chess player can follow them. This is the way it goes. Someone makes a proposal which is accepted by the other side, with three qualifications. They are then accepted by the other side with three qualifications to each of the first three qualifications. It was an old Chinese way to be sure nothing would happen.

Well, fighting broke out again in 1946, and Chiang Kai-shek then decided he was going to occupy North China and Manchuria. General Marshall argued against it, and General Wedemeyer argued against it, but he went ahead. We furnished him equipment, money, and a waterlift to Manchuria, and he sent the best divisions he had, well trained and well armed, to Mukden. They stayed there until finally the whole thing disintegrated, and they surrendered.

They would make a series of extended movements into the country in North China and take up a position in a walled city. Chiang's commanders were very poor. They had a walled-city complex. They thought the open country was dangerous. Open country was the one place in which they should have been. But they thought a walled city was fine; they could see people coming. Of course no one came, and they stayed in the city. The communists cut their communication lines and broke up their single-track railroad so it was no good to them.

At the beginning of 1947 General Marshall threw in the towel. He said that both parties were unwilling to carry out their agreements. Chiang Kai-shek would not heed the advice of one of the greatest military strategists in history and lost to the communists.

There is no question that Marshall's mission failed to yield the results he and I had hoped for. Fighting soon enveloped all of China, and it did not end until the communists were masters of the land and Chiang Kai-shek, with the remnants of his army, sought refuge on Formosa.

The Marshall mission had been unable to produce results because the government of Chiang Kai-shek did not command the respect and support of the Chinese people. The generalissimo's attitude and actions were those of an old-fashioned warlord, and, as with the warlords, there was no love for him among the people. There is no doubt in my mind that if Chiang Kai-shek had been only a little more conciliatory an understanding could have been reached.

I am not one to believe in the value of hindsight. Whether or not I was right in sending General Marshall to China does not depend on what some think they know today. It depends only on what we were able to know in 1945.

Neither Marshall nor I was ever taken in by the talk about the Chinese communists being just "agrarian reformers." The general knew he was dealing with communists, and he knew what their aims were. When he was back in Washington in March, he told me that their chief negotiator, Chou En-lai, had very frankly declared that, as a communist, he believed firmly in the teachings of Marx and Lenin and the eventual victory of the proletariat. Marshall's messages from China show, also, that he fully assumed that the Chinese communists would, in the end, be able to count on Russian support.

What I hoped to achieve was to see China made into a country in which communism would lose its appeal to the masses because the needs of the people and the voice of the people would have been answered.

I knew that peace in the world would not be achieved by fighting more wars. Most of all, I was always aware that there were two enormous land masses that no western army of modern times had ever been able to conquer: Russia and China. It would have been folly, and it would be folly today, to attempt to impose our way of life on these huge areas by force!

In the end, of course, Chiang was defeated by loss of support among his own people and by American arms, as many of his own generals took their armies, equipped through our aid, into the enemy

After World War II the United States was concerned about communist aggression in Asia and in Europe. This cartoon shows Stalin with several nations he hoped to make his puppets.

camp. It was when that sort of surrender began to occur on a large scale that I decided to cut off further shipments to China.

It is important to repeat that Marshall was advising, not dictating. I had sent him to China not to intervene in the affairs of that country but to render whatever aid we could to the cause of peace there. He was not sent to do Chiang Kai-shek's job for him. If General Marshall returned from his mission without results, it was because neither of the parties really wanted to live up to the agreement to form a coalition government to unite China.

Adapted from *Memoirs by Harry S. Truman: Years of Trial and Hope* (New York: Doubleday & Co., Inc., 1956).

READING REVIEW

1. What war strategy of the nationalists did Truman think contributed to their defeat?
2. What attitude of Chiang Kai-shek did Truman feel contributed to his losing China?
3. **Distinguishing Fact From Opinion** Give two facts and two opinions in Truman's description of Marshall's mission.

Introduction Martin Russ served with the United States Marines in Korea from December 1952 to September 1953. In this excerpt from his diary, he describes one mission of his platoon and how he felt during the raid.

Vocabulary Before you read the selection, find the meaning of these words in a dictionary: vague, illumination, precarious, skirmish.

The front, or front lines, are rarely referred to as such. "MLR" is used instead. It stands for "main line of resistance." In our case the MLR is a deep trench, from five to seven feet in depth, running along the ridgeline of the hill mass occupied by our platoon. Theoretically the MLR is a continuous avenue from coast to coast, cutting the peninsula of Korea in half. If this were so, it would not be unreasonable to assume that I could find my brother Tim if I followed the trench east for a few miles.

Our bunkers are situated on the reverse slope of the ridge, out of sight from the enemy trenches. A Yukon stove in each bunker provides heat. Candles provide light inside the bunkers. It is impossible to keep anything clean; showers of dirt fall every time an incoming shell lands anywhere nearby. These bunkers were probably built more than a year ago and, as far as improvements go, there is not much more that can be done.

Two days later, in early January 1953

The platoon staged a raid several nights ago. I've put off writing about it for one or two vague reasons.

The raiding party was divided into four groups. Each group was briefed separately by Lt. Casimetti, the company executive officer. The general mission of the unit was to capture a prisoner. The specific mission was to assault an enemy outpost known as Little Rock.

We filed out through an opening in the sandbags and climbed down the steep, icy slope, supporting ourselves by a rope bannister attached to iron barbed-wire stakes. Without the aid of this bannister we would have slid all the way to the bottom.

We made the climb to the top of Texas Ridge and turned left. The terrain up there is covered with little pine trees, and it was necessary to move quite slowly. Even so, we made a racket—which made some of us extremely nervous. The element of surprise would be lost, but there was nothing we could do. If we weren't crunching through patches of snow, we were crunching through patches of dry leaves. All this commotion angered me; I visualized groups of Chinese on Little Rock preparing themselves leisurely while we stumbled and slid toward them.

We remained where we were for several minutes, both units, awaiting the regimental T.O.T. (Timed on Target), the first of two preraid barrages. The impact of this volley was tremendous, including ten 4.2-inch white phosphorous projectiles which blasted the top of hill Detroit. The illumination allowed us to view our objective, Little Rock, a wide terrain finger running south from Detroit. A mine-detector operator from First Engineer Battalion had volunteered to clear a path in the minefield. He was accompanied across the paddy by another volunteer named Carl Pugnacci, a Pfc. They disappeared into the darkness and we waited. The presence of the mine-detector man seemed to indicate that none of our patrols had entered that area for some time. Fifteen minutes later they returned, having cleared a path. What a precarious stroll that must have been. They had crossed the paddy to the bottom of the Little Rock slopes.

The column was formed and we began to cross the paddy, maintaining an interval of five yards between each man. We crept along a series of ridges, no more than two feet high, called dikes. These little humps of earth are part of every rice paddy I've ever seen. They separate the little fields where the rice once grew, forming terraces to hold each shallow body of water. They are irregular and intersect at many points. It would have been possible to take a wrong turn were it not for the strip of white cloth the mine-detector man laid down for us to follow.

Lt. Buell immediately pointed out our defensive positions. It was necessary for the mine-detector operator to precede us.

Little Rock is not a large terrain feature. The distance from the base of the slope to the enemy trench, as we learned later, is not more than 100 yards.

It was very cold now because we were not moving. The field jacket meant nothing against the wind. I was so cold that when the second mortar barrage commenced, I thought of the explosions as fires, warmth. The barrage was startling: a flurry of 60-millimeter shells whistled through the air and screamed downward into the area above the jump-off point. The ground shook with the impact and more shells came plummeting down.

The machine-gun unit, led by Sgt. Kovacs, had been set up on Texas Ridge, 200 yards behind us. At 3:30 they commenced fire—sudden, rapid, overhead fire. I was ready to meet my maker at this point. This overhead fire lasted for one or two minutes. When it ceased, several things happened at once. As we learned later, Sgt. Kovacs moved his men swiftly to another position along the ridge. As they were moving out, a number of Chinese mortar rounds raked the area which they had just left, and the placement of this barrage looked perfect—the Chinese have the reputation of being expert mortarmen. Due to Sgt. Kovacs's foresight none of his men were injured. And at the same time, Lt. O'Dwyer and his men began the assault.

First each man heaved a grenade in the direction of the enemy trench, and then they moved in a skirmish line up the slope. The Chinese were ready; they must have heard us coming. Concussion grenades—we carried none—began exploding above us, flurries of them. Thirty would be a good guess. The ground shuddered and the dead leaves on the branches shook with the rushes of air. Next we heard the sound of two or three BARs and a group of carbines. Next—and it was in this order—we heard the BRRRRP! sound of one Chinese pp-S or "burp gun" as it is called. This was followed immediately by a burst from a carbine. That was all; there was no more shooting. The actual fire fight could not have lasted more than 20 seconds.

A moment later a figure appeared along the path. We challenged him; he gave the countersign and moved past us. Another figure, perhaps the same man, came up to us from the rear, carrying a stretcher and followed by two Koreans. He said to us, "Let's go. We need help." This man was probably a navy corpsman. In file, we climbed the slope and came upon a group of four men, kneeling and crouching around a fallen marine.

The Koreans helped extend the long stretcher. There was complete silence as we lifted the man onto it. He moaned softly as we began to step down the incline. The last concussion grenade exploded above us, but near. The force of the rushing air smacked into my right side and I lost balance. We dropped the stretcher. The wounded man rolled out of it and turned over once before coming to rest against a prone Korean. We reloaded the stretcher. He had stopped moaning and had in fact stopped living. Three other wounded men were brought down the hill.

It is difficult to put into words the urgency of the situation. The remaining members of the assault squad moved past us. They walked backwards, peering intently at the skyline. This bothered me very much. It was at this point that I began to get really frightened. I saw no reason why the Chinese would not follow us. Lt. Buell appeared and told us, the covering squad, to remain where we were, and that he would give us the word when to pull out, which would be after the stretcher-bearers had crossed the paddy.

Medve and I crawled forward and lay down on either side of the straw-covered path. My weapon had been cocked for some time and I clutched a grenade. A minute or two of breathless listening, then the lieutenant crept up to us and whispered, "Move out!" The three of us practically ran to the edge of the paddy, found the marking of white tape, and stepped up on one of the dikes.

Reforming a column along Texas Ridge, we retraced our route and reached home at 5:30 A.M.

Most of us crowded into the command post and drank coffee and ate sandwiches. There had been a death, and some of the men looked sick. Others pretended to be casual about it. Others appeared to be callous. All four casualties had been sent to the rear area before we arrived. Obviously the "raid" was a failure. The support barrages probably caused some damage, and one member of the assault squad swore that he hit the burp gunner—the only Chinese who actually fired. These facts, balanced by our own score of one dead, three wounded, do not sit evenly. And no enemy prisoner. It was the concussion grenades that halted the assault in its tracks.

I won't deny that I was excited about taking part in the raid. When the bombardment and the shooting started, I was so fascinated by the idea that people were out there who were trying to kill each other that I wasn't afraid—a stupid fool. Not appalled, fascinated. During the withdrawal, when I saw that people were hurt and that one of them was dead, I became very much afraid.

From *The Last Parallel* by Martin Russ. Copyright © 1957 by Martin Russ. Reprinted by permission of Holt, Rinehart and Winston, Publishers.

READING REVIEW

1. What was the MLR?
2. What was the goal of Martin Russ's platoon?
3. **Analyzing a Primary Source** What factors indicate that the platoon's mission failed?

★ 17-4 Shot Down Over Soviet Territory ★

Introduction To all appearances, Soviet Premier Nikita Khrushchev and President Dwight D. Eisenhower were on the way to relaxing the tensions between the two nations. After Khrushchev's friendly visit to the United States and his meeting with Eisenhower at Camp David, plans were made for a summit conference in Paris in May 1960. But then an event occurred that changed everything. This selection describes what happened.

Vocabulary Before you read the selection, find the meaning of these words in a dictionary: reconnaissance, designation, chafed, clandestinely.

Among the military jets crowding the United States base at the Turkish city of Adana in late April 1960, the low black plane with the high tail looked out of place. Its wings were so wide and thin that they drooped. Its landing gear, like that of no other plane, was rigged bicycle-fashion—a wheel under the nose and another under the tail, with flimsy, wheeled "pogo sticks" under the wingtips that could be dropped off as soon as the plane was airborne. The plane bore no identifying marks whatsoever. Its pilot—there was room for no other crewman beneath the glass canopy—seemed equally odd: he wore a special partial-pressure flying suit with oxygen tubes dangling from it at several points, and there was a revolver slung on his hip.

Francis Gary Powers was the senior pilot in the supersecret 10/10 squadron at Adana that was engaged in making reconnaissance flights at fantastically high altitudes over the Soviet Union. The jet had made its first flight in August 1955, and it was given the designation "U-2." Besides the pilot, the jet carried heavy electronic gear and a battery of cameras that he could turn on at the flick of a button. The cameras recorded the photographic information which, when developed and interpreted by experts, told the CIA what the directors of United States defense wanted perhaps more than anything else in the world to know: the location and activities of Soviet military elements, above all, of its missile forces.

On every mission Powers's U-2 broke the world's official altitude record for airplanes. Very probably he flew as high as 100,000 feet. At such levels his jet was not even visible from the ground. But that did not mean the Russians were unaware that he was up there. His jet carried electronic gear that picked up the indications of Russian radars tracking him, and American radiomen south of the border could hear Russians excitedly barking messages of his course and speed.

The United States government considered the sending of such U-2 missions over the Soviet Union an act essential to national survival in the Cold War days of the 1950s. Though Powers saw little of the pictures developed from his film and rushed off each time by special courier plane to Washington, it was evident enough from things said that "Operation Overflight" was a source of highly valued intelligence.

Premier Khrushchev knew all about these secret flights and had chafed at Russian helplessness to prevent them. At least once in 1956, immediately after an official visit to Moscow by General Nathan Twining, chief of the United States Air Force, an American plane flew clandestinely into Russia and penetrated as far as Kiev. "The question arose," Khrushchev said much later, "should we protest or not? I suggested not sending any protest. We learnt our lesson from the fact and stepped up our production of rockets and fighter planes." Later, in the intimate atmosphere of Camp David, Khrushchev had felt, he said, like asking Eisenhower why he was allowing U-2 flights over Russia, but decided it was too embarrassing.

The President also said nothing, but by the following spring U-2 flights were few and far between. After a long pause one was carried out from Turkey on April 9. Then, late in the month, Gary Powers was alerted for the next flight.

The first leg of the flight was uneventful, with considerable cloud cover around the Cosmodrome. But between Chelyubinsk and Sverdlovsk, when the Urals were coming up snow-topped in sunlight on the left, Powers's automatic pilot went out of whack. He switched to manual and pressed determinedly on. No U-2 had ever flown over Sverdlovsk before, and his cameras were working. About 30 to 40 miles northeast of Sverdlovsk he made a 90-degree turn and rolled into a flightline that would take him over the southwestern edge of the city. He was marking the time, altitude, speed, exhaust-gas temperature and engine-instrument readings in his log when "suddenly there was a dull thump, the aircraft jerked forward, and a tremendous orange flash lit the cockpit and sky."

For Powers there was just "time enough to think the explosion was external to the aircraft and, from the push, somewhat behind it." The plane fell away into an uncontrollable spin. Powers, thrown forward, did not use the ejection seat. Instead he reached over his head and unlocked the canopy, which sailed off into space. Without stopping to pull the switches that would have exploded the plane, he scrambled out, dangled frantically on his oxygen hoses till they snapped, and then fell free. At 15,000 feet his parachute opened automatically. As he floated down he remembered a suicide device that the "agency" man had handed him before takeoff. It was a poison pin inside a hollowed-out silver dollar. He unscrewed the enclosing loop, slipped out the pin and put it in his pocket, and flung the dollar to the Siberian winds.

The moment Powers hit the ground less than 100 yards from a village, citizens

After the death of Stalin there was a "thaw" in the cold war. During the thaw, Soviet premier Nikita Khrushchev toured the United States. This photograph was taken on a visit to a farm in Iowa.

out for the May Day holiday gathered round him. Someone took his pistol. On the barrel was the inevitable "USA." In his seatpack was an American-flag poster with "I am an American" printed on it in 14 languages. This spy in the sky, expecting to land in Norway, had also brought along his overnight kit. In it was his wallet with all his identification cards, his Social Security card, pictures of his wife Barbara. Flown to Moscow, Powers told the whole story of his spy flight from takeoff in Turkey to bailout over Sverdlovsk.

Adapted from Carl Solberg, *Riding High: America in the Cold War* (New York: Mason & Lipscomb, Publishers, 1973).

READING REVIEW

1. What information was the United States seeking by using the U-2?
2. Why did Khrushchev say he was "embarrassed" to mention the U-2 flights to Eisenhower?
3. **Relating Cause and Effect** Based on your reading in Chapter 17, what effect did the U-2 incident have?

★ 17-5 The Hungarian Revolution Fails ★

Introduction In 1956 nationalistic feelings in Hungary erupted into a revolt against Soviet domination. Although the revolutionary government had no official delegate at the United Nations at the time, Prime Minister Imre Nagy appealed to that body for help. The Soviet Union, however, had no intention of allowing new freedoms in a nation under its control. This selection presents Hungary's plea and the general world response.

Vocabulary Before you read the selection, find the meaning of these words in a dictionary: perplexed, impenetrable, ambiguity, hypocrisy, conspiratorial, ominous, initiative, abstentions, credentials, vindicated.

—I request Your Excellency promptly to put on the agenda of the forthcoming General Assembly of the United Nations the question of Hungary's neutrality and the defense of this neutrality by the four Great Powers. Signed: Imre Nagy, President of the Council of Ministers of the Hungarian People's Republic, designated Minister of Foreign Affairs.

The desperate appeal disappeared into a huge pile of papers on the desk of the United Nations secretary general, who was out to lunch.

It was only under persistent questioning by journalists quoting European sources on Hungary's declaration of neutrality that the United Nations press chief salvaged the message and read it to reporters at 2:00 P.M.

A perplexed world followed the events in Hungary, the fighting in the streets of Budapest, with admiration and sympathy. Demonstrations against the Soviet Union were staged in many cites.

Political action was concentrated at the United Nations, where all the attempts to counter what was happening were lost in an impenetrable tangle of goodwill, hesitation, ambiguity, incompetence, hypocrisy and hostility.

It looked like conspiratorial timing but it was, I believe, simply ominous historical coincidence that Britain, France, and Israel should have launched their attack on Egypt [to regain the Suez Canal, seized earlier by Egypt] on October 29, 1956. The Suez conflict put a different perspective on the world, setting friends and allies against each other and providing the Russians with the opportunity and excuse they needed. The United Nations was preoccupied with Suez and the ensuing confusion was an invitation to the Soviet government to move easily, forcefully, and brutally against Hungary.

Hungary's fate was sealed. In the early hours of November 4, the mighty Soviet onslaught was unleashed. In New York it was nearly midnight, November 3. In the United Nations General Assembly's continuing emergency session on Suez, the American chief delegate, Ambassador Henry Cabot Lodge, was recognized on a point of order and informed the hushed chamber that Budapest was under heavy bombardment.

Within three hours—by which time it was already 10:00 A.M. on November 4 in Budapest—the Security Council had been called to order. But a United States draft resolution to look into the Hungarian state of affairs was defeated by a Soviet veto. Nevertheless, by invoking the "Uniting for Peace" resolution, the council managed to bypass the Soviet veto. It voted by ten to one to call an emergency session of the General Assembly "to make appropriate recommendations concerning the situation in Hungary."

At emergency sessions of the General Assembly held between November 4 and 9 and at meetings of its regular Eleventh Session between November 19 and December 12, a series of resolutions was adopted—calling for a cease-fire, condemning the Soviet Union for brutal military intervention, requiring the withdrawal of Soviet troops from Hungary and granting the Hungarians free elections.

When time for the General Assembly's regular session ran out on January 10, 1957, a special committee was set up to investigate the situation "created by the intervention of the Soviet Union, through its use of armed forces and other means, in the internal affairs of Hungary in order to report its findings to the General Assembly."

The committee's conclusions are already history. The uprising had been spontaneous. The revolutionary councils and the government had come into being on the initiative of the Hungarian people. The revolution had its roots in the Hungarians' past and was inspired by their traditional love of freedom.

On the evening of June 17, 1957, Radio Budapest announced the execution of Imre Nagy, General Pal Maleter, and two of their associates. The Thirteenth Session of the General Assembly placed the Hungarian question on its agenda once more. After a solemn debate on December 11 and 12, 1958, a strongly worded resolution was adopted, censuring the communist regime of Hungary and the Soviet Union for the barbarous murders and for continuing violation of human rights.

The last shots were fired over Hungary at the United Nations in the early 1960s. On December 20, 1962, by a sub-

In the 1950s the countries in the Soviet bloc grew increasingly resentful of Soviet domination. Nationalists in Hungary rebelled in 1956, but Soviet tanks quickly crushed the rebellion. Here, Hungarians burn pictures of Stalin.

stantial majority the General Assembly reaffirmed its earlier resolutions, including its request for the withdrawal of Soviet troops from Hungary and assurance of the Hungarian people's fundamental rights, freedom and independence. It also resolved that its special representative was no longer needful and asked the secretary general to take "any initiative that he deems helpful in relation to the Hungarian question." The vote was 53 to 13 with 43 abstentions. Twelve members were absent.

The credentials of the representatives of the new government in Budapest were finally accepted by the assembly on January 8, 1963. Their acceptance was received with jubilation in the nonfree world and sadness by Hungarians. A small nation's hopes for justice and freedom had been destroyed. Why and how did this finally happen?

Maybe responsibility lies with the United States, but President Eisenhower vindicated himself and his country in a television interview with Walter Cronkite on November 23, 1961:

Topic 17

There was no European country, and indeed, I don't believe ours, ready to say that we should have gone into this thing at once and tried to liberate Hungary from communist influence. I don't believe that we had the support of the UN to go in and make this a full-out war. We had no government (in Hungary) that was asking us to come in and it wasn't until there was a sort of, I think, a very brief revolutionary government was set up, that we had any communication with them. So I don't know."

The last word belongs to Robert Murphy, undersecretary of state at the time of the Hungarian Revolution, who wrote in his memoirs: "Perhaps history will demonstrate that the free world could have in-tervened to give the Hungarians the liberty they sought, but none of us in the State Department had the skill or the imagination to devise a way."

An honest assessment.

Adapted from *The Hungarian Revolution of 1956 in Retrospect*, ed. Bela K. Kiraly and Paul Jonas (Boulder, Colo.: *East European Quarterly*, 1977).

READING REVIEW

1. What international event helped to divert attention from what was happening in Hungary?
2. What action did the United States take about events in Hungary?
3. **Distinguishing Fact from Opinion** Give two facts and two opinions expressed in the selection.

Topic 18 The Search for Stability (1945–1960)

★ 18-1 A Whistle-Stop Campaign ★

Introduction In the presidential election of 1948, Republican candidate Thomas E. Dewey was widely expected to win. Postwar strikes, shortages, inflation, and unemployment had cost President Harry S. Truman much support. Moreover, the Democratic party had split, with Henry Wallace representing a new Progressive party and Strom Thurmond a States' Rights party. But Truman was a fighter and took his case before the public in a whistle-stop campaign. Here his daughter Margaret Truman, his biographer, describes Truman's whistle-stop technique.

Vocabulary Before you read the selection, find the meaning of these words in a dictionary: spontaneously, scrutinized, authentic, uninhibited, impromptu.

The whistle-stop routine seldom varied. As we pulled into the station bands would blare "Hail to the Chief" and the "Missouri Waltz." Dad, usually accompanied by three or four local politicians, would step out on the back platform of the train, and they would present him with a gift—a basket of corn, a bucket of apples, or some item of local manufacture. Then one of the local politicians would introduce the President, and Dad would give a brief fighting speech, plugging the local candidate, and asking the people for their support. But the heart of these little talks was a local reference, sometimes supplied by Dad spontaneously, more often by careful advance research on the part of the staff.

Whenever possible, my father preferred to say something that he knew or felt personally. He told his listeners in Clarksburg: "I've always had a warm spot in my heart for Clarksburg. I have been a student of the War Between the States, and I remember that Stonewall Jackson was born here in Clarksburg." At Hammond, Indiana, where many of the tanks for our World War II armies were produced, he drew on his knowledge of our war effort, which he had scrutinized intensively, as head of the Truman Committee in the Senate. "Our armies all over the world were grateful for the high quality of work you turned out," he told the crowd. This was authentic. It was not just something he was reading off a card. He knew and felt these things.

I have always believed that the great difference between Harry S. Truman and Thomas E. Dewey in 1948 was Dad's uninhibited refusal to be anyone but himself. At Dexter, Iowa, I think he won thousands of farm votes with an impromptu talk he gave after his formal speech. "I can plow a straight furrow," he said. "A prejudiced witness said so—my mother."

After his whistle-stop talks, Dad would introduce first my mother and then me. Mother was introduced as "the boss," and me as "the one who bosses the boss." We never did get him to stop introducing us this way in spite of numerous demands. He was equally stubborn about other routines. Hitting hard at the Republican Congress's failure to do something about the housing shortage, he often included himself in the problem. In Ogden, Utah, for instance, he suggested that if the voters did the right thing on the second of November, "that will keep me from suffering from a housing shortage on January 20, 1949." In Colorado Springs he told the crowd: "If you go out to the polls and do your duty as you should, I won't have to worry about moving out of the White House; and you won't have to worry about what happens to the welfare of the West."

Frantic memorandums and letters from White House staffers and friends in the sophisticated East warned that these housing remarks did not "help create a picture of strength and confidence." My father ignored them. He knew that the people were delighted to find their President talking their language, on this and all other points. . . .

My father's speeches reflected his dislike of big words and flowery language because they gave the audience the impression the orator was showing off—and they also interfered with the communication of

Shortages, strikes, and inflation threatened Truman's chances for election in 1948. However, Truman made a whirlwind whistle-stop campaign by train. The election results upset all predictions. Here Truman proudly displays the mistaken headline in the Chicago Daily Tribune.

the facts. When it came to deciding how to phrase something, he had only two rules: no "two-dollar words," and make the statement as simple and understandable as possible. "Let's not weasel-word it," he often said.

The simplicity was another reason my father loved the whistle-stops best. There was no need to get into elaborate discussions about foreign or domestic policy. There simply wasn't time. So he could tell the crowd what he thought of the Eightieth Congress in the plainest, bluntest terms. At a whistle-stop he also got the kind of feedback that he loved. "Give 'em hell, Harry," someone invariably yelled, and Dad would beam and promise to give them exactly that.

From pages 22, 23, and 26 in *Harry S. Truman* by Margaret Truman. Copyright © 1972 by Margaret Truman Daniel by permission of William Morrow & Company.

READING REVIEW

1. What was the "whistle-stop routine" that Truman followed?
2. How did the White House staff react to Truman's speeches?
3. **Ranking** (a) List the factors that made Truman's campaign a success. (b) Which do you think was most important? Why?

Introduction In the early 1950s Senator Joseph R. McCarthy of Wisconsin spearheaded an attack against Americans in government who he suspected were "soft" on communism. Many people objected strongly to McCarthy's method of making accusations without proof. Others, however, accepted his crusade as necessary to prevent treason. In this selection, a historian points out that long before the McCarthy era Americans opposed ideas they considered radical.

Vocabulary Before you read the selection, find the meaning of these words in a dictionary: effluvia, articulation, crystallized, espionage, allegations.

What came to be called "McCarthyism" was grounded in a set of attitudes, assumptions, and judgments with deep roots in American history. There has long been a popular fear of radicalism in this country. Its effluvia are scattered throughout the past—the Alien and Sedition acts, immigration restriction, the Haymarket affair, the Palmer raids, Sacco and Vanzetti. Since the Bolshevik Revolution these fears and suspicions have been generally identified with the Soviet Union, making of Russia and the communist experiment a "menace" and a "threat" to American institutions. The United States did not recognize the new government of Russia until 16 years after the revolution, and then only grudgingly. At home, even during the New Deal, most Americans favored denying freedom of speech, press, and assembly to native communists. The mobilization and political articulation of these fears is the anticommunist "persuasion." As such it has informed and in some instances dominated American politics for more than 50 years.

In domestic affairs the anticommunist persuasion often found expression in the identification of all social change with communism. Conservative critics accused New Dealers and Fair Dealers of "leading the country down the road" to collectivism. The latter, captives themselves of the persuasion, spent much of their time trying to free their own programs from any taint of suspicion. In foreign affairs the anticommunist persuasion crystallized about the postwar debate over American policy toward the Soviet Union. It replaced the old and threadbare quarrels between isolationists and internationalists with an entirely new set of emotionally charged issues and slogans. Republicans accused the Democrats of "selling out" Eastern Europe and China and "appeasing" the Russians. The Democrats insisted, somewhat less successfully, that they were as "hard" on communism as anyone.

A third expression of the anticommunist persuasion, extreme and yet characteristic, was the charge of "communists in government" and treason in high places. After 1950 this came to be identified with Joe McCarthy. Yet to call it "McCarthyism" is to obscure the fundamental fact that it had been in the works for more than a decade before the Wisconsin senator made his national debut. The communists-in-government issue went back at least to the late 1930s, when Democrat Martin Dies and his Special House Committee on Un-American Activities turned it upon the Roosevelt administration.

It was the Dies committee, for example, that popularized in the United States the technique of guilt by association, through which a person is considered suspect because of the organizations to which he belongs or the friends whose company he keeps. The committee also established the value of ex-communist witnesses, and it carefully cultivated a growing body of these disillusioned extremists.

The membership of the Dies committee perfected all the gambits that McCarthy would later use: "I have reliable evidence which I am not at liberty to disclose at the present time." Or, if the Justice Department will only investigate, it will "have no difficulty getting the facts."

But it was not until the end of World War II that the issue of communism in government began to gather momentum. The attendant causes were no doubt the anxiety and frustration of the cold war and revelations of Russian espionage in

Canada, Great Britain, and the United States.

The charge of communism in government was a broad one, covering a wide variety of allegations ranging all the way from espionage (a concrete and specific act), to the mere presence of communists or "fellow travelers" in government agencies, to vague and often unsubstantiated charges of communist "influence" or communist "thinking."

Adapted from Robert Griffith, *The Politics of Fear: Joseph R. McCarthy and the Senate* (Lexington, Ky.: University Press of Kentucky, 1970).

READING REVIEW

1. According to Griffith, which techniques used by McCarthy were first used by the Dies committee?
2. What events helped create public acceptance of McCarthy's efforts?
3. **Recognizing a Point of View** What statements in the reading show the author's attitude toward McCarthy and his methods?

Senator Joseph McCarthy, at left, accused United States Army officials of communist activities. Little evidence was uncovered to support McCarthy's wide-ranging charges of treason in government, and his influence waned.

18-3 ★ Eisenhower Proposes a Middle Way ★

Introduction Republican Dwight D. Eisenhower was elected President by a landslide in 1952. The country was seeking stability, and Eisenhower proposed to keep national affairs on an even keel. In this selection from a speech given on Labor Day 1949 to the American Bar Association, he gives his views of the "creative area" of government.

Vocabulary Before you read the selection, find the meaning of these words in a dictionary: provocation, shibboleth, debris, inequities, knave, disintegration, annihilation, derided, aspirations, unanimous, arbitrary, stamina.

A little more than a century ago the *Communistic Manifesto* of Karl Marx was published, preaching the falsehood of an inescapable class warfare that would continue within society until by violence the workers erased all traces of traditional government. If Marx were right, this day should be, in all our great country, an annually recurring provocation to riot, physical strife, and civil disorder. The factual evidence of his blunder is so clear that it ought not to require emphasis.

Nevertheless, with a full century of contrary proof in our possession and despite our demonstrated capacity for cooperative teamwork, some among us seem to accept the shibboleth of an unbridgeable gap between those who hire and those who are employed. We miserably fail to challenge the lie that what is good for management is necessarily bad for labor; that for one side to profit, the other must be depressed. Such distorted doctrine is false and foreign to the American sense where common ideals and purpose permit us a common approach toward the common good. It must be combated at every turn by both clear word and effective deed.

Of course, our path in places is still obstructed by unfinished business, the debris of inequities and prejudices not yet overcome. But, strong in the fundamental principles of American life, we have, in less than two centuries, accomplished more for the community of men than was won in the previous forty.

For us today, those principles still dictate progress down the center, even though there the contest is hottest, the progress sometimes discouragingly slow. The frightened, the defeated, the coward, and the knave run to the flanks, straggling out of the battle under the cover of slogans, false formulas, and appeals to passion—a welcome sight to an alert enemy. When the center weakens piecemeal, disintegration and annihilation are only steps away, in a battle of arms or of political philosophies. The clear-sighted and the courageous, fortunately, keep fighting in the middle of the war. They are determined that we shall not lose our freedoms, either to the unbearable selfishness of vested interest or through the blindness of those who, protesting devotion to the public welfare, falsely declare that only government can bring us happiness, security, and opportunity.

During the 1950s many Americans embraced traditional values of home, religion, and patriotism. This painting by Norman Rockwell, "After the Prom," reflects the simple pleasure of dressing up for a school dance.

The middle of the road is derided by all of the right and of the left. They deliberately misrepresent the central position as a neutral, wishy-washy one. Yet here is the truly creative area in which we may obtain agreement for constructive social action compatible with basic American principles and with the just aspirations of every sincere American. It is the area in which is rooted the hopes and allegiance of the vast majority of our people.

Thus, the American system, in line with its principles, can and does, by governmental action, prevent or correct abuses springing from the unregulated practice of a private economy. In specific cases local governments have, with almost unanimous approval, provided needed public services so that extraordinary power over all citizens of the community might not fall into the hands of the few. In all cases we expect the government to be forehanded in establishing the rules that will preserve a practical equality in opportunity among us.

We, in turn, carefully watch the government—especially the ever-expanding federal government—to see that, in performing the functions obviously falling within governmental responsibility, it does not interfere more than is necessary in our daily lives. We instinctively have greater faith in the counterbalancing effect of many social, philosophic, and economic forces than we do in arbitrary law. We will not accord to the central government unlimited authority, any more than we will bow our necks to the dictates of the uninhibited seekers after personal power in finance, labor, or any other field.

Adapted from Dwight D. Eisenhower, "The Middle Way," *Vital Speeches of the Day* (New York: City News Publishing Co., 1949).

READING REVIEW

1. Which points of view does Eisenhower view as threats to freedom?
2. According to Eisenhower, what happens when the political center weakens?
3. **Summarizing** List the reasons Eisenhower gives for preferring a middle-of-the-road policy of government.

Introduction When the fighting men returned to their civilian jobs after World War II, many women who had worked in the industrial war effort returned to full-time homemaking. During the 1950s newspapers, magazines, radio, and television stressed the importance of mothers staying at home. This selection is by Agnes Meyer, a trustee of Barnard College serving in the Midcentury White House Child Conference.

Vocabulary Before you read the selection, find the meaning of these words in a dictionary: enhance, sublimates, beneficent, vicarious, depreciated, sterilized, self-abasement, masochistic, parity.

Women have many careers but only one vocation—motherhood. As a result their most successful careers are motherhood substitutes such as teaching, nursing, social work, as well as medical, psychiatric, and other scientific professions that protect the child and the family. A woman confronting the world has no greater resources than those she finds within herself. Education can do no worse than to destroy those instinctive resources. It can do no better than to enhance them. When woman sublimates her mother instinct in a career, she can achieve a rich, beneficent, and rewarding life. But only if she follows her vocation can she live in the fullest sense of the word. It is for woman as mother, actual or vicarious, to restore security in our insecure world—not the economic security on which we now lean far too much, but the emotional security for which the world longs as much as it longs for its daily bread.

Woman is the cement of society. Since time immemorial it has been woman who has held the family, society, and life itself together. She did it instinctively to protect herself during pregnancy and to protect her children during their long period of helplessness. Through this fundamental need for family solidarity it is woman who has developed the art of human relationships and an appreciation of the vital importance of human behavior.

Now that we have amassed so much factual knowledge of the importance of the home as the basis of society, of the importance of marital relationships, of child guidance and education in general, the role of wife and mother has become infinitely more exacting and difficult. Instead of apologizing for being a "mere housewife," as so many do, women should make society realize that upon the housewife now fall the combined tasks of economist, nutrition expert, sociologist, psychiatrist, and educator. Then society would confer upon the status of housewife the honor, recognition, and acclaim it deserves. It is one thing if women wish to work or must do so to help support the family. It is quite another thing—it is a destructive influence—if society forces women into the labor market in order that they may respect themselves and gain the respect of others.

Women must boldly announce that no job is more exacting, more necessary, or more rewarding than that of housewife and mother. Then they will feel free to become once more the moral force of society through the stabilization of the home. With all scientific knowledge we have amassed, women can and should be the standard bearers of a civilization higher in every respect than any we have ever known before. But they can only do this if they will accept the fact that their functions as women are very different from those of men. What modern woman has to recapture is the wisdom that just being a woman is her central task and her greatest honor. It is a task that challenges her whole character, intelligence, and imagination.

If we look at the social scene about us we find very hopeful indications that women, especially the young married women, have begun to realize these fundamental truths. The high birth rate is in itself a promising symptom. But further than that, many of these young women are carrying out their duties toward their husbands, their children, and the physical maintenance of the home with joyous intelligence and great ability. It is fair to say that there have probably never been in any civilization so many ideal marital partnerships in which husband and wife respect each other's sphere of activity and in which both share the responsibility for the education of the children.

On the other hand, it is no less true that there have never been so many women who are dissatisfied with being women and therefore with being wives and mothers. There have never been so many women who are unnecessarily torn between marriage and a career. There have never been so many mothers who neglect their children because they find some trivial job more interesting.

I am not trying to drive all women back into the home. The married woman who is rebellious about family life does her children more harm by staying home in such a frame of mind than by leaving them to some kindly relative or sending them to boarding school. It is the frame of mind of such women that is wrong, that must be understood and changed. For these women are equally disastrous as an influence in their working environment. God protect us all from the efficient, go-getter businesswoman whose feminine instincts have been completely sterilized. Wherever women are functioning, whether in the home or in a job, they must remember that their chief function as women is a capacity for warm, understanding, and charitable human relationships. Women are throwing their greatest natural gift out of the window when they cease to function as experts in cooperative living.

I am not asking women to overdo self-sacrifice to a point of self-abasement. We all know extreme feminine types who use this masochistic weapon not out of a desire to serve, but to conquer and subdue their victims. Women must learn to keep self-respect and self-sacrifice, the social and the biological functions, in balance. Such women have the most friends because they defend their own personalities while giving free play to the expansion of other personalities. Those are the women who are called blessed because they constitute the happiness of their families and of the whole community.

Such women, moreover, are not concerned with the modern cry for equal rights because they are too sure of themselves and of what they have to give to the world. They seek not parity but partnership with men.

Adapted from Agnes E. Meyer, "Women Aren't Men," *Atlantic*, 186 (1950), 2.

READING REVIEW

1. According to Meyer, what has been women's historical role in society?
2. What indications were there in 1950 that women were accepting this role?
3. **Relating Past to Present** (a) What role does Meyer recommend for women? (b) What other roles do women assume today?

★ **18-5   The Montgomery Boycott**   ★

Introduction In Montgomery, Alabama, in 1955, Rosa Parks refused to obey the law that forced blacks to sit in the back of public buses. When Parks was arrested, blacks in Montgomery responded by boycotting the bus system. On the first day of the boycott, civil rights leader Reverend Martin Luther King, Jr., gave a speech in the Holt Street Church in Birmingham. In this selection, King describes that day.

Vocabulary Before you read the selection, find the meaning of these words in a dictionary: dispelled, academic, rostrum, mammoth, fervent, perpetuation, intimidation, coercion, shrouded.

Within five blocks of the church I noticed a traffic jam. Cars were lined up as far as I could see on both sides of the street. It was a moment before it occurred to me that all of these cars were headed for the mass meeting. I had to park at least four blocks from the church, and as I started walking I noticed that hundreds of people were standing outside. In the dark night, police cars circled slowly around the area, surveying the orderly, patient, and good-humored crowd. The three or four thousand people who could not get into the church were to stand cheerfully throughout the evening listening to the proceedings on the loudspeakers that had been set up outside for their benefit. And when, near the end of the meeting, these speakers were silenced at the request of the white people in surrounding neighborhoods, the crowd would still remain quietly, content simply to be present.

It took fully 15 minutes to push my way through to the pastor's study, where Dr. Wilson told me that the church had been packed since five o'clock. By now my doubts concerning the continued success of our venture were dispelled. The question of calling off the protest was now academic. The enthusiasm of these thousands of people swept everything along like an onrushing tidal wave.

It was some time before the remaining speakers could push their way to the rostrum through the tightly packed church. When the meeting began it was almost half an hour late. The opening hymn was the old familiar "Onward Christian Soldiers," and when that mammoth audience stood to sing, the voices outside swelling the chorus in the church, there was a mighty ring like the glad echo of heaven itself.

Rev. W. F. Alford, minister of the Beulah Baptist Church, led the congregation in prayer, followed by a reading of the Scripture by Rev. U. J. Fields, minister of the Bell Street Baptist Church. Then the Chairman introduced me. As the audience applauded, I rose and stood before the pulpit. Television cameras began to shoot from all sides. The crowd grew quite.

Without manuscript or notes, I told the story of what had happend to Mrs. Parks. Then I reviewed the long history of abuses and insults that Negro citizens had experienced on the city buses. "But there comes a time," I said, "that people get tired. We are here this evening to say to those who have mistreated us so long that we are tired—tired of being segregated and humiliated; tired of being kicked about by the brutal feet of oppression." The congregation met this statement with fervent applause. "We had no alternative but to protest," I continued. "For many years, we have shown amazing patience. We have sometimes given our white brothers the feeling that we liked the way we were being treated. But we come here tonight to be saved from that patience that makes us patient with anything less than freedom and justice." Again the audience interrupted with applause.

Briefly I justified our actions, both morally and legally. "One of the great glories of democracy is the right to protest for right." Comparing our methods with those of the White Citizens Councils and the Ku Klux Klan, I pointed out that while "these organizations are protesting for the perpetuation of injustice in the community, we are protesting for the birth of justice in the community. Their methods lead to violence and lawlessness. But in our protest there will be no cross burnings. No white person will be taken from his home by a hooded Negro mob and brutally murdered. There will be no threats and intimidation. We will be guided by the highest principles of law and order."

With this groundwork for militant action, I moved on to words of caution. I urged the people not to force anybody to refrain from riding the buses. "Our method will be that of persuasion, not coercion. We will only say to the people, 'Let your conscience be your guide.'" Emphasizing the Christian doctrine of love, "our actions must be guided by the deepest principles of our Christian faith. Love must be our regulating ideal. Once again we must hear the words of Jesus echoing across the centuries: 'Love your enemies, bless them that curse you, and pray for them that despitefully use you.' If we fail to do this our protest will end up as a meaningless drama on the stage of history, and its memory will be shrouded with the ugly garments of shame. In spite of the mistreatment that we have confronted we must not become bitter and end up by hating our white brothers. As Booker T. Washington said, 'Let no man pull you so low as to make you hate him.'" Once more the audience responded enthusiastically.

Then came my closing statement. "If you will protest courageously, and yet with dignity and Christian love, when the history books are written in future generations the historians will have to pause and say, 'There lived a great people—a black people—who injected new meaning and dignity into the veins of civilization.' This is our challenge and our overwhelming responsibility."

As I took my seat the people rose to their feet and applauded. I was thankful to God that the message had gotten over and that the task of combining the militant and the moderate had been at least partially accomplished. The people had been as enthusiastic when I urged them to love as they were when I urged them to protest.

As I sat listening to the continued applause I realized that this speech had evoked more response than any speech or sermon I had ever delivered, and yet it was virtually unprepared. I came to see for the first time what the older preachers meant when they said, "Open your mouth and God will speak for you." While I would not let this experience tempt me to overlook the need for continued preparation, it would always remind me that God can transform man's weakness into his glorious opportunity.

From pages 60–63 from *Stride Toward Freedom*, by Martin Luther King, Jr. Copyright © 1958 by Martin Luther King, Jr. Reprinted by permission of Harper & Row, Publishers, Inc.

READING REVIEW

1. What was the mood of the crowd Martin Luther King addressed?
2. What did King hope to accomplish by his speech?
3. **Finding the Main Idea** What type of behavior did King urge upon his listeners?

Topic 19 A Turbulent Decade (1960–1969)

★ 19-1 Kennedy Warns the Russians ★

Introduction The Cuban missile crisis was one of the most decisive events of the cold war. On October 14, 1962, an American plane brought back photographic evidence of Soviet missile launch sites in Cuba. Eight days later, President Kennedy issued the public warning printed here. Note that Kennedy uses the term "quarantine" when referring to the American plan to turn back ships. He avoided the term "blockade" because international law generally regards a blockade as an act of war.

Vocabulary Before you read the selection, find the meaning of these words in a dictionary: surveillance, eventualities, retaliatory, clandestine, provocative.

This government as promised has maintained the closest surveillance of the Soviet military build-up on the island of Cuba.

Within the past week unmistakable evidence has established the fact that a series of offensive missile sites is now in preparation on that imprisoned island.

The purpose of these bases can be none other than to provide a nuclear strike capability against the Western Hemisphere.

Upon receiving the first hard information of this nature last Tuesday morning at 9:00 A.M., I directed that our surveillance be stepped up. And having now confirmed the evidence and our decision on a course of action, this government feels obliged to report this new crisis to you in fullest detail.

This urgent transformation of Cuba into an important strategic base by the presence of these large long-range and offensive weapons of sudden mass destruction constitutes a threat to the peace and security of all the Americas. It is in deliberate defiance of the Rio Pact of 1947, the traditions of this nation and hemisphere, the joint resolution of the Eighty-seventh Congress, the Charter of the United Nations, and my own public warnings to the Soviets on September 4 and 13.

This action also contradicts the repeated assurances of Soviet spokesmen that the arms build-up in Cuba would retain its original defensive character and that the Soviet Union had no need or desire to station strategic missiles on the territory of any other nation.

Neither the United States of America nor the world community of nations can tolerate deliberate deception and offensive threats on the part of any nation, large or small. We no longer live in a world where only the actual firing of weapons represents a sufficient challenge to a nation's security to constitute maximum peril.

Our own strategic missiles have never been transferred to the territory of any other nation under a cloak of secrecy and deception. And our history, unlike that of the Soviets since the end of World War II, demonstrates that we have no desire to dominate or conquer any other nation or impose our system upon its people.

Our policy has been one of patience and restraint, as befits a peaceful and powerful nation which leads a worldwide alliance.

We have been determined not to be diverted from our central concerns by mere irritants and fanatics. But now further action is required. And it is underway. And these actions may only be the beginning.

We will not prematurely or unnecessarily risk the course of worldwide nuclear war in which even the fruits of victory would be ashes in our mouth. But neither will we shrink from that risk at any time it must be faced.

Acting, therefore, in the defense of our own security and of the entire Western Hemisphere and under the authority entrusted to me by the constitution as endorsed by the resolution of the Congress, I have directed that the following initial steps be taken immediately.

First, to halt this offensive build-up, a strict quarantine on all offensive military equipment under shipment to Cuba will begin. All ships of any kind bound for Cuba from whatever nation or port will, where they are found to contain cargoes of offensive weapons, be turned back. This quarantine will be extended if needed to other types of cargo and carriers.

We are not at this time, however, denying the necessities of life as the Soviets attempted to do in their Berlin blockade of 1948.

Second, I have directed the continued and increased close surveillance of Cuba and its military build-up.

I have directed the armed forces to prepare for any eventualities. And I trust that in the interests of both the Cuban people and the Soviet technicians at the sites, the hazards to all concerned of continuing this threat will be recognized.

Third, it shall be the policy of this nation to regard any nuclear missile launched from Cuba against any nation in the Western Hemisphere as an attack by the Soviet Union on the United States requiring a full retaliatory response upon the Soviet Union.

Fourth, as a necessary military precaution, I have reinforced our base at Guantanamo, evacuated today the dependents of our personnel there, and ordered additional military units to be on a standby alert basis.

In 1962 air force photographs of missile bases in Cuba shocked the nation. President Kennedy warned the Soviet Union that no further military development would be allowed, and the Soviets dismantled the bases.

Fifth, we are calling tonight for an immediate meeting of the Organization of American States to consider this threat to hemispheric security.

Sixth, under the Charter of the United Nations we are asking tonight that an emergency meeting of the Security Council be convoked without delay to take action against this latest Soviet threat to world peace.

Seventh, and finally, I call upon Chairman Khrushchev to halt and eliminate this clandestine, reckless, and provocative threat to world peace and to stable relations between our two nations.

I call upon him further to abandon this course of world domination and to join in an historic effort to end the perilous arms race and to transform the history of man.

Adapted from John F. Kennedy, "Arms Quarantine of Cuba," *Vital Speeches of the Day* (New York: City News Publishing Co., 1962).

READING REVIEW

1. What, according to Kennedy, was the purpose of the Soviet missile bases in Cuba?
2. Why does he say the United States must take action right away?
3. **Analyzing** (a) What seven steps does Kennedy outline? (b) Which of these involve actions by the United States government? (c) Which steps concern international organizations?

★ 19-2 The First American in Orbit ★

Introduction The 1962 space journey of John Glenn was historic not only because he was the first American to orbit the earth. He was also the first astronaut to transmit back to earth a running commentary of the flight. This selection gives some highlights of Glenn's commentary.

Vocabulary Before you read the selection, find the meaning of these words in a dictionary: contrail, yaw, orientation, jettisoning, drogue.

Just after blast-off from earth, at 9:47 A.M. on February 20, the astronaut's report began.

Colonel Glenn: "We're under way. It is a little bumpy along about here. Some vibration area coming up here now.

"A little contrail went by the window, or something.

"We're smoothing out some now, getting out of the vibration area. Coming out real fine. Flight very smooth now. Pressure coming down—5.7 [pounds per square inch]."

At this point, about three minutes after the launch, the capsule's escape tower separated and pressure built up again as the sustainer engine accelerated.

Colonel Glenn: "I see the tower go. I saw the smoke go by the window. Still have about one and a half Gs [one G equals the pull of gravity]. Gs starting to build again a little bit."

A few minutes later, astronaut Glenn was in orbit. He was then 503 miles out over the Atlantic, 100 miles in altitude, and traveling at a speed of 17,530 miles an hour. Over the Bermuda area, he reported again.

Colonel Glenn: "Zero G [weightless] now, and I feel fine.

"Oh, that view is tremendous. Turnaround has started. Capsule turning around, and I can see the booster doing turnarounds just a couple of hundred yards behind. It looks beautiful.

"Can see clear back, a big cloud pattern way back across toward the cape. Beautiful sight.

"We're doing real fine up here. Everything is doing very well."

At 10:09 A.M., EST, a tracking station in Africa contacted the fast-moving space capsule, approaching that continent.

Colonel Glenn: "The horizon now is a brilliant blue. I have the mainland in sight at present time coming up on the scope, and have the Canaries [islands off the African coast] in sight through the window. Picked them up on the scope just before I saw them out the window."

After crossing Africa in about 10 minutes, he sped out over the Indian Ocean and on toward Australia. In about 45 minutes after his early-morning takeoff, the astronaut was on the nighttime side of the earth. He was asked to check stars, which could be seen much more clearly outside the earth's atmosphere.

Colonel Glenn: "That was about the shortest day I've ever run into.

"I have the Pleiades [a small cluster of stars also known as the Seven Sisters] in sight, very clear. Picking up some of these star patterns now a little better than when I was just off Africa."

Soaring on over Australia, the American spaceman was told that the town of Perth had turned on all of its lights in his honor. Here, he was about 120 miles above the earth and still in darkness.

Colonel Glenn: "Just to my right, I can see a big pattern of light, apparently right on the coast. I can see the outline of a town and a very bright light just to the south of it. The lights show up very well and thank everybody for turning them on, will you?"

The orbiting capsule by now was flying over the southwestern Pacific, where local time was after midnight and the date was Wednesday, February 21. Then, in mid-Pacific, the capsule crossed the international dateline and the date was again February 20. The Pacific crossing was otherwise without incident. Over the United States, some trouble was reported with the automatic controls that kept the capsule in a constant attitude in relation to the earth—a potentially dangerous situation.

Colonel Glenn: "I'm going on fly-by-wire [manual control of the attitude of the space craft] so I can control more accurately. It [trouble] just started as I got to Guaymas [Mexico] and appears to be—it drifts off in yaw to the right and about 1 degree per second. It will go over to an attitude of about 20 degrees and hold at that. And when it hits about a 20-degree point, it then goes into orientation mode and comes back to zero. It was cycling back and forth in that mode. I am on fly-by-wire now and controlling manually.

"Having no trouble controlling. Very smooth and easy. Controls very nicely."

With Glenn controlling it by hand, the capsule soared over a point marking the end of its first orbit just 88.29 minutes after launch. As the second orbit began, the astronaut reported again.

Colonel Glenn: "I have a beautiful view out the window of the coast at the present time. Just departing. Can see way down across Florida.

"Only really unusual thing so far besides ASCS [automatic stabilization control system] trouble were the little particles—luminous particles—around the capsule, just thousands of them right at sunrise over the Pacific."

Glenn was so interested in these swarms of fireflylike objects that clustered about his space capsule each time he headed into the sunrise that he turned his capsule completely around with the manual controls to get a better look.

He was also impressed by the contrast of leaving darkness and heading into full light in a matter of minutes.

Colonel Glenn: "I have the cape in sight. I can see the whole state of Florida just laid out like a map. Beautiful. I can still see clear back to the Mississippi Delta, and it looks very good down that way. It looks like we will have no problem on recovery."

The astronaut this time crossed the Atlantic farther south, hit the coast of Africa at the Equator, then crossed the track of his earlier orbit far south of India and passed over the center of Australia. His time was spent making countless checks and tests, reporting technical data to tracking stations along the route. Over Hawaii, a decision had to be made whether to try for a third orbit. The astronaut was asked how he felt about it, after the trouble that developed with the capsule's automatic controls.

Colonel Glenn: "I am 'go' for the third."

All went well as the capsule followed its third-orbit path, crossing the southern tip of Africa and the northern coast of Australia.

It was over the Pacific that indications of really serious trouble appeared. Island tracking stations picked up a signal that indicated the vital heat shield on the broad base of the capsule had come loose. The shield would provide the astronaut's only protection against the searing 3,000-degree heat of atmospheric friction during the reentry phase. If loose, it could come off. One indication that all was well would be if the retrorockets attached to the heat shield fired normally.

Just before Glenn reached the West Coast, the rockets were fired at 2:20 P.M., EST, to slow the capsule for its reentry curve down to earth.

Colonel Glenn: "Retros fired normally. I felt like I was going back the other way—clear back to Hawaii."

This indicated that the trouble was probably only a faulty signal. But it was decided to leave the retrorockets attached to the shield as a precaution against jarring it, instead of jettisoning the rockets over Texas as planned earlier. Now the capsule descended through the earth's atmosphere, its shield glowing as the spaceship crossed the United States and headed for its Caribbean landing area.

Colonel Glenn: "Boy, that was a real fireball."

Slowed by the atmosphere, then by a drogue parachute and a regular parachute, the capsule dropped in the Caribbean at 2:43 P.M., 800 miles southeast of Cape Canaveral and just 6 miles from the nearest rescue ship. By 3:04 P.M., it was lifted aboard the destroyer *Noa*. The astronaut climbed down on deck at 3:22. He grinned and gave his final report.

Colonel Glenn: "My condition is excellent."

Adapted from "An American in Orbit Talks to His Planet," *U.S. News & World Report*, March 5, 1962. Copyright © 1962 by United States News Publishing Corp.

READING REVIEW

1. What trouble developed during the third orbit?
2. On the basis of this selection, do you think Glenn was courageous? Why or why not?
3. **Understanding Geography** Use a globe to trace Glenn's orbits as described in the selection.

★ 19-3 LBJ in Action ★

Introduction Whether or not people approved of his goals, everyone agreed that Lyndon Johnson was a supremely persuasive politician. He accomplished a great deal in his early years as President. This selection is two anecdotes told by men who worked closely with him. Wilbur Cohen was Assistant Secretary of the Department of Health, Education, and Welfare. Willard Wirtz was Secretary of Labor.

Vocabulary Before you read the selection, find the meaning of these words in a dictionary: liaison, extemporaneously, aura, bumpkin.

Wilbur J. Cohen: "Now I'm going to tell you a very important story. It's one of the most important I know about Johnson. At the end of January 1965, shortly after he'd been inaugurated, Johnson called a meeting of the so-called congressional liaison officers of the various departments.

"He came in and sat down with us for what we thought would be five or ten minutes to wish us good luck, but he stayed for at least an hour, maybe an hour and a half.

"During that time he talked extemporaneously, and what he said was a three-hour credit course in American political history. He said, 'Look, I've just been elected and right now we'll have a honeymoon with Congress. With the additional congressmen that have been elected, I'll have a good chance to get my program through. Of course, for that I have to depend on you, the 20 or 30 people who are in this room.

"'But after I make my recommendations, I'm going to start to lose the power and authority I have, because that's what happened to President Woodrow Wilson, to President Roosevelt, and to Truman and to Kennedy.' He said, 'Every day that I'm in office and every day that I push my program, I'll be losing part of my ability to be influential, because that's in the nature of what the President does. He uses up his capital. Something is going to come up, either something like the Vietnam War or something else where I will begin to lose all that I have now.

"'So I want you guys to do everything possible to get everything in my program passed as soon as possible, before the aura and the halo that surround me disappear.

"'Don't waste a second. Get going right now. Larry, Wilbur—just remember I want this program through fast, and by fast I mean six months, not a year.'

"Of course, I don't mean to imply that if things had gone right he wouldn't have run again. But to my mind what he was saying was that he had to put everything on the line, and if that meant I've got only one full term, that's fine. At least I'll get my program through. I would rather use up everything in one term than be cautious and play around and run for a second.

"And I think he had a correct historical evaluation, much better than Wilson, who was a great historian, and certainly better than Kennedy, who was cautious because he thought Goldwater would run against him in 1964 and that he'd beat him and then he could do what he wanted and get his program enacted.

"Johnson—here was this country bumpkin who had, like Truman, a more correct evaluation of the historical forces affecting the president than almost anybody else."

Willard Wirtz: "I remember in a cabinet meeting that year John Gardner,* was talking along, very conversationally, and he came to some item or other, I've forgotten about what, and he said, all of sudden, 'Of course, Mr. President, you know we can't do that.'

"And Lyndon Johnson leaped out of his chair and leaped halfway across the table and he pointed his finger at John and said, 'Mr. Secretary, don't ever say that.' And then he started around that room, just looking everybody in the eye, and pointing his finger at everybody at the table. He said, 'There is nothing this country can't do. Remember that.'

---

*Gardner was Secretary of Health, Education, and Welfare.

Lyndon B. Johnson came to the White House with 20 years of experience in Congress. As President, he began a War on Poverty, a program that included loans, job training, and assistance to the poor. Here President Johnson visits an unemployed man and his family in eastern Kentucky.

"Well, now, he believed that. And domestically he was doggone close, very doggone close. My gosh, when you think of what happened in 1965, you turn around two centuries. Just take civil rights and women, to mention two—he turned the whole country around."

Reprinted by permission of the Putnam Publishing Group from *Lyndon: An Oral Biography* by Merle Miller. Copyright © 1980 by Merle Miller.

READING REVIEW

1. Why do you think Cohen says his story is "one of the most important" he knows about Johnson?
2. What is the significance of the anecdote told by Wirtz?
3. **Recognizing a Point of View** (a) How would you describe the attitude each of these two men had toward Johnson? (b) Do you feel that their views are objective? Why or why not?

Introduction Fannie Lou Hamer first came to national attention at the Democratic national convention of 1964. There she and other blacks from Mississippi tried but failed to be seated as delegates. In this interview, she describes her attempt to register to vote.

Vocabulary Before you read the selection, find the meaning of these words in a dictionary: registrar, de facto.

"So then that was in 1962 when the civil rights workers came into this county. Now, I didn't know anything about voter registration or nothin' like that, 'cause people had never been told that they could register to vote. And livin' out in the country, if you had a little radio, by the time you got in at night, you'd be too tired to listen at what was goin' on. So they had a rally. I had gone to church that Sunday, and the minister announced that they were gon' have a mass meeting that Monday night. Well, I didn't know what a mass meeting was, and I was just curious to go to a mass meeting. So I did, and they was talkin' about how blacks had a right to register and how they had a right to vote. Just listenin' at 'em, I could just see myself votin' people outa office that

I know was wrong and didn't do nothin' to help the poor. I said, you know, that's sumpin' I really wanna be involved in, and finally at the end of that rally, I had made up my mind that I was gonna come out there when they said you could go down that Friday to try to register."

She remembers the date precisely: August 31, 1962. She and 17 others climbed aboard an old bus owned by a black man from neighboring Bolivar County. SNCC had chartered it for the 30-mile ride to the county seat in Indianola. Once there, she was the first into the registrar's office.

He brought a big old book out there, and he gave me the sixteenth section of the Constitution of Mississippi, and that was dealing with de facto laws, and I didn't know nothin' about no de facto laws, didn't know nothin' about any of 'em. I could copy it like it was in the book, but after I got through copying it, he told me to give a reasonable interpretation and tell the meaning of that section that I had copied. Well, I flunked out.

"So then we started back to Ruleville and on our way back to Ruleville, this same highway patrolman that I had seen steady cruisin' around this bus stopped us. We had crossed that bridge, coming

In 1965 the Reverend Martin Luther King, Jr., led a demonstration of over 200,000 people in Washington, D.C. The marchers, black and white, demanded an end to racial discrimination and segregation.

over from Indianola. They got out the cars, flagged the bus down. When they flagged the bus down, they told all of us to get off the bus. So at this time, we just started singing "Have a Little Talk with Jesus," and we got off the bus, and all they wanted then was for us to get back on the bus. They arrested Bob [a SNCC worker] and told the bus driver he was under arrest. So we went back then to Indianola. The bus driver was fined $100 for driving a bus with too much yellow in it. Now ain't that ridiculous?"

"For what?"

"Too much yellow. Said the bus looked to much like a school bus. That's funny, but it's the truth. But you see, it was to frighten us to death. This same bus had been used year after year hauling cotton choppers and cotton pickers to Florida to try to make a livin' that winter, and he had never been arrested before. But the day he tried to carry us to Indianola, they fined him $100, and I guess it was so ridiculous that they finally cut the fine down to $30 and all of us together—not one, but all us together—had enough to pay the fine. So we paid the fine, and then we got back on the bus and come on to Ruleville."

Hamer was threatened by the owner of the plantation where she and her husband lived and worked as sharecroppers. She was either to abandon her efforts to register or leave the plantation. She left.

"I stayed away, 'cause things then—you could see 'em at night. They would have fires in the middle of the road. You wouldn't see no Klan signs, but just make a fire in the middle of the road. And it was so dangerous, I stayed in Tallahatchie County all of September and then October, and then November I come back to Ruleville. I was comin', I didn't know why I was comin', but I was just sick of runnin' and hadn't done nothin'. I started tryin' to find a place to stay, 'cause we didn't have nothin'.

The woman who had been her sixth-grade school teacher put her in touch with a black woman who had a three-room house for rent "for $18 a month and that was a lotta money." She and her family moved in on December 3.

"That was on Sunday, and that Monday, the fourth of December, I went back to Indianola to the circuit clerk's office and I told him who I was and I was there to take that literacy test again.

"I said, 'Now, you cain't have me fired 'cause I'm already fired, and I won't have to move now, because I'm not livin' in no white man's house.' I said, 'I'll be here every 30 days until I become a registered voter.' 'Cause that's what you would have to do: go every 30 days and see had you passed the literacy test. I went back then the tenth of January in 1963, and I had become registered. I passed the second one, because at the second time I went back, I had been studying sections of the Mississippi Constitution, so I would know if I got one that was simple enough that I might could pass it.

"I passed that second test, but it made us become like criminals. We would have to have our lights out before dark. It was cars passing that house all times of the night, driving real slow with guns, and pickups with white men in it, and they'd pass that house just as slow as they could pass it, three guns lined up in back. All of that. This was the kind of stuff. Pap couldn't get nothin' to do.

"So I started teachin' citizenship class, and I became the supervisor of the citizenship class in this county. So I moved around the county to do citizenship education, and later on I become a field secretary for SNCC—I guess being about one of the oldest people at that time that was a field secretary, 'cause they was real young."

Reprinted by permission of the Putnam Publishing Group from *My Soul Is Rested: Movement Days in the Deep South Remembered* by Howell Raines. Copyright © 1977 by Howell Raines.

READING REVIEW

1. Why did Hamer become involved in the civil rights movement?

2. What kinds of harassment were used against Mississippi blacks who tried to register to vote?

3. **Using an Interview as Historical Evidence** (a) If you were interviewing Hamer, what additional questions would you ask her? (b) Would you try to interview other people involved in the incidents she describes? If so, whom?

Introduction During the Great Depression, the family of Cesar Chavez lost its farm in Arizona and moved to California to find work as migrant laborers. Chavez's experiences with backbreaking labor, low pay, and substandard housing and education led him to organize farm workers into a union, the United Farm Workers. Here he tells how the movement started in Delano, California.

Vocabulary Before you read the selection, find the meaning of these words in a dictionary: continuous, respectability.

In community organizing you need a continuous program that meets the needs of the people in the organization. I have seen many groups attempt community organization and many have failed. The biggest reason for this is that there is a big emphasis on meetings and discussion and writing up programs and not on working with the people. Many organizers get lost in the shuffle of going to meetings, and somehow those who are being organized are lost. Too often we see as a remedy to this people suggesting that you should have a survey or a study made.

Anyone who has done any community organizing would agree with me that you can't have a program until you have the people organized. I don't mean you have to wait until you're fully organized, but how can you write a program without the participation of those you are trying to organize?

Another problem is respectability. If a minority group does "nice" things, like taking a petition to the mayor or having tea parties with the PTA, it's going to become respectable. And once you become a respectable group, you're not going to fight anymore. I've had a lot of experience in that. So if your group is going to city hall or the police department and fight with the police chief, and someone on your executive board is friends with him, you're going to think twice before attacking him.

If an organizer comes looking for appreciation he might as well stay home.

He's not going to get any, especially out of a group that's never been organized or had any power before.

A lot of people have asked me why Delano, and the answer is simple. I had no money. My wife's family lived there, and I have a brother. And I thought if things go very bad we can always go and have a meal there. Any place in the valley would have made no difference.

I had some ideas on what should be done. No great plans; just that it would take an awful lot of work and also that it was a gamble. If I can't organize them to a point where they can carry on their own group then I'm finished, I can't do it, I'd move on and do something else.

I went around for about 11 months, and I went to about 87 communities and labor camps, and in each place I'd find a few people who were committed to doing something. Something had happened in their lives and they were ready for it. So we went around to the town, played the percentages, and came off with a group. We had a convention here in Fresno, the first membership meeting, to set up a union—about 230 people from as many as 65 places. We knew the hardest thing would be to put across a program that would make them want to pay the $3.50 monthly dues, because we were dependent on that. I felt that organizing couldn't be done on outside money.

We had signed up about 1,100 people. The first month 211 paid. At the end of three months we had 10 people paying. Talk about being scared! But we went back and kept at it. By this time Dolores Huerta was helping me up in the northern part of the valley, and I was getting help from Gilbert Pedilla, both of whom are vice-presidents now. Gradually the membership was increasing. At the end of six months we were up to about 200 members. Instead of going all over the valley, as I did at first, I started staying in one place long enough for them to get in touch with me if they wanted to. We put a lot of emphasis on the people getting members.

Adapted from Cesar Chavez, "Why Delano?" in *Aztlan: An Anthology of Mexican American Literature*, ed. Luis Valdez and Stan Steiner (New York: Alfred A. Knopf, Inc., 1972). Copyright © 1972 by Alfred A. Knopf, Inc.

READING REVIEW

1. According to Chavez, why do community organizations often fail?

2. Why, in his view, is "respectability" a problem when trying to organize community action?

3. **Summarizing** What were the main steps Chavez took when he started to organize the farm workers?

★ 19-6 Trial After a "Fish-In" ★

Introduction Many Indian protests of the 1960s involved what were seen as threats to ancient fishing rights. In western Washington, a group of Tulalip and Puyallup Indians held a "fish-in"—modeled after the sit-ins of the black civil rights movement. They chose their usual site, where the state had forbidden them to fish. They were arrested and later tried. In this selection one of the participants, Laura McCloud, tells what happened at the trial.

Vocabulary Before you read the selection, find the meaning of these words in a dictionary: obstructing, depleted, summations.

On October 13, 1965, we held a "fish-in" on the Nisqually River to try and bring a focus on our fishing fight with the State of Washington. The "fish-in" started at 4:00 P.M. and was over at about 4:30 P.M. It ended with six Indians in jail and dazed Indian kids wondering what happened.

My parents Don and Janet McCloud, Al and Maiselle Bridges, Suzan Satiacum, and Don George, Jr., were arrested that day. They were released after posting bail a few hours later. The charges against these six Indians was "obstructing the duty of a police officer." Now all we could do was wait till the trials started. There was a seventh Indian who was later arrested for the same charge, Nugent Kautz. And he had not been at Frank's Landing on that day.

The trial was to begin on January 15, 1969, at 9:30 A.M. We went into the courthouse that Wednesday certain that we would not receive justice as was proven to us in other trials. As we walked into the hallways there were many game wardens standing there, some dressed in their uniforms and some in plain clothes, but we recognized all of them.

The first witness for the State was a field marshal for the game department—Zimmerman. He stated that he was directing the game wardens at the landing on October 13. He was in charge of the reinforcements from all over the state that came down on us like a sea of green. At the time of the fish-in I thought that there were about a hundred game wardens.

The next state witness was the public relations man for the game department. He had 16-millimeter motion pictures to show. He had been posing as a newsman on the day of the fish-in. Our attorney objected to the pictures because they could

In the 1960s Native Americans, like other minority groups, demanded equality. Vernon Bellecourt, shown here, was a leader of AIM, the American Indian Movement.

have been cut and fixed to the state's advantage or taken for the state's advantage. But the state got their way and the motion pictures were shown. And to this moment I cannot understand why they wanted these pictures shown because they sure looked better for our side than for theirs.

The parade of state witnesses were all either game wardens or fisheries patrolmen. All these men swore oaths to their God to tell the truth. Every one of them lied under oath. They were all asked if any of them carried weapons or if they had seen any wardens carrying weapons. After these game wardens went on the stand the prosecuting attorney said they had one more witness but he could not be there until the next day. So the judge said the trial would be adjourned until 9:30 the next morning.

The trial started late again the next morning. The state started off with their last witness, State Fisheries Biologist Lasseter. He talked about how we Indians are the ones who depleted the fish in the Puyallup River and if we weren't controlled we would do the same to the Nisqually River. The Puyallup River is filled with pollution more than it is with water. And why would we want to wipe out our livelihood? Our attorney made Lasseter state that it could have been the pollution, not the Indians, who depleted the fish in the Puyallup River.

Now, it was our turn! The first witness for our defense was Bob Johnson. At the time of the fish-in he was the editor of the *Auburn Citizen* newspaper. He told of the tactics the game wardens used on us. Mr. Johnson also had evidence with him, pictures of the game wardens, showing billy clubs and seven-celled flashlights. The prosecuting attorney got real shook up about these. It seemed like he was saying "I object" every few minutes.

The next witness was a Mrs. Flanigan, a psychologist who had been with Bob Johnson, to be an impartial witness. She said she thought that this fish-in would be boring because of the other one she had attended at Brando's Landing at the Puyallup River. But after this incident she became a believer and it had led her to help start an organization to help the Indian people.

The next defense witness was Janet McCloud, Tulalip Indian. She told the facts about why the Indians had had the fish-in demonstration on that day and what the mood was the Indians had before the fish-in. This was important because the state thought we were after blood that day. And we were not expecting any violence because all my brothers and sisters were there and the youngest was 4 at that time. And if we had expected any violence none of the children would have been there. She told how she felt when she realized that the game wardens were going to ram our boats and how she felt when she realized these men meant business with their seven-celled flashlights, billy clubs, and brass knuckles. My two little brothers were in that boat when it was rammed. The youngest was 7 and could not swim.

The next witness was Don McCloud, Puyallup Indian. He was one of the Indian men in the boat that day. He told how the boat was rammed. (Oh, incidentally, the game wardens said that they did not ram the boat.) He also said how he had seen a game warden with a steel pipe.

The next witness was Nugent Kautz, a Puyallup Indian. He told how he had not been present at the fish-in but was in school at Tacoma.

With all this testimony and evidence, it was plain to see that the game wardens had lied. We only hoped that the jury would believe our side of the fish-in story.

After the two lawyers gave their summations the jury went into session. This was at ten o'clock at night. They were out until midnight. The foreman came in first and said, "The rest are afraid to come in." I thought, here comes another guilty. When the foreman handed the judge the decision the room became very silent. Then the judge read, "The jury finds the defendant Nugent Kautz not guilty." He read the rest of the names with the same verdict. I didn't believe it. I turned to my cousin and said, "Did I hear right?" She nodded her head, yes. Everyone was happy, except for the state. The game wardens were very hostile after this.

© 1971 American Heritage Publishing Co., Inc. Reprinted by permission from *Red Power: The American Indians' Fight for Freedom* by Alvin M. Josephy, Jr. (Adapted from "Is the Trend Changing?" by Laura McCloud.)

READING REVIEW

1. According to McCloud's account, what happened at the fish-in?
2. (a) What was the verdict of the jury? (b) Did the author agree with the verdict?
3. **Analyzing a Primary Source** (a) In what ways does the writer indicate her feelings about the fish-in and the trial? (b) Do you think the defendants received a fair trial? Why or why not?

★ 19-7   A New Kind of Woman   ★

Introduction In 1966 journalist Caroline Bird was asked by a magazine to write an article about the hurdles American women faced. Bird conducted about 100 interviews as she researched the topic. When the magazine turned her article down because it was "shrill," she expanded it into a book, *Born Female*, published in 1968. Four years after her original research, Bird did a follow-up study. This became the last chapter of the book's second edition. This selection is from that chapter, called "A New Kind of Woman."

Vocabulary Before you read the selection, find the meaning of these words in a dictionary: coerced, venerable, assertive, innovation, autonomous.

The successful women I interviewed in 1966 were still spending a lot of energy proving that their husbands and children were not neglected, protesting their "femininity" by tottering around in tight shoes or inappropriately frilly clothes, and proclaiming that they liked men better than women. They could say that they envied this or that privilege of men, if they smiled or shrugged when they said it. But they could not say that they wished they were male, that they preferred to be single or childless, or that they liked the company of women better than that of men.

In 1970, women all over the country were saying all of these things. In four short years a surprising number of institutions stopped practices that coerced women into family roles. Colleges abandoned all responsibility for the private lives of women students. Some newspapers stopped classifying job ads by sex.

Women were admitted to scores of clubs, restaurants, colleges, and jobs formerly closed to them. And every Ivy League college had women students on some basis or other. Congress removed the legal barrier to women generals and admirals. The venerable Protestant Episcopal Church—always slower to change its constitution than its social policies—had abolished its women's division and was considering the elevation of women to the priesthood.

Women were gaining at work. Favorable court decisions were striking down the state labor laws that had "protected" factory women from the hours and duties that led to promotion and competition with union men. The proportion of women in graduate schools began to rise, and the gap between the starting salaries of men and women college graduates began to narrow.

Women were more assertive of their rights. They were filing charges of discrimination under Title VII [of the 1964 Civil Rights Act]. Everybody in the women's rights movement moved to new, more radical, ground.

But the most startling innovation since 1966 was the appearance of a new kind of woman, more alien to American tradition than the flapper of the 1920s, the man-suited, career spinster of the 1930s, or the Rosie who riveted the bombers in World War II. Virtually nonexistent in 1966, the new, liberated woman could be found on every college campus and in every sizable American city in 1970.

The American woman she most resembles is the politically alert, fiercely autonomous, and sometimes man-hating suffragette who had won the vote for

Topic 19

women at the end of World War I by militant hunger strikes and street demonstrations. But the new liberated woman of 1970 is not an old battleax. Well-educated, privileged, she is often attractive and almost always young—in 1970, seldom over 25. She is, in addition, idealistic, intense but soft-spoken, and she is furious.

Men can't believe her even when they see her. In their book she's an impossibility: a beautiful or potentially beautiful woman who is deliberately throwing away the advantages of her sex.

She is liberating herself not so much from sex, but from what goes with being a girl—all that sugar and spice and everything nice.

Liberated women are rebelling most angrily of all against the privileges of their sex. They don't like to have men open doors, pay bills, or change their tires, and many of them are "hardening" their muscles and learning karate to defend themselves against muggers or unwelcome males. "Hit her! She's your equal," one liberated woman shouted to a man under attack by another liberated woman during a demonstration.

The new women are not out to broaden their horizons to include man's world (the new Establishment position). They scorn requesting, politely or otherwise, that men please move over and give them a piece of the action (the middle-of-the-road New Feminism of the National Organization for Women). They want what every feminist of history with a grain of political sense has always denied wanting. "If we draft women, who will do the housework?" a World War I congressman asked, and none of the fire-breathing suffragettes dared to say, "Why not you, sir?"

Adapted from Caroline Bird, *Born Female: The High Cost of Keeping Women Down.* Reprinted by permission of Russell I. Volkening., Inc., as agents for the author. Copyright © 1968, 1970 David McKay Company, Inc.

READING REVIEW

1. What were some of the changes that affected women between 1966 and 1970?

2. (a) How does Bird describe the "new kind of woman" that emerged during this period? (b) In Bird's view, what does this new woman want?

3. **Comparing Points of View** (a) Compare Bird's view of the new woman of 1970 with the view of women in the 1950s in Reading 18-4. (b) Do you agree with either view? Why or why not?

★ 19-8 The Death of a Village ★

Introduction The United States Army found that fighting in Vietnam presented a host of problems for which it was ill prepared. American forces learned that in a guerrilla war it was often difficult to recognize the enemy. And it was almost impossible to use conventional military tactics against them. One new method that was developed was the "new-life hamlet," here described by an infantry medic who spent 17 months in Vietnam.

Vocabulary Before you read the selection, find the meaning of this word in a dictionary: reprisal.

There was a village called Ben Suc which was in the Iron Triangle area, on the Saigon River north of where we were, and essentially it was considered a communist hamlet. We had pulled Medcaps [medical aid missions] there probably a dozen times. It was one of those places we went back to a number of times. I learned to speak a little Vietnamese and I got to where I felt I knew some of the people.

Ben Suc was a very nice old village in a beautiful setting by the river. The graveyard was interesting because the tombstones were really old and in different shapes and sizes. They would have Buddhist or Taoist symbolism and some Christian symbols, too, for people who were Catholic. The whole place had a sense of antiquity and yet was very much here-and-now.

We started out one morning on these 40-foot-long miniature LST boats. We went up the river in a convoy of about 16 and landed at Ben Suc. The infantry was dropped in ahead of us and they met some fairly light contact.

We brought in Chinooks, Hueys, Skytrains [helicopters]. Trucks were brought in, Rome plows, bulldozers, and ultimately what happened was we took all the villagers out and relocated them into what was called a new-life hamlet, which for all practical purposes was a concentration camp. We were told that the purpose of these was to keep the Viet Cong out, to prevent reprisals against these good Saigon allies, when in fact these people were the communists and the camps were to keep them under control.

They were just flown out, so I didn't know where they ended up. We had been to that village a dozen times before. Nobody had ever shot at us, nobody even bothered us. We would come in, do our medical stuff and leave. People were happy to see us. We brought medicine. Medicine was very hard to get hold of out there. A tooth abscess could actually cause death in that environment because there's nothing to stop infection.

We would usually have a couple of people assigned for security. We're talking of anywhere from 15 to 50 people who were going to put on a real show—it depended on how many doctors we were taking. Essentially we would organize the villagers and run them through an assembly-line procedure—there were so many people who needed treatment and such inadequate time to do it in the way it would normally be done. . . . Given the medical need, it was conducted pretty professionally.

But we burned the village down. Any kind of holes that were found in the ground were blown up. There were a couple of weapons found, nothing significant. A fair amount of rice was destroyed, and the graveyards were bulldozed. The whole thing was turned into a big parking lot.

What I remember most about the village was this one old woman. We had taken care of her once when she was in great pain. She came back and brought other members of her family, and the third time we were up there she invited me over to their place to eat lunch. So when we'd go up there I'd always have

United States involvement in Vietnam developed gradually. Eventually over half a million American troops were sent there.

lunch with these people. And now soldiers were taking her and her family and a couple of pigs and their chickens—they didn't have that much—and loading them on a Chinook. She ran up and put her arms around me and wanted me to do something about it. There wasn't anything I could do. And that's when I started having second thoughts about the war. I still can see her face clear as day. I have no idea how her story ended. She reminded me a lot of my mother, always watching out for the kids, scolding, but very loving about it.

Adapted from *Everything We Had: An Oral History of the Vietnam War by Thirty-three American Soldiers Who Fought It*, ed. Al Santoli (New York: Random House, Inc., 1981). Copyright © 1981 by Albert Santoli and Vietnam Veterans of America. Reprinted by permission of Random House, Inc.

READING REVIEW

1. Why was Ben Suc destroyed?
2. (a) According to the medic, what was a new-life hamlet supposed to be? (b) What did he say it was in reality?
3. **Analyzing a Primary Source** From what the medic says, do you think he favored or opposed United States involvement in the Vietnam War? Explain.

Topic 19

20 Challenges at Home and Abroad (1969–1976)

★ 20-1 Nixon Visits China ★

Introduction President Nixon's 1972 visit to China was one of the highlights of his long career in politics. In this selection from his memoirs Nixon describes his first meeting with Chou En-lai, the prime minister, and Mao Tse-tung, chairman of the Chinese Communist Party.

Vocabulary Before you read the selection, find the meaning of these words in a dictionary: immaculately, self-deprecation, clique, substantive, animated, nuance, discreetly.

Our plane landed smoothly, and a few minutes later we came to a stop in front of the terminal. The door was opened, and Pat and I stepped out.

President Richard Nixon's visit to China in 1972 symbolized a new friendship between the United States and China. Diplomatic relations and scientific and cultural exchanges followed.

Chou En-lai stood at the foot of the ramp, hatless in the cold. Even a heavy overcoat did not hide the thinness of his frail body. When we were about halfway down the steps, he began to clap. I paused for a moment and then returned the gesture, according to the Chinese custom.

I knew that Chou had been deeply insulted by Foster Dulles's refusal to shake hands with him at the Geneva Conference in 1954. When I reached the bottom step, therefore, I made a point of extending my hand as I walked toward him. When our hands met, one era ended and another began.

After being introduced to all the Chinese officials, I stood on Chou's left while the band played the anthems. "The Star-Spangled Banner" had never sounded so stirring to me as on that windswept runway in the heart of communist China.

The honor guard was one of the finest I have ever seen. They were big men, strong-looking, and immaculately turned out. As I walked down the long line, each man turned his head slowly as I passed, creating an almost hypnotic sense of movement in the massed ranks.

Chou and I rode into the city in a curtained car. As we left the airport, he said, "Your handshake came over the vastest ocean in the world—25 years of no communication." When we came into Tienamen Square at the center of Peking, he pointed out some of the buildings; I noticed that the streets were empty.

Madame Chou was waiting for us when we arrived at the two large government guesthouses where our official party was to stay. We had tea in the sitting room, and then Chou said that he was sure everyone would like to rest before the state banquet.

About an hour later Kissinger burst in with the news that Chairman Mao wanted to meet me. I waited about five minutes while Henry went downstairs, and then we drove to the residence.

Several Chinese photographers had rushed in ahead of us in order to record our first meeting. We all sat in overstuffed armchairs set in a semicircle at the end of the large room. While the photographers continued to bustle around, we exchanged bantering small talk. Kissinger remarked that he had assigned Mao's writings to his classes at Harvard. Indulging in characteristic self-deprecation, Mao said, "These writings of mine aren't anything. There is nothing instructive in what I wrote." I said, "The chairman's writings moved a nation and have changed the world." Mao, however, replied, "I haven't been able to change it. I've only been able to change a few places in the vicinity of Peking."

Although Mao spoke with some difficulty, it was clear that his mind was moving like lightning. "Our common old friend Generalissimo Chiang Kai-shek doesn't approve of this," he said, with a sweeping gesture that might have meant our meeting or that might have taken in all China. "He calls us communist bandits. He recently made a speech. Have you seen it?"

"Chiang Kai-shek calls the chairman a bandit," I replied. "What does the chairman call Chiang Kai-shek?"

Mao chuckled when my question was translated, but it was Chou who answered. "Generally speaking, we call them 'Chiang Kai-shek's clique,'" he said. "In the newspapers sometimes we call him a bandit; he calls us bandits in turn. Anyway, we abuse each other."

Referring to our presidential election, Mao said that in honesty he had to tell me that if the Democrats won the Chinese would deal with them.

"We understand," I said. "We will hope that we don't give you that problem."

"I voted for you during your last election," Mao said with a broad smile.

"When the chairman says he voted for me," I replied, "he voted for the lesser of two evils."

"I like rightists," Mao responded, obviously enjoying himself. "People say that you are rightists—that the Republican Party is on the right."

"Mr. Chairman," I said, "I am aware of the fact that over a period of years my position with regard to the People's Republic was one that the chairman and the prime minister totally disagreed with. What brings us together is a recognition of a new situation in the world and a recognition on our part that what is important is not a nation's internal political philosophy. What is important is its policy toward the rest of the world and toward us."

Although the meeting with Mao dealt mainly with what he called the "philosophy" of our new and potential relationship, I raised in general terms the major substantive questions we would be discussing.

Mao was animated and following every nuance of the conversation, but I could see that he was also becoming very tired. Chou had been discreetly glancing at his watch with increasing frequency, so I decided that I should try to bring the session to a close.

"I would like to say, as we finish, Mr. Chairman, that we know you and the prime minister have taken great risks in inviting us here. For us also it was a difficult decision. But having read some of your statements, I know that you are one who sees when an opportunity comes and then knows that you must seize the hour and seize the day."

Mao's face beamed when the translator came to these words from his own poem.

Adapted from Richard Nixon, *RN: The Memoirs of Richard Nixon* (New York: Grosset & Dunlap, Inc., 1978). Copyright © 1978 by Richard Nixon.

READING REVIEW

1. (a) How did Nixon and Chou greet each other? (b) Why were these initial moments important?

2. How would you describe the atmosphere at the meeting?

3. **Making Inferences** On the basis of this selection, what do you think were the main points Nixon wanted to communicate to the Chinese at this first meeting?

Introduction A persistent problem throughout the 1970s was high inflation. In this selection, journalist Theodore White traces its beginnings.

Vocabulary Before you read the selection, find the meaning of these words in a dictionary: shortfall, morbid, deficit, entourage, indexing, ratchets, fluctuate, obsession, perquisites.

Historic disasters usually come labeled with day and year—sometimes even with the hour. Not so with the Great Inflation. October 29, 1929, Black Tuesday, had been the day the stock market crashed and the depression began. At 7:56 on the morning of Sunday, December 7, 1941, the Japanese bombed Pearl Harbor and America was at war. At 12:40 P.M., Friday, November 22, 1963, John F. Kennedy was shot—and a dream was lost. Before dawn on Wednesday, January 31, 1968, a Viet Cong suicide squad burst into the American Embassy in Saigon: the Tet offensive had begun and the Vietnam War was lost.

But inflation has no date of beginning. Inflation is the cancer of modern civilization, the leukemia of planning and hope. As with all cancers, no one can say when it begins or how fast it may spread. It is a disease of money, and when money goes, order goes with it. Inflation comes when a government has made too many promises it cannot keep and papers over the shortfall with currency which, ultimately, becomes confetti—and faith is lost.

In the Great Inflation of the United States, we have all lived through an era when the burdens accepted by government at home and abroad have bewildered American understanding. But this bewilderment became apparent only in the decade between 1971 and 1980.

At this point, as we try to trace the Great Inflation, we must invite the reader to chew on the juiceless gristle and bones of events, and in particular, on the events of a year of no great memories, 1971. It was then that the President of the United States, Richard Nixon, realized that the architecture of the world he had inherited no longer sheltered America from the demands of the world we had made.

Ever since the 1890s, America had shipped out to the world more than it imported. And the world had struggled with the "dollar gap." In April of 1971, however, the Department of Commerce posted a morbid figure: a monthly deficit in the trade balance. In May came another deficit, establishing the first two-month deficit in 22 years. In June, yet another. In July, a fourth deficit. And thus came the first great run on the dollar, in the summer of 1971. If the everlasting American trade surplus was vanishing, it was better to convert American dollars, whether paper or on credit ledgers, to the gold they promised, rather than to hold the dollar as a guarantee.

By midsummer of 1971, the American hoard of pure gold, those golden bars at Fort Knox, Kentucky, had shrunk to only $10.5 billion (from a postwar high of $25 billion). Outstanding against this hoard were $100 billion in foreign banks and accounts, plus billions more in American promises. If those dollars were only paper promises, then the time to grab at the gold they promised was now.

On Fridy, August 13, Nixon summoned his entourage of house economists to one of the first of those countless conferences which are all called Camp David summits. On Sunday, he appeared before the nation to announce a startling new economic policy. Of this Nixon new economic program, two hard items must be remembered.

First, Nixon declared that America was going off the gold standard. The United States would no longer redeem dollars in gold. Second, Richard Nixon seized the opportunity to impose on the United States a system of wage–price controls. He had very early spotted the pressure and direction of prices in American life—up, and up, and up—and now, in 1971, inflation was speeding at the then unbelievable rate of 6 percent a year. It must be stopped. Nixon decided he must act. He announced that while America would no longer enforce the discipline of gold on trade, he would impose discipline on American prices and wages. There would be a three-month freeze on all wages and prices, to be followed (as it turned out) by another year of price controls until the system of control collapsed.

We were, by the decisions of 1971, all at once adrift in a trade world that had no standards of values except for squeezing the last profit out of the marketplace. And at home, we were locked by a government that felt it could regulate values, from the wages of cannery workers to the price of canned pineapple, from the wages of garment workers to the price of a man's suit. Other nations would soon learn that the American marketplace set a ceiling on prices which they could approach (and undercut) without penalty. And over all this reigned the sense and sentiment of American political thinking. Tradition required us to go on helping the undernourished of the world, tradition required us to continue opening our markets to fair trade.

At least three more major markers on the way to the inflationary crisis of 1980 should be added to the date of 1971.

The first was the war in Vietnam. Most thoughtful economic historians—with whom I generally agree—feel that it was war that let slip the thongs of money discipline at home.

The second marker came in 1972, with the indexing of Social Security payments to the cost of living.

The third—and by far the most important—marker was set by the outside world as it tightened a new set of ratchets. That concerned the price of oil, which means the price of energy, and energy is what makes the wheels go round.

So important is this third marker that it deserves a capsule of history all its own. America, under John D. Rockefeller, had introduced the world to this energy that comes from fluid hydrocarbons. Then, without realizing it, American built an independent system of life based on the abundance of cheap energy. This sense of independence eroded only slowly, and then very subtly. It was in 1948 that America first imported more oil than it shipped out. But America then still produced enough oil to fuel the American automobiles that took workers to their jobs, families to the suburbs, and mothers to the shopping malls.

By the early 1970s, that innocent assumption of enduring American abundance had been totally undermined. America, almost as much as Europe and Japan, was dependent on oil not only from Arabia, but from Algeria, Libya, Africa, Indonesia.

This was a condition that could not be concealed from the rulers of the oil-producing states of the Middle East, so many of whose administrators had been trained in American schools of business or geology. They had learned about America's vulnerability. Thus, in 1973, they closed the noose. Oil was selling on the world market at $3.41 a barrel at the beginning of 1973. It would go to $11.11 in 1974, to $14.54 in 1978, to $28.00 in the spring of 1980, and then fluctuate between $32.00 and $41.00 as 1980 came to its end.

When it was that the Great Inflation migrated from the back pages of the business news sections to the front pages and evening television shows no one can say with certainty. But shortly after the oil crisis of 1973-1974, the Great Inflation had become the obsession of common talk. The costs of a new pair of shoes, of the children's orthodontist, of eating out in a restaurant, of lawyers' fees, of pensions and perquisites, were gloomily accepted as dinner table conversation.

Abridged pages 137–138, 141–144, 150–153 from *America in Search of Itself: The Making of a President 1956–1980*, by Theodore H. White. Copyright © 1982 by Theodore H. White. Reprinted by permission of Harper & Row, Publishers, Inc.

READING REVIEW

1. With what other "historic disasters" of the 1900s does White compare "the Great Inflation"?

2. Why is inflation so damaging to modern civilization?

3. **Understanding Economic Ideas** (a) What two steps to control inflation did Nixon take in 1971? (b) Why did these decisions cause problems? (c) What three additional "markers" led the way to inflation?

Introduction After the Watergate scandal, humorist Art Buchwald published his newspaper columns on the subject in the book "*I Am Not a Crook*." (This was a statement Nixon made late in 1973.) Buchwald dedicated his book to the President and thanked him for providing him with "two glorious years of material."

Vocabulary Before you read the selection, look up these words in a dictionary: motley, courtiers, docile.

Once upon a time there was a king who ruled over a vast land from one ocean to another. Such was his power and wealth that he had a palace in the west, a palace in the east, a palace in the south, and on weekend he had one in the mountains.

The king surrounded himself with a motley group of courtiers who were not above stealing, lying, and cheating to keep him on the throne. Many of the king's rich subjects were forced to pay tribute to the palace in exchange for special favors and goodwill.

Although the king knew what his courtiers were doing, he shut his eyes to their behavior because being king was the most important thing in his life.

But, alas, one day the courtiers tried to take over a water gate, and this was too much, even for the docile people who inhabited the land.

The king, realizing his subjects were angry, issued a proclamation saying he was appalled by the corruption in his palace, and he would find the guilty people and banish them from his court forever.

He called in the king's prosecutor, an honest and devoted servant, and said, "I want to leave no stone unturned to find the people who have brought disgrace and shame on my kingdom."

The king's prosecutor asked, "Sire, does that mean I may investigate everyone in the palace?"

"Of course. What kind of king do you think I am that would prevent my own prosecutor from rooting out evil in the land?"

The prosecutor took the king at his word and started talking to the counselors in the palace. Each one had a different story to tell, and it was impossible for the prosecutor to know who was telling the truth.

He went back to the king and said, "Sire, we have heard many versions of the same story, but we have no proof as to which one is correct."

The king said angrily, "No proof? What kind of king's prosecutor are you if you cannot product proof?"

"We know who has the proof."

Senator Sam Ervin of North Carolina, center, conducted Senate hearings about the Watergate scandal. At Ervin's left is Senator Howard Baker.

"Then drag him here and pull his toenails out."

"This is difficult, sire," the prosecutor said, staring at the king's toenails. "If we could just have your scrolls recording your conversations with your counselors . . ."

"Have you gone mad?" the king shouted. "I am the king. No one sees my scrolls. They shall go with me to my grave."

"Then," the prosecutor said, "it is impossible for me to find the guilty parties, sire."

"You fool," the king said. "My subjects are angered. If we allow corruption in the palace to go unpunished, they will try to throw me off my throne."

"But what can I do if you refuse to let me see the scrolls?"

"Let me think a minute," the king said. "If I do not produce the scrolls, the populace will believe I am trying to hide my guilt. But, on the other hand, if I produce the scrolls, they will know I'm guilty. Did any king ever face such a painful dilemma?"

"What is your decision, sire?"

"Alas, I have no choice," the king said. "Guards, take this man to the dungeon and chop off his head."

"But, sire," the poor prosecutor cried, "why me?"

"We can always get another king's prosecutor," was the reply, "but where can the people get another king?"

Reprinted by permission of the Putnam Publishing Group from *I Am Not a Crook* by Art Buchwald. Copyright © 1973, 1974 by Art Buchwald.

READING REVIEW

1. Who are the king and his "motley group of courtiers"?
2. Who is the "king's prosecutor" and why does he run into trouble?
3. **Using Fiction as Historical Evidence** (a) What can you learn about the public's attitude toward Watergate from a humorous newspaper column such as this one? Explain. (b) Do you think this selection is funny? Why or why not?

★ 20-4 Watergate: The Judge's Viewpoint ★

Introduction John Sirica had been on the point of retirement when the Watergate cases came before his court. As a longtime Republican, he felt that charges of partisanship would be lessened if he himself presided at the trials. In this selection he sums up his reactions to the trials.

Vocabulary Before you read the selection, find the meaning of these words in a dictionary: trauma, scrutiny, indictments, thwart, perpetrators, invulnerable, arrogance, nurtured.

And now, although I still sometimes marvel that we came through that awful mess with our government intact, Watergate is finally over. My initial suspicions that no one but top party leaders could have authorized the burglary were proved true by President Nixon's own tapes. And although our nation went through a trauma which could easily have led to a severe constitutional crisis, I believe the United States is stronger for having successfully weathered that storm.

Had there been no Watergate, wealthy contributors might still be pumping undisclosed millions into political campaigns in hopes of buying favor with elected officials. Now we have an independent Federal Election Commission and a stronger campaign law, which demands that all candidates for national offices disclose their sources of funding in writing.

Had there been no Watergate, it is unlikely that we would have seen the tremendous increase in the public scrutiny of federal officials' conduct, a scrutiny which has led to investigations and indictments such as those involving the General Services Administration.

And had there been no Watergate, Congress would probably not even be discussing public financing of federal election campaigns. Although there is a great number of unanswered questions about this issue, I believe some type of legislation to reduce politicians' reliance on contributions from special interests would in the long run benefit the entire nation.

Most important, Watergate, unlike any previous scandal in our political history, was both a crisis and a reaffirmation of our constitutional form of government. Unlike past episodes of dishonesty in Washington, it was a product not of greed in the usual sense, but of greed for power.

The country should take great pride that this naked attempt to thwart the Constitution of the United States—to substitute the will of a few powerful men for the rule of law which we have struggled so long and so hard to win and to protect—was in the end defeated, with the perpetrators driven from office and brought to justice. Yet I can never forget Senator Ervin's observation that "they almost got away with it." I think it's worth asking, Why didn't they get away with it?

Everyone has a tendency to find heroes, to claim that individual acts of decency or bravery or devotion bring about great historical events. But I think the lesson of Watergate is quite the opposite. I firmly believe it was our system of government and our system of law that ended that crisis and saved the very constitutional form of government that gave us that system and those laws.

Naturally, I have a special feeling about the role of the courts in the whole crisis. I feel that without the courts, without their ability to get to the facts, to compel testimony and the production of evidence, the Watergate case might never have been cracked. The press played a critical role, of course, but the press cannot subpoena witnesses, it cannot demand the truth under any penalty other than temporary embarrassment; it can only help force further public attention and investigation.

I have always felt that no matter how bitter the experience one endures, and surely Watergate was a bitter experience, there are some beneficial lessons to be learned. Watergate taught us that our system is not invulnerable to the arrogance of power, to misdeeds by power-hungry individuals, and that we must always be on guard against selecting such people as our leaders. It taught us that our system of law is the most valuable asset in this land and that it must be nurtured, protected, and respected. The misuse of campaign funds was exposed during the Watergate investigations, and we have moved, though not perfectly to be sure, to make our presidential elections more fair by preventing single, large contributors from having too great an influence on the outcome of those elections. Likewise, we have strengthened the laws that force public officials (including judges) to disclose their financial assets and income, so that the public can be reassured that those officials have not been bought and paid for by some special interest.

Most important, I hope we have learned the value of citizens who do their duty, who do the work set out for them by our laws and our system of government. Like the scores of common citizens who served unselfishly on the grand juries and trial juries in the Watergate cases. Or the lawyers who prosecuted and defended in those cases to the very best of their ability. Or members of Congress who put politics aside to do their unpleasant jobs. Or the news reporters who wouldn't drop a story when they were under pressure to do so. The so-called heroes of Watergate were no more than people doing what was right, doing their jobs whether they were scared or exhausted or being criticized or were all alone.

After my sudden heart attack in February 1976, I awoke from a long period of unconsciousness. One of my doctors, Stephen Nealon, was with me in the hospital as I began to realize how close to death I had come and in how much danger I remained. He told me later that I said to him, "If I go out, I'd like to think that I did something for my country."

I think I did do something for my country. I think I did my job as best I could. I think I did my duty as a citizen and as someone fortunate enough to hold a position of public responsibility in our system of government.

Adapted from *To Set the Record Straight: The Break-in, the Tapes, the Conspirators, the Pardon*, by John J. Sirica, by permission of W.W. Norton & Company, Inc. Copyright © 1979 by John J. Sirica.

1. What reforms in government resulted from the Watergate affair?

2. (a) In Judge Sirica's view, what was the most important factor in ending the crisis? (b) What "beneficial lessons" did Watergate teach?

3. Recognizing a Point of View (a) On the basis of this selection, how would you describe Sirica's attitude toward President Nixon? (b) How did he feel toward the press? (c) What was his attitude toward the American system of government?

★ 20-5 Ford vs. Carter From a Front-Row Seat ★

Introduction In 1976, reporter Elizabeth Drew kept a detailed journal of the major events of the presidential election campaign. Here she writes about the first television debate between President Gerald Ford and challenger Jimmy Carter. As one of the three panel members who questioned the candidates, she had a close-up view of the event.

Vocabulary Before you read the selection, find the meaning of these words in a dictionary: glib, repartee, rebuttal, advocated, exuberantly, magnitude, spontaneity.

September 23, Thursday, Philadelphia.

The first Presidential debate is to take place here tonight. I have had serious doubts about the idea of these debates—doubts that have been increased by the fact that they have received such a build-up. Moreover, they seem to be based on the concept—and this has increased the anticipation and the build-up—that the candidates for the presidency of the United States should meet as two gladiators in the arena. The object of the exercise would appear to be to score points off one another. It seems that the debates have been anticipated more for their possible entertainment value than for their possibilities for showing us the differences between the two candidates on some of the important questions facing our country. . . . The debates place a high value on being glib of tongue, effective on television. The qualities that they reward have little to do with

being President: memorizing a lot of data, being quick at repartee. They don't put any particular premium on wisdom, patience. Being quick on one's feet in the Oval Office can lead to trouble. There has been a lot of talk about who will "win" the debates. The idea that someone will "win" is what's wrong.

I have been asked to participate in the first debate as one of the panel of three questioners, and, despite misgivings about the whole enterprise, have decided to see what might be done with this opportunity to get some questions raised. . . .

As the debate opens, the first question, about jobs, is put to Carter, and as he answers, Ford watches him intently. This is probably as close to each other as they have ever been—at least, for this length of time. Carter says that we could get unemployment down to 4 or 4.5 percent by the end of his first four years in office, with a "controlled inflation rate." He lists a number of particulars about how he would get there—clearly intent on dispelling the idea that he is "fuzzy." Asked if he thinks wage and price controls might be necessary, he says, "We have a long way to go in getting people to work before we have the inflationary pressures"—which begs the question. . . . Ford, in his rebuttal, eager to strengthen the idea that Carter is "fuzzy," says, "I don't believe that Mr. Carter has been any more specific in this case than he has been on many other instances." It is clearly a line that Ford had planned to say no matter what Carter said. . . .

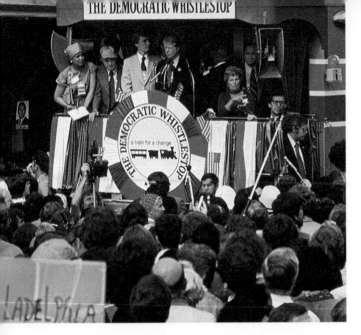

In 1976 the Democrats nominated former Georgia governor Jimmy Carter for President. Although comparatively unknown, Carter's effective campaigning brought his strong points home to the voters. Here he speaks from the back of a train.

Carter is asked how he would pay for all the programs that he has advocated or lent his support to (jobs, health insurance, child care, federal absorption of welfare costs, housing, aid to cities, a higher earnings limit on Social Security, federal aid to education) and, as he has pledged, balance the budget by the end of his first term. He does not really answer. He says that the Congressional Budget Committees estimate that if unemployment was reduced to 4 or 4.5 percent, there would be an extra $60 billion in federal revenues. But neither committee has made such an optimistic estimate. . . .

In Ford's rebuttal to Carter, he exuberantly suggests that if there is a $60-billion increase in revenues, "I think the American taxpayer ought to get a tax reduction of that magnitude." It is the politician's reflex: the sort of thing he might have said, without thought, on the floor of the House of Representatives in order to make a point, or on the stump at a time when it didn't matter so much what he said. . . . Both of them are talking about tax relief of the sort that cannot be wrung from tax reform—unless they are willing to advocate reductions in tax preferences of the sort that few politicians are willing to advocate. . . .

Carter seems uncertain tonight, not in command. . . . The President, it is clear, has been advised by his aides to look stern—as in his "No more Mr. Nice Guy" campaign photo—and it is the one expression he seems to have all evening. He is wearing a vest, which makes him look like a conservative banker. He is forceful in his way of speaking, but he doesn't say very much. Talking about jobs, he says we have to stimulate the economy and then he says we have to hold down spending. Carter, at last, injects a note of humanity when he talks about unemployment. But both of them seem overbriefed and overguarded, almost afraid of spontaneity. Even Ford's gestures—facing Carter and waving his arms—seem studied. Neither of them suggests that there are hard questions and real choices that have to be made. . . . Asked if he thinks there should be new statutes governing the intelligence agencies, Ford doesn't seem to get the point.

And then, as Carter is giving his rebuttal (he doesn't seem to get the point, either) word comes that, unbelievably, the audio has gone off, and the two candidates for the presidency stand there silently while we wait for it to go back on. Carter is one of the most impatient people I know of, and the President looks none too pleased. . . . Assured that the cameras are not on them, the two men glance at each other and then wipe their faces. Apart from that, they do not acknowledge each other's presence; they speak not a word to each other. Ford stares straight ahead, lips set; Carter, from time to time, manages a wan smile. I try to think of what other, more spontaneous politicians might have done in this situation. . . . This has to be the greatest electronic foul-up of all time. The President and the would-be President are like prisoners behind their lecterns.

Finally, at 11:17, 27 minutes after it went off, the sound comes back on. Carter, as if he were a wound-up doll, simply resumes where he left off, and says one sentence: "There has been too much government secrecy and not enough respect for the personal privacy of American citizens."

In his closing statement, Carter reverts to the sort of sermonette he gave on the trail during the primaries, and he now seems more natural than he has all night. What he says has nothing to do with the debate subjects, but so be it. Hand moving up and down, palm out, in the familiar gesture, he says, "For a long time, our American citizens have been excluded." He says, "I owe the special interests nothing." . . .

Ford says that "one of the major issues in this campaign is trust." Repeating a theme from his State of the Union Message, he says, "A President should never promise more than he can deliver and a President should always deliver everything that he has promised." . . . Then, identifying himself with the working people, and also using his wife, who is generally considered quite popular, he says, "Betty and I have worked very hard to give our children a brighter future." He closes, and both he and Carter gaze at the camera sincerely.

From *American Journal: The Events of 1976*, by Elizabeth Drew. Copyright © 1976, 1977 by Elizabeth Drew. Reprinted by permission of Random House, Inc.

READING REVIEW

1. (a) Why does Drew have "serious doubts" about presidential debates? (b) Why does she take part despite her doubts?

2. How does she characterize the two presidential candidates? Be specific in your answer.

3. **Supporting Generalizations** In the first paragraph, Drew criticizes the debate as an exercise for the candidates to "score points off one another." What examples does she give in the rest of this selection to support her generalization?

Topic

21 Beginning the Nation's Third Century
(1977–Present)

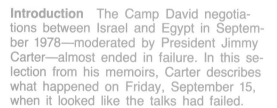

★ 21-1 Tense Days at Camp David ★

Introduction The Camp David negotiations between Israel and Egypt in September 1978—moderated by President Jimmy Carter—almost ended in failure. In this selection from his memoirs, Carter describes what happened on Friday, September 15, when it looked like the talks had failed.

Vocabulary Before you read the selection, find the meaning of these words in a dictionary: rupture, fervently, unilaterally, onus, adamant, repudiating.

I awoke to the realization that we could go no further. I called the American delegation to Aspen, and we discussed how to deal with our failure. I would spend the day getting proposals from Sadat and Begin, so that I could summarize the differences and prepare the final document on Saturday.

After Harold* and I had been at work for about 20 minutes, Vance burst into the room. His face was white, and he announced, "Sadat is leaving. He and his aides are already packed. He asked me to order him a helicopter!"

It was a terrible moment. Now, even my hopes for a harmonious departure were gone. I sat quietly and assessed the significance of this development—a rupture between Sadat and me, and its consequences for my country and for the Middle East power balance. I envisioned the ultimate alliance of most of the Arab nations to the Soviet Union, perhaps

---

*The participants mentioned by Carter include Harold Saunders, secretary of state for Near Eastern affairs; Secretary of State Cyrus Vance; Frederick Brown, in charge of State Department press relations; and Moshe Dayan, Israeli foreign minister.

joined by Egypt after a few months had passed. I told Vance that the best thing for us to do now, to salvage what we could, would be to refuse to sign any document with either country—just to terminate the talks and announce that we had all done our best and failed.

Then I asked Brown and Vance to leave me. When they were gone, I remained alone in the little study where most of the negotiations had taken place. I moved over to the window and looked out to the Catoctin Mountains and prayed fervently for a few minutes that somehow we could find peace.

Then, for some reason, I changed into more formal clothes before going to see Sadat. He was on his porch with five or six of his ministers, and Vance and Brown were there to tell them all good-bye.

I nodded to them, and walked into the cabin. Sadat followed me. I explained to him the extremely serious consequences of his unilaterally breaking off the negotiations: that his action would harm the relationship between Egypt and the United States, he would be violating his personal promise to me, and the onus for failure would be on him. I described the possible future progress of Egypt's friendships and alliances—from us to the moderate and then radical Arabs, thence to the Soviet Union. I told him it would damage one of my most precious possessions—his friendship and our mutual trust.

He was adamant, but I was dead serious, and he knew it. I had never been more serious in my life. I repeated some of the more telling arguments I had previously used at our meeting by the swimming pool. He would be publicly repudiating some of his own commitments, damaging his reputation as the world's foremost peacemaker, and admitting the fruitlessness of his celebrated visit to Jerusalem.

His worst enemies in the Arab world would be proved right in their claims that he had made a foolish mistake.

I told Sadat that he simply had to stick with me for another day or two—after which, if circumstances did not improve, all of us simultaneously would take the action he was now planning.

He explained the reason for his decision to leave: Dayan had told him the Israelis would not sign any agreements. This made Sadat furious. He had accused Dayan of wasting our time by coming to Camp David in the first place. His own advisers had pointed out the danger in his signing an agreement with the United States alone. Later, if direct discussions were ever resumed with the Israelis, they could say, "The Egyptians have already agreed to all these points. Now we will use what they have signed as the original basis for all future negotiations." It was a telling argument. I thought very rapidly and told him that we would have a complete understanding that if any nation rejected any part of the agreements, none of the proposals would stay in effect.

Sadat stood silently for a long time. Then he looked at me and said, "If you give me this statement, I will stick with you to the end." (He kept his promise, but it never proved necessary to give him any such statement.)

Adapted from Jimmy Carter, *Keeping Faith: Memoirs of a President* (Toronto: Bantam Books, Inc., 1982). Copyright © 1982 by Jimmy Carter.

READING REVIEW

1. What arguments did Carter use to try and persuade Sadat not to leave?
2. Why did Sadat stay?
3. **Relating Cause and Effect** Based on your reading in Chapter 21, what was the effect of Sadat's decision to stay?

★ 21-2   The Meaning of the Hostage Crisis ★

Introduction Four months after the American hostages returned from Iran, *The New York Times* printed a special report summarizing the crisis and analyzing its meaning for the United States. This selection is from the conclusion of that report.

In November 1979, Iranian militants took 54 Americans hostage in the United States embassy in Teheran. This photograph of one of the hostages with his captors shocked and angered Americans at home.

Vocabulary Before you read the selection, find the meaning of these words in a dictionary: impotence, jeopardized, hypothetical, latitude, extricate, punitive, conciliatory, abyss, callousness, embodiment, poignant, ineffectual.

More than anything else, Americans encountered in Iran a symbol of their impotence. A nation yearning to believe in itself again, after Vietnam and Watergate, instead became enmeshed in a struggle with an ancient religious culture whose record of misunderstanding and hostility with the West dates from ancient times.

The hostage crisis illuminated the extent to which the United States could prove itself unable to protect its vital strategic and economic interests, as well as its citizens. It will be remembered further as a lesson in the limitations of force, since an invasion or blockade might have thrown the United States into a confrontation with the Islamic world, strained relations with its allies, jeopardized the West's oil supply, invited Soviet intervention, and threatened the lives of the hostages themselves.

But the spectacle of American failure in Iran will long haunt Americans, especially because it was driven home by yet another blow to their self-assurance. For a society that believes almost religiously in technology, the breakdown of three helicopters in a desert dust storm was a bitter setback. Fifteen years ago, the American military failure in Vietnam had spoken of the futility of trying to stop a revolution by force. On the sands of Dasht-e-Kavir Desert, the failure spoke of courage undermined by poor maintenance and planning.

If President Carter had gotten the hostages out, he might well have won reelection. If, on the other hand, he had failed where he succeeded—in negotiating an end to the hostage crisis before leaving office—he would have left his successor with a set of dismal choices that would have changed the character of Ronald Reagan's presidency.

Historically, however, the Iran crisis is likely to have some less hypothetical effects. Just as the Vietnam War led to new restrictions on a President's ability to commit the United States overseas, the hostage crisis will likely give the President fresh latitude to respond to acts of terrorists. A President in the years ahead may find the nation once again held hostage but less willing to endure 444 days of mostly fruitless negotiations to extricate itself. Americans are likely to demand a policy that falls between the tough, punitive bombing pursued by President Nixon in Vietnam, and the milder, more conciliatory approach of President Carter.

Also, Iran provided Americans a look into the abyss of hatred for America abroad that is going to make it more difficult, especially on an emotional level, for the nation to do future business with the third world. The hostage crisis reawakened the United States to an old reality: that its good intentions are not enough; that the world is a complex place, even if its complexities are reduced each night to a grotesque television drama—a screeching collision of two cultures fated to misunderstand the righteous indignation and callousness of each other.

Having stared into the face of what it regarded as the embodiment of "evil," America is now probably more likely than ever to assert, free of guilt, the "virtue" of its own self-interest around the globe. The United States could therefore become more distrustful of the demands of the people whose cultures it does not readily understand.

It will be the task of historians to sort out the contradictions of our behavior during the crisis. They are likely to find it odd, for instance, that a nation willing to lose 57,000 lives in Vietnam later became so obsessed with saving the lives of a few score men and women that it restrained its response. Historians will also have to account for the fact that what might well have been an occasion for humiliation blossomed instead into a cause for celebration. The hostages returned home to a heroes' welcome made poignant by the simple but awesome heroism of people who did little more than survive with grace and dignity.

In the years ahead, it probably will become clear that America's communal obsession with the fate of the captives helped produce the nation's ineffectual response to their plight. Many experts already believe that a policy of ignoring or deemphasizing the sense of crisis might have caused the Iranians to lose interest in holding the Americans captive. In any case, the emotional reaction will tell historians much about what kind of nation we were as we headed into the 1980's.

Adapted from Steven R. Weisman, "For America, A Painful Reawakening," in *America in Captivity: Points of Decision.* Copyright © 1981 by the New York Times Company. Reprinted by permission.

READING REVIEW

1. In what ways did the hostage crisis deal a blow to American self-assurance?
2. To what "contradictions" in American behavior does the author refer?
3. **Making Predictions** Weisman predicts several possible outcomes of the hostage crisis. (a) What are they? (b) Have any come true?

★   21-3   American Traditions in Today's World   ★

Introduction President Reagan has often emphasized the importance of American political and religious traditions in today's world. In 1983, addressing the National Association of Evangelicals, he spoke of America's religious principles and described the Soviet Union as an "evil empire."

Vocabulary Before you read the selection, find the meaning of these words in a dictionary: secularism, superintending, permeates, invocation, phenomenology, theologians, enjoined, legacy, transcending, phenomenon, omnipotence, blithely, verifiable, bizarre.

This administration is motivated by a political philosophy that sees the greatness of America in you, her people, and in your families, churches, neighborhoods, communities—the institutions that foster and nourish values like concern for others and respect for the role of law under God.

Now I don't have to tell you that this puts us in opposition to, or at least out of step with, a prevailing attitude of many who have turned to a modern-day secularism, discarding the tried and time-tested values upon which our very civilization is based.

No matter how well intentioned, their value system is radically different from that of most Americans.

And, while they proclaim they are freeing us from superstitions of the past, they have taken upon themselves the job of superintending us by government rule and regulation. Sometimes their voices are louder than ours, but they are not yet a majority.

Freedom prospers when religion is vibrant and the rule of law under God acknowledged.

When our founding fathers passed the First Amendment, they sought to protect churches from government interference. They never meant to construct a wall of hostility between government and the concept of religious belief itself.

The evidence of this permeates our history and our government: The Declaration of Independence mentions the Supreme Being no less than four times; "In God We Trust" is engraved on our coinage; the Supreme Court opens its proceedings with a religious invocation; and the members of Congress open their sessions with a prayer.

I'm sure you must get discouraged at times, but there is a great spiritual awakening in America, a renewal of the traditional values that have been the bedrock of America's goodness and greatness.

One recent survey by a Washington-based research council concluded that Americans were far more religious than the people of other nations. Ninety-five percent of those surveyed expressed a belief in God and a huge majority believed the Ten Commandments had real meaning for their lives.

I repeat: America is in the midst of a spiritual awakening and a moral renewal. With your biblical keynote, I say today let "justice roll on like a river, righteousness like a never-failing stream."

Now, obviously, much of this new political and social consensus I have talked about is based on a positive view of American history, one that takes pride in our country's accomplishments and record. But we must never forget that no government schemes are going to perfect man. We know that living in this world means dealing with what philosophers would call the phenomenology of evil or, as theologians would put it, the doctrine of sin.

There is sin and evil in the world, and we are enjoined by Scripture to oppose it with all our might. Our nation, too, has a legacy of evil with which it must deal. The glory of this land has been its capacity for transcending the moral evils of our past. Especially in this century, America has kept alight the torch of freedom—not just for ourselves but for millions of others around the world. And this brings me to my final point today.

During my first press conference as President, in answer to a direct question, I pointed out that as good Marxists–Leninists the Soviet leaders have openly and publically declared that the only morality they recognize is that which will further their cause, which is world revolution.

In the early 1980s tensions grew between the United States and the Soviet Union. However, in the fall of 1984 President Reagan met with Soviet ambassador Andrei Gromyko. The meeting was the first step toward new talks on limiting nuclear war.

Topic 21

I think the refusal of many influential people to accept this elementary fact of Soviet doctrine illustrates an historical reluctance to see totalitarian powers for what they are. We saw this phenomenon in the 1930s; we see it too often today. This does not mean we should isolate ourselves and refuse to seek an understanding with them.

I intend to do everything I can to persuade them of our peaceful intent. I will remind them that it was the West that refused to use its nuclear monopoly in the forties and fifties for territorial gain. And it is the West that now proposes 50-percent cuts in strategic ballistic missiles and the elimination of an entire class of land-based, intermediate-range nuclear missiles.

At the same time, however, they must be made to understand we will never compromise our principles and standards. We will never give away our freedom. We will never abandon our belief in God.

Let us pray for the salvation of all those who live in totalitarian darkness, pray they will discover the joy of knowing God.

But until they do, let us be aware that while they preach the supremacy of the state, declare its omnipotence over individual man, and predict its eventual domination of all peoples of the earth—they are the focus of evil in the modern world.

So in your discussions, I urge you to beware the temptation of pride—the temptation blithely to declare yourselves above it all and label both sides equally at fault, to ignore the facts of history and the aggressive impulses of an evil empire, to simply call the arms race a giant misunderstanding and thereby remove yourself from the struggle between right and wrong, good and evil.

I ask you to resist the attempts of those who would have you withhold your support for this administration's efforts to keep America strong and free, while we negotiate real and verifiable reductions in the world's nuclear arsenals and one day, with God's help, their total elimination.

While America's military strength is important, let me add here that I have always maintained that the struggle now going on for the world will never be decided by bombs or rockets, by armies or military might.

The real crisis we face today is a spiritual one; at root, it is a test of moral will and faith.

I believe we shall rise to this challenge. I believe that communism is another sad, bizarre chapter in human history whose last pages even now are being written. I believe this because the source of our strength in the quest for human freedom is not material but spiritual, and, because it knows no limitation, it must terrify and ultimately triumph over those who would enslave their fellow man.

Adapted from Ronald Reagan, speech to the National Association of Evangelicals, Orlando, Florida, March 9, 1983.

READING REVIEW

1. Reagan says that the founding fathers "never meant to construct a wall of hostility" between government and religious belief. What evidence does he give to support his statement?

2. What, according to Reagan, is the "elementary fact of Soviet doctrine"?

3. **Finding the Main Idea** On the basis of the parts of Reagan's speech quoted here, what do you think is the main idea of the speech?

★ 21-4   Are Computers Alive? ★

Introduction Sherry Turkle, a teacher with advanced degrees in both sociology and psychology, spent six years interviewing people about computers. She was interested not only in how they used the machines, but also in how electronic technology had affected their ways of looking at the world. For computers are not ordinary machines. They raise questions about the meaning of intelligence and of life itself. This selection is from the book she wrote based on those interviews.

Vocabulary Before you read the selection, find the meaning of these words in a dictionary: optimal, disdain, metaphysical, evocative, mutilation, gibberish, resuscitating.

In the 1980s computers became standard technology in government, industry, and education. Young children frequently introduced their parents to computers.

It is summer. Robert, 7, is part of a play group at the beach. I have been visiting the group every day. I bring a carton filled with small computer toys and games and a tape recorder to capture the children's reactions as they meet these toys. Robert is playing with Merlin, a computer toy that plays tic-tac-toe. Robert's friend Craig has shown him how to "beat" Merlin. There is a trick: Merlin follows an optimal strategy most of the time, and if neither player makes a bad move every game will end in a draw. But Merlin is programmed to make a slip every once in a while. Children discover a strategy that will sometimes allow them to win, but then when they try it a second time it usually doesn't work. The machine gives the impression of not being "dumb enough" to let down its defenses twice.

Robert has watched Craig perform the "winning trick" and now he wants to try it himself. He plays his part perfectly, but on this round Merlin too plays a perfect game, which leads to a draw. Robert accuses it of being a "cheating machine. And if you cheat you're alive." Children are used to machines being predictable. The surprising is associated with the world of the living. But this is a machine that surprises.

Robert throws Merlin into the sand in anger and frustration. "Cheater. I hope your brains break." He is overheard by Craig and Greg, aged 6 and 8, who sense that this may be a good moment to reclaim Merlin for themselves. They salvage the by now very sandy toy and take it upon themselves to set Robert straight.

Craig: "Merlin doesn't know if it cheats. It won't know if it breaks. It doesn't know if you break it, Robert. It's not alive."

Greg: "Someone taught Merlin to play. But he doesn't know if he wins or loses."

Robert: "Yes, he does know if he loses. He makes different noises."

Greg: "No, stupid. It's smart. It's smart enough to make the right kinds of noises. But it doesn't really know if it loses. That's how you can cheat it. It doesn't know you are cheating. And when it cheats it doesn't even know it's cheating."

Jenny, 6 interrupts with disdain. "Greg, to cheat you have to know you are cheating. Knowing is part of cheating."

The conversation is over. I found it a striking scene. Four young children stand in the surf amid their shoreline sand castles and argue the moral and metaphysical status of a machine on the basis of its psychology: does the machine know what it is doing? Does it have intentions, consciousness, feelings?

What is important here is not the yes or no of whether children think computers cheat or even whether computers are alive. What is important is the quality of the conversation, both psychological and philosophical, that the objects evoke.

Millions of parents have bought computer toys hoping they will encourage their children to practice spelling, arithmetic, and hand–eye coordination. But in the hands of the child they do something else as well: they become the occasion for theorizing, for fantasizing, for thinking through metaphysically charged questions to which childhood searches for a response.

Sit silently and watch children pulling the wings off butterflies, staring at the creatures with awesome concentration. When they do this, children are not simply being thoughtless or cruel. They are not playing with butterflies as much as with their own evolving ideas, fears, and fantasies about life and death, about what is allowed and what is not allowed, about what can be controlled and what is beyond control.

In my research on how computers enter children's thinking, I asked children direct questions, but I did something else as well. I observed what children did with computers and computer toys in natural settings where computers provoked excitement, conversation, and disagreement. Sometimes children who would say computers were "not alive" betrayed more complex feelings by treating them as though they were.

The butterfly can play its role as an evocative object because it is on a threshold, alive enough to fly, yet seemingly far enough from being alive in the way that a person is alive to make its mutilation and killing almost acceptable. And when the butterfly's wings have been torn from it, it is placed in another situation betwixt and between. When does it stop being a butterfly? At what point is it dead? The computer too evokes feelings and thoughts related to life, death, and the limits of permissibility and control. It too is seen as marginal, in some ways alive and in many not. Thus it is like bugs and butterflies. But it introduces something very new.

The world of bugs and butterflies is like the world of Humpty Dumpty: "All the king's horses and all the king's men couldn't put Humpty together again." Computers belong to a different world. They offer an experience of restoring "life" as well as ending it. The computer's interactivity and complexity—the fact that it is "smart" and "talks back"—make some children see it as one of those things on the margin of being alive.

It is also possible to play with the idea of "killing" the computer. Certain inputs will "crash" it: the program, unable to cope, is thrown into a nonfunctioning state. The crash, an event often accompanied by a violent burst of gibberish on the screen, can carry a high emotional charge. Watching children go through cycles of crashing and reviving, of "killing" and "resuscitating" their machines, suggests that they are using them to work through feelings about endings and beginnings, about life and death.

Adapted from Sherry Turkle, *The Second Self: Computers and the Human Spirit* (New York: Simon & Schuster, Inc., 1984).

READING REVIEW

1. Why does Merlin, the computer toy, provoke an argument among children at the beach?

2. What does Turkle find striking about this discussion?

3. **Comparing** (a) Why does Turkle compare computers with butterflies? (b) Do you agree with her comparison? Why or why not?

★ 21-5 The Energy Dilemma ★

Introduction Many problems the United States faces today—unemployment, inflation, slow economic growth—tend to persist year after year. Economist Lester Thurow believes that these problems can be solved, but only if Americans decide how to balance economic gains and losses. The economy, he says, is a zero-sum situation, like a sporting event; for every winner there is a loser. Here he analyzes the energy situation in terms of winners and losers.

Vocabulary Before you read the selection, find the meaning of these words in a dictionary: dilemma, status quo, morass.

Nowhere is the nature of our fundamental dilemma more clearly illustrated than in energy. High prices, shortages, and supply disruptions are serious. They threaten future growth in our standard of living and are the main driving force behind an accelerating rate of inflation. They disrupt and disturb our lives in countless ways. At the same time, we have been unable to solve the problem. President Nixon could announce a Project Independence, and succeeding Presidents could announce that the energy problem was the "moral equivalent of war." But almost a decade later we are further from energy independence than we were at the beginning. This has occurred in spite of the fact that we are a country rich in energy resources.

The lack of action does not spring from a lack of solutions, but from the fact that each solution would cause a large, real income decline for some segment of the population. Everyone is in favor of energy independence in the abstract. But each path to energy independence is vigorously opposed by some significant group that would suffer large income declines if this particular solution were chosen. In the process, all solutions are vetoed and we remain paralyzed. The status quo is painful, but we cannot move.

One solution to the energy problem is simply to let the price of energy rise in accordance with that of imported oil. This would solve the problem in the sense that there would be no gas lines, no shortages, and no Energy Department full of complex and sometimes counterproductive regulations. Supply and demand pricing would work, but at the same time it would involve an enormous change in the distribution of income.

While a 100-percent increase in the price of energy would reduce the real income of the average American by 9.9 percent, it would have reduced the real income of the poorest tenth of families by 34 percent and the richest tenth by 5 percent. The real income effects among the poor are almost seven times as large as they are among the rich.

While it is relatively easy to calculate whose income would go down as energy prices rise, it is much harder to calculate whose income would go up. The income of those who own energy resources would go

After an oil embargo in the 1970s created a severe fuel crisis, Americans looked for alternative forms of energy. In 1980 oil prices dropped, but solar and other sources of power seemed a good way to avoid future dependency on foreign oil. The solar panels on this roof use sun rays to heat the house.

up, but who are they? No one knows with any certainty, but it is possible to find an approximate answer. Since most of our energy resources are owned by corporations, the ownershp of energy is probably very similar to the ownership of corporate stock. Here we know that the top 10 percent of all households owns over 90 percent of all corporate stock.

If we assume the same situation is true with respect to energy resources (the top 10 percent owns 90 percent), most of the income transfers among Americans will go to the top 10 percent of the population. When the pluses and minuses are added up, their income will go up, and the income of the remaining 90 percent will go down. Since the income gains to the top 10 percent from owning energy resources would be about five times as large as their income losses from having to pay higher energy prices, a free market for energy would have resulted in a sharp shift toward inequality in the distribution of income.

The same problem of economic losses can be seen in the political stalemate over energy independence. While many countries cannot become energy self-sufficient since they lack the necessary resources, the United States could easily achieve energy independence from a technical perspective. Our coal reserves alone are so enormous that they could fill all of our needs for the foreseeable future.

Many other forms of energy—nuclear, small-scale hydroelectric, solar, wind—could be harnessed to provide some of our energy needs. Technologically energy independence is well within our reach. Politically it may not be within our reach at all. Every path to energy independence requires a sharp reduction in the income of some group, and as a result every path to energy independence has its political foes. Even if these foes cannot muster the votes to cleanly defeat a particular path, they can raise costs and delay the projects so long that the path loses its appeal.

The costs of all alternative energy sources are highly dependent upon the regulatory environment in which they are to be used. Coal is cheap in a world where no one cares about the environmental damage occurring when it is mined or burned. But coal can be a very expensive alternative energy source in an economy with strict pollution controls.

Similarly, nuclear energy is cheap or expensive depending upon the risks that one is willing to take with exposure to radiation. If one wants to reduce the risks close to zero, nuclear energy is very expensive. If one is willing to take substantial risks, nuclear energy is cheap. Individuals differ on the risks they are willing to take, but our willingness to tolerate nuclear accidents also has something to do with how close each of us lives to a nuclear power plant.

The regulatory environment is a major part of the costs of alternative energy sources. But the conflicts about what constitutes the "right" regulatory environment are even more costly. Changes in the health, safety, or environmental standards when a plant is half-built or fully built are much more expensive than any set of stable requirements known before construction begins. But not having arrived at an agreed upon set of environmental standards, no one can promise a stable set of requirements. The result is great uncertainly with lengthy time delays as we fight over what environmenal standards should be imposed.

The same distributional problems occur with other energy sources. Each has noncontroversial applications and areas where it is cheap (solar power to heat swimming pools or hot water, wind power to pump water for cattle in isolated locations). But each is expensive and controversial when expanded to fill the enormous gap now filled with imported oil.

To think of alternative energy sources is to think of vigorous well-organized opponents. In some cases the opponents may be a minority, but they are perfectly capable of causing lengthy political and legal delays. The most visible are those who oppose nuclear power (cheap or expensive). But I have yet to meet anyone who wants a coal-fired, electrical-generating plant next to him. Environmentalists want coal mined and burned safely and cleanly without disturbing the topography at either end. It is not at all certain that this can be done, but certainly it cannot be done cheaply.

We are in a morass from which we cannot escape. The President proposes timid energy legislation that could not possibly solve the basic problems, but Congress cannot digest even this. The basic problem exists, persists, and becomes more painful. But no solutions are possible since they all result in a shift in the distribution of income. Not having a clear idea of what constitutes a desirable distribution of income, we are unwilling to accept or ratify any of these changes. We have no way to decide *when* compensation should be forced to suffer real income declines. We sink because we will not swim.

From *The Zero-Sum Society: Distribution and the Possibilities for Economic Change* by Lester C. Thurow. © 1980 by Basic Books, Inc., Publishers. Reprinted by permission of the publisher.

1. Why is the energy situation a serious one according to Thurow?

2. (a) What is the first solution Thurow suggests for coping with the energy crisis? (b) What benefits would it provide?

3. **Supporting Generalizations** Thurow says that the United States cannot solve many of its economic problems because of indecision about who will win and who will lose in a zero-sum society. How does he support this generalization?

Topic
22 The United States: Yesterday and Tomorrow

★ 22-1 Americans on the Move ★

Introduction In 1831 a young Frenchman named Alexis de Tocqueville docked at Newport, Rhode Island. He spent the next several months traveling around the United States, talking and observing and writing down his impressions. The resulting book, *Democracy in America*, was and remains one of the most insightful works ever written about America and Americans. Just 150 years later, political writer Richard Reeves retraced Tocqueville's footsteps. Here are some observations Reeves made at Louisville, Kentucky.

Vocabulary Before you read the selection, find the meaning of these words in a dictionary: repression, fervently, trauma, impenetrable.

Moving away is the American way. "We are a nation of leavers," Ellen Goodman said. The country was founded and built by people moving away, from repression or lack of opportunity in the Old World, from repression and lack of opportunity in Connecticut or Massachusetts or Oklahoma. Tocqueville was surprised to discover that the settlers at the frontier of 1831, Michigan and Ohio, were not from Europe but from Connecticut. They were moving away, seeking more opportunity, a chance, a new beginning.

People were leaving Louisville at the rate of perhaps 75,000 every ten years.

Thirty thousand different people were coming in—for a while. That wasn't always obvious. When I asked Barry Bingham and Wilson Wyatt whether there really was a separate place named Louisville, whether people considered themselves part of that place, both men, both over 70, answered, "Oh, yes!" They figured that 95 percent of the people in Louisville were "from someplace around here." When I asked the same question of Dann Byck, in his early forties, and his wife, Marsha Norman, at 31 considered one of America's most promising dramatists, they said that more than half the people they knew in Louisville came from other parts of the country. Byck's 17-year-old daughter, Amy, said only a quarter of the people she knew came, originally, from Kentucky. When Byck, out of curiousity, tried to trace the family of John Brent McIlvaine, the "greatest merchant" who talked with Tocqueville, he found only one McIlvaine listed in the area telephone books. He called and asked the woman who answered, "Has your family been in Louisville a long time?"

"Yes," she said. "We came here six years ago from Pittsburgh."

"This may sound trivial," said Barry Bingham in one of our conversations, "but one of the greatest changes I've noticed in my lifetime is the erasing of distinctions between rural and city people. Country people used to look and talk differently,

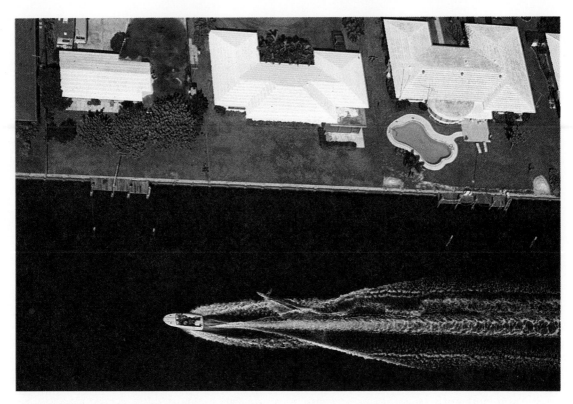

During the 1970s and 1980s millions of Americans moved to the South and Southwest in search of warm weather and good jobs. This aerial photo of Florida shows some of the sunbelt's attractions.

probably thought differently. Now you can't tell the difference—education, travel, television, I guess."

It did not sound trivial at all to me. I had found the differences in Americans, no matter how fervently celebrated locally, overwhelmed by the similarities. The sameness of tract homes, shopping centers, and hamburger stands—man's contributions to the countryside, rural and urban, northern and southern, eastern and western—seemed a deliberate, if unconscious, defense against the trauma of mobility.

Most Americans moving away do not have to go to a strange place. There is relocation without dislocation—the highways built to the rigid specifications of the federal government, the homes built from efficient standard plans, the hamburgers prepared to a juiciness determined in Chicago by market research. It is not new, it is progressive—and inevitable. "The man you left behind in the streets of New York," Tocqueville wrote in an essay, "you

will find him again in the midst of almost impenetrable solitudes: same dress, same spirit, same language, same habits and the same pleasures."

Adapted from Richard Reeves, *American Journey: Traveling with Tocqueville in Search of Democracy in America* (New York: Simon & Schuster, Inc., 1982). Copyright © 1982 by Richard Reeves.

READING REVIEW

1. Why, according to Reeves, do Americans move?

2. (a) How do Louisville residents of different ages perceive the city's population? (b) Can you think of any reason for the difference in their views?

3. **Relating Past to Present** (a) How does Reeves use quotations from Tocqueville to underscore his own points? (b) On the basis of this selection, would you say that Tocqueville was a good prophet? Why or why not?

Introduction The place: Chicago. The time: today, more or less. The speaker: Mary Lou Wolff, an Italian American mother of nine—housewife and, much to her surprise, political activist. In this selection she describes how she became increasingly involved in local politics.

Vocabulary Before you read the selection, find the meaning of these words in a dictionary: musty, soldered, confrontation.

We had history in school. I always felt a little uneasy with it. When I was a kid, if I went to the Chicago Historical Society, I felt strange there. I thought that was just for high-class people. I just felt foreign. I'd see some of the suits Abraham Lincoln wore or something. But I remember just feeling ill at ease. The words "democracy" and "government," they just reminded me of school and the nuns giving lessons. As if what they were talking about was musty and had nothing to do with living on Chicago Avenue. Yet I knew things were happening to me. . . .

I was beginning to meet a type of people I never met before. There were people from Europe, from worker movements, who would occasionally stop by. There were students. I liked hanging around and talking to these people. They seemed to treat me seriously, as if I understood what they were talking about. Often I didn't, but they assumed I did. I liked that. . . .

I worked at a series of dead-end jobs. I made paper boxes. I soldered radio parts. I was a waitress. I was not successful at any of these things. Suddenly I realized how boring all this is. I was confused. . . .

Finally, I gave all that up and got married. I was 20. After I had a few kids, I'd be reading the paper and I'd think about those people from the days before, and I missed them. . . .

I had nine children. It was absolutely full-time. Once in a while somebody would remember and say: "Could you come and give a speech?" I'd always say: "No, I'm a mother, I'm too busy." . . .

My friends were all very nice. We'd get together and exchange recipes for coffee cake. We'd talk about the drapes we were gonna make. I enjoyed all that. But I'd always come home feeling vaguely discontented. I spent a lot of time reading, though not in any disciplined way. I'd just pick up a book here, sometimes it would be a classic, but I'd find myself wishing there were somebody around I could talk about the book with. There was nobody. . . .

Every once in a while I'd pick up a newspaper and read about CAP, Campaign Against Pollution. Father Dubi was the young priest at the head of it. They broke rules. They carried on a fight against Commonwealth Edison and finally won an antipollution ordinance. They went into other issues and changed their name to Citizens Action Program.

Our neighborhood was right at the cross section where the Crosstown Expressway is going to be built. People are asking us where is the expressway going to be built, so we know what street it's gonna go down. Should we be opposed to it if it's on this street or opposed if it's on that street? Finally somebody said: "Why should we be for it at all?" There was a moment of silence. We all looked. That's right. We don't want it at all! Somebody else said: "That's silly. You don't think there's any way you're gonna stop 'em. That's all set for years." The rest of us said: "No. We're not gonna have it come through."

CAP was organizing against it and asked if we'd be interested in meeting with some other people. We were invited to go on an action, which we'd never heard of. This was a new step in organizing. . . . I began to realize I liked direct action. Not only was it more exciting, but it was a glimmering of the idea that you don't get anywhere if you talk too much. At some point, you must act.

Action. The word came into my vocabulary. They'd call up from CAP and say: "We're gonna have an action tomorrow morning at city hall." It would be a confrontation with some official. We were trying to see the plans for Crosstown. The officials wouldn't let us see them. It was simple as that at first. They'd say: "We don't have them ready, we're studying

As the proportion of elderly in the United States population increased, many joined groups such as the Grey Panthers to lobby for their interests.

them." We heard that many times. They'd been studying for several years.

Here, suddenly, was a group of people I liked, admired, saying: "You don't have to always be polite." This was a complete shock. That's something you're taught from the time you're a baby. If you want to get anywhere, you have to be polite. Follow the rules. If officials say, "Sit down and wait," you sit down and wait.

These people were saying you can stand up and demand things. At first, I was troubled by this. What does that mean? Do you insult people? I began to realize, no, I don't see anybody insulting anyone. I see people acting nervy. They're not doing anything wrong. They're just not agreeing to follow somebody else's rules. . . .

I was always a very quiet, polite person. If I had to speak in front of anybody, my face would flush. I would get embarrassed. But the people from CAP seemed

to see something different in me. They began to treat me in a way that I wasn't even treating myself. They expected me to do things I never thought I could do. Maybe I was different than I thought I was.

People were saying that I'm an organizer. I didn't know exactly what an organizer did. I thought of them as mysterious people. Later I found there was nothing mysterious about them. It was just the work they did. They gave me serious books to read about corporate America, things about expressways. Normally I would think: Let my husband read them. Housewives don't have time for this. But they'd say: "Read it and let us know what you think." I was flattered. At first I reacted out of flattery. But after a while, I began to realize they actually think I'm intelligent enough to know something serious. I was getting some knowledge of politics, and some deep personal changes were coming about as well.

They were gonna have a meeting at McCormick Place, about five or six hundred people. We needed somebody for a keynote speaker, somebody who's gonna turn the crowd on. I was wondering who they were gonna get. Father Dubi said: "I propose we have Mary Lou." I was absolutely stunned. My past reaction would have been to say: "Oh, no, I don't think I can do it." But now I thought: If they think I can do it, though it scares me, I'll try. So I went home and wrote my speech myself. The day came, lo and behold, I got up and I knew it was a good speech 'cause the crowd was reacting.

At the end, I said—it was a little corny—any time there's a gathering like this, of people coming together and deciding they have to fight, if Jefferson or those people are around anywhere, they must be thrilled, they must be saying: This is what we had in mind.

From that moment on, I began to think it was possible, though difficult, to have a democracy. It was an experiment, risky, chancy. But you couldn't say: "Okay, we got a democracy." It's an ongoing process that has to be carried on with each generation. All that occurred to me as I was writing the speech. I've done more reading and thinking about it since. And I know that's right. It was the first time I realized what that was about.

One election day, after our workers covered every precinct, an elderly man with a heavy German accent came up to me and said: "This is the first time I ever voted." I thought he was a new citizen. He said: "No, you don't understand. I voted for years, but this is the first time I ever really voted. I knew why I was voting a certain way. This is the first time I ever understood what democracy was about."

From *American Dreams: Lost and Found,* by Studs Terkel. Copyright © 1980 by Studs Terkel. Reprinted by permission of Pantheon Books, a division of Random House, Inc.

READING REVIEW

1. How did Wolff react to the idea of democracy when she was a student?
2. Why do you think Wolff speaks of democracy as "an experiment, risky, chancy"?
3. **Comparing Points of View** Another activist who tells her story in her own words is Fannie Lou Hamer in Reading 19-4. Compare the two women in terms of motivation, issues, background, and personality.

★ 22-3 In Praise of Productivity ★

Introduction Henry Fairlie, born in England, has lived in the United States since the 1960s. He admires the country's informality, ethnic diversity, and—as he explains here—its methods of coping with problems.

Vocabulary Before you read the selection, find the meaning of these words in a dictionary: copse, coherence, decadent, unflagging, innovation, languish.

An English economist once said that it was America that had taught the world that it need not starve. Consider that. It cannot be denied. The achievements of American agriculture are one of the wonders of the modern world. Americans consume each year only a third of the wheat which American farmers produce. There is no other valley in the world which has been made, by irrigation, as fertile as the Central Valley of California. But it is not only such facts and figures that tell the wonder. One must look down the vastness of the Middle West, as the English poet Louis MacNeice did in 1940, "astonished by its elegance from the air. Elegance is the word for it—enormous plains of beautifully inlaid rectangles, the grain running different ways, walnut, satinwood or oatcake, the whole of it tortoiseshelled with copses and shadows of clouds."

It is common for the American when he is in Europe to gasp at the hedgerows of England or the terraced vineyards of Italy, kept for centuries. But the gasp of the Englishmen is no less when he gazes on a continent, immense in scale, still fabulous in its diversity, which not only is cultivated but has by its cultivation been given its own coherence; which unlike Europe has been made one. Who but the Americans would, so early, have made the Great Plains yield so much—those semi-arid lands which even they, at first, called "the Great American Desert"?

But let us return to small things. If America was to produce, it had also to invent. The English critic T. R. Fyvel once told a story of a friend, also English, who had "found himself for a fantastic weekend in a society of Texas millionaires who whizzed around in their private aircraft, dropping in on parties hundreds of miles away." The friend found this unexpectedly refreshing. He was even more impressed when he saw the children of his host "buzzing around in special little pedal motor cars which were air conditioned." But one night his Texas millionaire host turned to him and said something like: "You know, Bob, I ask myself if our machine civilization isn't shot all to pieces." The Englishman, horrified, burst out to his host: "Don't have those decadent thoughts! Don't have any thoughts! Leave them to us—while you stay just as you are!" I understand his response. There seems to be nothing, however fanciful, that the American, with his unflagging inventive genius, will not attempt.

How I have come to take it all for granted was brought home to me not long ago, when I was sitting in my house with a friend visiting from England. It was a quiet afternoon in early summer. The windows were open, I could hear the birds chirping in the garden. My friend suddenly exclaimed: "How can you bear to live in all this noise?" What noise? "All this noise in the house," he said. "Something is always switching itself off or on, humming or purring." He had destroyed my own peace, for I noticed it from then on.

It is no wonder that America consumes so much energy. The electric gadgetry in an American home makes it its own Disney World. But to most Englishmen it is the physical evidence of a society that does not tire of innovation; which by its inventiveness still seems to keep the future open; and in whose inventiveness ordinary people find convenience.

The inventiveness and gadgetry of the American reflects the spirit of a society which echoes the song: "It ain't necessarily so." If houses are insufferably cold, you invent a stove, and then you invent central heating. And if anyone writes in to say that the Romans had central heating, the important point is that the common man in Rome did not have it. Ben Franklin invented a prefabricated stove which could be produced for the common man. Such a stove in Europe at the time would have been produced by craftsmen for the few.

But then it has always been the American way as well, when faced with any injustice or harshness in this society, to say that "it ain't necessarily so," and to do something about it. If ever this spirit is allowed to languish, whether in the invention of things or the improvement of its society, America will have ceased to be what it means to the rest of the world.

Adapted from Henry Fairlie, "Why I Love America," *The New Republic*, July 4, 1983.

READING REVIEW

1. How does Fairlie compare the American landscape with those of Europe?
2. Why does the author admire American inventiveness?
3. **Expressing an Opinion** Name two American innovations other than central heating that you think Fairlie would admire. Explain your answer.

★ 22-4 A New Way to Look at the World ★

Introduction Looking back over the long sweep of human history, Alvin Toffler divides it into three great eras, or waves. The First Wave, was the period when all the world's people depended on agriculture. The Second Wave started with the Industrial Revolution of the 1700s. The Third Wave is beginning now. One of its characteristics, says Toffler in his book *The Third Wave* is an increased need for worldwide thinking.

Vocabulary Before you read the selection, find the meaning of these words in a dictionary: drastically, sovereign, ecological, catastrophes, naive, permeable, inadvert, porous, potent, affiliate, proliferation, horticulture, odontological.

The Third Wave brings new problems, a new structure of communications, and new actors on the world stage—all of which drastically shrink the power of the individual nation-state.

Just as many problems are too small or localized for national governments to handle effectively, new ones are fast arising that are too large for any nation to cope with alone. "The nation-state, which regards itself as absolutely sovereign, is obviously too small to play a real role at the global level," writes the French political thinker, Denis de Rougement. "No one of our 28 European states can any longer by itself assure its military defense and its prosperity, its technological resources, the prevention of nuclear wars and of ecologi-

Modern science and technology often bring nations together in economic enterprises. This photograph shows a paper mill built in Japan being towed up the Amazon River for paper production in Brazil.

cal catastrophes." Nor can the United States, the Soviet Union, or Japan.

Tightened economic linkages between nations make it virtually impossible for any individual national government today to manage its own economy independently or to quarantine inflation. National politicians who claim their domestic policies can "halt inflation" or "wipe out unemployment" are either naive or lying, since most economic infections are now communicable across national boundaries. The economic shell of the nation-state is now increasingly permeable.

Furthermore, national borders that can no longer contain economic flows are even less defensible against environmental forces. If Swiss chemical plants dump wastes into the Rhine, the pollution flows through Germany, through Holland, and ultimately into the North Sea. Neither Holland nor Germany can, by itself, guarantee the quality of its own waterways. Oil tanker spills, air pollution, inadvertent weather modification, the destruction of forests, and other activities often involve side effects that sweep across national borders. Frontiers are now porous.

The new global communications system further opens each nation to penetration from the outside. Canadians have long resented the fact that some 70 United States television stations along the border telecast programs to Canadian audiences. But this Second Wave form of cultural penetration is minor compared with that made possible by Third Wave communications systems based on satellites, computers, teleprinters, interactive cable systems, and dirt-cheap ground stations.

All such developments—the new economic problems, the new environmental problems, and the new communications technologies—are converging to undermine the position of the nation-state in the global scheme of things. What's more, they come together at precisely the moment when potent new actors appear on the world scene to challenge national power.

The best-publicized and most powerful of these new forces is the transnational or, more commonly, the multinational corporation. What we have seen in the past 25 years is an extraordinary globalization of production, based not merely on the export of raw materials or finished manufactured goods from one country to another, but on the organization of production across national lines.

The transnational corporation (or TNC) may do research in one country, manufacture components in another, assemble them in a third, sell the manufactured goods in a fourth, deposit its surplus funds in a fifth, and so on. It may have operating affiliates in dozens of countries. The size, importance, and political power of this new player in the global game has skyrocketed since the mid-1950's. Today at least 10,000 companies based in the noncommunist high-technology nations have affiliates outside their own countries. Over 2,000 have affiliates in six or more host countries.

Of 382 major industrial firms with sales over $1 billion, fully 242 had 25 percent or more "foreign content" measured in terms of sales, assets, exports, earnings, or employment. And while economists disagree wildly on how to define and evaluate (and therefore classify and count) these corporations, it is clear that they represent a crucial new factor in the world system—and a challenge to the nation-state.

Though they are the best known, the transnational corporations are not the only new forces on the global stage. We are witnessing, for example, the rise of transnational trade union groupings—the mirror image, as it were, of the corporations. We are also seeing a growth of religious, cultural, and ethnic movements that flow across national lines and link up with one another. We observe an antinuclear movement whose demonstrations

in Europe draw protesters together from several countries at a time. We also are witnessing the emergence of transnational political party groupings.

Paralleling these developments, meanwhile, is a rapid proliferation of nongovernmental transnational associations. Such groups devote themselves to everything from education to ocean exploration, sports to science, horticulture to disaster relief. They range from the Oceania Football Confederation or the Latin American Odontological Federation to the International Red Cross, the International Federation of Small and Medium-sized Commercial Enterprises, and the International Federation of Women Lawyers.

The nation-state's role is still further diminished as nations themselves are forced to create supranational agencies. Nation-states fight to retain as much sovereignty and freedom of action as they can. But they are being driven, step by step, to accept new constraints on their independence.

European countries, for example, grudgingly but inevitably have been driven to create a Common Market, a European parliament, a European monetary system, and specialized agencies like CERN—the European Organization for Nuclear Research.

What we are creating is a new multilayered global game in which not merely nations but corporations and trade unions, political, ethnic, and cultural groupings, transnational associations and supranational agencies are all players.

Excerpts abridged from pp. 334, 336, 339, 340–341 in *The Third Wave* by Alvin Toffler. Copyright © 1980 by Alvin Toffler. By permission of William Morrow & Company.

READING REVIEW

1. What are two of the problems, in Toffler's view, that national governments cannot handle effectively?
2. How do modern forms of communication affect the nation-state?
3. **Classifying Information** Toffler discusses "new actors on the world stage" that limit national power. Name and describe three of them.

Skill Lessons

Historians use primary sources to learn about the past. A *primary source* is firsthand information about people or events of the past.

Paintings are one kind of primary source. They show how the people of a certain time and place saw themselves. Often, they give useful evidence about aspects of daily life such as food, clothes, games, and homes.

The picture below was painted on the walls of a Maya temple. Use the following steps to learn how to use a painting as a primary source.

1. **Identify the subject of the painting.** Study the painting carefully. (a) List three things the people are doing. (b) What kinds of plants and animals are shown? (c) What title would you give to this painting? (d) Explain why you chose this title.

2. **Decide what the painting tells about the life of the people.** Study the painting and review what you have read about the life of the Mayas. (a) Where was the painting found? (b) Describe the houses of the people. (c) From this painting, what conclusions can you draw about the daily life of the Mayas?

3. **Decide if the painting is a reliable source.** A painting does not always tell the full story. An artist may have painted it for a special reason or may have left out some details. You need to decide whether it is a reliable source of information. (a) Do you think that the artist showed everything exactly as it was? Explain. (b) Does this painting give you a complete idea of the daily life of the Mayas? Explain.

Among the many kinds of primary sources are photographs and written records. Written records are primary sources if they are firsthand information from people who were involved in an event. Letters, diaries, contracts, laws, and treaties are all primary sources.

The excerpt below is adapted from Gottlieb Mittelberger's *Journey to Pennsylvania*. The book was published after a trip in 1750. Follow these steps to practice using a primary source.

1. **Identify the source by asking who, what, when, and where.** (a) Who wrote the source? (b) What is it about? (c) About when was it written? (d) Where does it take place?

2. **Recognize the author's point of view.** Many eyewitnesses have a particular reason for writing about an event. And they want to share their views with their readers. When you read a primary source, you need to recognize the author's point of view. (a) What is Mittelberger's opinion about the journey to Pennsylvania? (b) What words or phrases show you that he feels strongly about the journey?

3. **Decide whether the source is reliable.** (a) Do you think that Mittelberger gives an accurate view of the journey? Why? (b) Do you think that there is anything left out of his account? (c) Would you say that this is a reliable source for learning about crossing the Atlantic in the mid-1700s? Explain.

 Journey to Pennsylvania

When the ships have weighed anchor, the real misery begins. Unless they have good wind, ships must often sail 8, 9, 10 or 12 weeks before they reach Philadelphia. Even with the best wind, the voyage lasts 7 weeks. . . . During the voyage people suffer terrible misery, stench, many kinds of seasickness, fever, dysentery, boils, scurvy, cancer, and the like, all of which come from old, sharply-salted food and meat and from very bad, foul water so that many die miserably.

Add to this misery, the lack of food, hunger, thirst, frost, heat, dampness, and fear. The misery reaches a peak when a gale rages for two or three nights and days so that every one believes that the ship will go to the bottom with all human beings on board.

When ships land at Philadelphia after the long voyage, only those who have paid for their passage are allowed to leave. Those who cannot pay must stay on board until they are bought and released from the ships by their buyers. . . . The sale of human beings in the market on board ship goes like this. English, Dutch, and Germans come on board to choose among the healthy passengers and bargain with them how long they will serve for their passage money. Adults bind themselves to serve anywhere from 3 to 6 years. Young people must serve until they are 21 years old.

Many parents must sell and trade away their children like so many head of cattle. It often happens that whole families are sold to different buyers.

Work and labor in this new and wild land are very hard. Work mostly consists of cutting wood, felling oak trees, and clearing large tracts of forest.

As you learned in Skill Lesson 2 (page 332), people usually have a reason for writing about events or developments in which they are involved. As a result, a primary source, or firsthand account, reflects the author's point of view. Two people writing about the same subject can have different points of view.

The letters below are written by Abigail and John Adams. During the Revolution, John Adams was away from home for long periods. His wife, Abigail Adams, wrote to him often. She kept him informed about their children and their farm, which she kept going. When the Continental Congress was preparing the Declaration of Independence, she wrote her husband the first letter reprinted below. The second letter is John Adams' reply to his wife.

Read the letters. Then compare the two points of view.

1. **Study the contents of each source.** (a) What does Abigail Adams want her husband to do? (b) What is John Adams' response to her request? (c) Who does John Adams mean when he says "another tribe, more numerous and powerful than all the rest"?

2. **Compare the points of view.** (a) What does Abigail Adams think men are like? (b) Does John Adams agree with his wife's view of men? Explain.

3. **Evaluate the usefulness of these sources.** (a) What do these letters tell you about American society in 1776? (b) Do you think these letters are a reliable source of information? Explain.

 Abigail Adams wrote:

I long to hear that you have declared independence. And by the way, in the new code of laws that I suppose you will make, I wish you would remember the ladies and be more generous and favorable to them than your ancestors. Do not put such unlimited power in the hands of husbands. Remember, all men would be tyrants if they could. If particular care and attention is not paid to the ladies, we are determined to stir up a rebellion and will not regard ourselves as bound by any laws in which we have had no voice or representation.

 John Adams replied:

As to your extraordinary code of laws, I can't help laughing. We have been told that our struggle has loosened the bonds of government everywhere, that children and apprentices were disobedient, that schools and colleges had grown turbulent, that Indians slighted their guardians and Negroes grow insolent to their masters. But your letter was the first hint that another tribe, more numerous and powerful than all the rest, had grown discontented.

Depend upon it, we know better than to repeal our masculine systems. Although they are in full force, you know they are little more than theory . . . in practice, you know, we are the subjects. We have only the title of masters, and rather than give this up, which would subject us completely to the power of the petticoat, I hope General Washington and all our brave heroes would fight.

Many primary sources, such as letters, diaries, and speeches, express the opinions of the people who wrote them. Therefore, when historians study primary sources, they have to recognize fact and opinion. A *fact* is something that actually happened. It is known to be true because it can be proved or observed. An *opinion* is a judgment that reflects a person's beliefs or feelings. It is not necessarily true.

Often, writers present a series of facts to back up an opinion. For example, in the Declaration of Independence, Jefferson listed facts to support the opinion that George III had tried to establish "an absolute tyranny over these states."

In the letter below, Alexander Hamilton writes about political differences between himself and the party led by Madison and Jefferson.

1. **Determine which statements are facts.** Remember that facts can be checked and thereby can be proved.

Use your reading in this chapter to help answer these questions. (a) Choose two statements of fact in Hamilton's letter. (b) How might you prove that each statement is a fact?

2. **Determine which statements are opinions.** Writers often show that they are giving an opinion by saying "in my view" or "I think" or "I believe." (a) Choose two statements in which Hamilton gives his opinion. (b) How can you tell each is an opinion?

3. **Determine how a writer mixes fact and opinion.** Reread the last sentence of the letter. (a) What did Hamilton mean by a "womanish attachment to France and a womanish resentment against Great Britain"? (b) Is it true that Jefferson supported France and opposed Britain? (c) What country did Hamilton want the United States to support? (d) Why do you think Hamilton mixed fact and opinion in the statement?

 Alexander Hamilton wrote:

It was not until the last session of Congress that I became completely convinced that Mr. Madison and Mr. Jefferson are at the head of a faction that is hostile toward me. They are motivated by views that, in my judgment, will undermine the principles of good government and are dangerous to the peace and happiness of the country.

Freneau, the present publisher of the *National Gazette,* was a known Antifederalist. It is certain that he was brought to Philadelphia by Mr. Jefferson to be the publisher of a newspaper. At the same time as he was starting his paper, he was also a clerk in the Department of State.

His paper is devoted to opposing me and the measures that I have supported. And the paper has a general unfriendly attitude toward the government of the United States.

On almost all questions, great and small, which have come up since the first session of Congress, Mr. Jefferson and Mr. Madison have been found among those who want to limit federal power. In respect to foreign policy, the views of these gentlemen are, in my judgment, equally unsound and dangerous. They have a womanish attachment to France and a womanish resentment against Great Britain.

Political cartoons can tell you a great deal about the past. For many years, cartoonists have tried to influence public feeling about important issues. To do so, they may exaggerate the facts. This is one reason why cartoons can often make a point more strongly than words can.

BORN TO COMMAND.

KING ANDREW THE FIRST.

Study the cartoon at left, which was published in the 1830s. Ask yourself what point about Andrew Jackson the cartoonist was trying to make. Then answer the following questions.

1. **Identify the symbols used in the cartoon.** Cartoons often use symbols. A *symbol* is something that stands for something else. For example, a skull and crossbones is a symbol for death. A dove is a symbol for peace. To understand a cartoon, you must know what its symbols mean.

   Figure out what the symbols in this cartoon stand for. (a) Who is pictured in the cartoon? (b) What is he holding in each hand? (c) What do these symbols stand for? (d) What is he wearing on his head? (e) What does this symbol stand for? (f) What is he standing on?

2. **Analyze the meaning of the symbols.** Use your reading of this chapter and the cartoon to decide what the symbols refer to. (a) What incident is probably referred to by the object in Jackson's left hand? (b) What event might the cartoonist have had in mind when he showed Jackson standing on the Constitution?

3. **Interpret the cartoon.** Draw conclusions about the cartoonist's point of view. (a) What do you think the cartoonist thought of President Jackson? Why? (b) How was the cartoonist trying to influence the public's attitude toward Jackson? (c) Does the cartoon give a balanced view of Jackson as President? Explain. (d) Study the painting of Jackson on page 296. Does the painting express an attitude toward Jackson different from that of the cartoon?

A diary is often a useful primary source because it tells you what the writer saw, heard, said, thought, and felt. It gives you firsthand information about people, places, and events. Because diaries are private, writers often say what they honestly think.

The excerpts below are from a diary kept by Amelia Stewart Knight. With her husband and children, she traveled the Oregon Trail in 1853. Her diary tells about the hardships the family faced on their way to a new life in Oregon.

1. **Identify the primary source.** (a) Who wrote the diary? (b) Under what conditions was it written? (c) Why do you think the writer wrote it?

2. **Analyze the information in the primary source.** Study the diary for information about how the writer lived.

(a) What does Knight say about hardships on the Oregon Trail? (b) Describe the geography of the area the Knight family traveled through. (c) What chores did Amelia Knight do? (d) What chores did the children do?

3. **Draw conclusions about the writer's point of view.** Decide how the writer felt about making the overland journey west. (a) How do you think Amelia Knight felt about the hardships of the journey? (b) How might keeping the diary have helped her face these hardships? (c) What personal qualities did a person need to make the journey? (d) Study the painting on page 309. What activities described in the diary can you see in the painting? (e) What other activities does the painting show?

 Amelia Stewart Knight's Diary

Monday, April 18th   Cold; breaking fast the first thing; very disagreeable weather; wind east cold and rainy, no fire. We are on a very large prairie, no timber to be seen as far as the eye can reach. Evening—Have crossed several bad streams today, and more than once have been stuck in the mud.

Saturday, April 23rd   Still in camp, it rained hard all night, and blew a hurricane almost. All the tents were blown down, and some wagons capsized. Evening—It has been raining hard all day; everything is wet and muddy. One of the oxen missing; the boys have been hunting him all day. (Dreary times, wet and muddy, and crowded in the tent, cold and wet and uncomfortable in the wagon. No place for the poor children.) I have been busy cooking, roasting coffee, etc. today, and have come into the wagon to write this and make our bed.

Friday, May 6th   We passed a train of wagons on their way back, the head man had drowned a few days before, in a river called the Elkhorn, while getting some cattle across. With sadness and pity I passed those who a few days before had been well and happy as ourselves.

Friday, August 19th   After looking in vain for water, we were about to give up, when husband came across a company of friendly Cayuse Indians, who showed him where to find water. The men and boys have driven the cattle down to water and I am waiting to get supper. We bought a few potatoes from an Indian, which will be a treat for our supper.

Sometimes, songs can give useful historical evidence. A song can tell you how people in an earlier time lived from day to day. The words in a song can help you understand how they thought about their world.

When using a song as evidence, you need to think carefully about what it says. Often, a song exaggerates the truth in order to be funny or sad. You must try to decide how much of the song is true.

The lines below are from a cowboy song of the late 1800s. It was sung by cowboys driving cattle from Texas to Kansas. At night, cowboys sang to calm the cattle and drown out noises that might cause a stampede. Singing songs was another custom that cowboys learned from Mexican vaqueros.

Read the verses from the song. Then use the following steps to analyze the song as evidence.

1. **Identify the subject of the song.**
   Read all five verses of the song. (a) What is the subject of the song? (b) About when was it written? (c) Who do you think wrote it? (d) Why do you think it was written?

2. **Study the content of the song.** Study the details about the life of a cowboy that the song gives. (a) When did cowboys begin work, according to the song? (b) When did they finish work? (c) What hardships did cowboys face?

3. **Use the song as historical evidence.** Try to decide how much of the song is true. (a) What evidence can you find that the song exaggerates hardships faced by cowboys? (b) Which line in the first verse hints that myths, or legends, were already growing up about the life of a cowboy? Explain. (c) Does the song make you think that you would have liked to be a cowboy? Explain. (d) Do you think this song is a good source of information about the life of a cowboy? Why or why not?

 Cowboy's Life

A cowboy's life is a dreary, dreary life;
Some say it's free from care,
Rounding up the cattle from morning till night,
On the bald prairie so bare.

Just about four o'clock old cook will holler out,
"Roll out, boys, it's almost day."
Through his broken slumbers the puncher he will ask,
"Has the short summer night passed away?"

The cowboy's life is a dreary, dreary life,
He's driven through the heat and cold;
While the rich man's a-sleeping on his velvet couch,
Dreaming of his silver and gold.

When the spring work sets in, then our troubles will begin,
The weather being fierce and cold;
We're almost froze, with the water in our clothes,
And the cattle we can scarcely hold.

The cowboy's life is a dreary, weary one,
He works all day to the setting of the sun;
And then his day's work is not done,
For there's his night guard to go on.

During World War I, both the Allies and the Central Powers used propaganda. Propaganda is a deliberate attempt to spread ideas that help a certain cause or hurt an opposing cause. Propaganda is used to shape public opinion.

Propaganda has been used throughout history. It is important to be able to recognize propaganda in order to understand historical events. During World War I, newspapers and governments on both sides used propaganda to win public support for the war effort. For example, both Britain and Germany used propaganda to convince Americans to enter the war on their side.

1. **Identify the facts.** Propaganda such as drawings or posters present facts and opinions in a visual way. Remember that facts can be shown to be true. Opinions are the beliefs or ideas of a person or group. They are not necessarily true. (a) What facts are shown in this drawing? (b) How do you know that these are facts? (c) What opinions are shown?

2. **Identify the propaganda technique.** Propaganda can shape public opinion through many different techniques. One technique is presenting half-truths. For example, a picture, newspaper article, or chart can show facts that are correct, but only show some of the facts.

A second propaganda technique is name-calling. One side might call the other side barbarians. A third technique is identifying a cause with a famous person or noble idea. A fourth is using symbols or pictures that show the other side in the worst possible light.

Study the drawing at left. (a) What symbol is used to represent Germany? (b) How are the Allies shown? (c) Which of the propaganda techniques listed above does this drawing use? (d) Do you think this drawing is an effective piece of propaganda? Why?

3. **Draw conclusions based on the evidence.** Study the drawing to figure out why it was used in the United States. (a) Which side do you think would have wanted this drawing published in the United States? Why? (b) Describe two ways in which this drawing might have affected public opinion in the United States.

4. **Make a generalization.** Based on your reading in this chapter, why do you think propaganda is often used in wartime?

When you do research for a report, you often will use secondary sources. **Secondary sources** are different from primary sources because they are not firsthand accounts. Instead, they are accounts based on the writings or evidence of others. Secondary sources include biographies and textbooks.

1. **Identify the parts of the book.** At the front, most books have a title page, copyright page, and table of contents. The **title page** lists the title, author, and publisher of the book. The **copyright page** is found right after the title page. It tells when the book was published. The **table of contents** is found near the beginning of a book. It includes a list of chapter titles and sometimes a list of maps or photographs in a book. Find a book on the 1920s. (a) List the full title, author's full name, and publisher of the book. (b) When was the book first published? (c) How many chapters are in the book?

2. **Study the table of contents.** By studying the table of contents, you can see at a glance the major subjects covered in the book. At right, is the table of contents of *Boom and Bust* by Ernest R. May. (a) How many chapters are in this book? (b) List three kinds of information the table of contents gives. (c) According to the table of contents, what is the book about?

3. **Practice using an index.** Most history books include an index at the end of the book. An **index** is an alphabetical list of the main subjects in a book. An index lets you find out if the book has information on a certain subject. Practice using the index at the back of this textbook. Notice that the index breaks some subjects down into subtopics. See the note at the beginning of the index. (a) Does the book have

CONTENTS

information on the Jazz Age? On Bessie Smith? (b) Besides listing subjects, what other information does the index give? (c) Where would you look in the index to find out if the book discusses the Sacco and Vanzetti trial?

4. **Practice skimming a chapter.** Another way to find information in a book is to skim a chapter. Skimming is a way of looking quickly at a chapter to see if it has information that you might find useful. To skim a chapter, read through the first paragraph. Then look at the first and last sentences of each paragraph. Using the book you selected for step 1, skim Chapter 2. (a) What does the first paragraph of Chapter 2 tell you about the chapter? (b) What are the main subjects covered in the chapter?

During the Great Depression, thousands of Americans wrote to the President and Mrs. Roosevelt. Letters such as the ones below are useful to anyone who studies how the depression affected ordinary people.

1. **Analyze each letter.** By reading each letter carefully, you can learn about the writer and the events of the time. (a) What does the first letter writer tell about conditions for blacks in Reidsville? (b) Was the second letter written by a man or a woman? (c) How can you tell? (d) Why do you think the third writer sent the letter to Mrs. Roosevelt?

2. **Identify the writer's point of view.** Many factors can affect a writer's point of view, including social background, age, or race. Each of these letter writers had a particular reason for writing to the President or Mrs. Roosevelt. (a) What is the major concern of each of the letter writers? (b) What factors do you think affected the point of view of each?

3. **Use the letters to help draw conclusions about the Great Depression.** Use the letters below and what you have read in this chapter to draw conclusions. (a) What hardships did families face during the depression? (b) Why did black Americans have an especially hard time? (c) How did older Americans want the President to help them? (d) Did the New Deal help any of these groups? Explain.

2.
From New Orleans, Louisiana

Dear President Roosevelt:
I take the pleasure of writing to you these few lines asking you if you could help me, please. I have 10 children. I have 4 children that go to school, and I can't get them any clothes. My husband is working for the city, but he doesn't work every day. Some weeks he makes three days' pay and some he makes four. And how could I pay rent and buy clothes for my children.

1.
From Reidsville, Georgia

Dear Mr. President:
Would you please direct the people in charge of the relief work in Georgia to issue the provisions and other supplies to our suffering colored people. I am sorry to worry you with this, Mr. President, but hard as it is to believe, the relief officials here are using up most everything that you send for themselves and their friends. They give us black folks nothing but a few cans of pickled meat. To white folks, they give blankets, bolts of cloth, and things like that.
Yours truly (can't sign my name, Mr. President, they will beat me up and run me away from here).

3.
From Petersburg, North Dakota

Dear Mrs. Roosevelt:
You must excuse me for writing to you, but I have heard that you would like the pension for old people to be set at $30 a month. Mrs. Roosevelt, I would be very thankful if you could force that through.
I am now 72 years old and have never had anything. I have always been poor and have always worked hard.
I am sure, Mrs. Roosevelt, that you will try all you can to help us old folks. From a poor Norwegian wife in North Dakota.

In a free society, newspapers play an important role. They print news articles. Most also print unsigned articles, called editorials. An **editorial** is an article that gives a newspaper's opinion on an issue.

Editorials are different from news articles. They mix both facts and opinions. Editorials have at least four different purposes: to criticize, persuade, explain, or praise. Often, editorials criticize a decision or action. Some try to persuade or encourage people to follow a certain course of action. Others explain or interpret an issue or event. Still others praise a person or organization for doing a good job.

1. **Identify the subject of the editorial.** Read the editorials reprinted below to decide what each is about. When you read Editorial A, keep in mind the fact that the white-controlled government of South Africa follows a policy of apartheid (uh PAHRT hayt). That is, it rigidly separates each racial group. Nonwhites have very little freedom and few political rights. (a) What is the subject of Editorial A? Editorial B? (b) In what newspaper did each appear? (c) When was each printed?

2. **Decide what position or opinion each editorial takes.** Review Skill Lesson 10 (page 232). (a) List two facts included in Editorial A. (b) Does Editorial A approve or disapprove of South Africa's policy? Explain. (c) What opinion does Editorial B express about the arms talks?

3. **Analyze how editorials might influence public opinion.** Newspapers have a large number of readers. Many readers want to know what the editors of the paper think about an issue or event. (a) Which of the four purposes described above do you think Editorial A has? Editorial B? (b) Which editorial do you find most convincing? Why?

 Editorial A

When President Reagan meets today with South African Bishop Desmond Tutu, he should heed the example of 25 congressional Republicans. . . .

In a letter this week to South Africa's ambassador to the United States, the congressmen expressed exasperation with apartheid policies that exclude South African blacks from civil rights and political power. "The reality of apartheid and the violence used to keep it in place," their letter said, undermine the good relations that this country seeks with South Africa's government. Reagan should make the same point. . . .

Minneapolis Star and Tribune, December 7, 1984
Minneapolis, Minnesota

 Editorial B

Moscow and Washington have announced that Secretary of State Shultz and Soviet Foreign Minister Gromyko will meet in Geneva on Jan. 7 and 8. According to the White House statement, they will "enter the new negotiations with the objective of reaching mutually acceptable agreements on the whole range of questions concerning nuclear and other space arms."

So, these are nothing more than talks about talks. They haven't even set the agenda yet for actual arms control. National Security Adviser McFarlane, with nice diplomatic understatement, says, "I would not say that this is a milestone of conclusion but, rather, an opening of a process that will be difficult and sustained over time."

The Dallas Morning News, November 24, 1984
Dallas, Texas

A Chronology of American History

This chronology includes some of the most important events and developments in American history. It can be used to trace developments in the areas of government and citizenship, exploration and invention, American life, and the world of ideas.

	Government and Citizenship	Explorers and Inventors
Prehistory– 1499	Mayan Empire reaches its height Crusades for Holy Land begin Aztecs establish empire in Mexico Strong monarchies develop in Europe Incas establish empire in South America	Mayas predict eclipses of sun Aztecs develop system of mathematics Marco Polo travels to China Columbus sails to America Vasco da Gama reaches India
1500– 1599	Cortés defeats Aztecs Pizarro captures Inca capital Spanish enact Laws of the Indies English colony established at Roanoke English defeat Spanish Armada	Spanish explore North America Magellan's expedition circles the globe Cartier sails up St. Lawrence River Drake sails around the world
1600– 1649	House of Burgesses set up in Virginia Mayflower Compact signed Massachusetts Bay colony founded Maryland becomes first proprietary colony	English joint stock companies sponsor settlement in North America Champlain founds Quebec Spanish found Santa Fe West Indian tobacco adapted to Virginia
1650– 1699	Town meetings held in New England Restoration of Charles II in England Royal colonies develop France claims Louisiana Glorious Revolution in England	Spanish explore Pacific coast Joliet and Marquette explore Mississippi River La Salle reaches Mississippi Delta
1700– 1749	Georgia founded Molasses Act passed English settlers move into Ohio Valley	Indigo developed as cash crop Benjamin Franklin develops scientific approach to medicine
1750– 1799	French and Indian War Intolerable Acts passed Declaration of Independence signed Revolutionary War Articles of Confederation ratified Constitution ratified	Watt patents steam engine Fitch launches first steam-powered boat Slater sets up textile mills in New England Eli Whitney invents cotton gin

Changes in American Life	The World of Ideas	
Agriculture develops in Americas Rise of merchants and bankers in Europe Trade between Europe and Asia expands Incas develop diverse economy	Mayas develop system of writing Aztecs build Tenochtitlan Renaissance begins in Europe Incas construct great cities	**Prehistory– 1499**

Native American population of Spanish
  America declines
Slave trade begins in Americas
French develop fishing and fur trading
  in North America
	Spanish try to convert Native Americans
	  to Christianity
	Universities open in Spanish America
	John White paints watercolors of life in
	  North America
		**1500–
		1599**

John Smith organizes life in Jamestown Slavery introduced in Virginia Bible Commonwealth in Massachusetts	Persecution of Puritans in England Harvard founded Public school law passed in Massachusetts Religious tolerance granted in Maryland	**1600– 1649**

New England becomes shipbuilding
  center
Navigation Acts passed
Royal African Company established
Bacon's Rebellion
	Quakers seek religious freedom in
	  Pennsylvania
	Spanish missions in Southwest
	Religious freedom granted in Massachusetts
	College of William and Mary founded
		**1650–
		1699**

Triangular trade flourishes Immigration to Middle Colonies grows Plantations expand in Southern Colonies Growth of port cities	Yale College founded First regular newspaper in colonies founded John Peter Zenger arrested for libel	**1700– 1749**

Proclamation of 1763
Parliament passes Sugar, Quartering,
  Stamp, Currency, and Townshend acts
Colonies boycott British goods
Northern states abolish slavery
Northwest Ordinance takes effect
	American literature reflects nationalism
	Southern states disestablish Episcopal
	  Church
	Noah Webster promotes an American
	  language
	National capital designed and built
		**1750–
		1799**

Government and Citizenship	Explorers and Inventors
1800–1824 Louisiana Purchase War of 1812 Missouri Compromise passed Monroe Doctrine	Lewis and Clark expedition Steamboats improved Steam-powered locomotives developed
1825–1849 Jacksonian democracy Indian Removal Act passed Texas wins independence Oregon divided along 49th parallel Mexican War	Erie Canal opened Mechanical reaper, steel plow, and telegraph developed First commercial railroads in use Gold discovered at Sutter's Mill
1850–1874 Compromise of 1850 Kansas-Nebraska Act passed Civil War Reconstruction Alaska purchased from Russia Warfare on the Great Plains	Passenger elevator, sleeping car, and air brake invented Bessemer process developed Pony Express founded Ironclad ships used in Civil War Transcontinental railroad completed

1875–1899 Battle of Little Big Horn
Populist movement
ICC created
Sherman Antitrust Act passed
Spanish-American War
	Refrigeration in meatpacking
	   developed
	Telephone, phonograph, incandescent
	   light bulb invented
	First skyscraper built

1900–1924 Progressive era Roosevelt Corollary World War I Fourteen Points Treaty of Versailles rejected Red Scare	Panama Canal built Assembly line introduced Scientific management introduced Synthetic fibers developed Electric appliances become widespread
1925–1949 Bonus Army New Deal World War II Truman Doctrine and Marshall Plan NATO created	Transatlantic telephone service begins First television pictures broadcast Lindbergh flies across Atlantic Iron lung developed Atomic bomb developed
1950–1974 Korean War McCarthyism Cuban missile crisis Vietnam War Watergate crisis	*Explorer I* launched into orbit Computers marketed commercially American astronauts land on moon Viking probe of Mars

1975–Present Diplomatic recognition of China
Camp David agreement on Middle East
Hostage crisis in Iran
Sandra Day O'Connor appointed to
   Supreme Court
	Genetic engineering, computers, lasers,
	   and artificial joints and organs
	   advance medicine
	Flights of *Columbia*
	Voyager expeditions pass Saturn

Changes in American Life	The World of Ideas	
Henry Clay's American System American Colonization Society Industry spreads in North Cotton growing expands in South	Religious revival movement develops Troy Female Seminary established Hudson River School of painting	**1800– 1824**

Temperance movement develops
The Liberator founded
National Trade Union organized
Seneca Falls Convention
California gold rush
	Mormon Church founded
	Mount Holyoke becomes first women's
	  college in United States
	Horace Mann leads movement to
	  establish free public education
		**1825–
		1849**

Homestead Act passed Emancipation Proclamation signed Cattle and mining boom in West Corporation becomes major business organization Knights of Labor founded	*The Scarlet Letter* published Free public education spreads in North *Uncle Tom's Cabin* published Wilberforce College founded First school of nursing established	**1850– 1874**
Trusts established AFL founded Rapid growth of cities Jim Crow practices in South Settlement house movement	Mass-circulation newspapers develop Progressive education movement American Realists school of painting Reformers expose urban problems through writing and photography	**1875– 1899**
Muckrakers expose social problems Pure Food and Drug Act passed NAACP formed Constitutional amendments on income tax, prohibition, women's suffrage Strict wartime controls on economy	Armory Show of modern art Jazz Age Harlem Renaissance Hollywood becomes world movie capital Commercial radio begins Lost Generation influences literature	**1900– 1924**
Stock prices soar Great Depression Recovery legislation passed Internment of Japanese Americans Wartime production ends depression	Golden years of Hollywood movies Effects of depression depicted by writers and photographers *Grapes of Wrath* published WPA sponsors artistic projects	**1925– 1949**

Rapid expansion of suburbs
Civil rights movement
Great Society programs
Arab oil embargo contributes to fuel
  shortages
	Rock 'n' roll becomes popular
	Abstract expressionism and pop art
	  affect visual arts
	Greater emphasis on science education
	  after Sputnik launch
		**1950–
		1974**

Inflation plagues economy Increase of women in work force Move to the sunbelt Reaganomics introduced	Computers revolutionize entertainment and communications Physical fitness craze	**1975– Present**

A *p* before an italicized page number refers to a picture on that page.

Illustration Credits

Frequently cited sources are abbreviated as follows: AMNH, American Museum of Natural History; LC, Library of Congress; MCNY, Museum of the City of New York; MFA, Museum of Fine Arts, Boston; MMA, Metropolitan Museum of Art, New York; NA, National Archives; NG, National Gallery of Art, Washington, D.C.; NMAA, National Museum of American Art; NYHS, courtesy of the New York Historical Society, New York; NYPL, New York Public Library; NYSHA, New York State Historical Association, Cooperstown; SI, Smithsonian Institution; UPI, United Press International; WW, Wide World; Yale, Yale University Art Gallery.

Key to position of illustrations:
b, bottom; *l*, left; *r*, right; *t*, top.

Cover Photo by Victoria Beller-Smith; **page 3** AMNH; **4** NYSHA; **5** *t* LC, *b* The Rockwell Museum; **6** NG, Gift of Edgar Wm. & Bernice Chrysler Garbisch; **7** NYHS.

Part One

THEME 1 Page 13 Bettmann Archive; **15** Fred J. Maroon/Louis Mercier; **17** AMNH; **18** AMNH; **21** AMNH; **23** Bibliotheque Nationale; **25** Bibliotheque Nationale; **27** National Gallery of Canada; **29** LC.

THEME 2 Page 30 Courtesy of Glenbow Museum, Calgary, Alberta; **33** National Gallery of Canada/Gift of the estate of the Hon. W.C. Edwards, Ottawa, 1928; **35** LC; **37** Dan McCoy/Rainbow; **39** NYPL; **40** NYPL/Stokes Collection; **42** North Carolina Archives; **45** Colonial Williamsburg; **47** Bettmann Archive; **48** NYPL; **51** Insurance Company of North America.

THEME 3 Page 53 *t* NYSHA, *b* Albany Institute of History and Art; **55** National Gallery of Canada; **57** LC; **59** LC; **61** Historical Society of Pennsylvania; **65** Wide World; **66** NYPL; **67** NYHS; **69** Mystic Seaport Museum; **70** NYHS.

THEME 4 Page 72 Washington University Gallery of Art, St. Louis, MO; **74** NYHS; **76** Historical Society of Pennsylvania; **79** NYPL; **81** NYHS; **84** Courtesy of the Museum of Fine Arts, Boston (M. and M. Karolik Collection); **86** LC.

THEME 5 Page 89 The Rockwell Museum; **90** Smithsonian National Collection of Fine Arts; **93** National Portrait Gallery, SI, Washington, DC/Lent by National Museum of American Art; **95** Oregon Historical Society; **96** Institute of Texan Cultures, San Antonio; **99** NYPL; **100** Peabody Museum of Salem; **103** LC; **105** LC; **107** Gemimi-Smith; **109** LC; **110** St. Louis Art Museum; **111** The Rockwell Museum.

THEME 6 Page 112 Musee de Pau; **113** *l* NA, *r* MMA, Gift of I.N. Phelps Stokes, Edward S. Hawes, Alice Mary Hawes, Marion Augusta Hawes; **116** NYPL; **119** The Granger Collection; **121** The Granger Collection; **123** NG, Gift of Edgar Wm. & Bernice Chrysler Garbisch; **127** LC; **129** *l* LC, *r* American Heritage Picture Collection.

Part Two

THEME 1 Page 132 Taft Museum, Cincinnati, Ohio; **133** Newberry Library; **135** University of Washington; **137** Granger Collection; **140** Wichita Art Museum; **142** Nebraska State Historical Society, Soloman D. Butcher Collection; **145** Culver Service; **147** MMA, Gift of Frederic H. Hatch, 1926; **148** Bettman Archive; **153** LC; **154** HYNH; **156** LC; **158** LC; **163** Edwin Levick; **164** Indiana Historical Society; **166** The Granger Collection; **167** NYPL; **169** LC; **171** Granger Collection; **172** LC; **175** Trustees of the British Museum.

THEME 2 Page 176 Museum of the City of New York; **177** Newberry Library; **179** International Museum of Photography at George Eastman House; **182** Newberry Library; **183** Charles Scribner's Sons; **184** National Portait Gallery, Smithsonian Institution; **187** LC; **189** The Granger Collection; **190** Bettman Archive; **191** The British Museum; **192** Granger Collection; **195** LC; **197** LC; **199** West Point Museum; **201** Granger Collection; **205** Imperial War Museum; **206** Chicago Tribune-New York News Syndicate, Inc.

THEME 3 Page 207 The New School for Social Research; **209** MMA, Gift of Abby Aldrich Rockefeller; **211** Phillips Collection; **214** Westport Schools Permanent Art Collection; **216** LC; **218** Brown Brothers; **220** LC; **222** NYHS.

THEME 4 Page 227 courtesy of the Bronx General Post Office, photograph by John Serafin; **228** Conde Nast Publications; **231** NA; **235** American Heritage; **237** NA; **238** Photo by the Detroit News; **241** LC; **243** LC; **244** NA; **247** LC; **249** New York Times Photos; **252** U.S. Navy; **256** Curtis Publishing Co.; **258** LC; **261** NA; **263** F.D.R. Library; **265** F.D.R. Library; **269** U.S. Army Photograph.

THEME 5 Page 270 MMA; **273** New York Times; **277** UPI; **279** Erich Lessing, Magnum Photos, Inc.; **281** UPI; **283** UPI; **284** courtesy Harry N. Abrams, Inc.; **289** U.S. Air Force Photo; **293** AP/Wide World Photos; **294** Francis Kelly, *Life* Magazine, © Time, Inc.; **297** Shostal Associates; **301** Pentagon; **302** John Dominis, *Life* Magazine, © Time, Inc.; **306** Owen Franken/Stock, Boston; **310** Peter Southwick/Stock, Boston; **313** AP/Wide World Photos; **315** David Marie/Folio, Inc.; **317** Kenneth Karp; **319** William Hubbell/Woodfin Camp & Assoc.; **322** Baron Wolman/Woodfin Camp & Assoc; **324** Elizabeth Crews/Stock, Boston; **327** Machete/Pictorial Parade.

Skill Lessons

Page 329 Peabody Museum, Harvard; **333** LC; **336** LC.

Chronology

Page 340 *l* Independence National Historical Park, *r* Peale Museum; **341** *l, r* Colonial Williamsburg Foundation; **342** *l* Chicago Historical Society, Solomon D. Butcher Collection, *r* Thomas Gilcrease Institute of American History and Art, Tulsa, Okla; **343** *l* Bethlehem Steel Corporation, *r* Joslyn Art Museum.

DATE DUE

WITHDRAWN